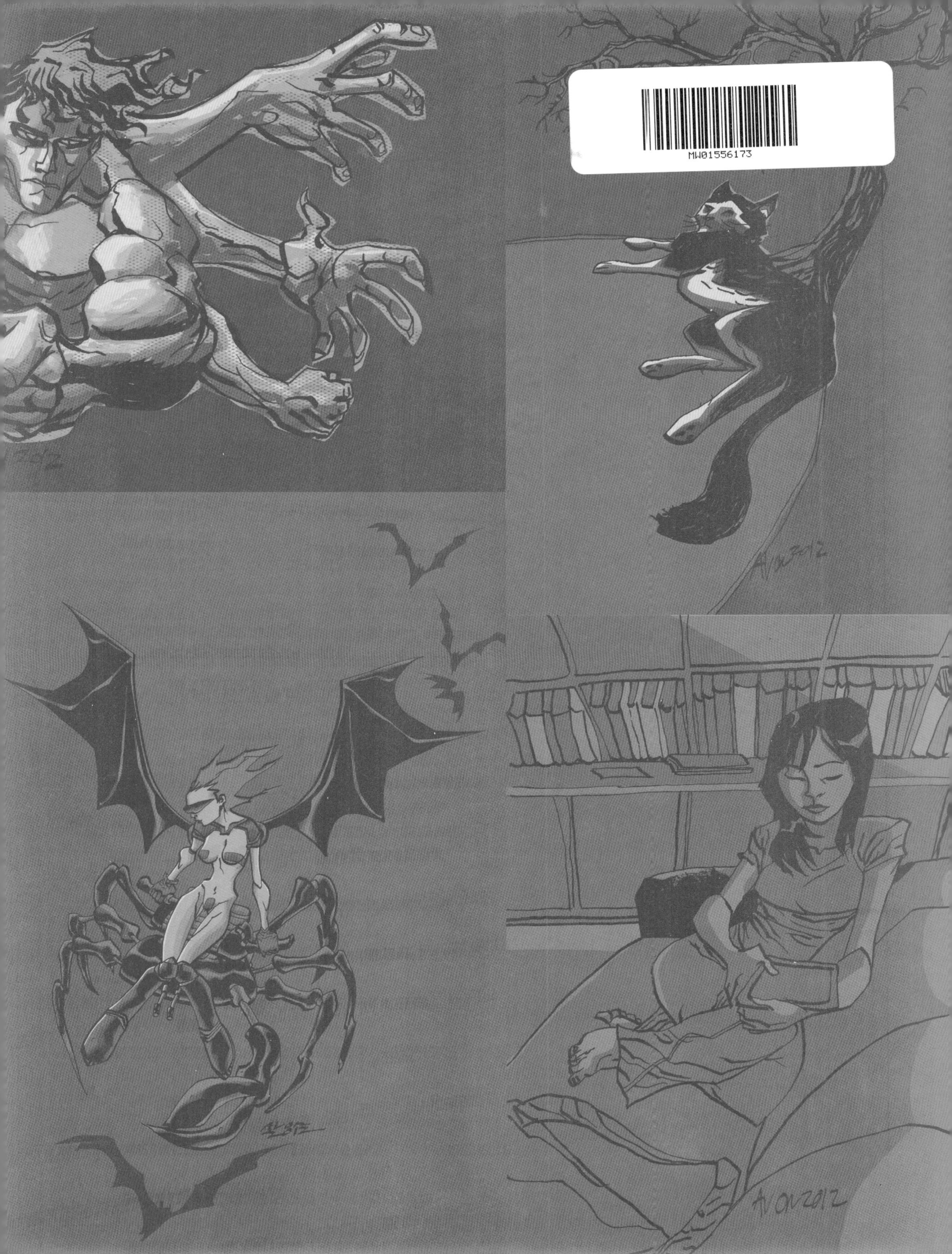

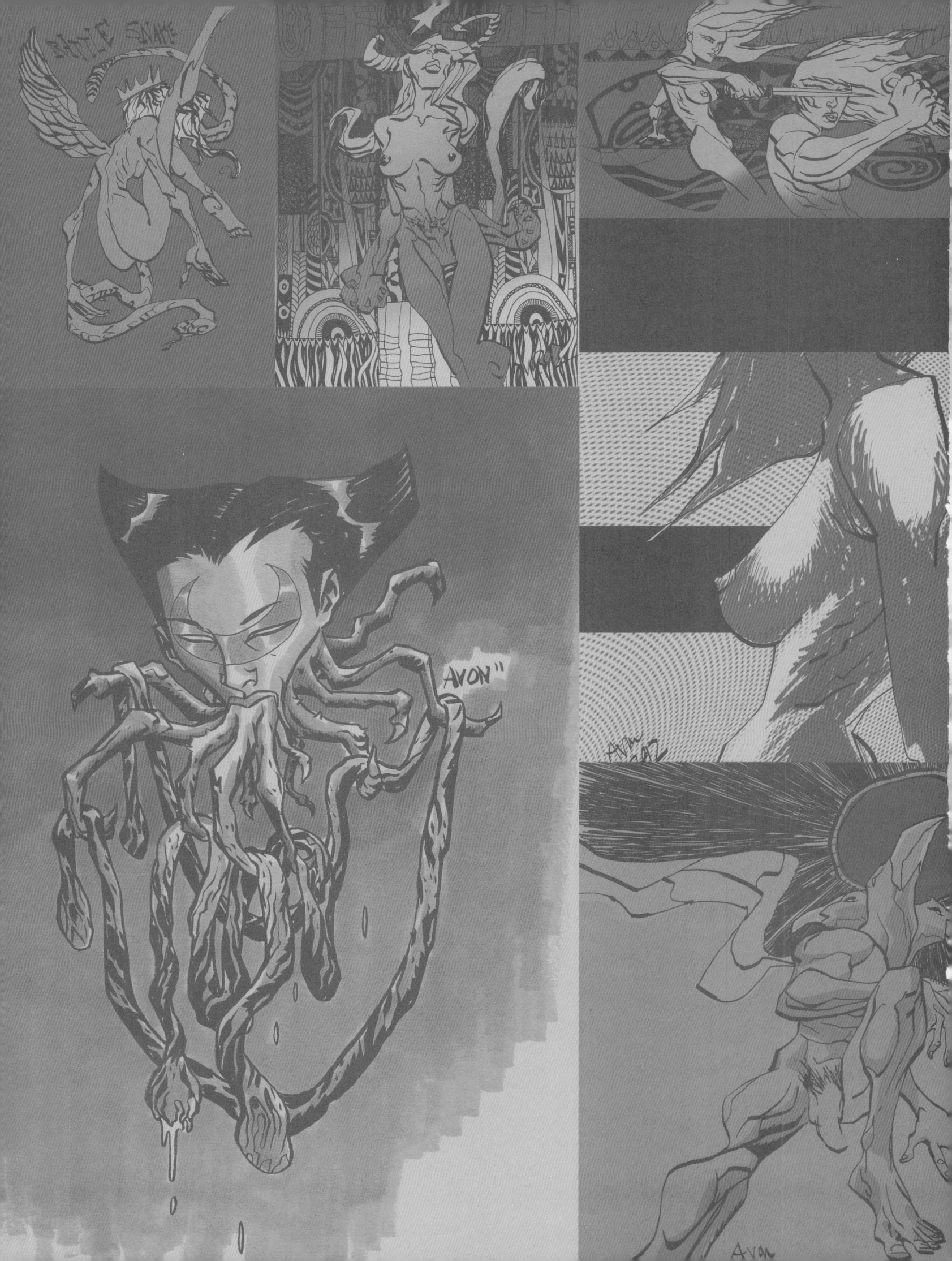

NO PLAN B
THE ART OF MICHAEL AVON OEMING

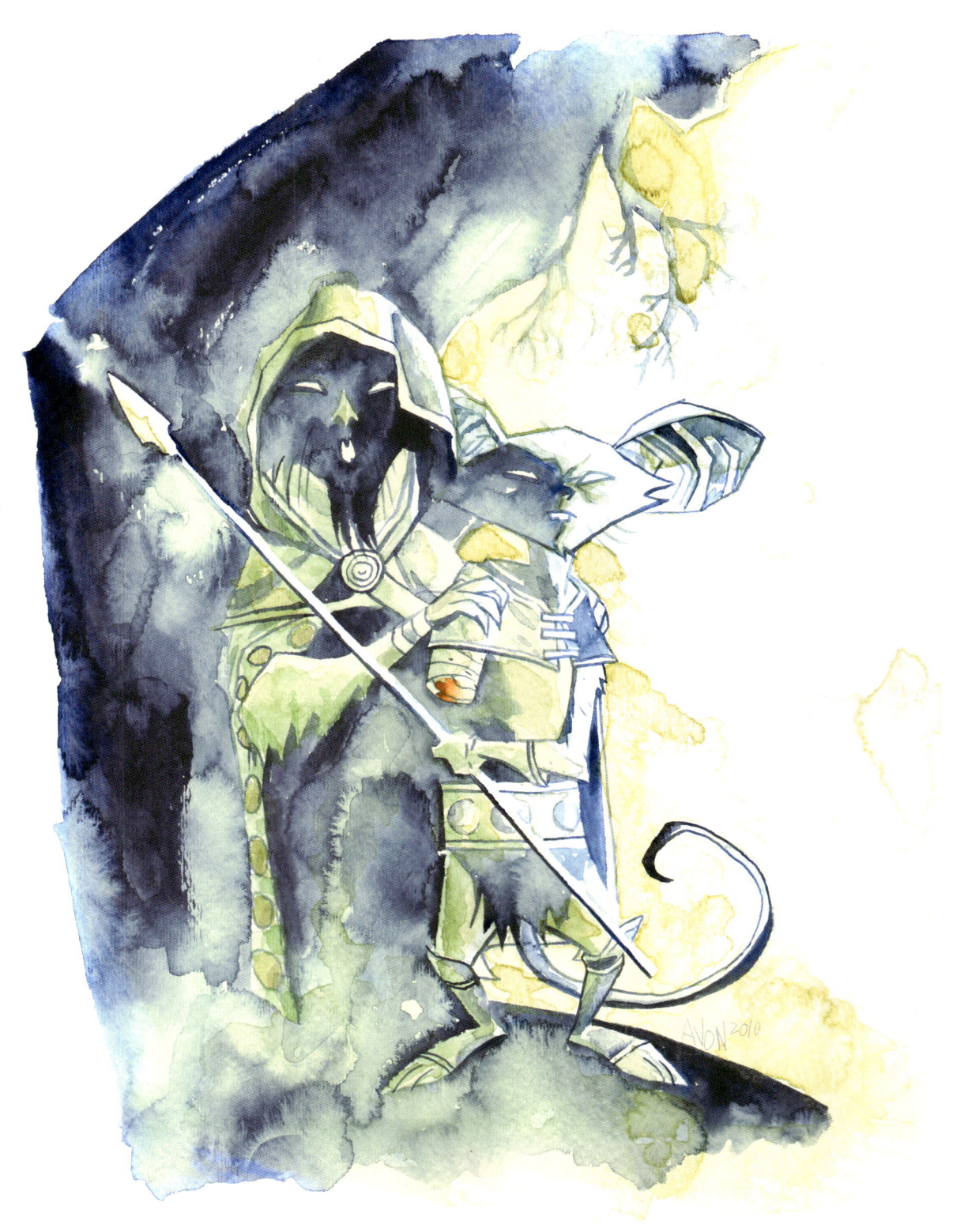

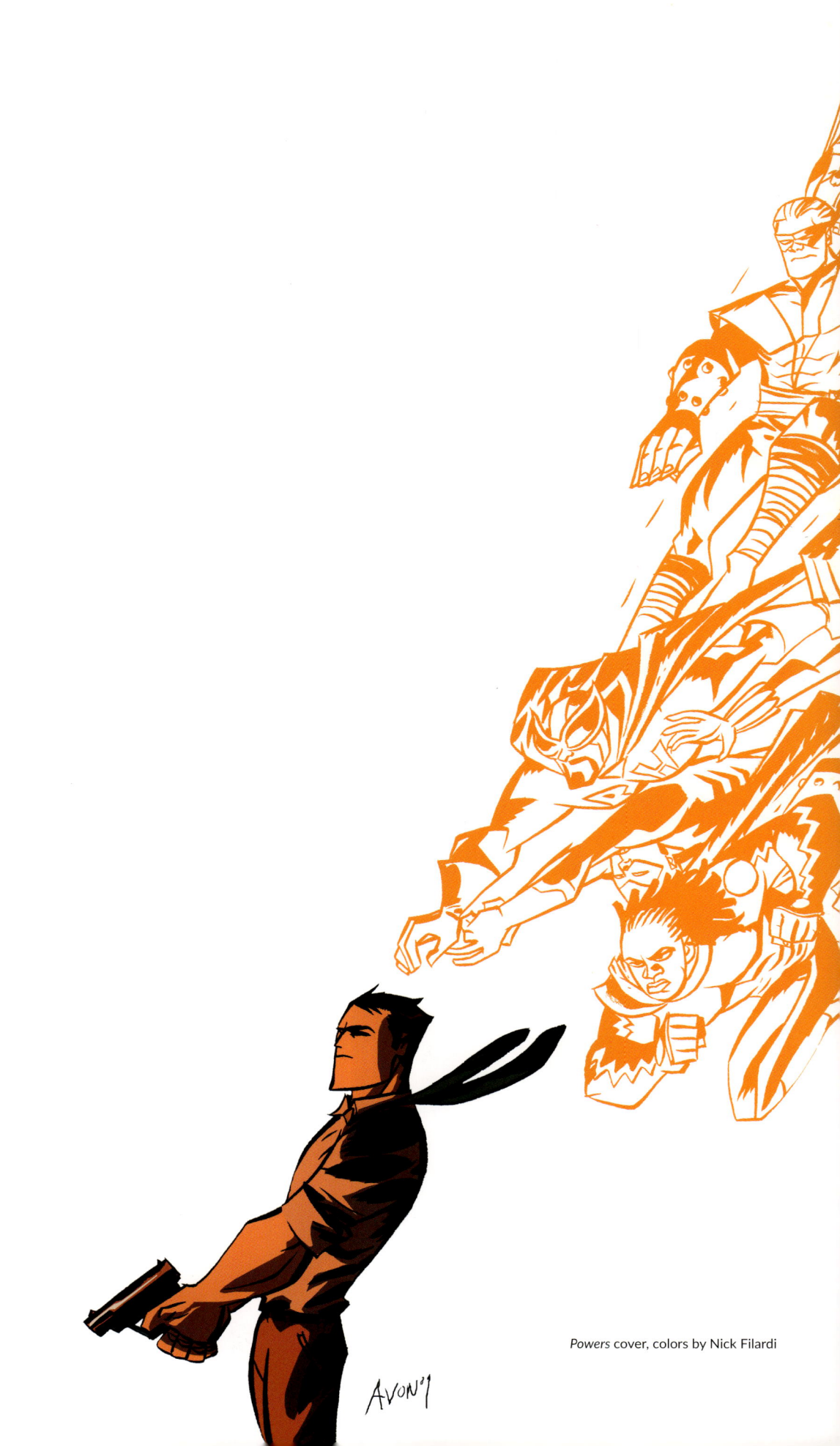

Powers cover, colors by Nick Filardi

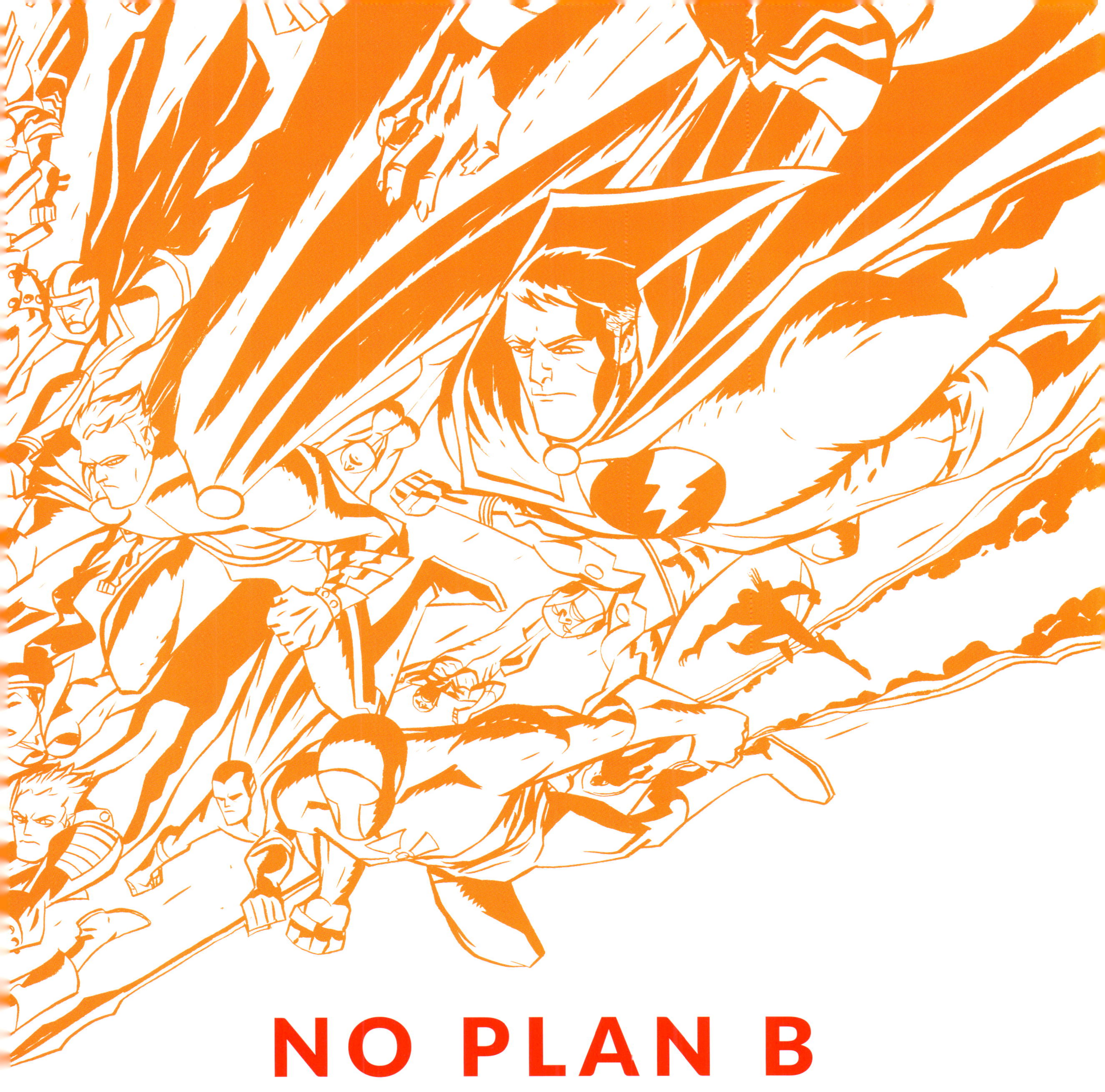

NO PLAN B

THE ART OF MICHAEL AVON OEMING

All art and colors by **OEMING** except where noted

Introduction by **BRIAN MICHAEL BENDIS**

Afterword by **DAVID MACK**

MICHAEL AVON OEMING interviewed by
JOHN SIUNTRES in January and February 2017

Cover colors by **DAVE STEWART**

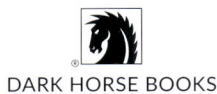

DARK HORSE BOOKS

PUBLISHER **MIKE RICHARDSON**

EDITOR **SCOTT ALLIE**

ASSISTANT EDITOR **KATII O'BRIEN**

DESIGNER **ETHAN KIMBERLING**

DIGITAL ART TECHNICIAN **CHRISTIANNE GOUDREAU**

SPECIAL THANKS TO Taki Soma, Brian Michael Bendis, David Mack, Jen Gruenwald, Jim Krueger, and Riley Pittenger.

Neil Hankerson, *Executive Vice President* · Tom Weddle, *Chief Financial Officer* · Randy Stradley, Vice President of Publishing · Matt Parkinson, *Vice President of Marketing* · David Scroggy, *Vice President of Product Development* · Dale LaFountain, *Vice President of Information Technology* Cara Niece, *Vice President of Production and Scheduling* · Nick McWhorter, *Vice President of Media Licensing* · Mark Bernardi, *Vice President of Book Trade and Digital Sales* · Ken Lizzi, *General Counsel* · Dave Marshall, *Editor in Chief* · Davey Estrada, *Editorial Director* · Scott Allie, *Executive Senior Editor* · Chris Warner, *Senior Books Editor* · Cary Grazzini, *Director of Specialty Projects* Lia Ribacchi, *Art Director* · Vanessa Todd, *Director of Print Purchasing* · Matt Dryer, *Director of Digital Art and Prepress* · Sarah Robertson, *Director of Product Sales* · Michael Gombos, *Director of International Publishing and Licensing*

Published by Dark Horse Books
A division of Dark Horse Comics, Inc.
10956 SE Main Street
Milwaukie, OR 97222

First edition: August 2017
ISBN 978-1-50670-307-7

10 9 8 7 6 5 4 3 2 1
Printed in China

International Licensing: (503) 905-2377
Comic Shop Locator Service: (888) 266-4226

No Plan B: The Art of Michael Avon Oeming © 2017 Michael Avon Oeming. Wild Rover, The Victories, 7 Nation Army, all ™ & © Michael Avon Oeming. Mice Templar ™ & © Michael Avon Oeming, Bryan J.L. Glass, and Victor Santos. Quixote, Ship of Fools ™ & © Michael Avon Oeming and Bryan J.L. Glass. Powers, Takio, United States of Murder Inc. ™ & © Michael Avon Oeming and Jinxworld, Inc. Rapture, Sinergy ™ & © Michael Avon Oeming and Taki Soma. God Complex ™ & © Michael Avon Oeming, Dan Berman and John Broglia. Hammer of the Gods ™ & © Michael Avon Oeming and Mark Wheatley. Half Moon © Michael Avon Oeming and Warren Ellis. The Circle © Michael Avon Oeming and Scott Allie. Mike Mignola's Hellboy, Abe Sapien, B.P.R.D. all ™ & © Michael Mignola. The Goon™ & © Eric Powell. Madman™ & © Mike Allred. Kabuki™ & © David Mack. Fight Club 2 ™ & © Chuck Palahniuk. Usagi Yojimbo™ & © Stan Sakai. Conan ® © Conan Properties International LLC. Aleister & Adolf™ & © Douglas Rushkoff. Alabaster™ & © Caitlín R. Kiernan. Emerald City Comicon Crusader and Crusaderette ™ & © ReedPOP. Will Eisner's The Spirit ™ & © Will Eisner Studios, Inc. Furious ™ © Bryan J.L. Glass and Victor Santos. Foot Soldiers ™ & © Jim Krueger. Galaga © Namco Ltd. Scarlet © Jinxworld, Inc and Alex Maleev. Captain Victory ™ & © Jack Kirby. A.K.A. One in the Chamber ™ & © Rob Reilly and Steven Walters. Head Lopper ™ & © Andrew MacLean. Bitch Planet ™ & © Kelly Sue DeConnick and Valentine De Landro. Pretty Deadly ™ & © Kelly Sue DeConnick and Emma Ríos. Lady Saber and the Pirates of the Ineffable Aether ™ & © Greg Rucka and Rich Burchett. Dark Horse Books® and the Dark Horse logo are registered trademarks of Dark Horse Comics, Inc. All rights reserved. No portion of this publication may be reproduced or transmitted, in any form or by any means, without the express written permission of Dark Horse Comics, Inc. Names, characters, places, and incidents featured in this publication either are the product of the author's imagination or are used fictitiously. Any resemblance to actual persons (living or dead), events, institutions, or locales, without satiric intent, is coincidental.

Library of Congress Cataloging-in-Publication Data

Names: Bendis, Brian Michael, writer of introduction. | Mack, David, 1969- writer of afterword. | Oeming, Michael Avon. Works. Selections.
Title: No plan B : the art of Michael Avon Oeming / introduction by Brian Michael Bendis ; afterword by David Mack.
Description: First edition. | Milwaukie, OR : Dark Horse Books, 2017. | "Michael Avon Oeming interviewed by John Siuntres in January and February 2017. Cover colors by Dave Stewart."
Identifiers: LCCN 2017015114 | ISBN 9781506703077 (hardback)
Subjects: LCSH: Oeming, Michael Avon--Criticism and interpretation. | BISAC: ART / Popular Culture. | ART / Individual Artists / General. | ART / General.
Classification: LCC NC1764.5.U62 O3936 2017 | DDC 741.6092--dc23
LC record available at https://lccn.loc.gov/2017015114

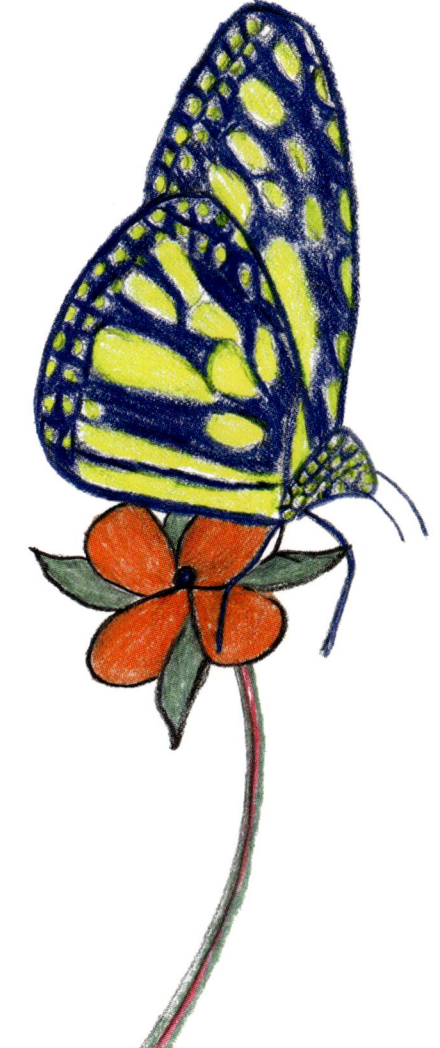

DEDICATED TO my three parents. To my mother Linda Mae Williams, Aunt Carol, and Uncle Larry Pastuszak. What would I have been without you?

OEMING!

By Brian Michael Bendis

Brace yourself. This is going to get mushy.

Why? Because this intro is coming from one of Michael's best friends and closest collaborators for over twenty years. In that time, we have developed our creative partnership into a friendship and then, even more surprisingly and importantly, we have become family. I actually know the story behind almost every single picture in this book. I know the stories of all of the pictures he didn't even put in this book. And, by the way, there are thousands of those too.

That's the first thing you need to know: Michael cannot stop drawing. The title of the book should have been *Obsessive-Compulsive Disorder: The Michael Oeming Story*. Sometimes when he is just hanging out and not working, I can see his hand moving as if it were drawing in the air. Like John Hurt's character in *Indiana Jones and the Kingdom of the Crystal Skull*, just put a pen in Mike's hand, hold up a pad in front of it, and see what you get.

So, the book is really called *No Plan B* because he can't stop drawing even if he wanted to. But, truth be told, this *No Plan B* philosophy is part of the glue that attracted us to each other in the first place.

I first met Michael at a store signing in Philadelphia. Claude's Comics, which I believe is no longer with us, had invited me, David Mack, Michael, and a few other buzzy indie artists of the time. We had just started producing our first signature works for independent comics, and this lovely store just liked our work and had us to Philadelphia to be part of their celebration. It was an act of fan over business, as we had absolutely no draw, but it was this very store signing that changed all of our creative lives. David and I were already friends, but we both met Michael this day and we liked him. Jerry Seinfeld used to have a joke about how only kids can walk up to another kid on the street or the playground and just say, "Hey, want to be best friends?" and then become best friends. Adults don't do that. Except, it seems, at indie comic book store signings in Philly. Mike, David Mack, and I did this. We met, said, "Let's be best friends," and then . . . we just did. And stayed that way for all these years. We even called ourselves the MOB because we just wanted people to know. Awwww . . .

Mike had quite a few credits under his belt, because, as I am sure will be well illustrated in this book, he broke into the industry at a very young age. An annoyingly young age. He was inking professional Marvel comics as a teenager! He was inking *Daredevil* as a teenager!! That's crazy.

Ask him about the cornucopia of graphic novel erotica that Michael produced in his early days. (*Edward Penishands* is my favorite.)

I'm sure John and Mike get into it, but Mike had to reinvent himself and start over at the ripe old age of twenty-one. The industry had some ups and downs, and Mike, at his young age, didn't understand that maintaining a career is harder than getting one. (He understands now.) At the time David and I met Mike, he was reestablishing his creative voice with the style that would become synonymous with *Powers*.

After our lovely weekend in Philadelphia, we all went home to work on our books that we hoped, hoped, hoped one day someone would care about. The next day, I got a fax (because I'm old). It was a Mike drawing of my character Jinx from a graphic novel I was working on at the time, but in his new, let's call it "*Powers* style." He also did a version of David Mack's Kabuki character. They were both outstanding, and I immediately found myself wanting to read *Jinx* written by me and drawn by Mike more than I was interested in *Jinx* written and drawn by me. I called David Mack and I asked, "Are we going to fight over him, or can I have him?"

I called Mike and started what would become our life-defining friendship. I also pitched what would eventually become *Powers*. He immediately sent back the first drawing attempts of Christian Walker, which were so close to what Walker actually ended up becoming that anyone could see we were going to be a very good partnership.

What I did not know at the time was that Mike was broke and living paycheck to paycheck from a job as a nighttime security guard at a New Jersey parking lot. I did not know, until I did, that Mike drew the first issues of *Powers* under the light of his security booth in the middle of the winter in the middle of New Jersey. I didn't realize that he was basically starting over from scratch. The market had shifted and he had run out of gigs. All I knew at the time was he knew how to produce professional, kick-ass, unique, energetic books.

So for those artists out there who bought this book with the only money you have, I hope the fact that so much of this was drawn in places like that New Jersey security booth means you will be inspired to not be beaten down by your personal situation and to keep making comics or art or music. It can be done. Mike did it. He really did.

Mike works every day. Every day. He works everywhere. Hurt his back? He'll draw upside down. This book could easily be ten times as long. That's how many drawings Mike has. Good drawings, too. All "Best of Mike" stuff. Paring this volume down must have been insane.

Back when *Powers* was first being assembled in the late nineties (Google it; it's a real decade), neither Mike nor I had individually produced a book that had generated orders over four thousand copies. So the fact that we were trying to produce a full-color book that needed at least twelve thousand to break even was asking a bit much from the universe. "But, God, we really like making comics together!" Thankfully, that's exactly what our first numbers were . . . twelve thousand. We were thrilled. We got to go to print. But then you have to worry about the second issue and the third issue and, historically, almost pathologically, those numbers go down, way down, because retailers are ordering *before* they find out if anybody even bought the first one. But because it was, I guess, *our time*, things just fell into place after many years of not. *Powers* actually increased in numbers, and by the end of our first story line we had tripled and quadrupled what the first issue's numbers were. That literally never happens. We had a hit. Our first.

Together.

We soon discovered that "hit book" means Hollywood calls. Sony called and made us an offer after the first issue. A real movie offer. Enough money to get Mike out of that security booth ASAP. And he never looked back.

Except one time.

So, many years later, in Atlanta, on the set of the *Powers* television show, I pulled my producer's car into our secured parking lot. I pulled up to a sign that read, "Powers Parking Only."

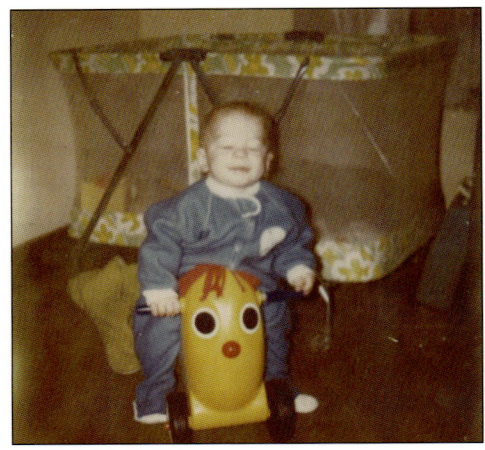 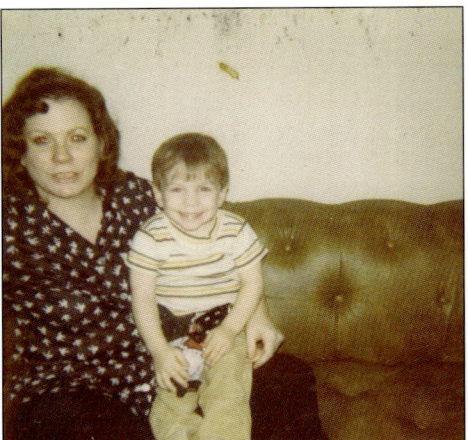 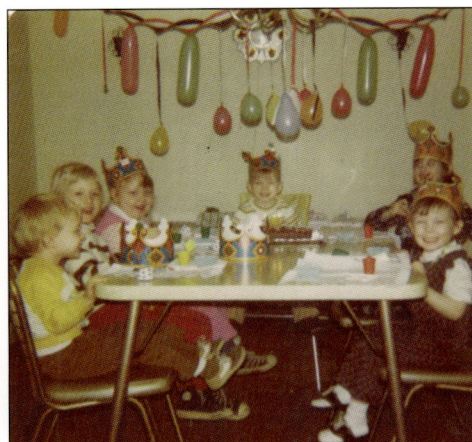

Oeming as toddler; with mother, Linda Mae Williams; fourth birthday, Bordentown, New Jersey

The book that started in the parking lot now had its own parking lot. I FaceTimed to show him. The moment landed. Now, that is full fucking circle.

Oh yeah, we got a TV show. After fifteen years of development roller coaster—and I don't call it *hell*, I call it a roller coaster because hell is just torture with no hope. Roller coaster is a completely different feeling. This was roller coaster.

After fifteen years of development, *Powers* turned from movie into a cable television show into the premiere broadcast show of a streaming service using technology that didn't exist when *Powers* was first born. Through that entire *crazy*balls process of Hollywood maybes, producer lies, defeats, successes, and all that that entails, my friendship and partnership with Michael grew. Maybe it was all the crazy, but where most creative teams split from the stress, we did the opposite . . . Why? Because of Mike.

Our partnership grew in leaps and bounds. We kept creating new books. Mike trusted everything would work out, and he was the only one. Oh, and he was right. Not only did we get a pilot from FX; we got to make two seasons of the show for PlayStation. Get a TV show if you can—it was pretty great.

So now our little book, which we were drawing in our basements, and in our security booth, was a multimillion-dollar Sony operation. Standing on set with Mike, sometimes even shoulder to shoulder, watching the crew and the cast make the show with the same amount of passion that Mike carries with him in his notebook, will always be one of the great joys of my adult life (that don't involve my wife or children).

I was so happy that both showrunners for *Powers* saw the value of Mike. Sometimes when a series gets turned into a television show or movie, the first thing that goes is the artist's unique vision. The artist has a line art and ink style that gets replaced by film and cinematography. Instead, Mike's invaluable graphics showed up as part of the story. It was the voice of Retro Girl's marketing campaign and how the Powers were sold as cartoon characters in the world of *Powers*. For season 2, they asked Mike to work with the people doing our credit sequence so that the credit sequence was a stronger reflection of the comic. Michael's graphic style will forever be part of the show.

Mike would sit on set and draw the actors in character, acting in scenes from the book he originally drew, and then give the sketches to the actors. Told you, *always* drawing.

Here we are on the other side. Our show is done, at least in this incarnation. Cancellation is heartbreaking. We are grateful that we had the show at all, and don't feel mad at anybody that it isn't there anymore, but at the same time we certainly would've liked to continue making it. I bring this up not because the wound is fresh—all my wounds are always fresh—but because how Mike handled it is why I love Mike. To me, cancellation is kind of like breaking up with someone that you still like. They don't like you, so there's not much to talk about, but it still hurts because you were feeling very good in the relationship.

But Mike? When I had to call Mike and tell him the bad news, he just said, "That was fun. Let's get back to work."

Let's. Get. Back. To. Work.

I love him so much. For Mike, it's all about the work. So Mike is never unsatisfied or dispassionate or bored, because he always has his work.

Just last week—here comes the mushy—my wife and I went on a double date with Mike and Taki, his wife, our friend, and I believe we laughed like idiots the entire time. Just four friends having been through everything and come out the other side, eager to have great Portland pie and talk about the past, present, and future.

It's easy to look at the crazy, big moments in life and celebrate the relationships around those, but as I get older it's the little moments that stick out. Like a double date just full of laughs.

All the while, Mike and I both know we may not have even scratched the surface of what we are capable of doing together. As this volume clearly illustrates, there is nothing, artistically, Mike is not capable of.

There is a line in the *Steve Jobs* movie that says you don't have to be an asshole to be gifted. That it is not binary. That you can be both gifted and kind. Mike is and will always be both. Mike has always and without question treated everyone he has ever met with respect and dignity.

So, you're about a hundred pages away from asking, "Then how can someone that nice draw such fucked-up stuff?"

(Another good title for the book.)

Because he does it right! He takes the crazy, rage, anger, fear, loathing, and all those other messy, gorgeous feelings we all have, and makes them art. That's what artists are supposed to do. If you are an artist, and you bought this book looking for knowledge, now you have it. ☺ I love that Mike almost subconsciously uses artwork to work out his issues, whether they be conspiracies or a divorce. He puts it all in the pages of his comics. I joked for years that I wrote the violence and sex scenes in *Powers* because if I didn't, Mike was going to put them in there anyhow—and there was a time he actually did that, so I thought I might as well make them part of the story. ☺

So, my darling friend Michael, I celebrate this book with you as I celebrate your life with you. You deserve this and so much more.

That sounded like a bar mitzvah toast. It might have been. I'll try again.

Here's to many, many more years, and many more decades, and many more projects together.

Okay, that sounded very bar mitzvah. I'm sorry. I love you.

BENDIS!
Portland, Oregon 2017

NO PLAN B

Michael Avon Oeming
From an interview with John Siuntres

My love of comics started in sixth grade after a second cross-country move.

I was born in El Paso, Texas, January 30, 1973. My mom had had a drinking problem since before I was born, and we moved to New Jersey before I was one to be near my aunt and uncle, Carol and Larry Pastuszak. My mother lost custody of me when I was four, and I moved in with Carol and Larry in Bordentown, New Jersey. Mom lived in halfway homes trying to get sober, but would write to me all the time, drawing clowns or flowers in her letters. My early connection with my mother was through art.

She got better, and regained custody of me in 1981, when I was eight, and we all lived together in Bordentown. Those were some of the best years. But Mom wanted a fresh start, and in 1982 she and I moved to Fort Worth, where her other sister Annette lived. I'd spent my childhood in the suburbs of New Jersey, so Texas was like another planet. I was guilty of a certain amount of northeastern snobbery, which I was unaware of at the time. I couldn't adjust or connect to anybody in Texas.

My mother took me to a flea market where guys were selling *Spider-Man* comics out of a long box. I flashed back to the *Electric Company* TV show and the old Ralph Bakshi *Spider-Man* cartoon. I brought the comics home and became obsessed, using tracing paper to copy panels, and realized this is what I wanted to do—draw comics.

We moved back and forth between Jersey and Texas for a few years. I could always find a 7-Eleven to buy comics. In the early eighties the art I saw was watered-down imitations of Jack Kirby's Marvel style. Then in 1985, while living in Jersey, I saw *X-Men Annual* #9. It was set in Asgard, which blew my mind—I was a big fan of Norse mythology but hadn't read the Marvel *Thor* comics. More importantly, Art Adams drew that annual, and it looked amazing. Not only did I want to draw comics professionally, I wanted to be Arthur Adams. Arthur's work led me to seek out other artists, like Rick Leonardi, Mike Mignola, and of course Walt Simonson's *Thor* run.

In 1986, an ad in the back of a Marvel book led me to my first real comics shop, Thunder Road Comics in Burlington, New Jersey, not far from where I lived, where I met another customer. Adam Hughes lived one town over from me. I'd met a few other aspiring artists from whom I learned a lot, but they never made it in comics. Adam became an early mentor and a good friend. He went through the same beginner challenges I was going through, but even before he got professional work, you could see his potential. He was already a great artist.

I met Neil Vokes and Rich Rankin through Adam. They were doing *Eagle*, a book from the black-and-white comics boom in the mideighties. Rich inked Neil, and Adam did pinups and backgrounds for them. I was in my early teens, and they were always there with advice. I learned about inking from Rich. An inker learns a lot from the pencillers he inks. Adam and Neil and some others gave me photocopies of their pencils, which I'd ink on vellum, as well as practicing over copies of Art Adams and Barry Windsor-Smith pages.

I'd send samples to an editor at one company or another, and he'd write back to tell me what I needed to work on. The lessons you learn through that rejection and failure are important. My greatest strength as an artist is getting through my weaknesses by working through my doubt. So many artists stop because of self-doubt. I'd rather finish a bad drawing and redo it later than continue to work to make it perfect. Finishing things is one of the greatest lessons an artist can learn.

Eventually I got some inking work from a company called Innovation. I was fourteen in 1987 and I'd broken into comics! But I was so inexperienced I didn't know how to get more work. I was in high school, so it's good I didn't pursue comics full-time immediately. I was still trying to draw like Art Adams, Michael Golden, and Kevin Nowlan—highly detailed, realistic stuff. I could never pull that off. It took a long time to decide which kind of style worked for me.

When I broke into comics full-time, on *Child's Play* for Innovation in 1990, it was still as an inker. Later I got some pencilling and

Jim Krueger's The Foot Soldiers

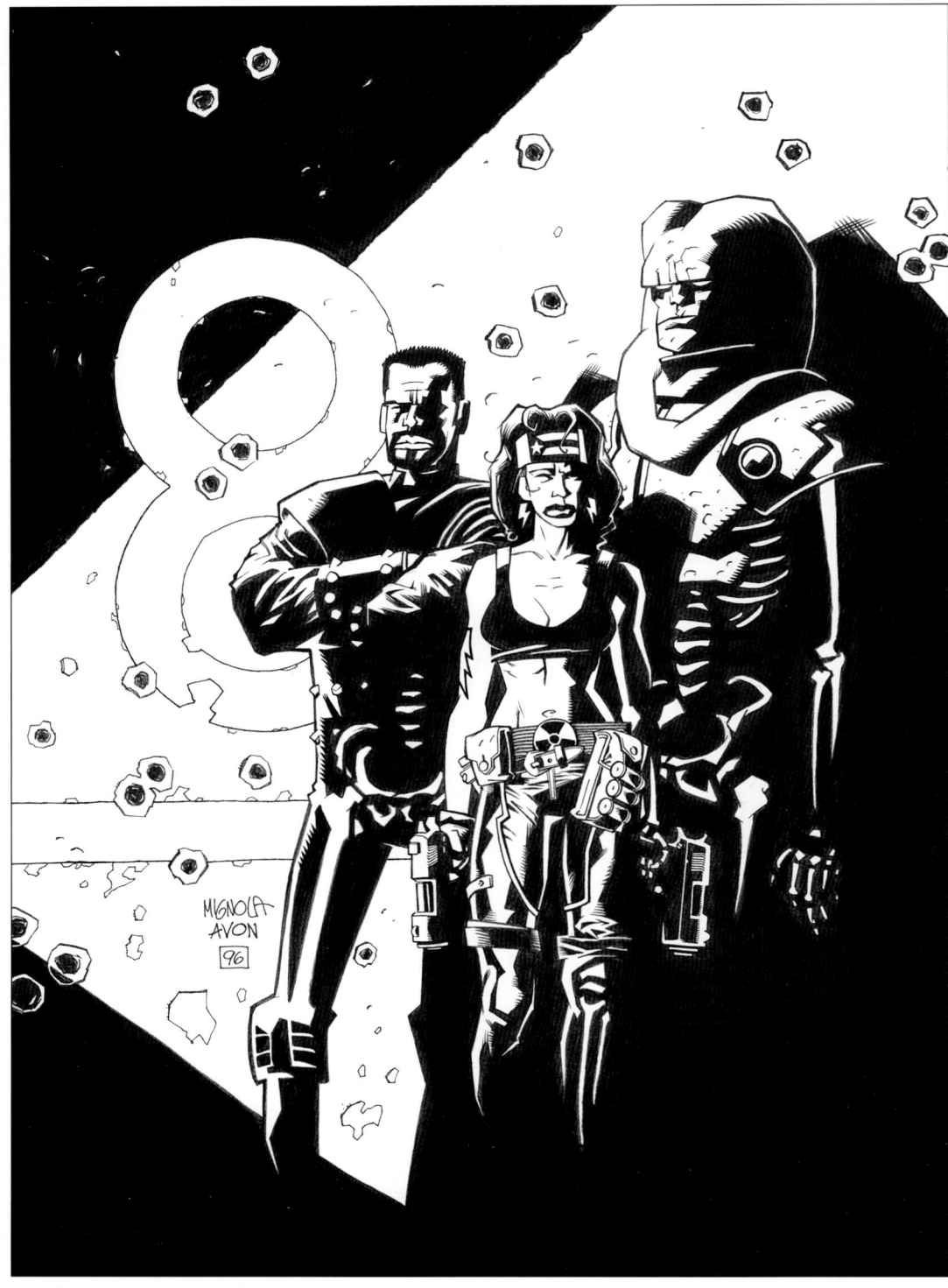

Ship of Fools cover, pencils by Mike Mignola, inks by Oeming

inking jobs. Speculators who'd driven comics sales to an unsustainable high left, and the market imploded in the mid-1990s. I'd been drawing *Judge Dredd* for DC when the paying work dried up.

While on *Dredd* I'd met Jim Krueger at a New York comics convention. He showed me designs for a series called *Foot Soldiers* that he wanted to write. We did the book for Dark Horse in 1994, and it's led to a lifelong friendship with Jim. *Foot Soldiers* is the earliest work I can look back on without cringing, but the industry was still suffering. Every time I looked up from my desk, another comics publisher was folding. Hundreds of stores were closing, and jobs were disappearing. *Foot Soldiers* couldn't pay the bills.

I went back to inking, but competition for inking jobs got stiff too. I inked *Ninjak* for Neil Vokes at Valiant until my son Ethan was born in 1996. I was twenty-three and couldn't support my family working in comics. I got a regular job for the first time in my life.

In 1998 I worked nights as a security guard in a small booth on a car lot, where I'd have some downtime to draw. I had so little time between work and having a son that I had to radically rethink the way I was drawing.

I tried to get work on DC's *Batman Adventures* books, based on the Bruce Timm TV series. I played around with this cartoony, nonrendered style, and people reacted to it strongly when I sold

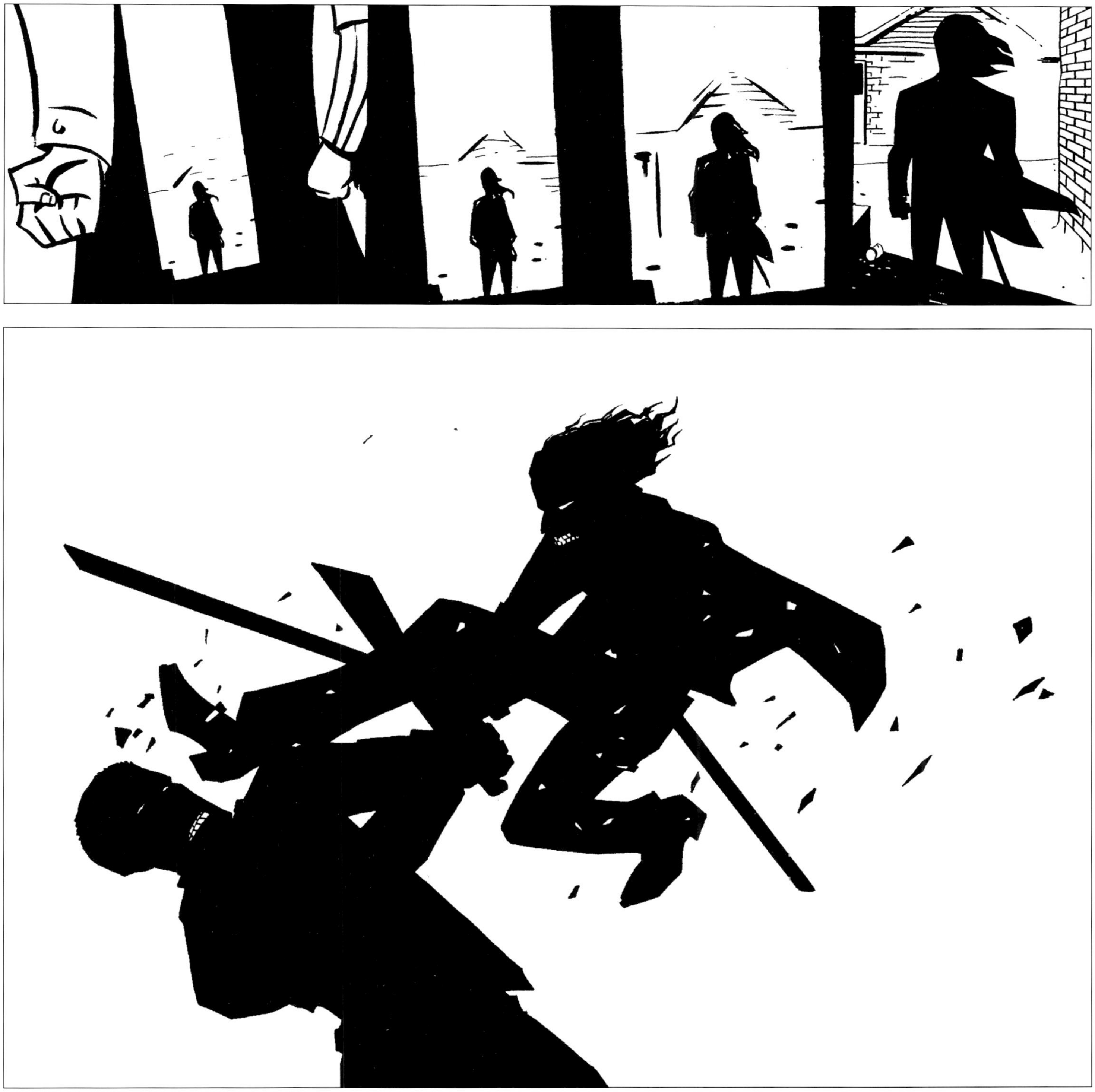

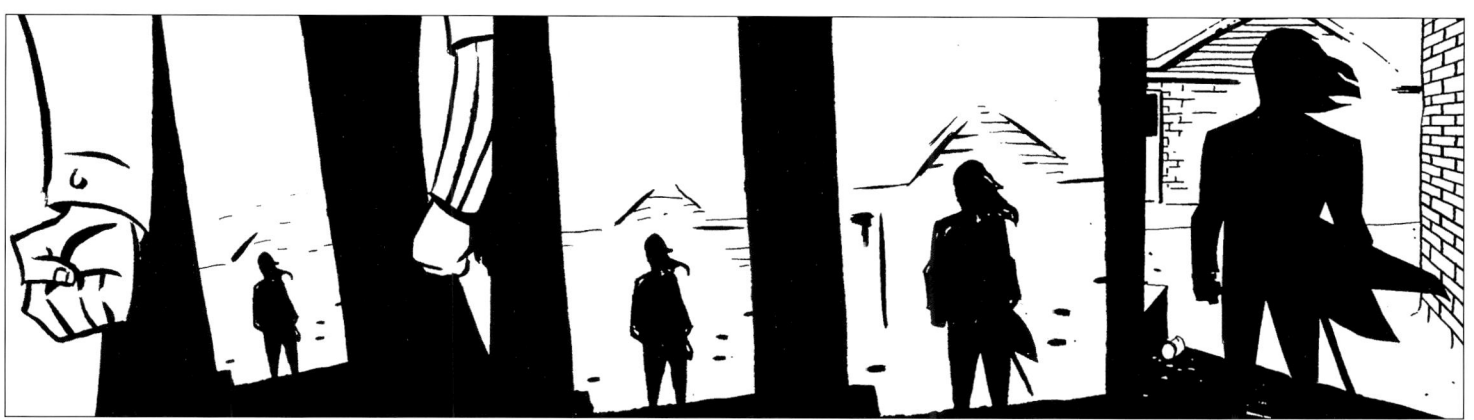

Quixote: A Novel interior art

pinups at conventions. I loved the style and decided this was the direction I needed to go in.

The anxiety about what editors wanted—about what style would please a publisher—was gone. I wasn't getting jobs anyway. I stopped sending samples in. I'd draw for myself, making indie comics while keeping a regular job. This was the great lesson from failure. I stepped out of comics to redefine the direction for my career—and everything turned around for me.

Adam Hughes had introduced me to a *Star Wars* role-playing group, led by Bryan Glass. Bryan wrote his own campaigns, something I hadn't known you could do. We'd start playing at 9 p.m. and go until 3 a.m. I was blown away by Bryan's storytelling. He and I started working on a comic about a modern-day Don Quixote set in a big city. Quixote was a crazy homeless person, with Sancho as his homeless sidekick. I'd given Bryan just the smallest idea—an image of a helicopter stuck on top of a building, looking like a windmill. That's all I had, and I loved Bryan's take on it.

We weren't able to finish it as a comic. Years later, I asked Bryan, "Why don't we do an illustrated novel?" I took art from the comic and added a bunch of new stuff. Bryan wrote the book. His brother, Jim Glass, did the production work. We published the novel through Image in 2005, the four hundredth anniversary of the original *Don Quixote* novel by Cervantes. It took us to Spain for book signings.

Bryan Glass was my first collaborator, and has been one of my longest friendships. The first thing we worked on was called *Spandex Tights*. We did a couple of other things with a company called Comics Zone.

I wanted to do a science-fiction book influenced by an old BBC TV series called *Blake's 7*, which had a main character called Avon, my middle name. It was the first time I heard the name without it being associated with cosmetics. This turned into *Ship of Fools*, the first creator-owned book Bryan and I did, in 1993. Poor Bryan had to suffer through my inexperience, but it was some of the best times we ever had.

I came up with *Mice Templar* while working in that security booth. The films *Watership Down* and *The Secret of NIMH* left a big impact on me. At the same time I was getting into J. R. R. Tolkien's stories. I knew I had to flesh this idea out. By 1998 Bryan was out of comics, working with a theater group, but I wanted to bring him back in. We went to a Robert McKee story seminar and I pitched him *Mice Templar*. We didn't get *Mice Templar* out into the world until 2007 at Image Comics, but Bryan took my six-issue outline and created a long-running series out of it.

Sometimes you have a certain project in mind and you want to collaborate. If you're lucky, there are people around that you know are perfect for it, and you tap them. That was the case with Bryan Glass and *Mice Templar*.

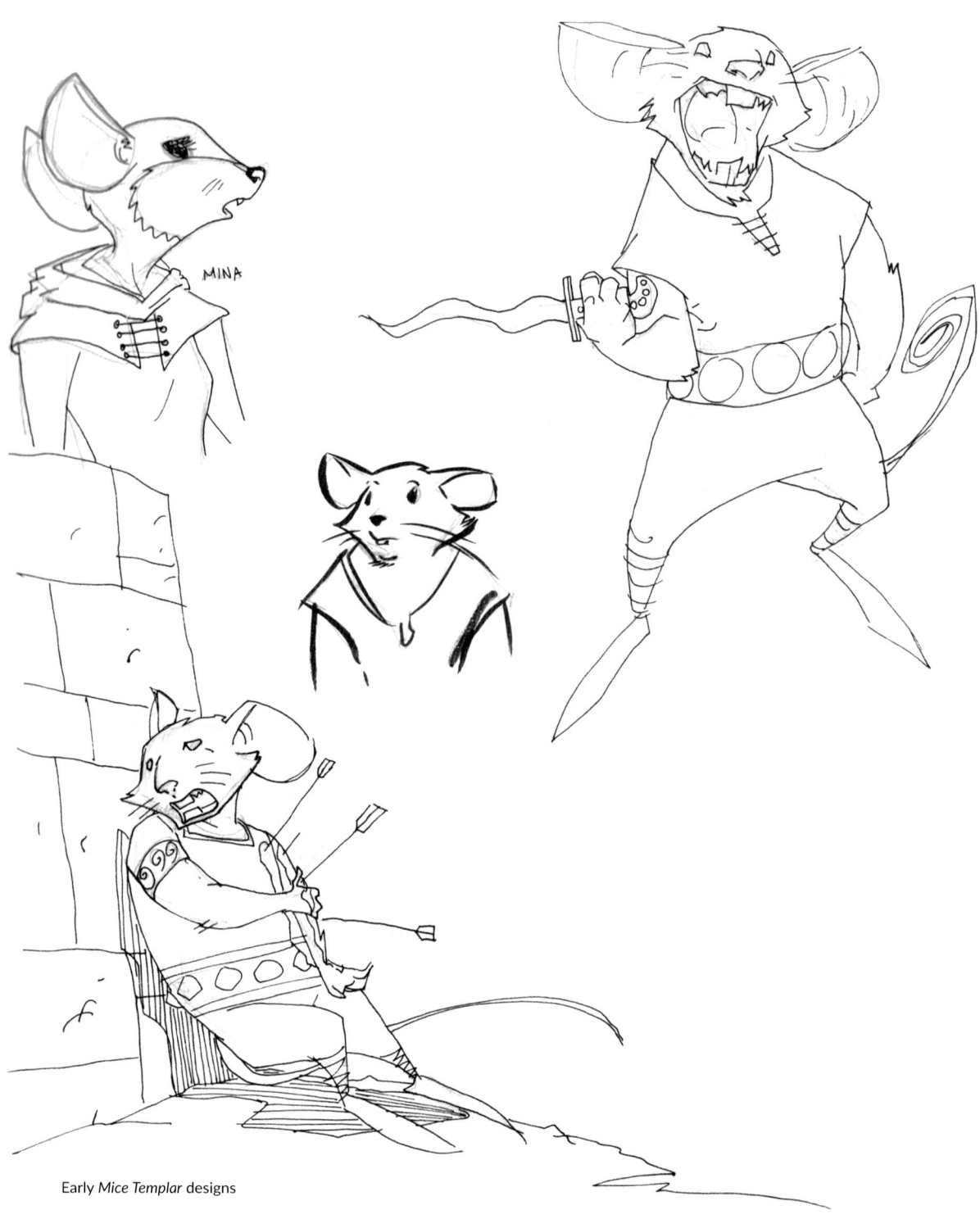

Early *Mice Templar* designs

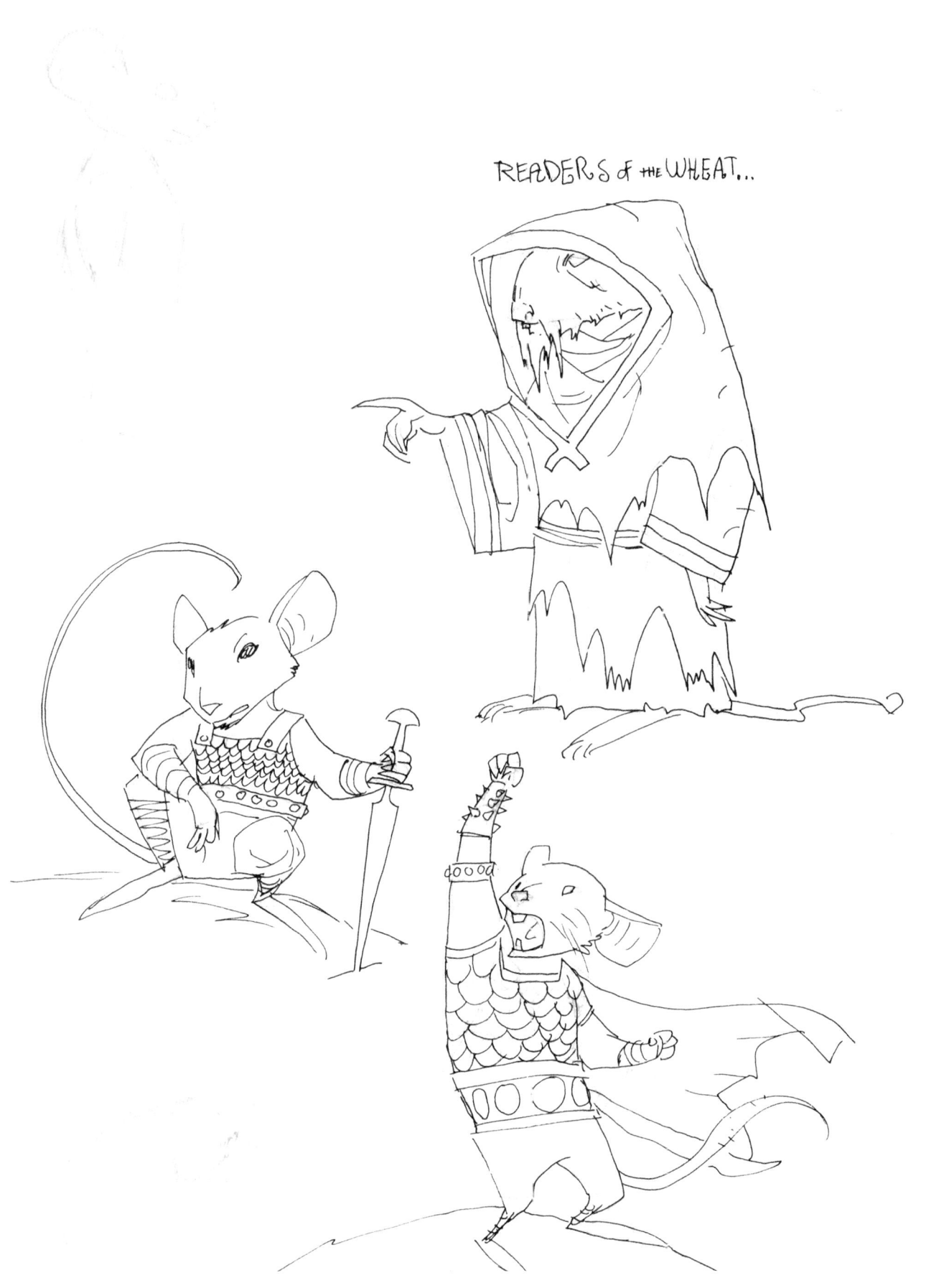

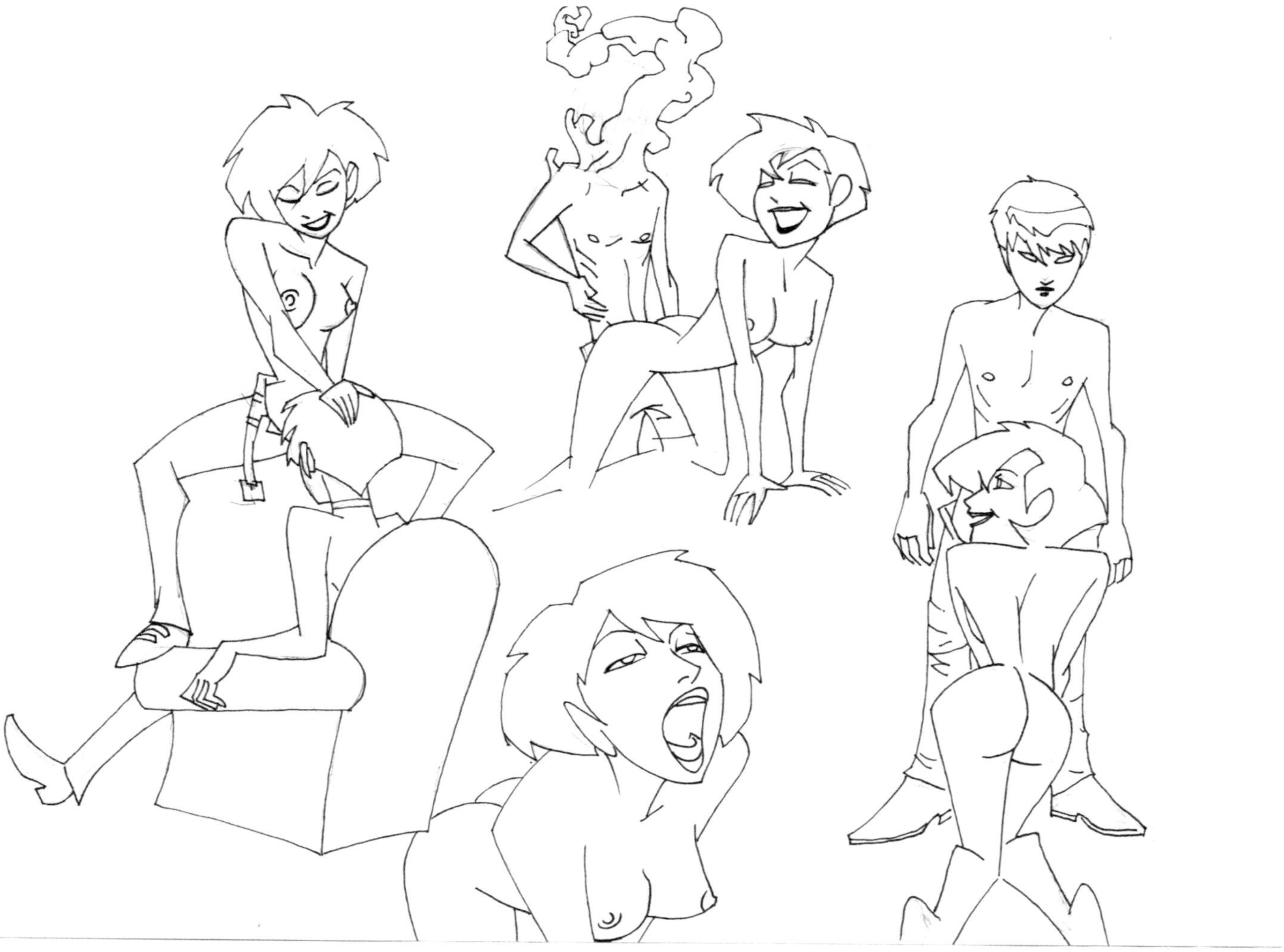

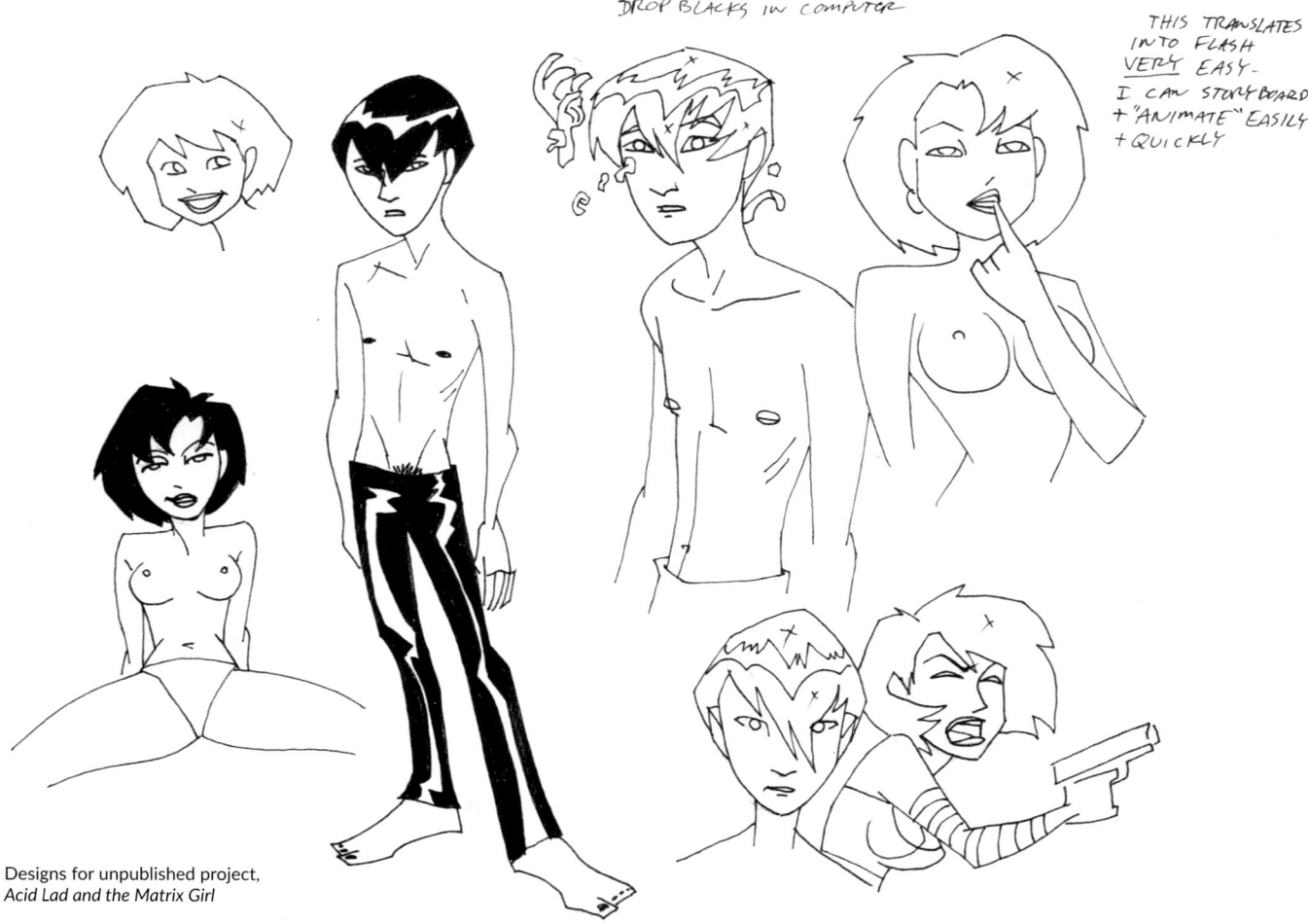

Designs for unpublished project, *Acid Lad and the Matrix Girl*

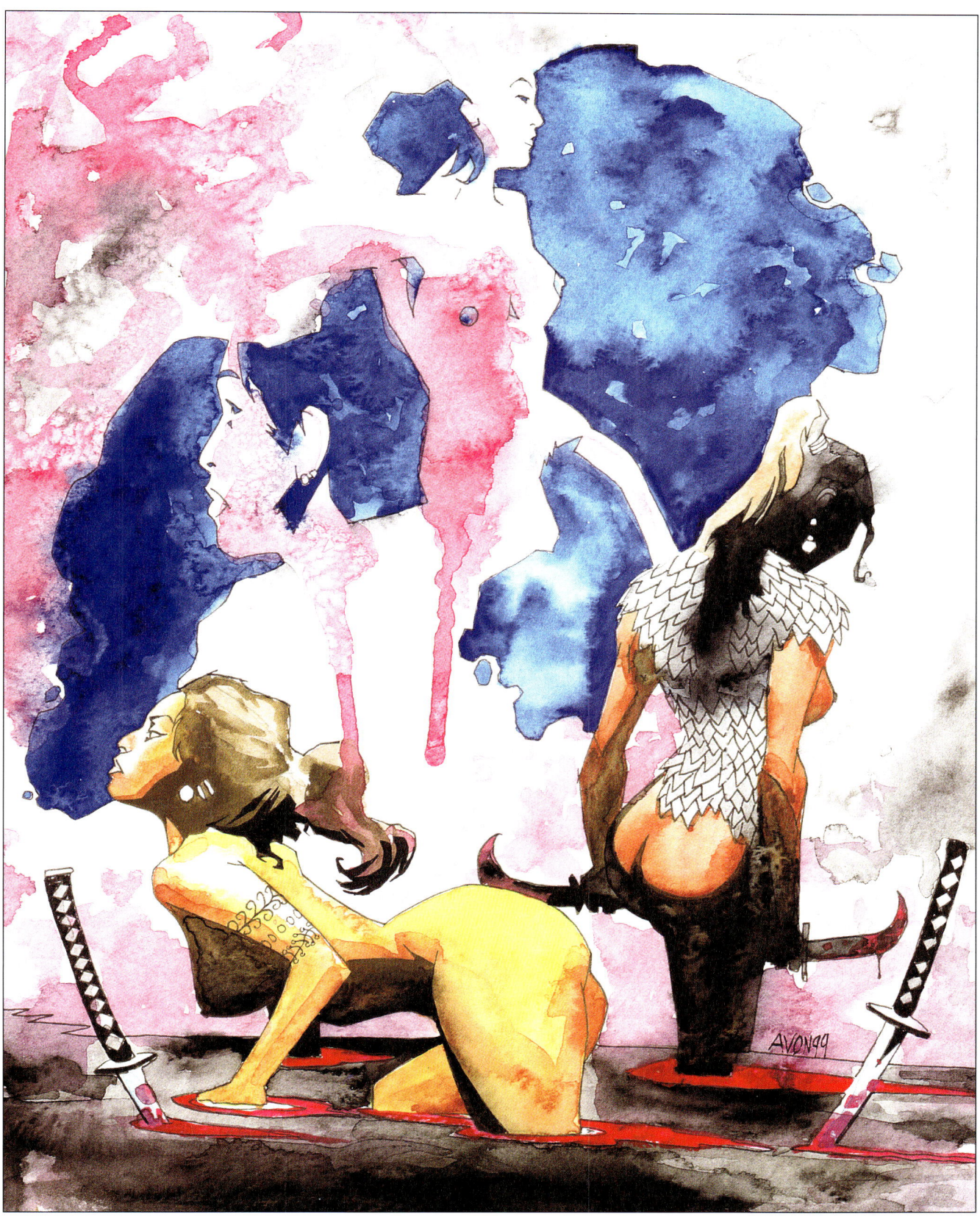

Even though David Mack and I have such different approaches to our art, his work has had a huge influence on me. I loved doing pinups for his *Kabuki* book, and my house is filled with paintings David has done of me, Taki, and our dog.

The very first book I drew after I met David was *Bulletproof Monk* in 1998 (Image Comics). Despite my turn to this new, cartoony approach in my art, *Monk* was a little more realistic because of what I was seeing in David's work. To emulate David's multimedia approach to his paintings, I used all sorts of design elements—triangles and abstract shapes that worked their way into the layout of the pages.

I've always loved how David uses watercolors. I like that they're not tight and controlled. I like colors to bleed and to do their own thing, and David has a perfect balance of total control while letting color speak for itself. I'm in awe of his work. When we get together I'll sketch him, and he'll sketch me. From the first time David and Brian Bendis and I all met doing a comic book signing in Pennsylvania, they've been two of my closest friends.

Before comics, my interests were dinosaurs, mythology, and Saturday-morning cartoons.

While other kids at the library picked out Dr. Seuss, I headed right for dinosaurs and mythology. I spent a lot of time in my own daydreams, amazed that dinosaurs had really existed, getting lost in the clues in the photographs of footprints and fossils.

I saw an extension of those ideas in the way some myths were connected to real places, or as metaphors for actual events, sometimes natural disasters or wars, like the Trojan War and Homer's *Iliad*. Gods were superheroes before I knew about comics. When Harryhausen's *Clash of the Titans* came out in 1981, I was overwhelmed with imagery.

Bordentown, New Jersey, was a rural town, where I could imagine dinosaurs in the woods and gods riding around on the clouds, every tree containing some hidden spirit.

When I got into comics, my early obsession with mythology was rekindled with Marvel's *Thor*, fueling my imagination. Norse mythology held my fascination more than the Greek because of how it combined pagan legends with Christianity. Odin's search for enlightenment involved him killing himself to be resurrected in a Christlike fashion. I saw the Christian Armageddon reflected in the death and renewal of Ragnarok, the Norse end-of-the-world scenario that I eventually got to play with when I wrote *Thor* for Marvel.

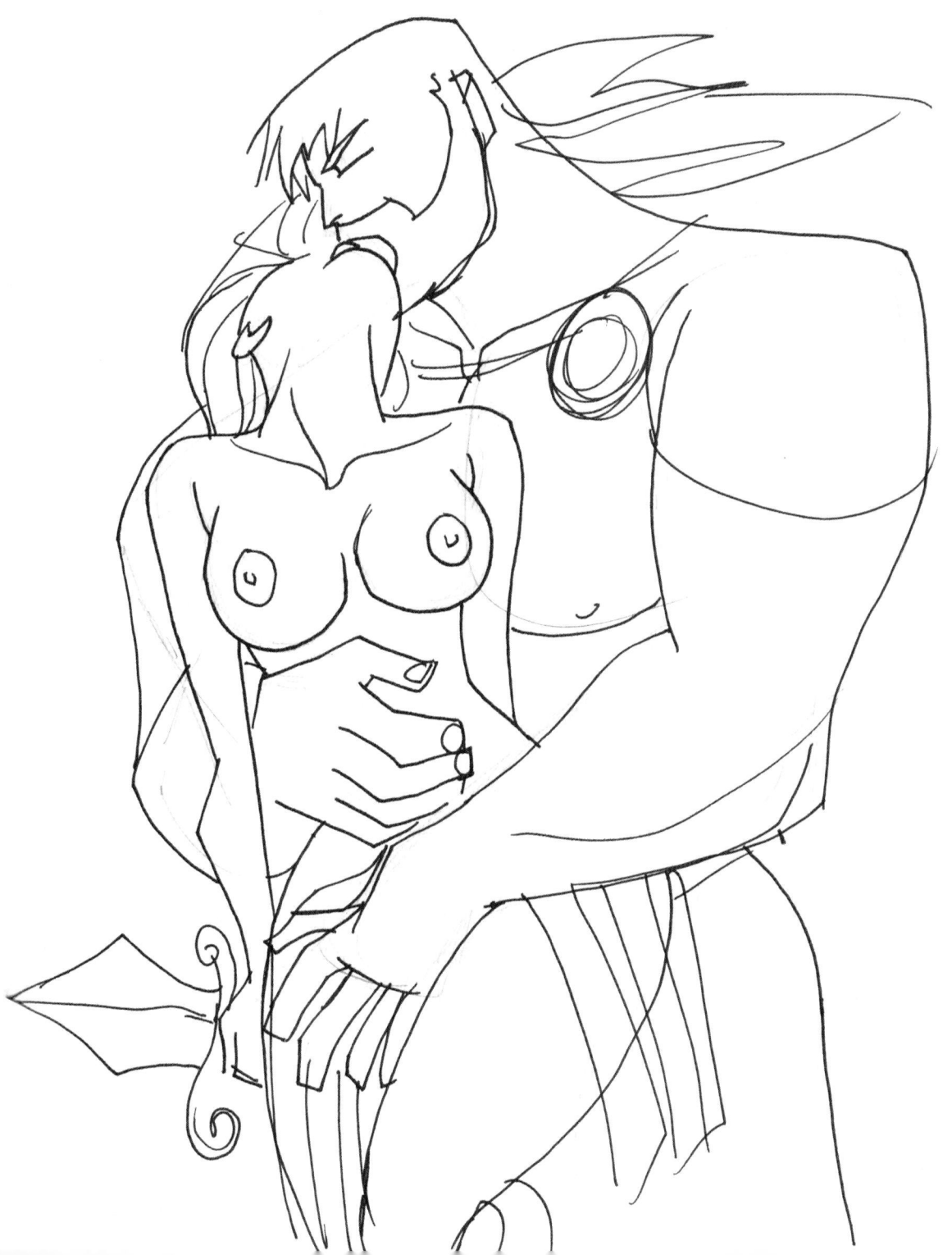

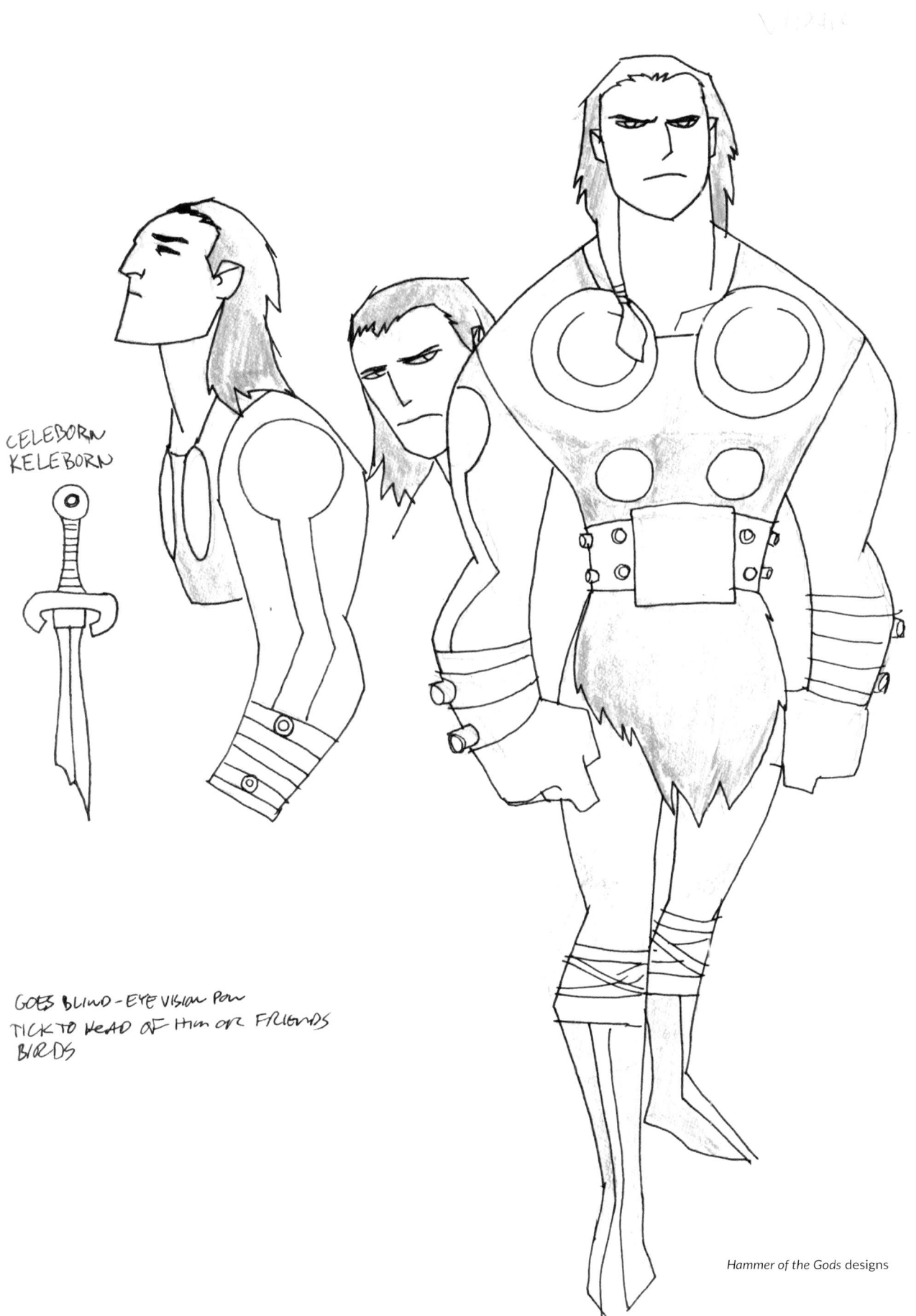

Hammer of the Gods designs

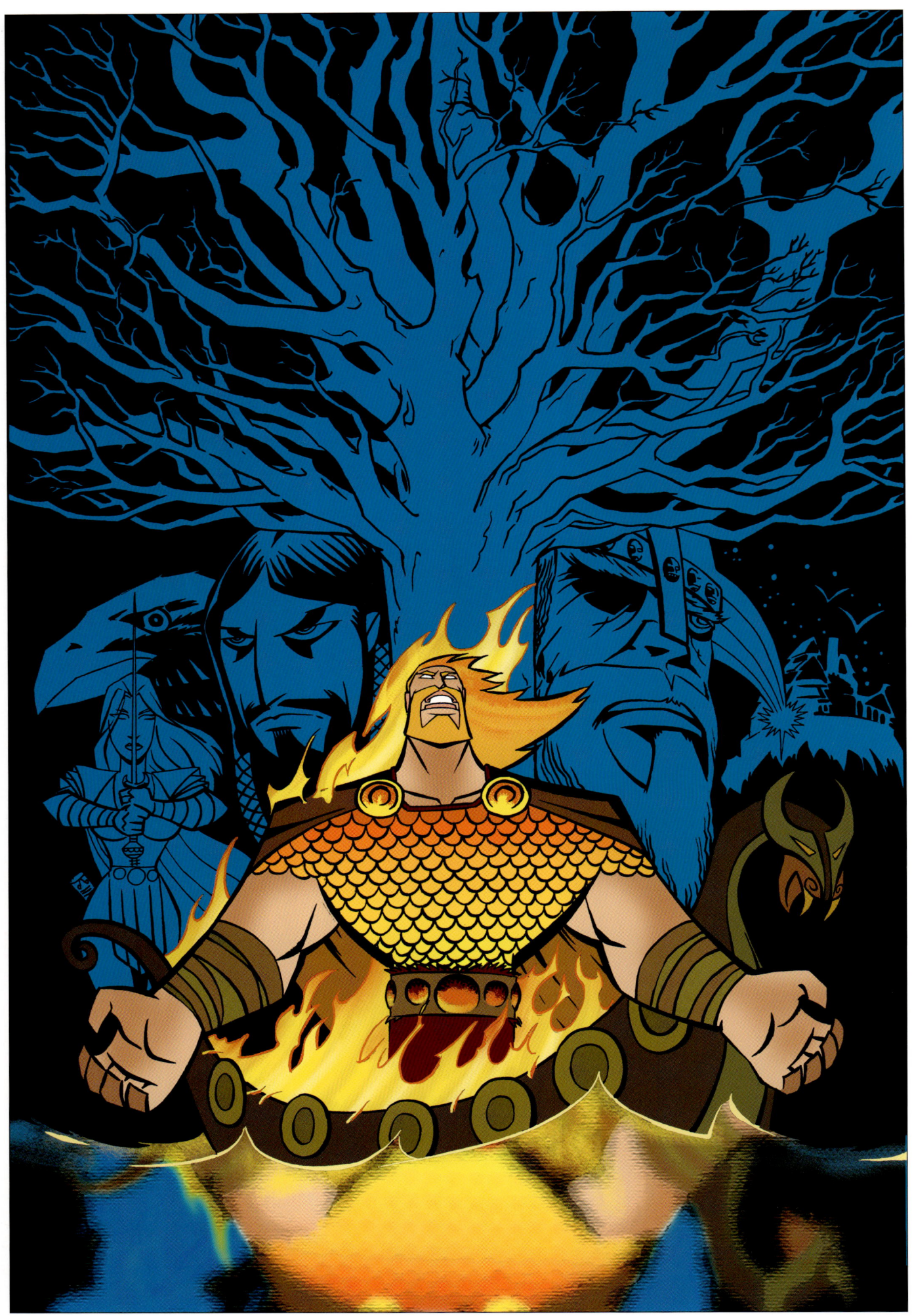
Hammer of the Gods cover, colors by Mark Wheatley

I met Mark Wheatley through Neil Vokes, and we shared a mutual interest in Norse mythology. I'd come up with the *Hammer of the Gods* plot when I was working in the security booth, but I didn't have a real ending. In 1998, just before *Powers*, I was working with Mark on a very early web comic called *Dr. Cyborg* by Alan Gross. Mark helped me work out the *Hammer* story, as well as finding a publisher (Insight Studio Group, later at Image Comics) and someone to do colors. We had a very easy working relationship.

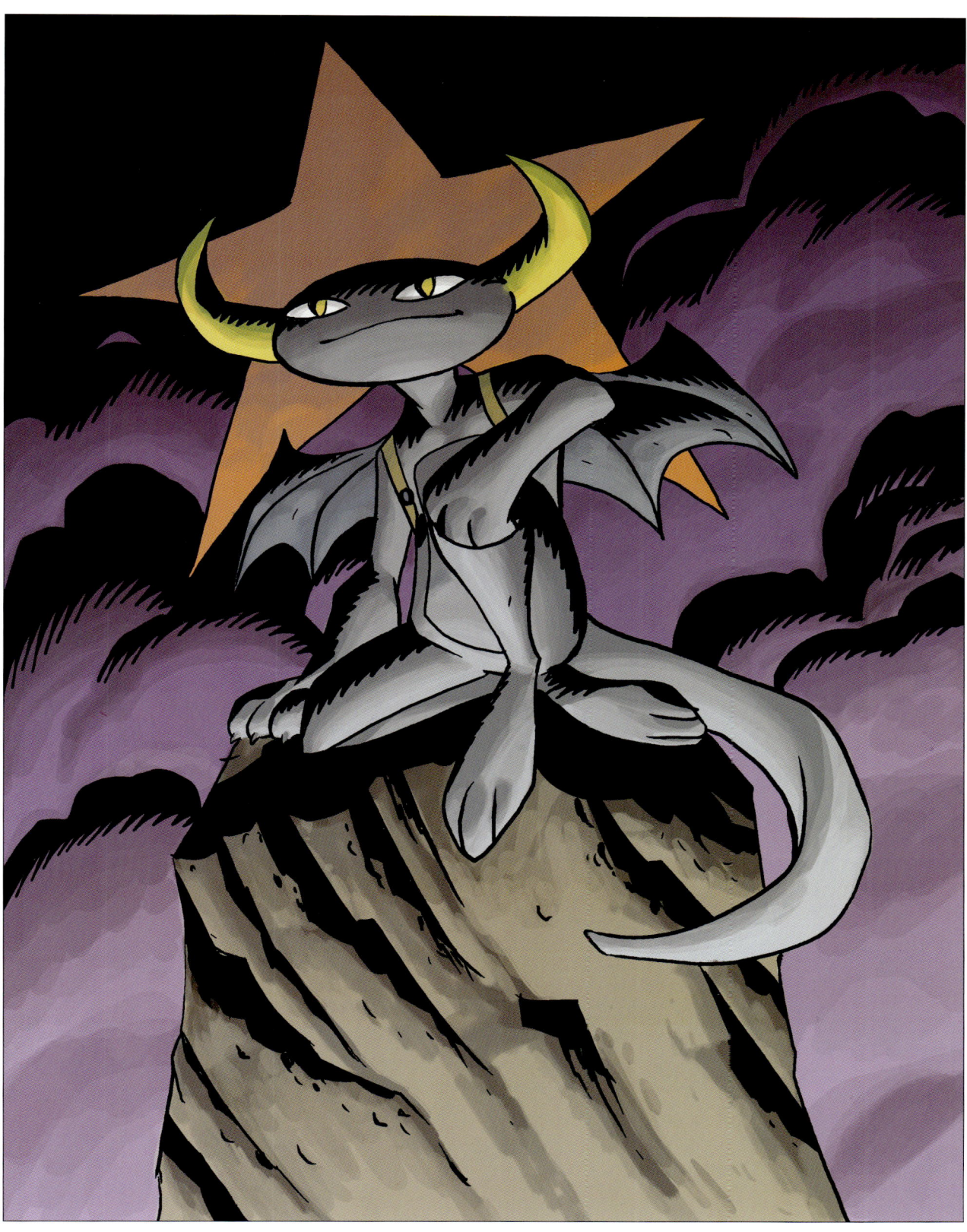

I don't have a title for this dragon guy. I've done a lot of illustrations for this idea over the last twenty years. I've always liked the Brothers Grimm fairy tales with their hidden allegories. And I love children's "road stories," like *Alice in Wonderland* and *Wizard of Oz*. Both were big influences on this project. I wanted to call it *The Last Dragon*, but for anyone my age that title's tainted by the movie with the El DeBarge song. It just can't be done.

I want to do it as an autobiographical story, but do I want it to be an all-ages story with adult undertones, or an adult story disguised as a children's piece? I'm still not sure.

NO PLAN B: THE ART OF MICHAEL AVON OEMING   17

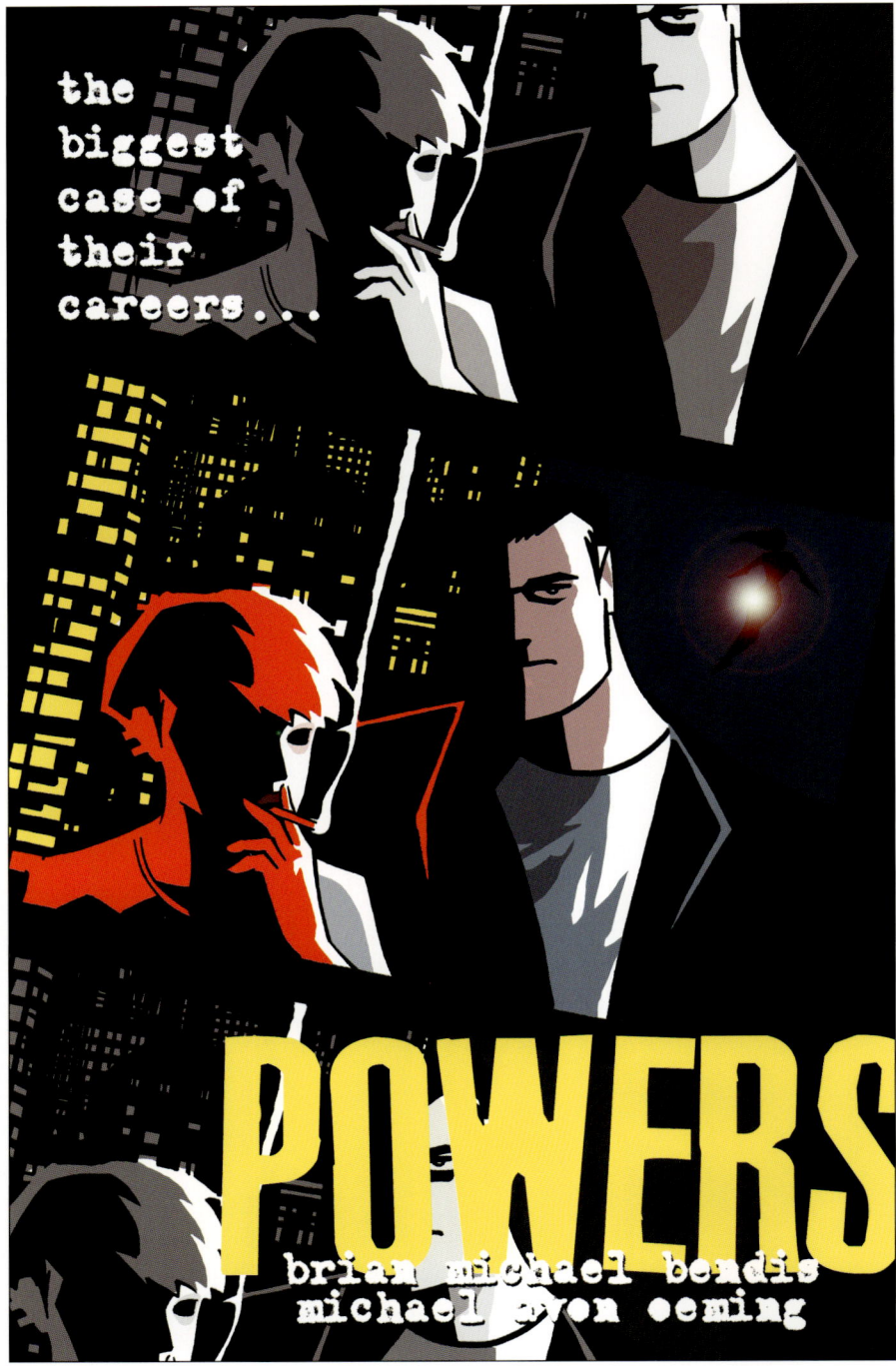

Powers covers, colors by Pat Garrahy

The idea of *Powers* goes back to when Bendis, David Mack, and I all first met. David and Brian had already been friends for a few years, traveling around the country promoting their independent books and doing all kinds of crazy, fun stuff. I met them at a signing at Claude's Comics in Pennsylvania. We all hit it off and stayed in contact. We each had books at Caliber Comics, so we started supporting each other's work, setting up at conventions together.

When I was done working with Bryan Glass on *Ship of Fools*, I wanted to break away from sci-fi/fantasy stories to do some crime noir, which I'd always loved in film. That's what Bendis was doing on *A.K.A. Goldfish* and his other Caliber books.

Around this time I was drawing Bendis's and David Mack's characters in a new, cartoony style I was trying out. Brian had just started *Sam and Twitch* for McFarlane and said he had an idea.

At first it sounded like superheroes, and I said I didn't want to do that. Brian said, "No, the superhero elements are really small. We'll only ever see them in glimpses. This is a cop book, like the TV show *Homicide*, except when you see dead bodies, they'll be superheroes."

We took a cue from the *Marvels* miniseries by Kurt Busiek and Alex Ross, seeing the superheroes from the citizen's point of view, the characters at ground level looking up to see a hero fly by in the sky, watching these gods fighting from a distance. Light and shadow would play big roles in the book. We talked a lot about the film *Taxi Driver*, and the use of light and shadow setting the mood for that film.

When I designed Walker—it's silly to think about it now—I wanted him to look like a cross between George Clooney and Ricky Martin. He needed to be a big guy, but I wanted Ricky Martin's hairstyle. I gave Walker what we call a "shovel face."

I gave Deena black hair at first, but Brian thought she looked like she could be Walker's sister. I made her blond after looking through fashion magazines to give her the right haircut. I fell in love with Alyssa Milano's hairstyle in the film *Double Dragon*, blond on top and dark on the sides, which became Deena's haircut. *Powers* debuted at Image Comics in April 2009 and moved to Marvel/Icon in 2004.

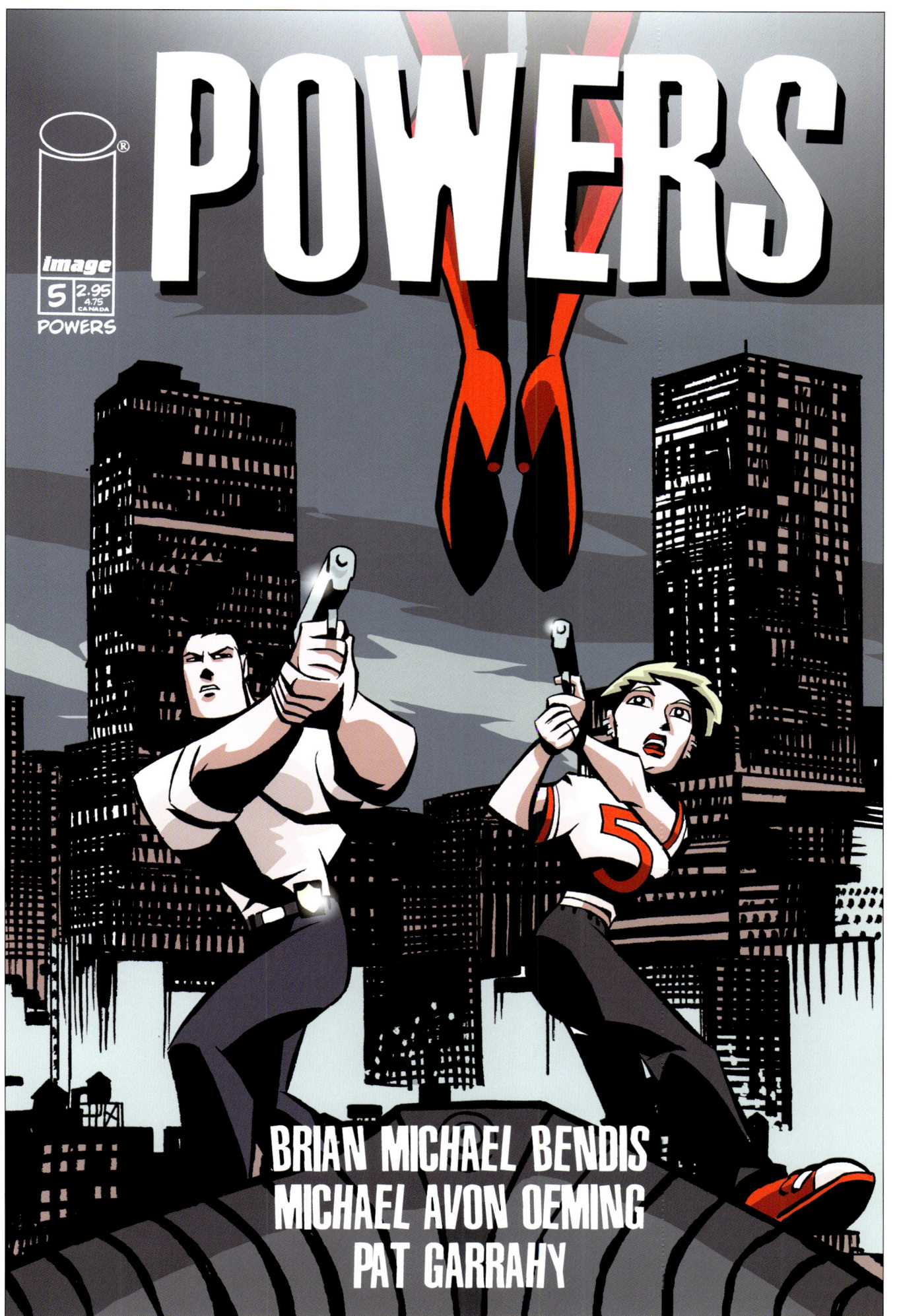

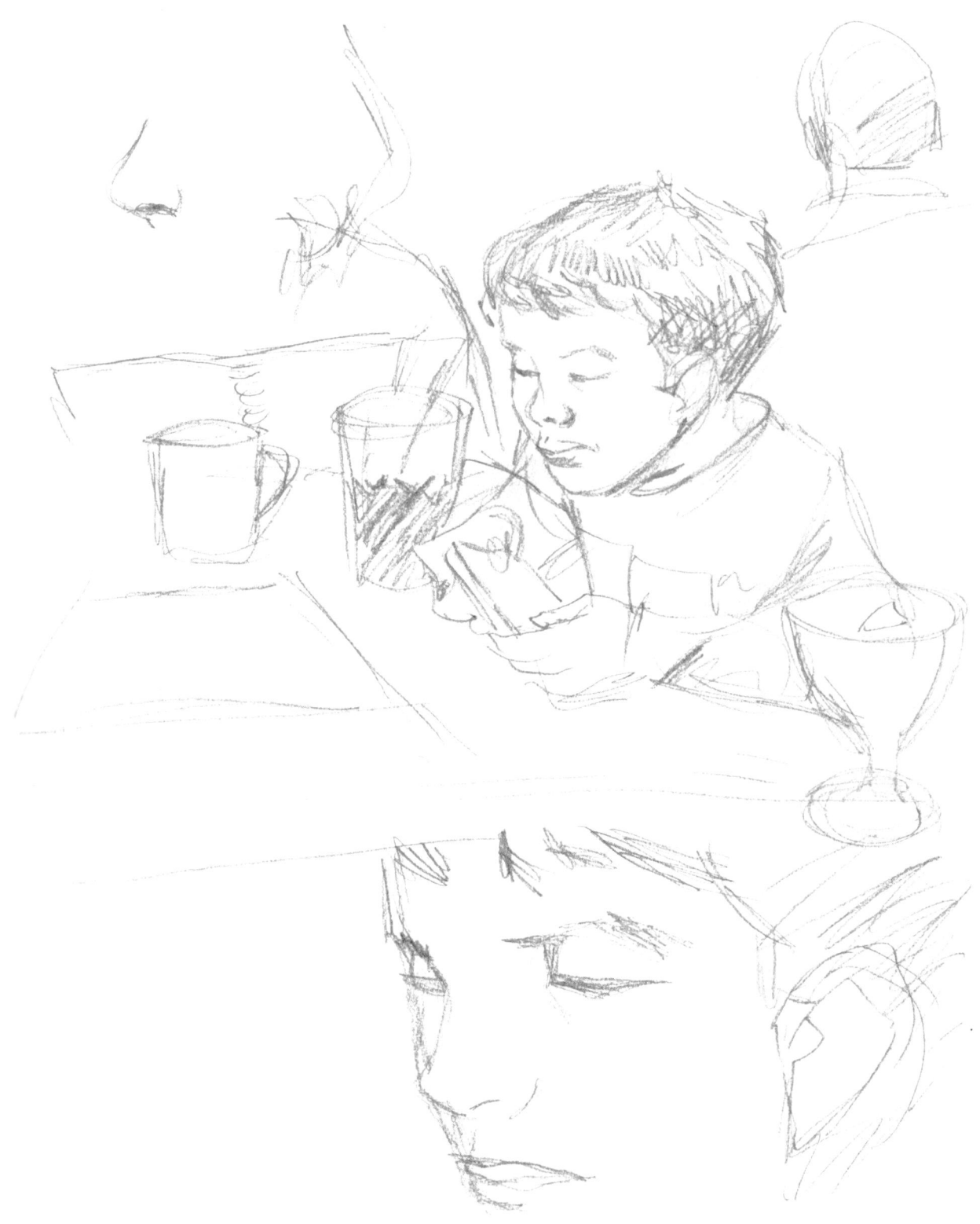

I first contacted Alex Toth just as I started drawing *Powers* in 2000. In my early days I'd send samples of my work to publishers and creators like Steve Rude and Mike Baron for feedback. Alex had become reclusive, doodling and letter writing all day, so I got his contact info, and I was surprised when he wrote back with great things to say about my art. I'd expected an ass whooping, because he was known as a harsh critic. But he was complimentary, citing my work to other artists and to the press as new work that he liked.

He told me to stop drawing "Bruce Timm–looking shovelheads" and draw faces in my own way, but I loved that look and wasn't going to stop. He also suggested I not overrender, and I still struggle with that in my art today.

My favorite period of Toth's art was his DC short stories of the 1970s into the early eighties. Toth's work was realistic but cartoony at the same time, and he used heavy black on the page. Toth taught us all how to appreciate and balance shadows and light, not only for composition but also to display character traits. Lighting would fall on the face of a character, or a body would appear in silhouette encircled by a flashlight. I always try to emulate Toth's philosophy of making shadow and light important in conveying emotional story moments.

When Toth went into the hospital I heard many fans were sending get-well letters to his room. I figured I'd wait till he was home to encourage him to get better, but he died in the hospital in 2006, and I didn't get a last chance to wish him well.

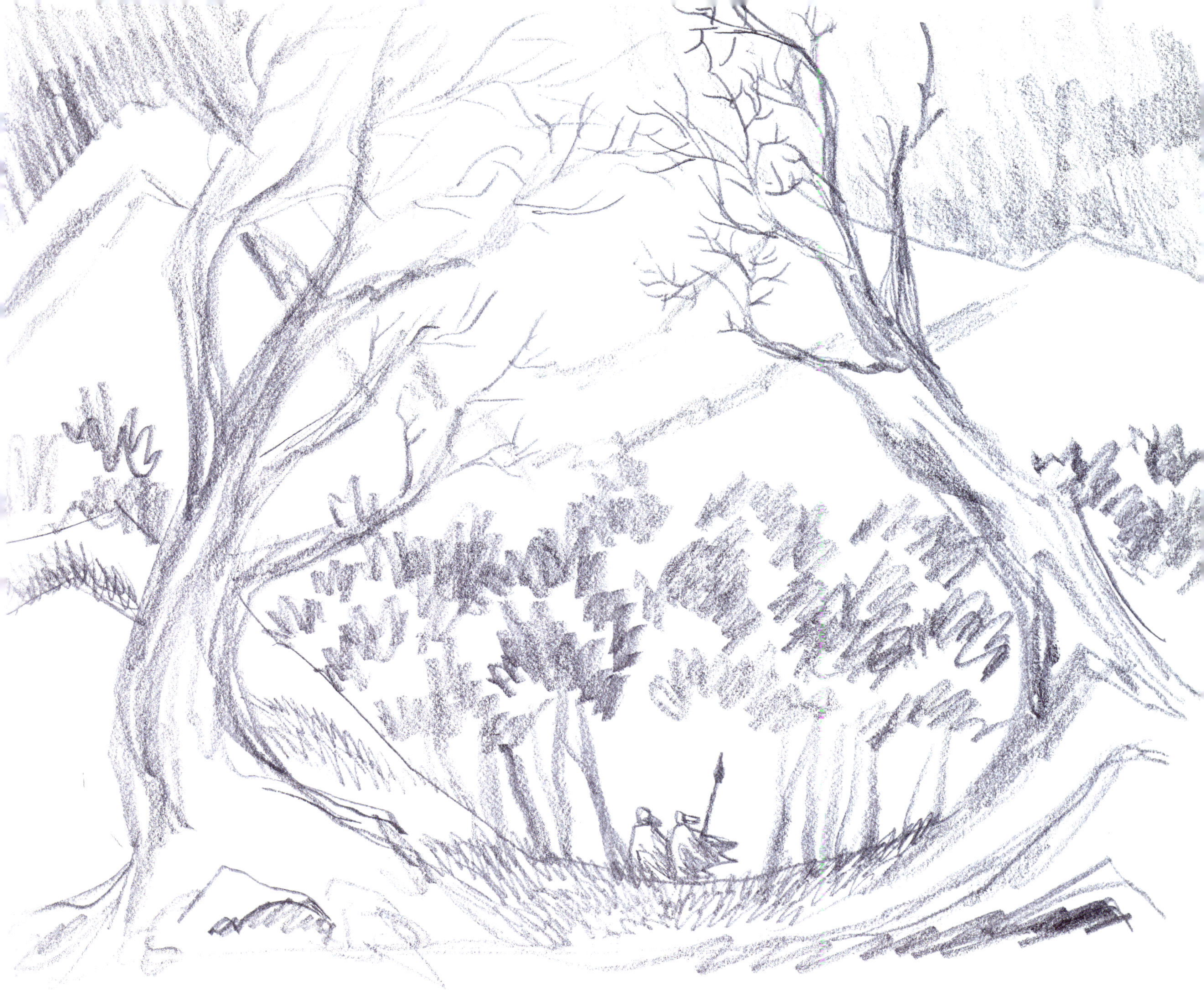

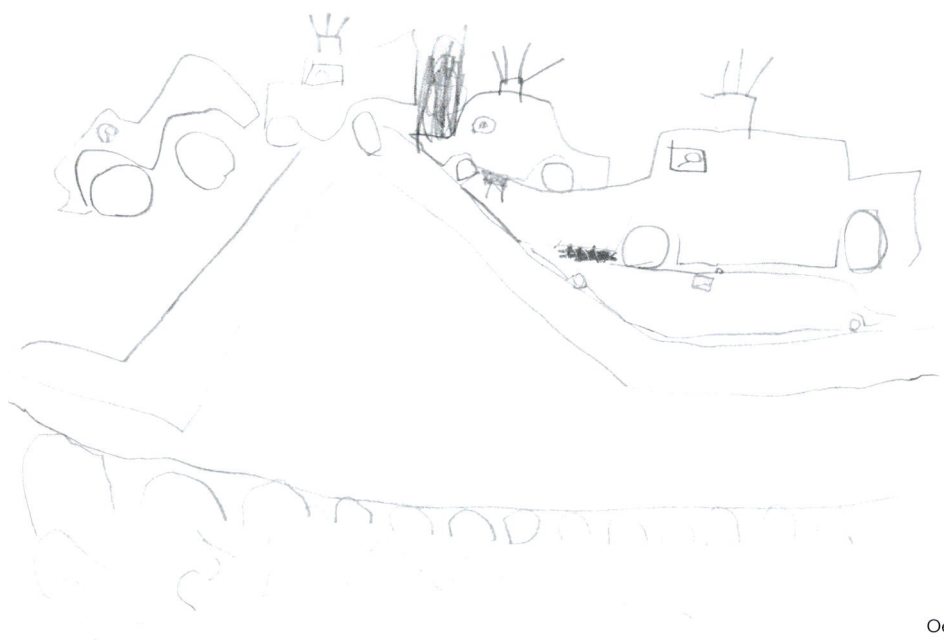

Drawing by
Oeming's son Ethan

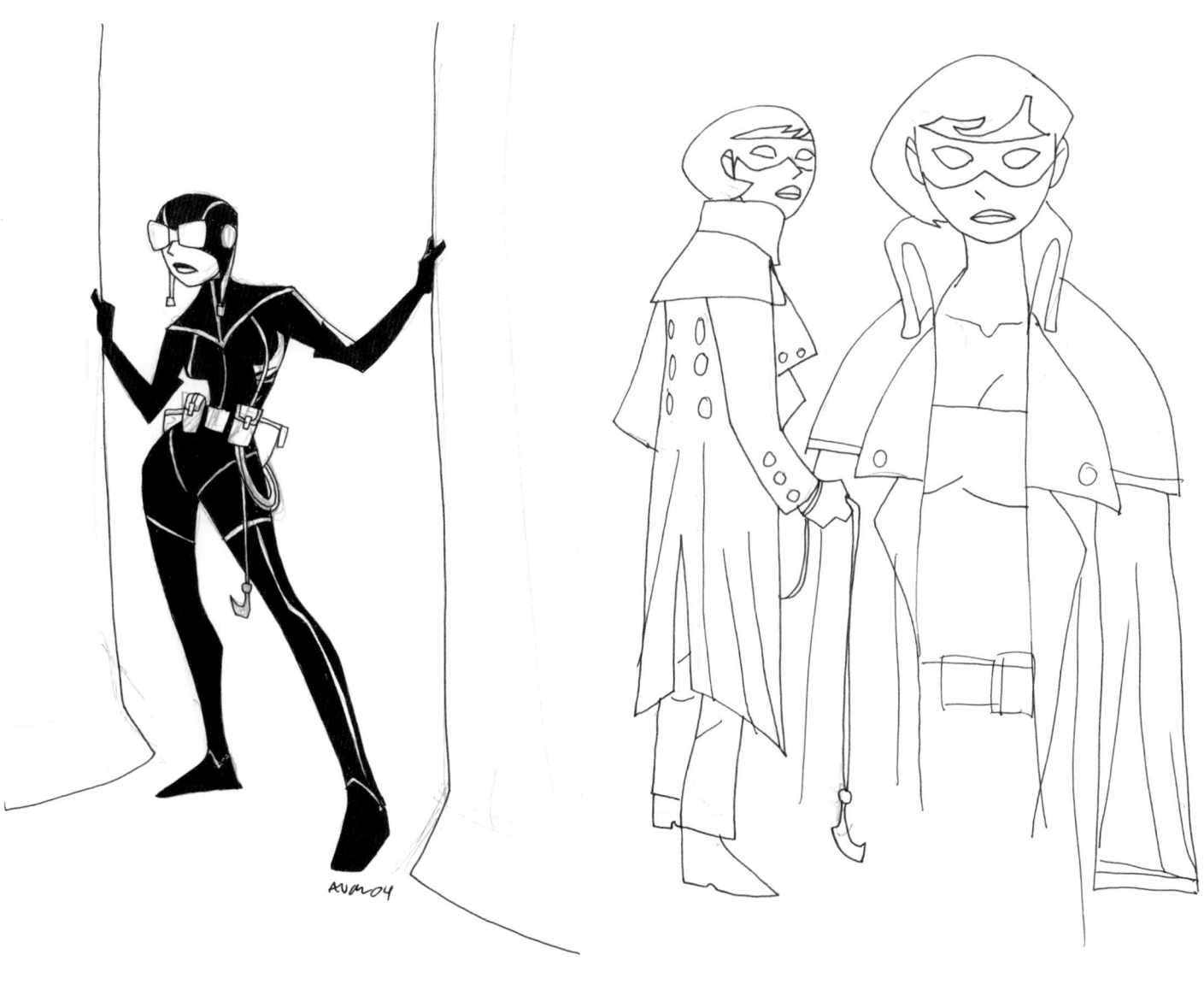

When I started reading comics in the mid-eighties, I mostly saw that watered-down, Marvel house style of art, but there were a few artists with their own distinct style. Mike Mignola stood out. There was a dream sequence in a Spider-Man story Mike did that blew my mind.

I'm just such a fan of his that when I draw his characters I throw away my brushes and use the kind of pen he does. I think Mike appreciates artists who don't ape his style, but do their own thing while having something in common with Mike's art. He breaks all the rules with his drawing. It's as enigmatic as his story choices.

I've worked with Mike now on *B.P.R.D.* and on other *Hellboy*-related projects, all at Dark Horse Comics—most recently a short story called "Mood Swings" with Chelsea Cain [*page 159*], and before that an issue of *Abe Sapien* [*page 114*] with Scott Allie, and a 2003 one-shot called *B.P.R.D.: The Soul of Venice* [*page 26*] that we cowrote with Miles Gunter.

When Mike was still living in New York we talked for maybe five minutes about working on something together. It involved a thief and a sort of mermaid split in half. I did a couple sketches, but we never followed up on it. I look back now and realize I was going to cocreate something with one of the people I admire most in comics—how the hell did I let the ball drop?

Cover to Brian Posehn's debut album *Live In: Nerd Rage*

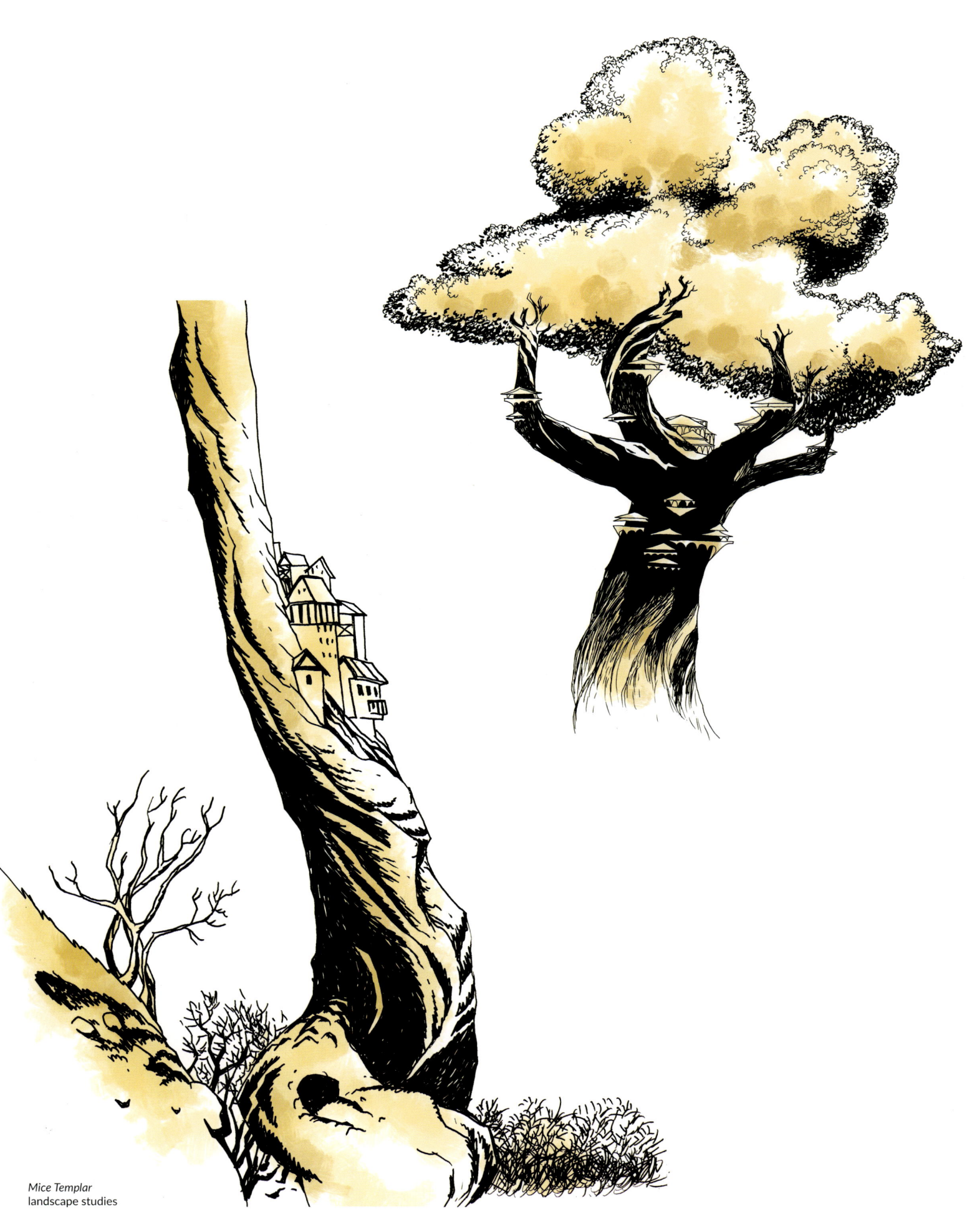

Mice Templar
landscape studies

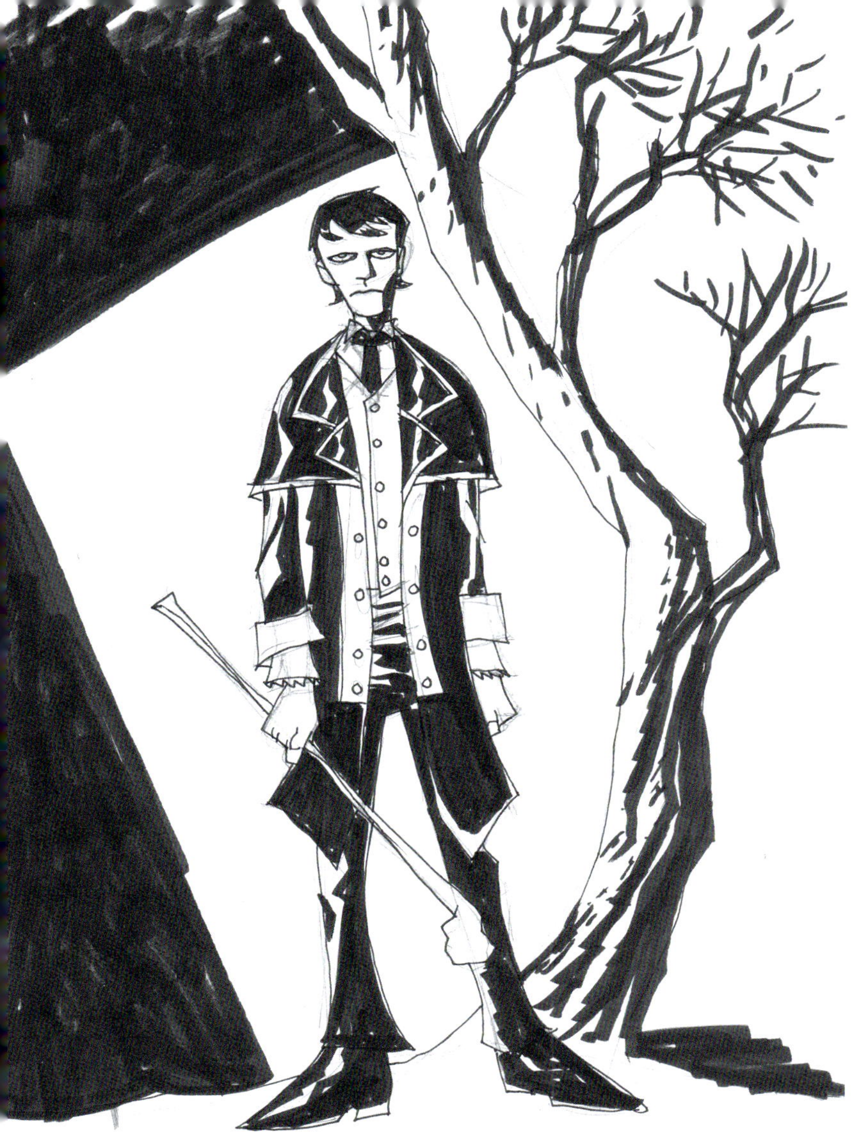

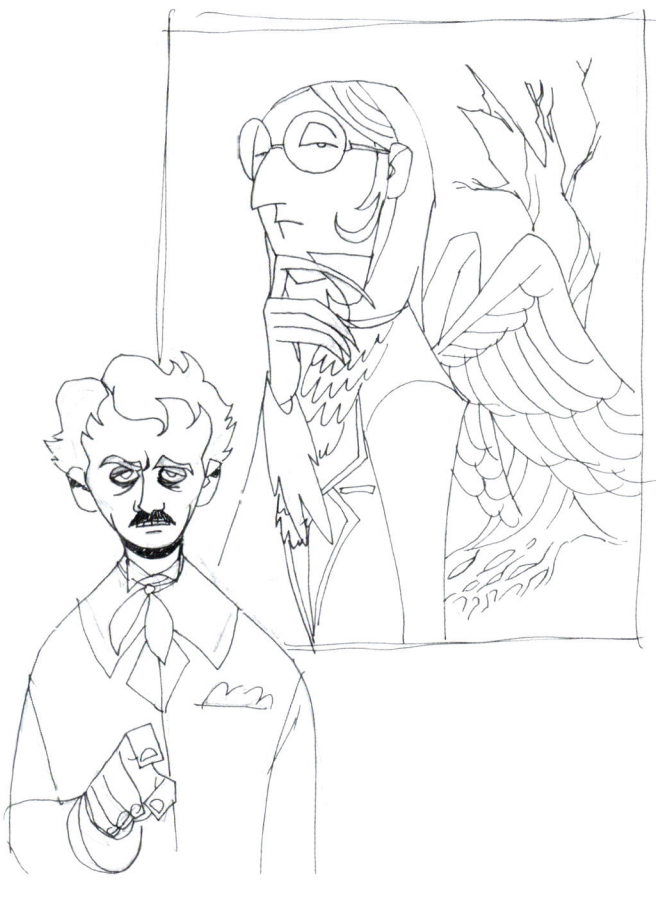

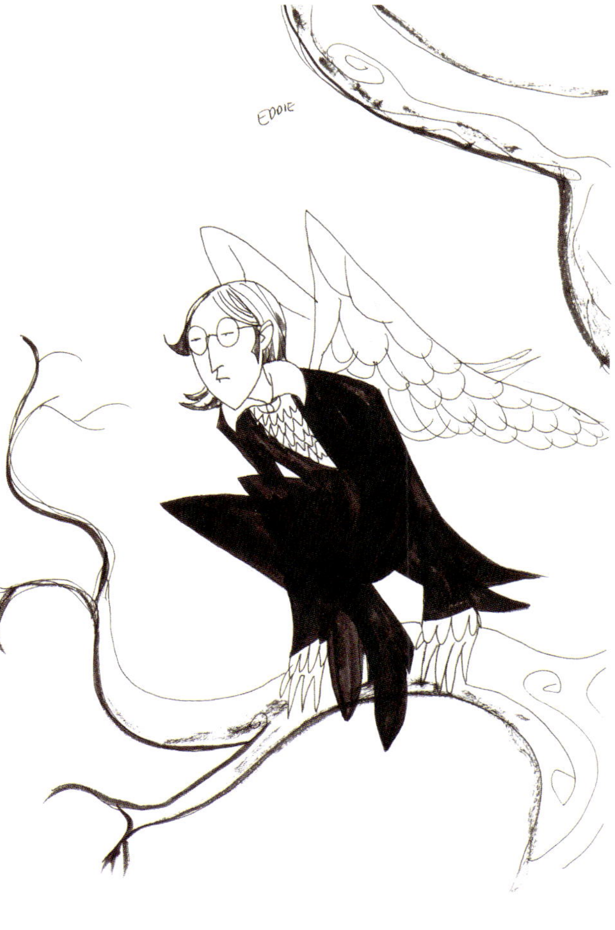

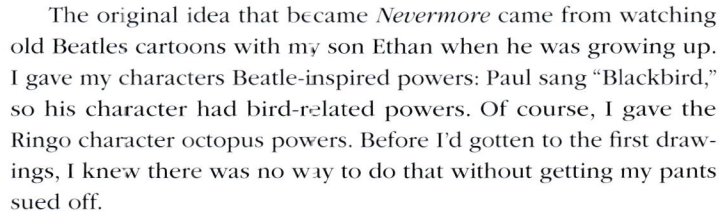

The original idea that became *Nevermore* came from watching old Beatles cartoons with my son Ethan when he was growing up. I gave my characters Beatle-inspired powers: Paul sang "Blackbird," so his character had bird-related powers. Of course, I gave the Ringo character octopus powers. Before I'd gotten to the first drawings, I knew there was no way to do that without getting my pants sued off.

I shifted to an Edgar Alan Poe–inspired idea. The blackbird became a raven. My villain was based on "The Masque of the Red Death." We did a short story in the back of *Hammer of the Gods* with a crazy Saturday-morning-cartoon vibe to it—a band of kids playing music and fighting monsters.

It was even more cartoony than what I'd later do with *Takio*, a very Edward Gorey look with its gothic tones, and what I now see was a late 1990s/early 2000s emo look to it. It feels dated. And adapting Poe's ideas into comics has been done to death. There's a lot of rich material to mine from Poe, and his ideas hold up even today. I don't know if my Poe ideas would stand out.

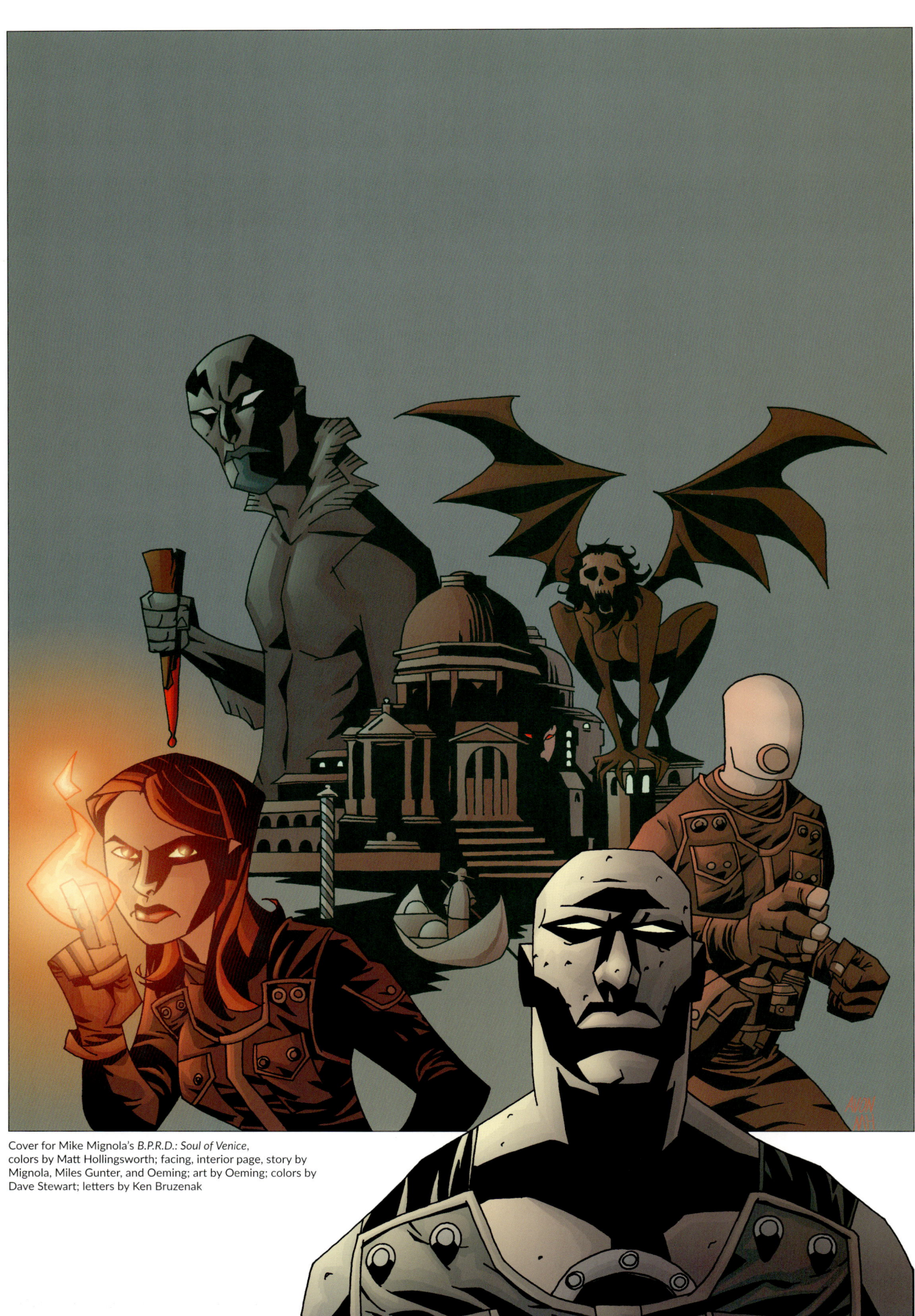

Cover for Mike Mignola's *B.P.R.D.: Soul of Venice*, colors by Matt Hollingsworth; facing, interior page, story by Mignola, Miles Gunter, and Oeming; art by Oeming; colors by Dave Stewart; letters by Ken Bruzenak

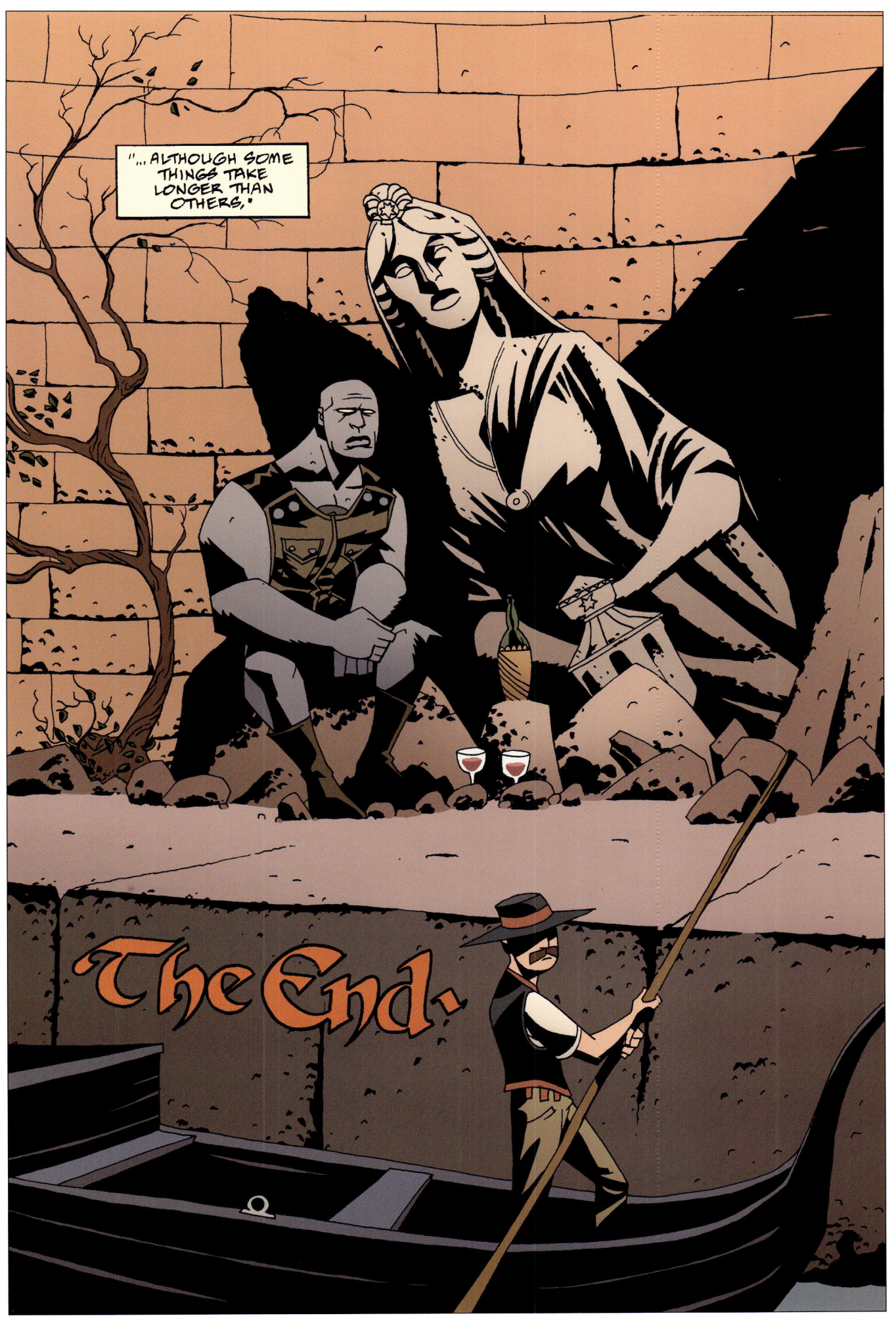

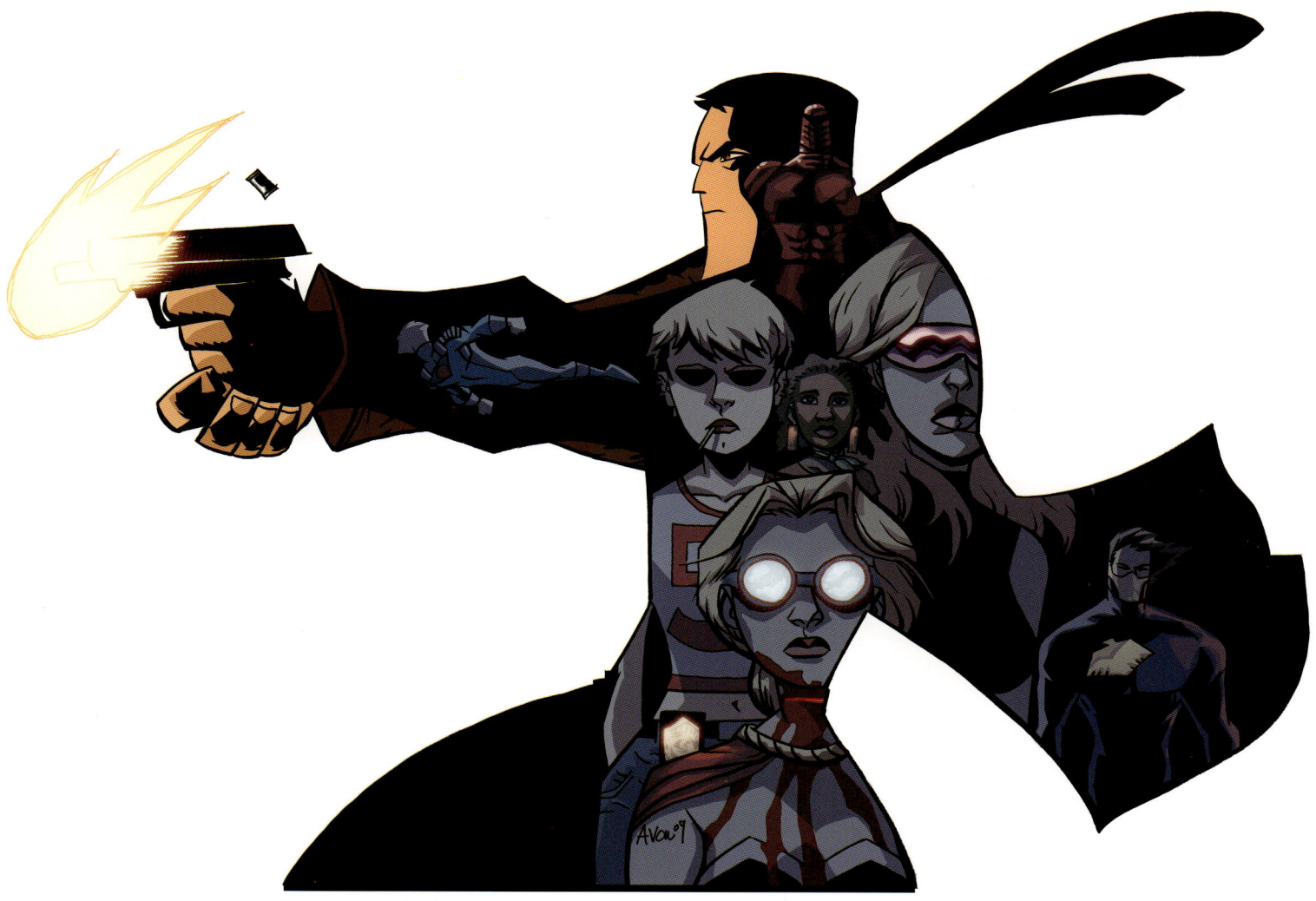

Powers covers, colors by Nick Filardi

I started working with Nick Filardi when Ivan Brandon suggested him as a colorist on *Cross Bronx* in 2006 (Image Comics). Nick's color sense brought something I'd never seen done in my work before: vibrant colors with a noir sensibility. He used textures in ways I never had.

We needed a new colorist for *Powers*—much like rock bands look for drummers, we burned through them trying to find the right person. We had Nick and one other very talented artist each do a sample piece for us, and ultimately we went with Nick. Outside of Taki Soma, I've never had a regular colorist other than Nick. I call Nick "my other wife" given the amount of work we do together.

When I was hired for *Cave Carson* in 2016 at Vertigo I sent Gerard Way examples of *The Victories*, which Nick colored. Gerard said, "Yes, I want this approach for *Cave*, but let's go even crazier!"

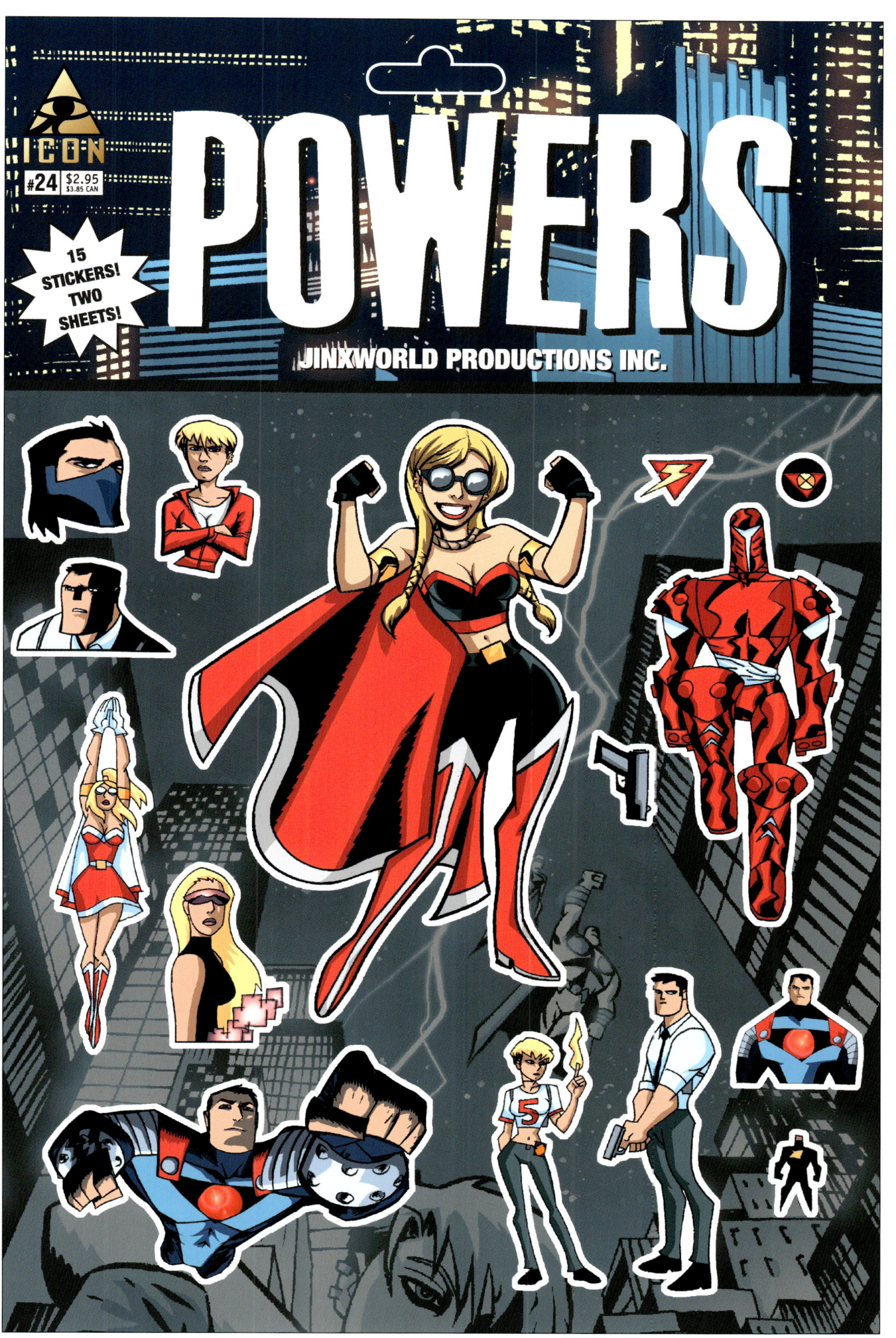

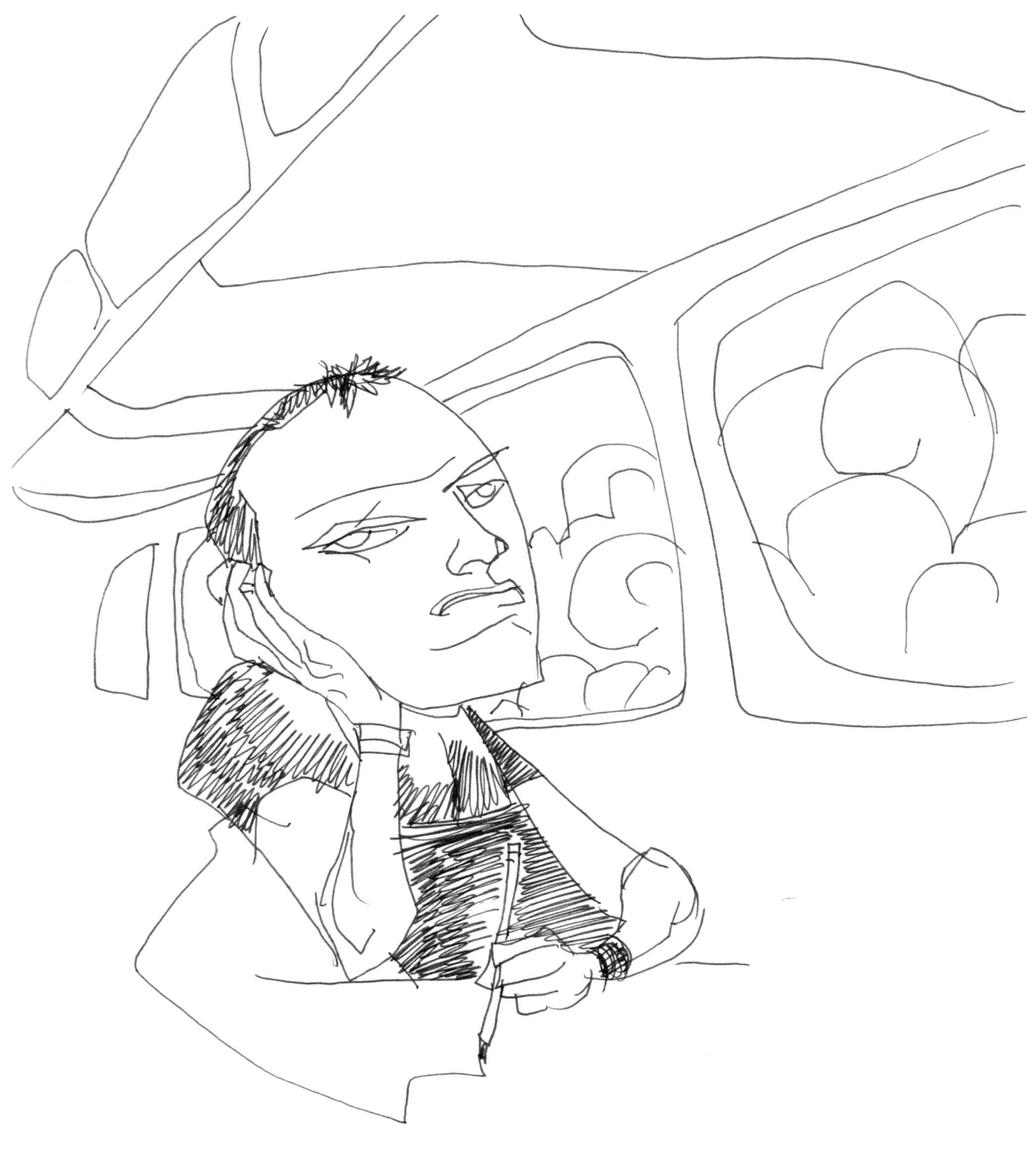

Self-portrait; facing, watercolor of Brian and Olivia Bendis

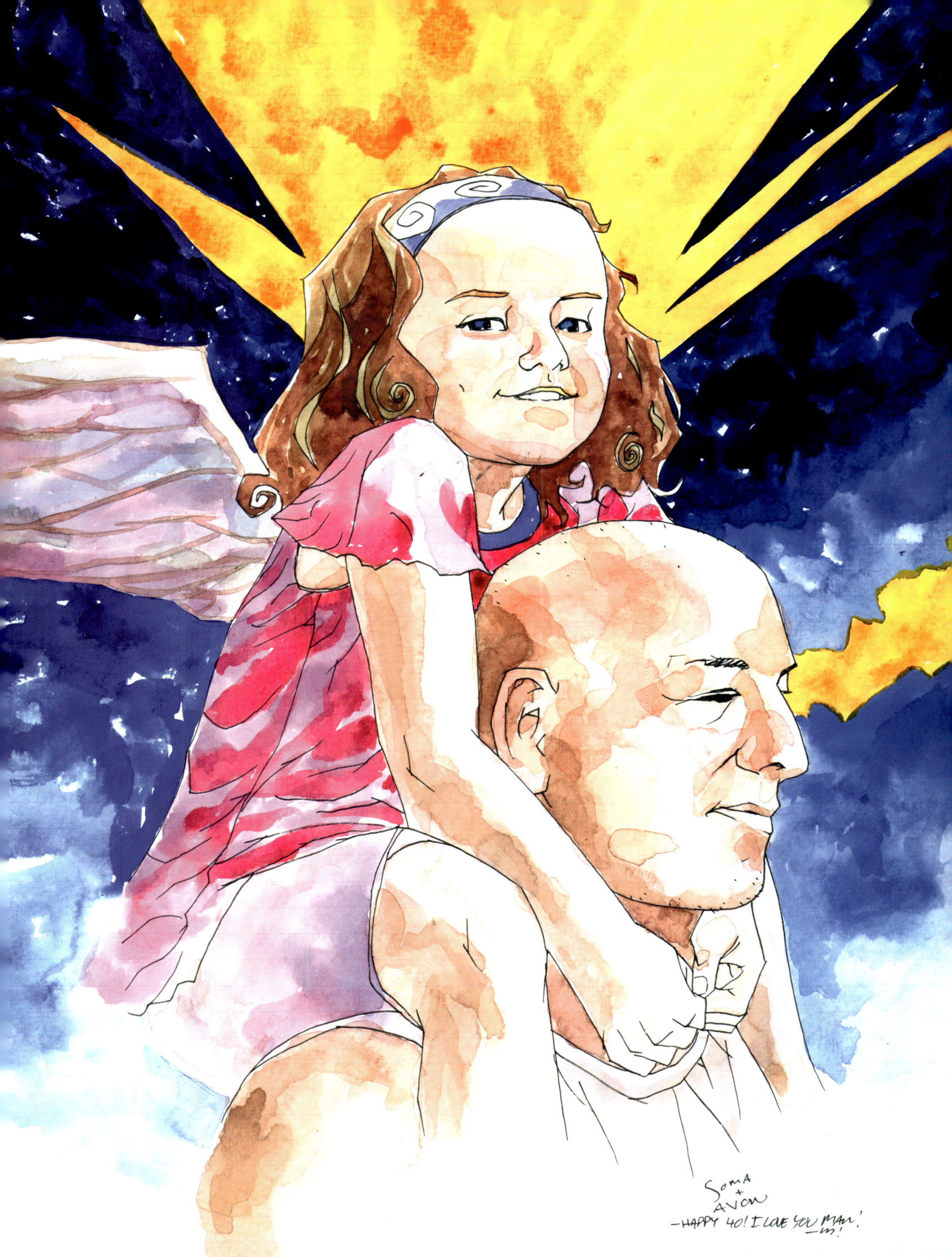

Zeus; facing, Ziggy

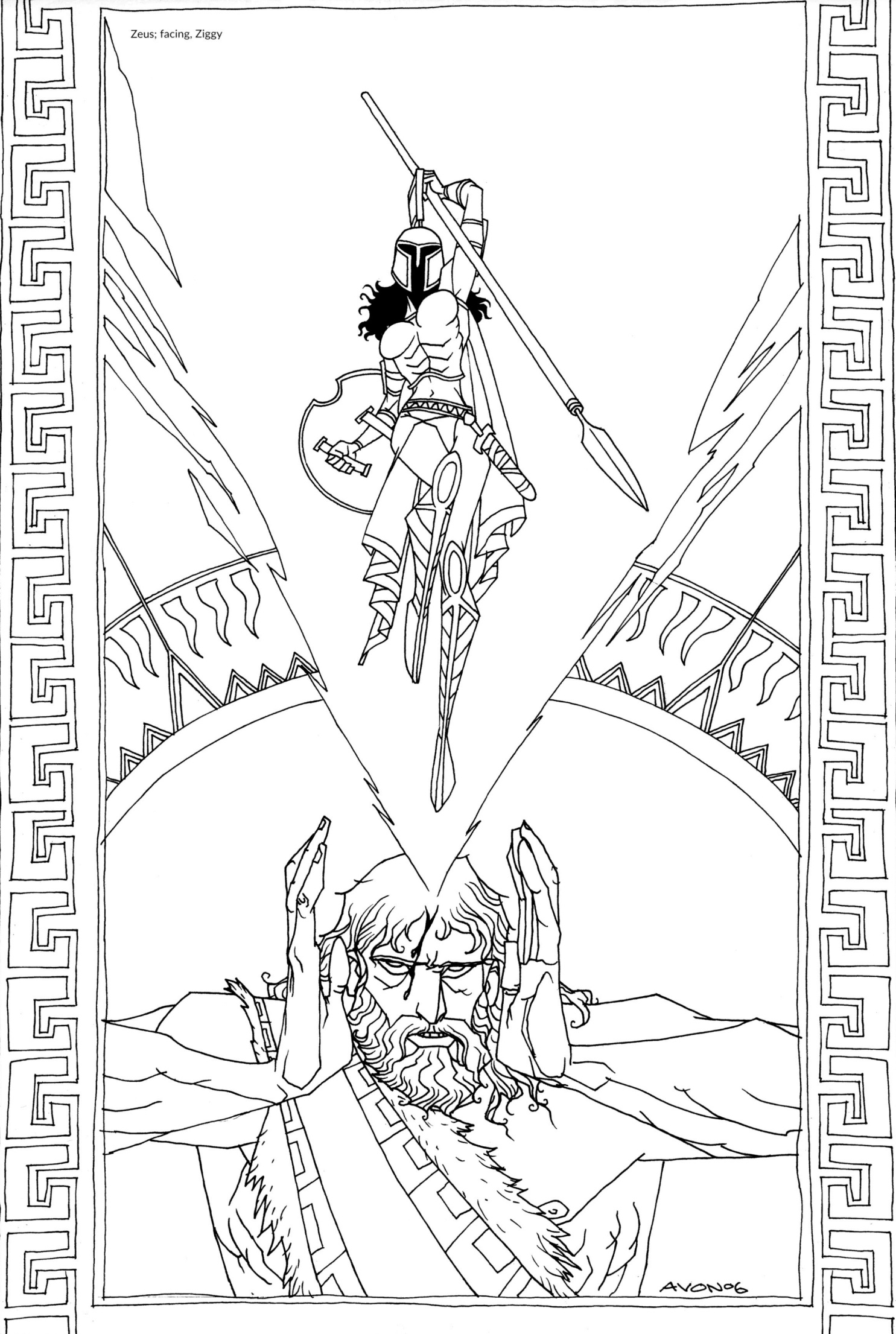

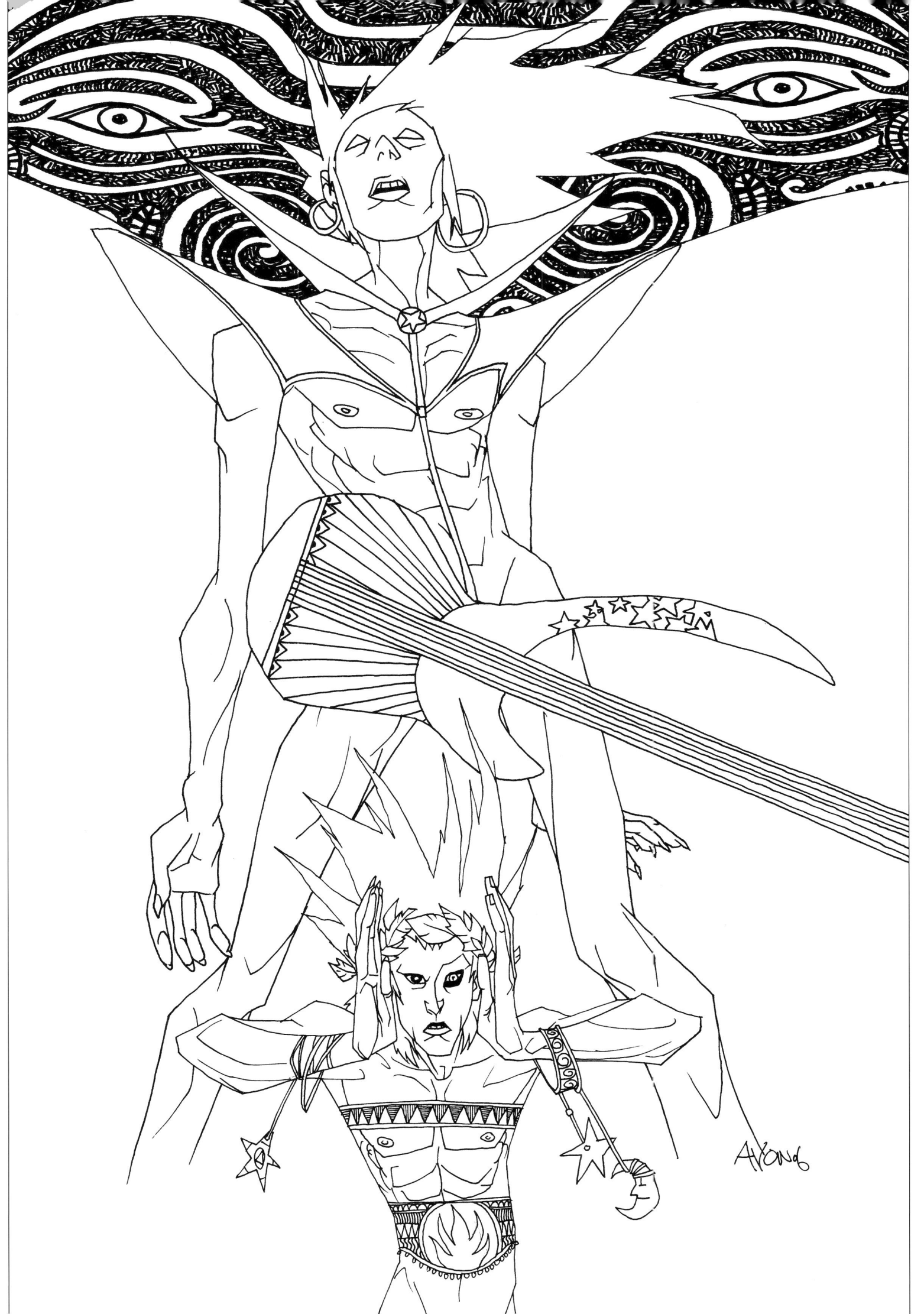

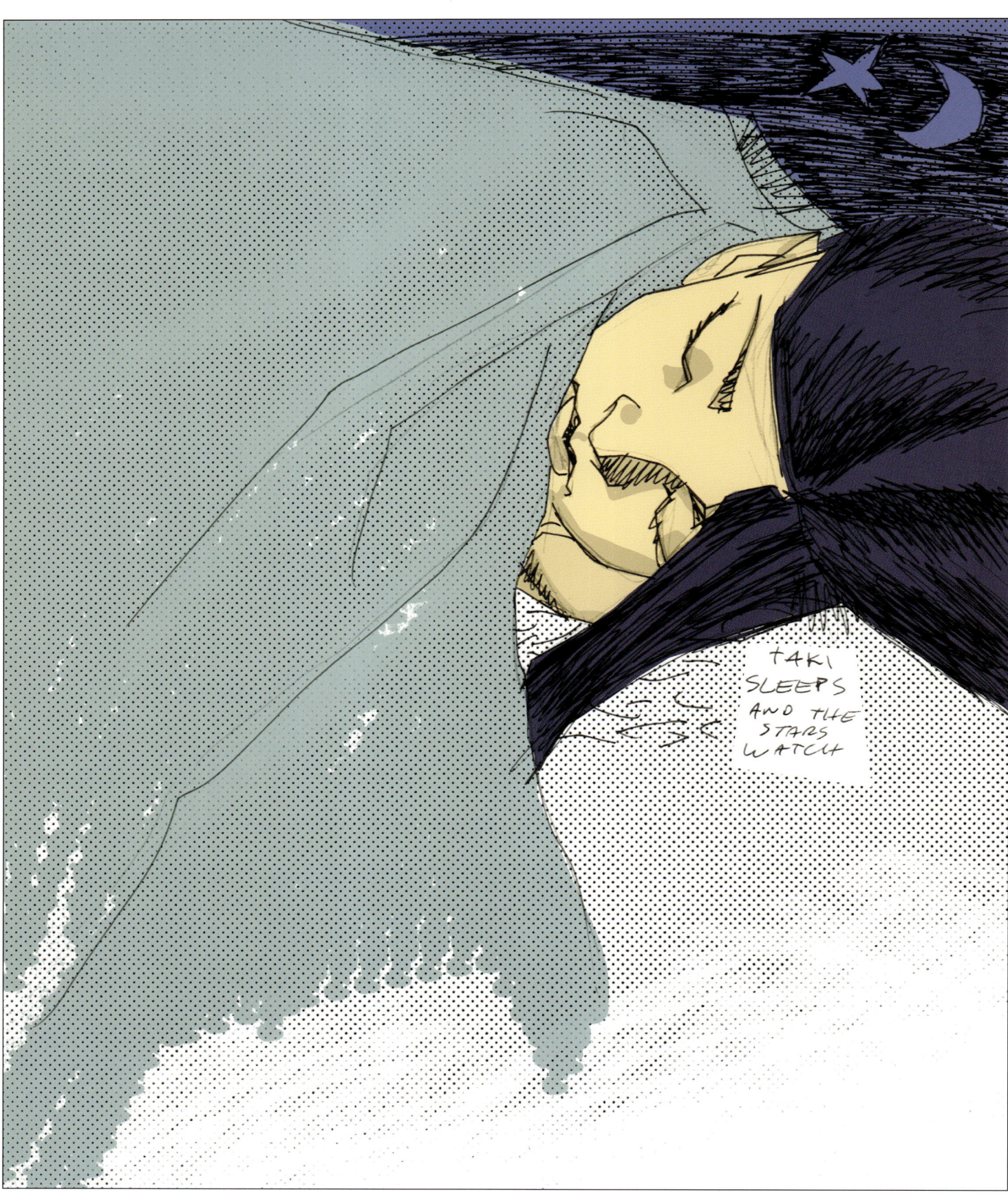

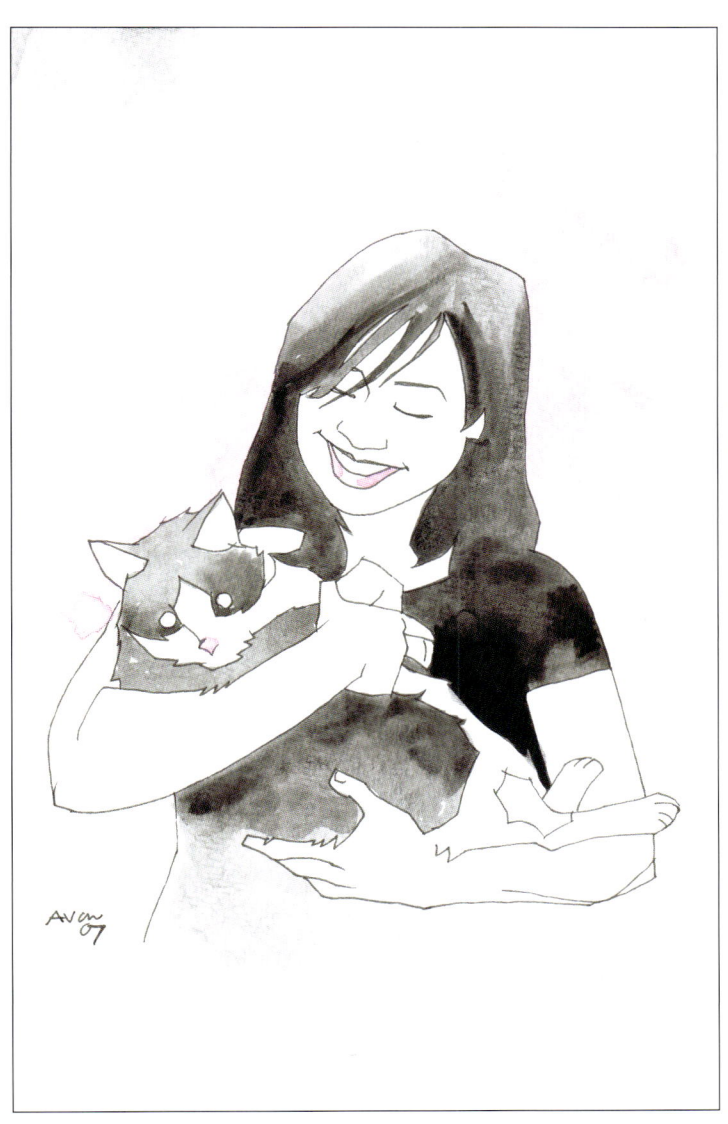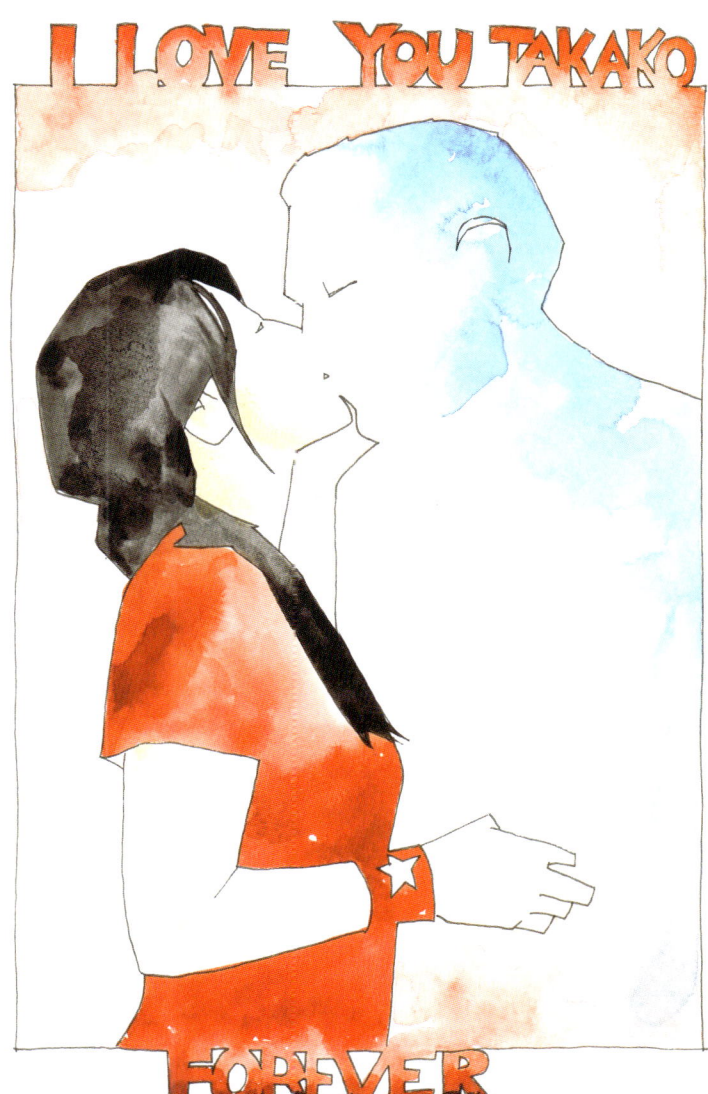

Oeming's favorite subject, Taki Soma; following pages, the gift that won her over

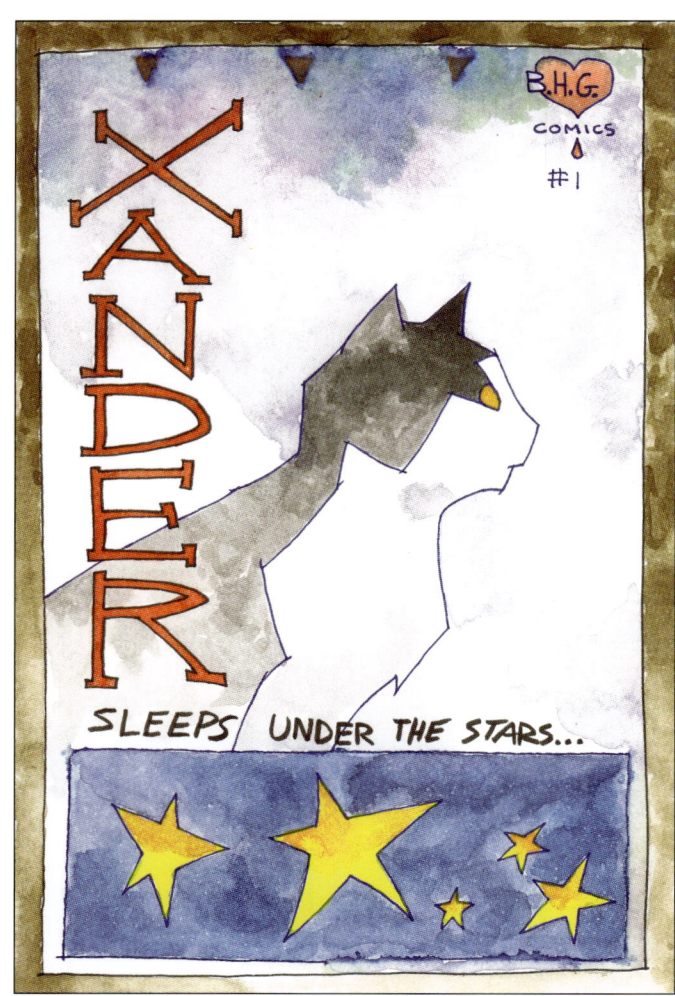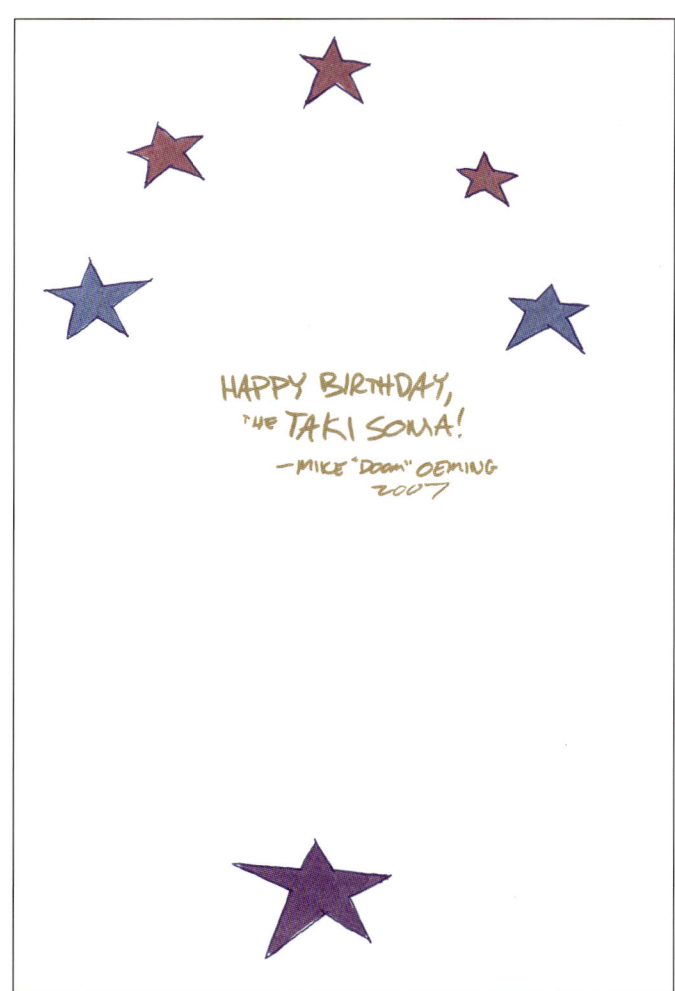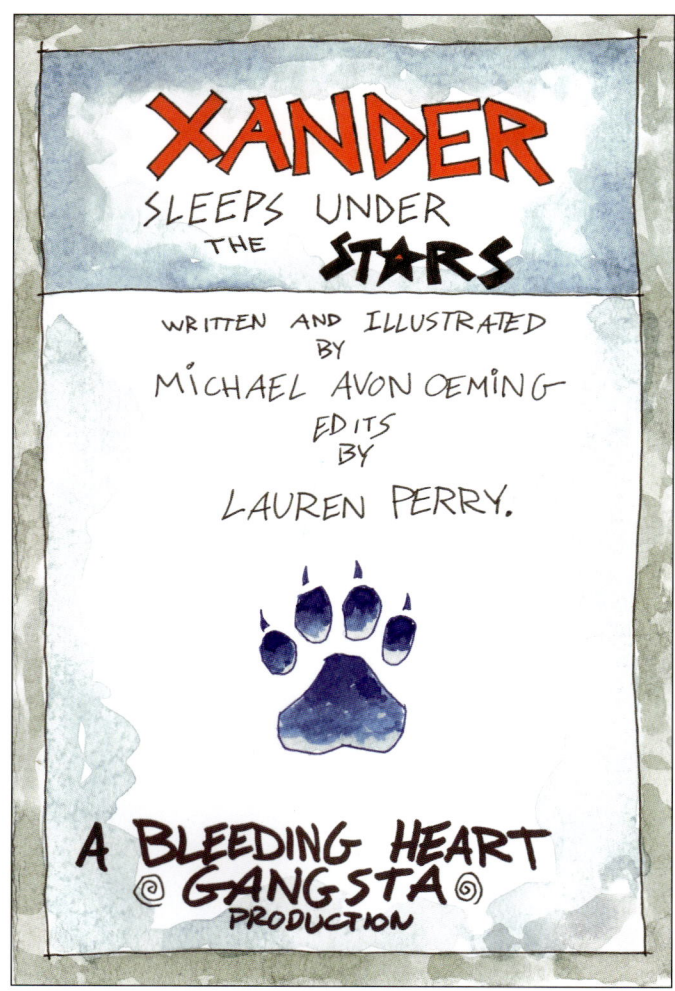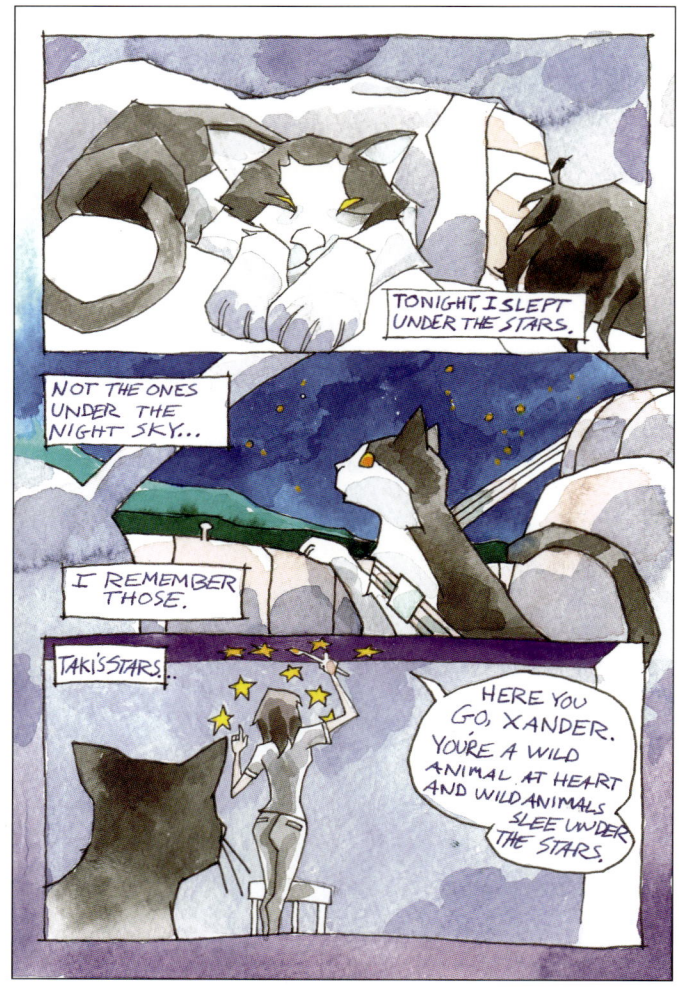

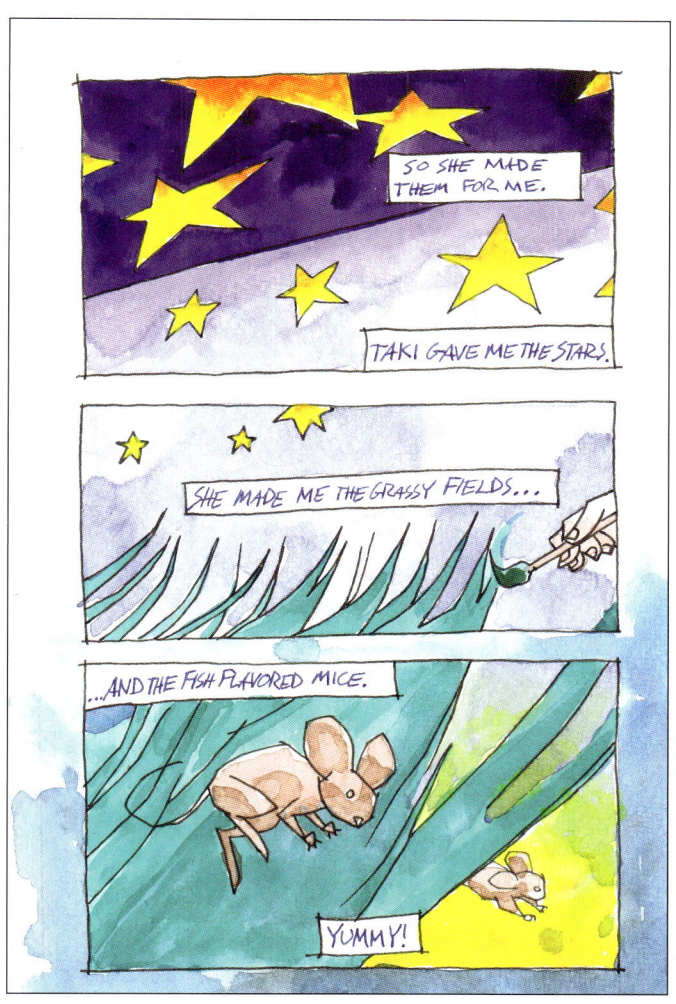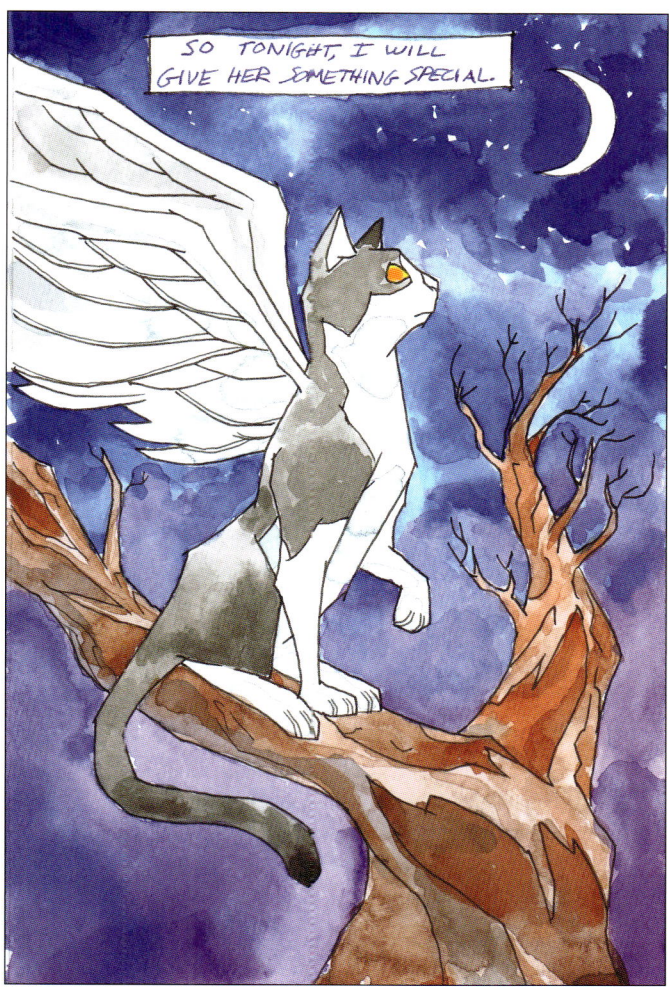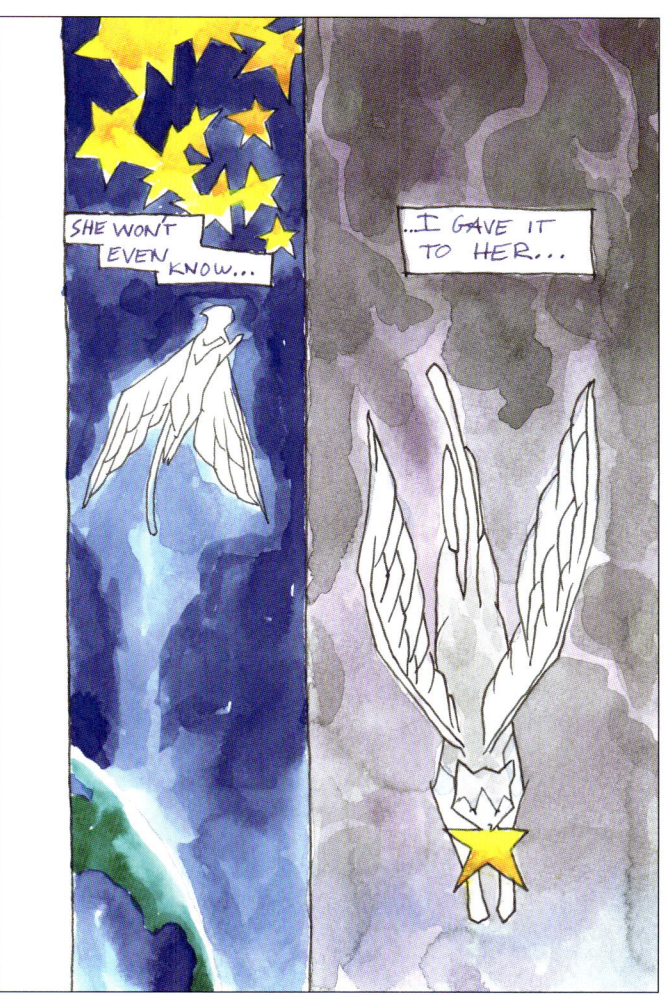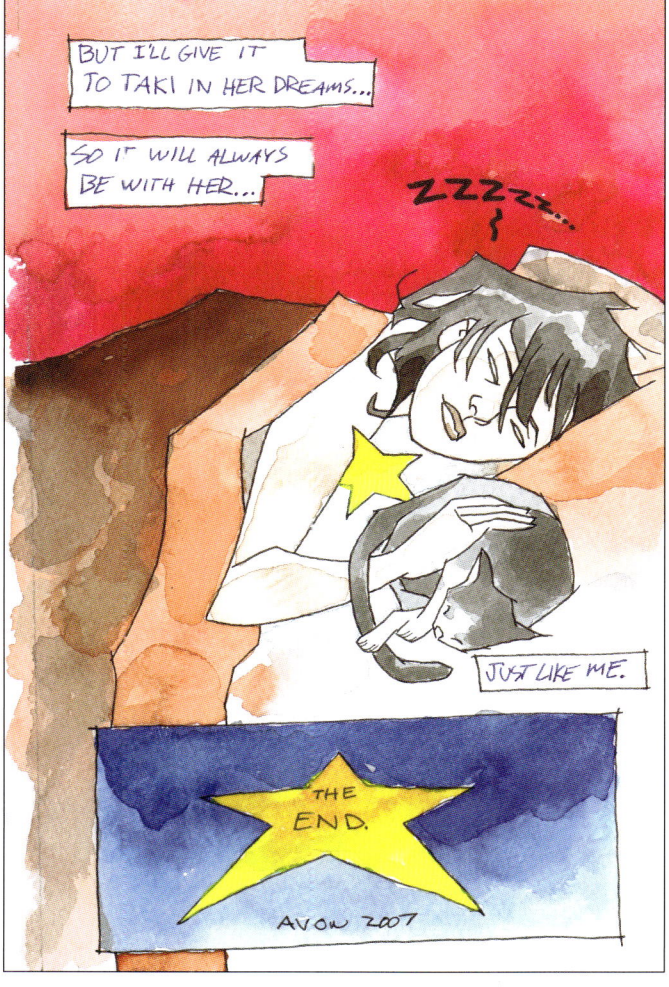

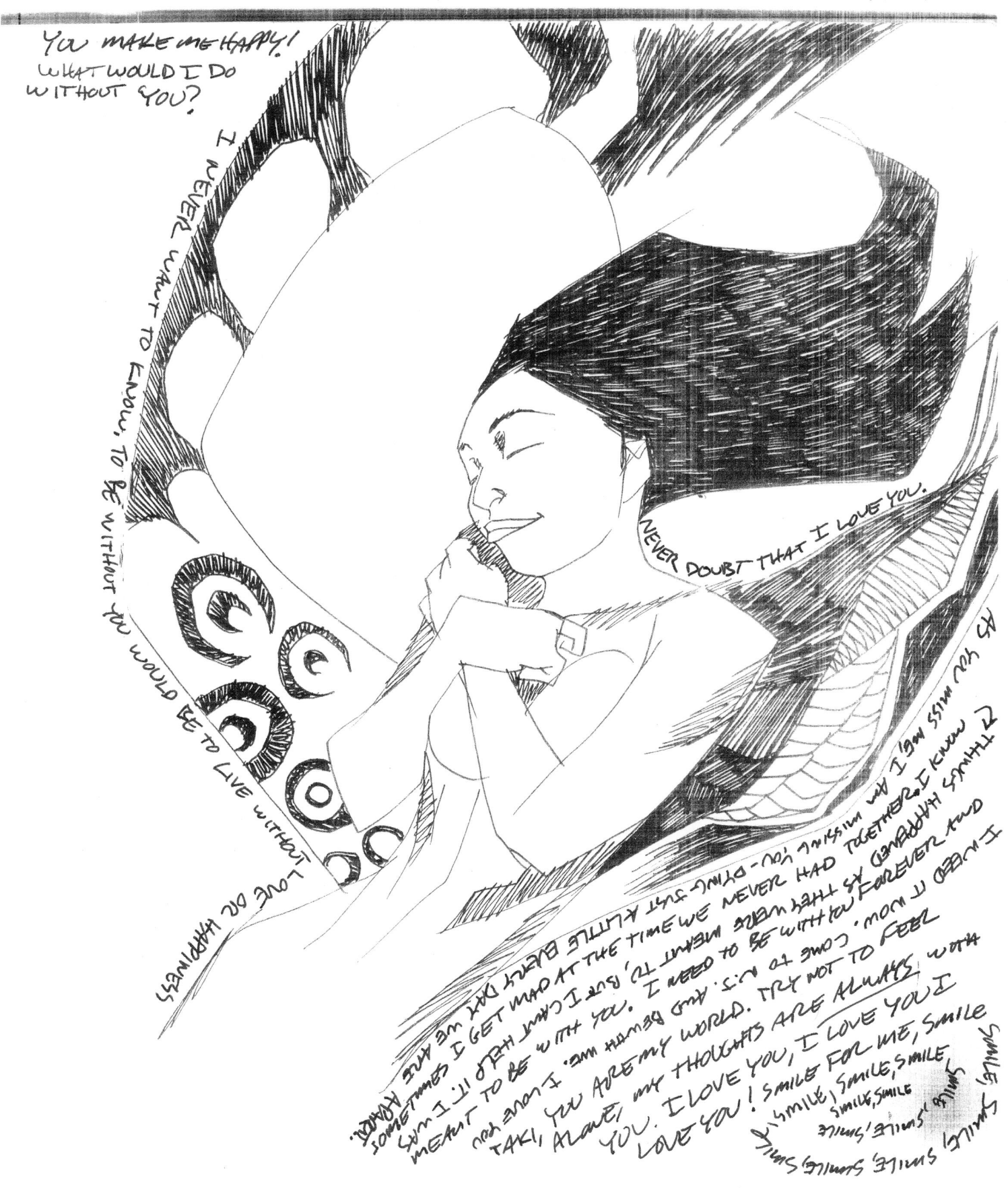

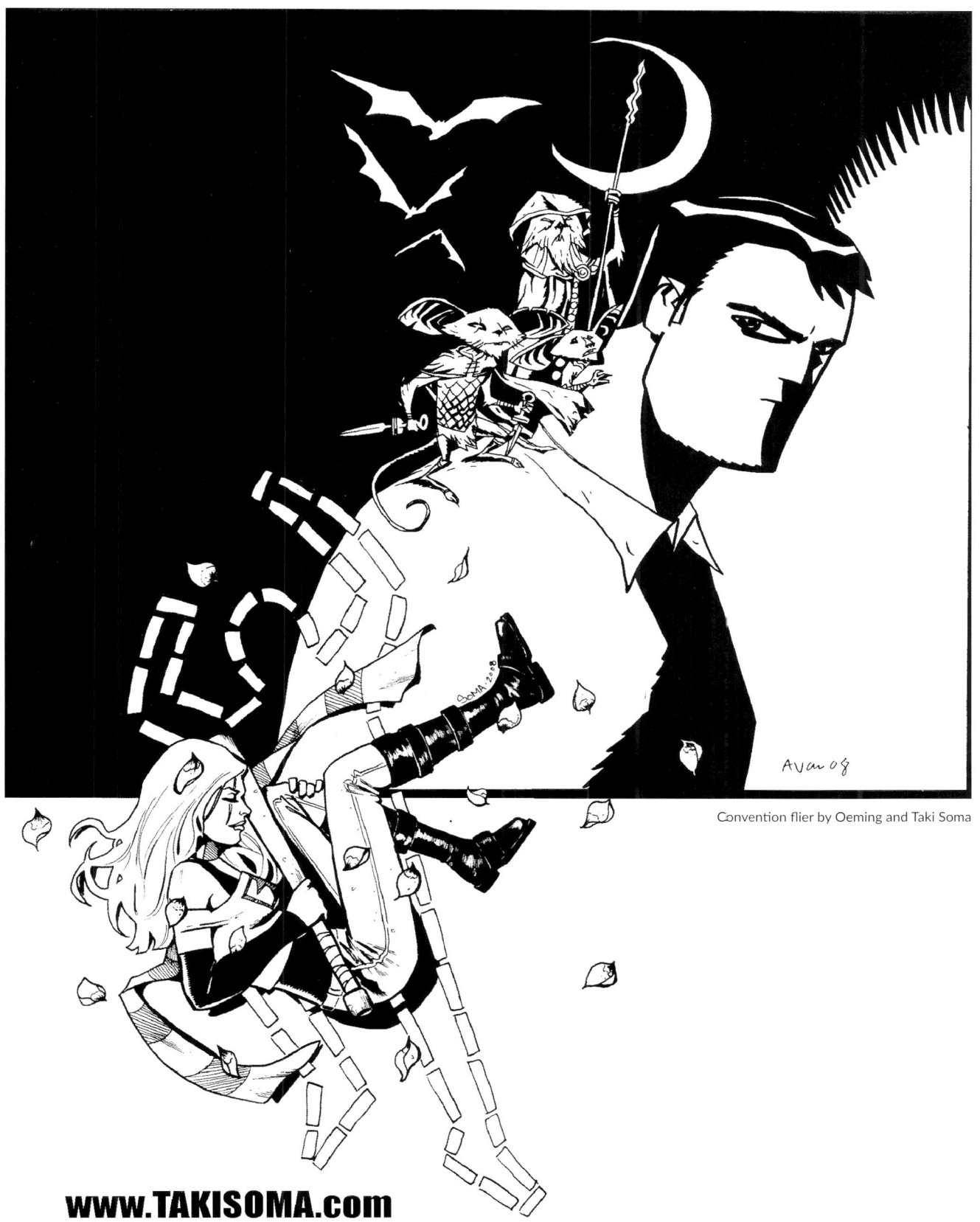

Convention flier by Oeming and Taki Soma

I married Taki Soma in 2009 at the Ground Kontrol arcade in Portland, Oregon, with David Mack officiating. We've worked together a lot, but there's never really been any problems balancing our working relationship and our personal relationship. Of course, we've gone through stuff in our personal relationship, but it's never been caused by work. It's amazing how well we work together. When you work with somebody, you're usually dealing with ego. You want to protect your ideas. Taki and I talk out everything in our life. We live together, we have our animals, we have my son. So when it comes to writing stories, it's easy to communicate and either shoot down or support the other person's ideas without any sort of weird feeling.

That might be different with most couples when it comes to creativity. Some couples can work together, while others who love each other just as much and have just as beautiful a relationship don't want to cross that work line. Taki and I work together on some things, but not everything. We make sure we each have enough time for our own work.

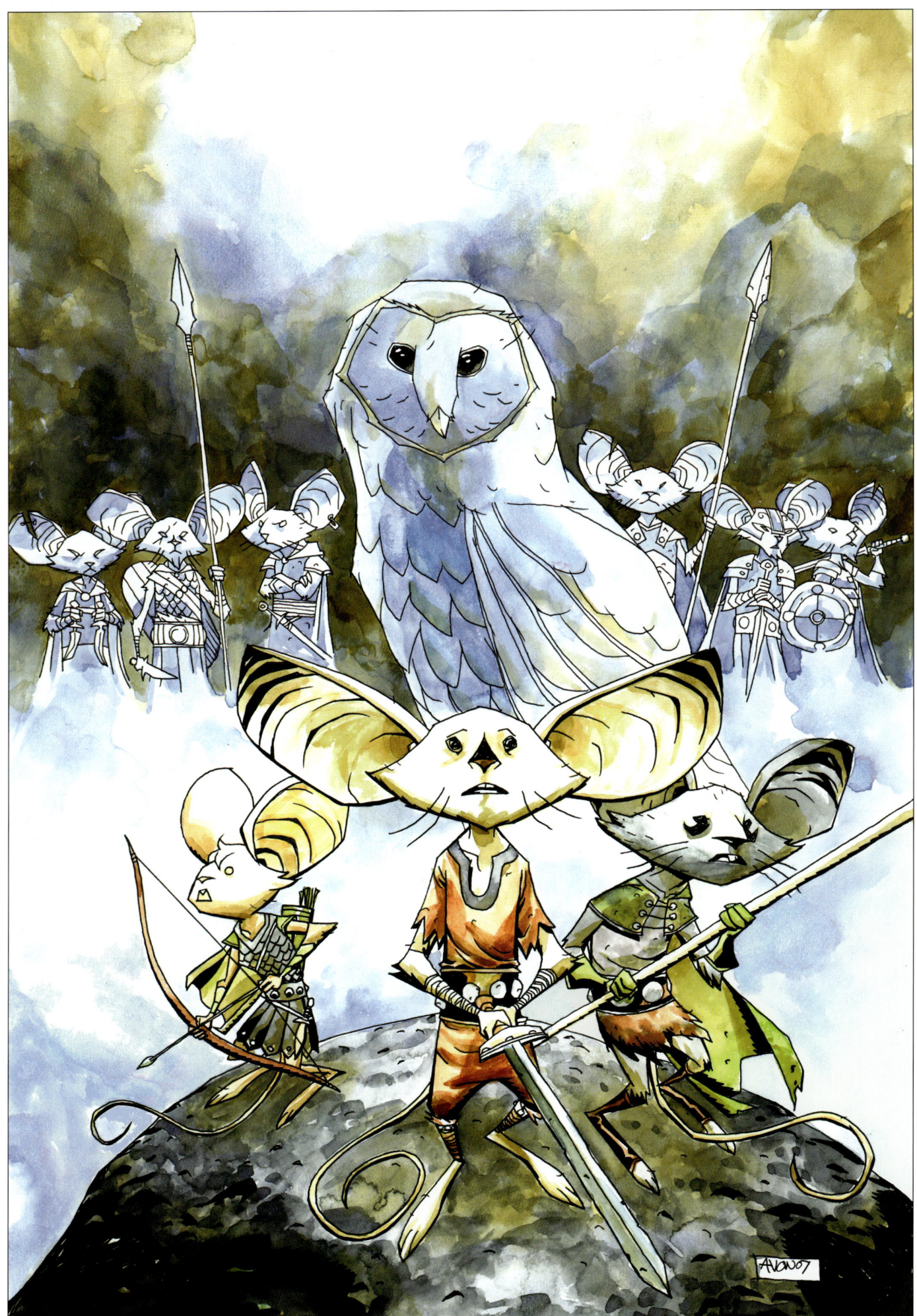
Mice Templar covers

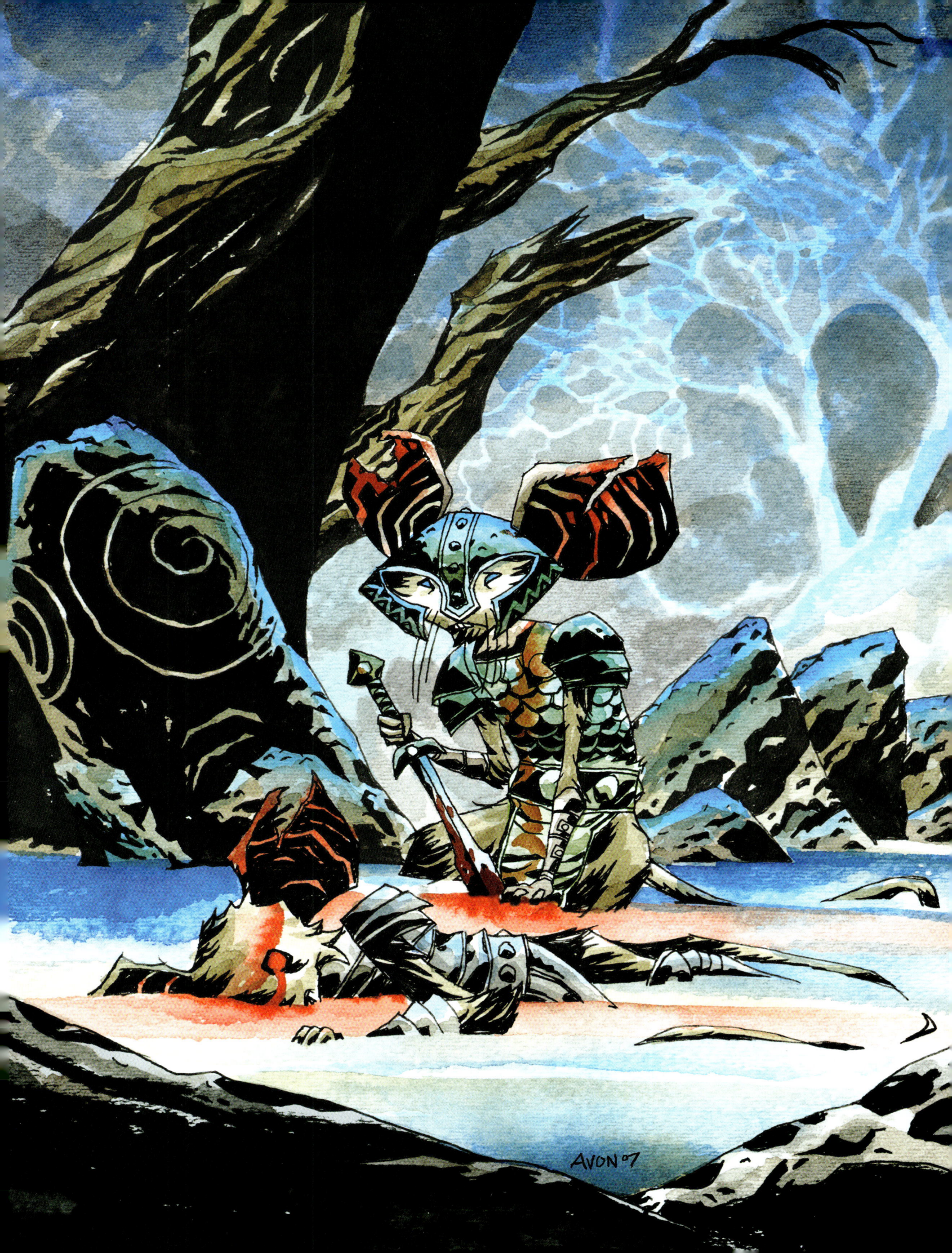

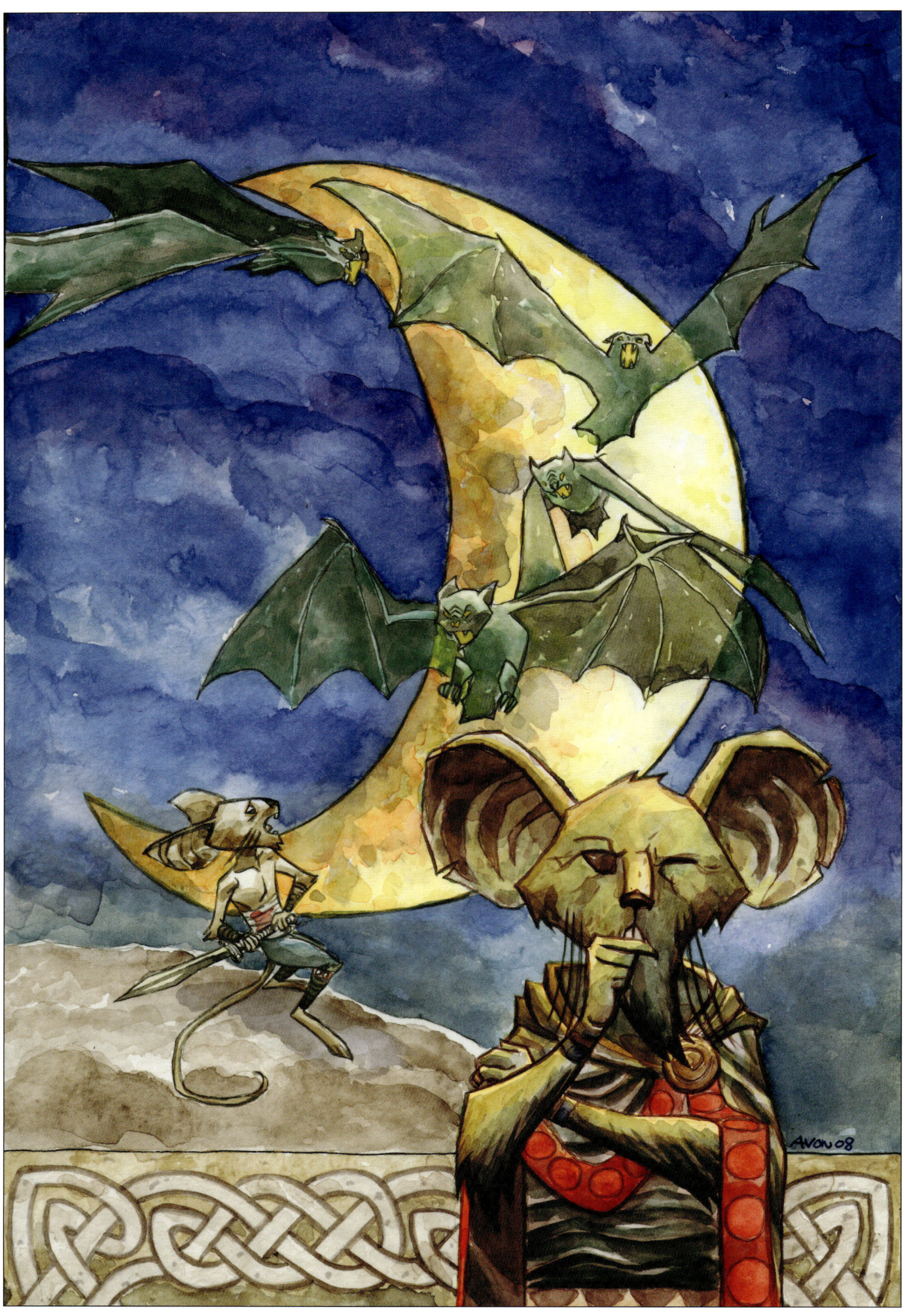

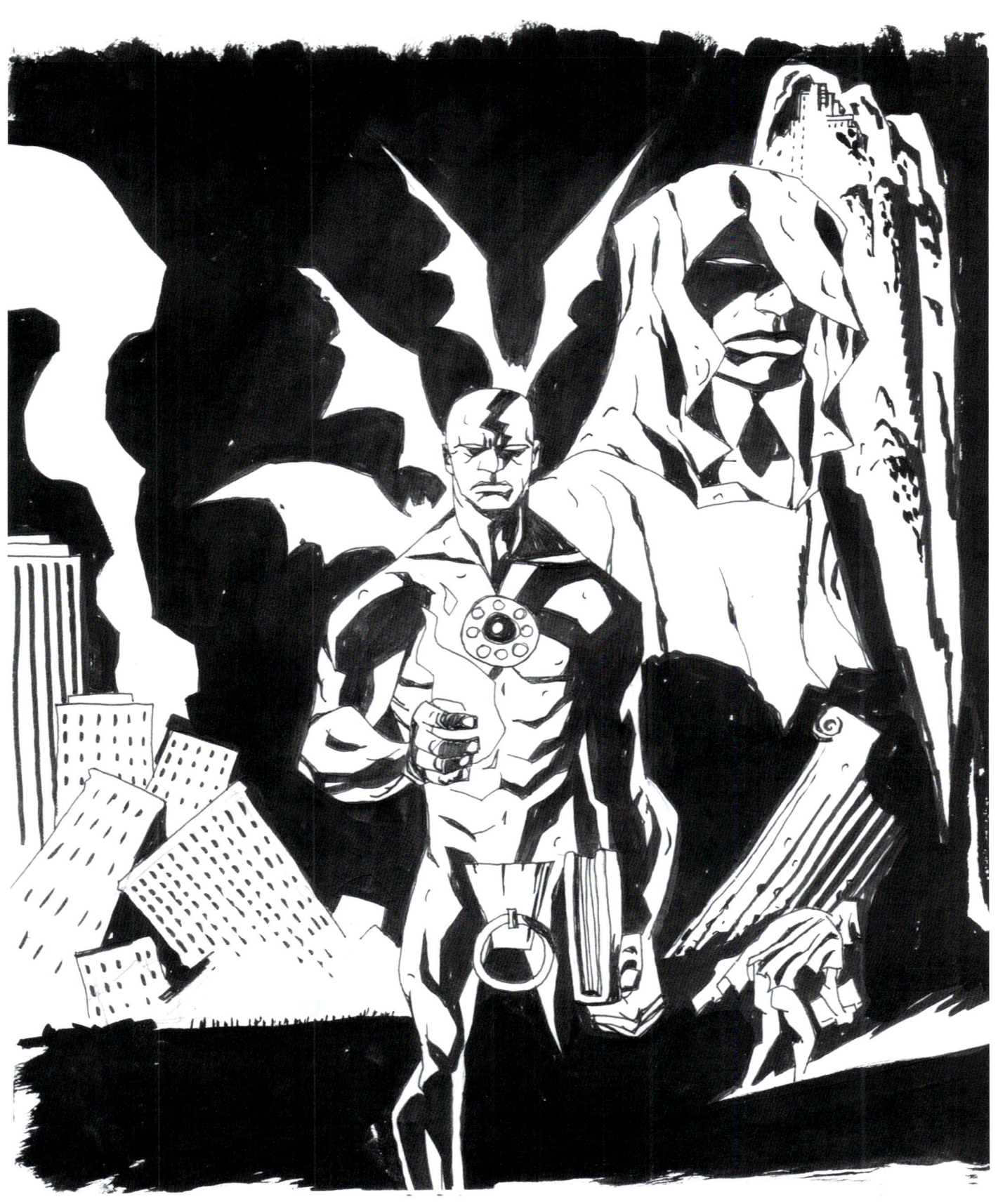

Oeming's idea for a story about Mignola's Roger the Homunculus in Hell, before he knew Mignola planned to do *Hellboy in Hell*

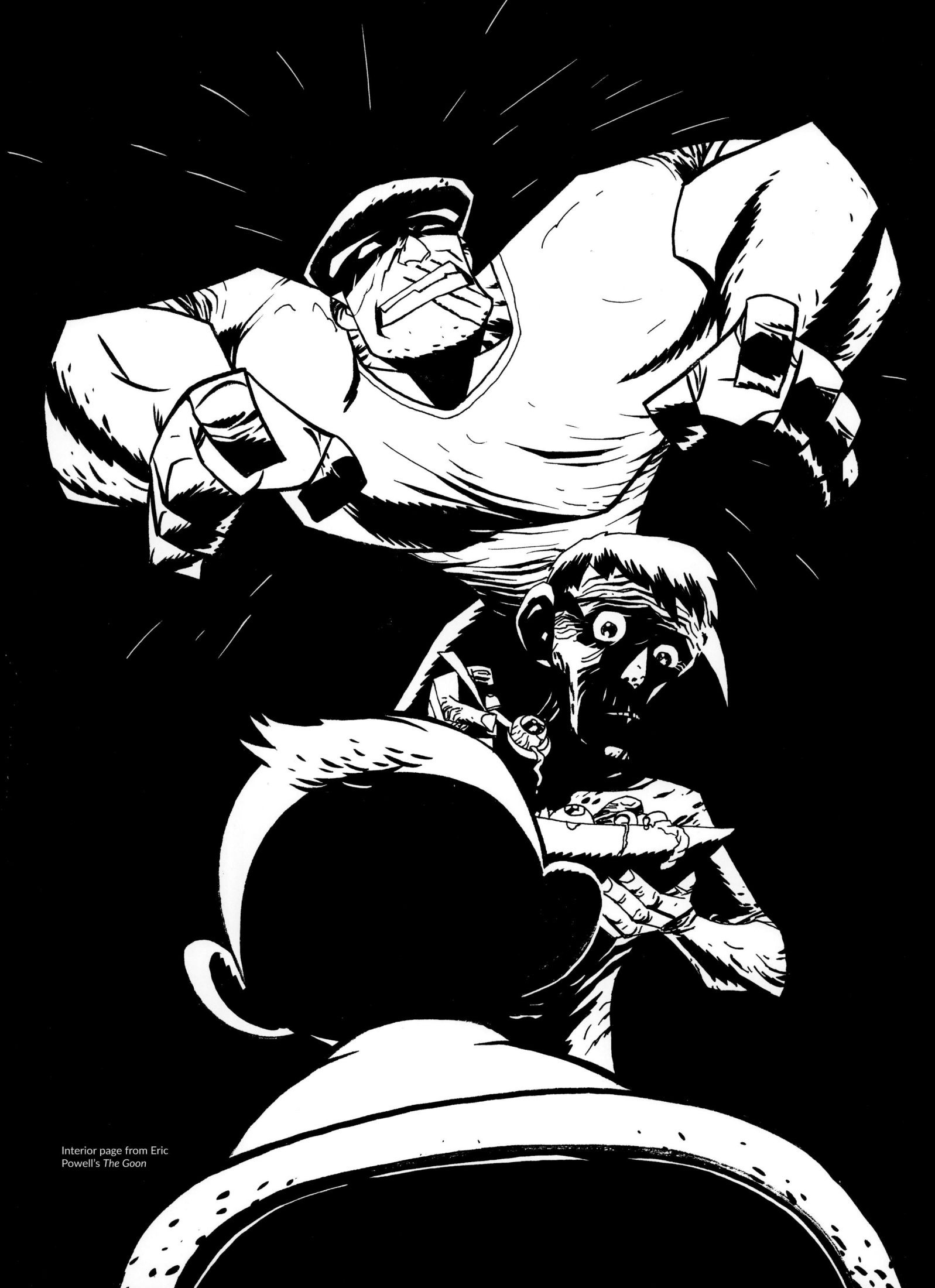

Interior page from Eric Powell's *The Goon*

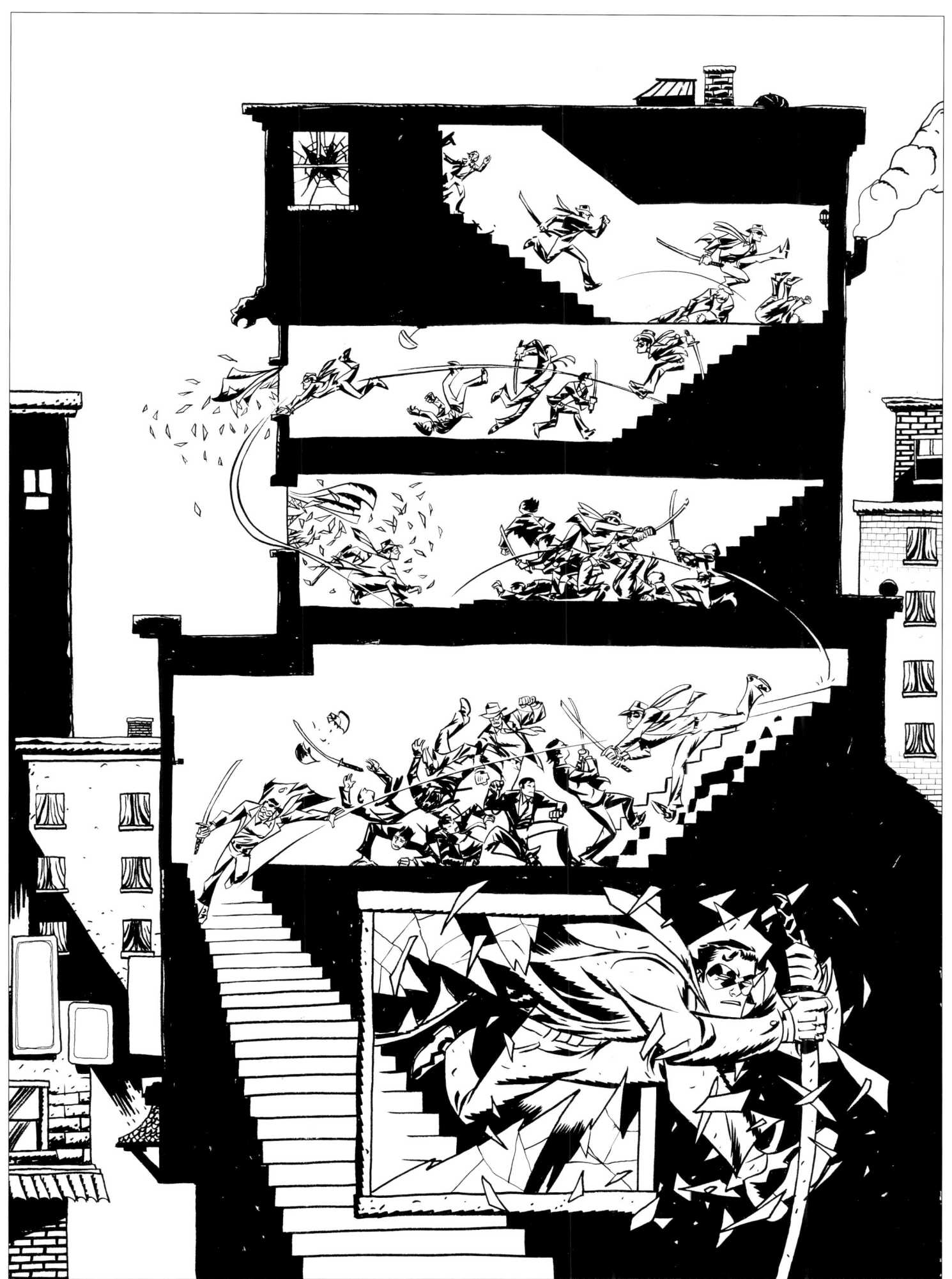

Interior page from Will Eisner's *The Spirit*

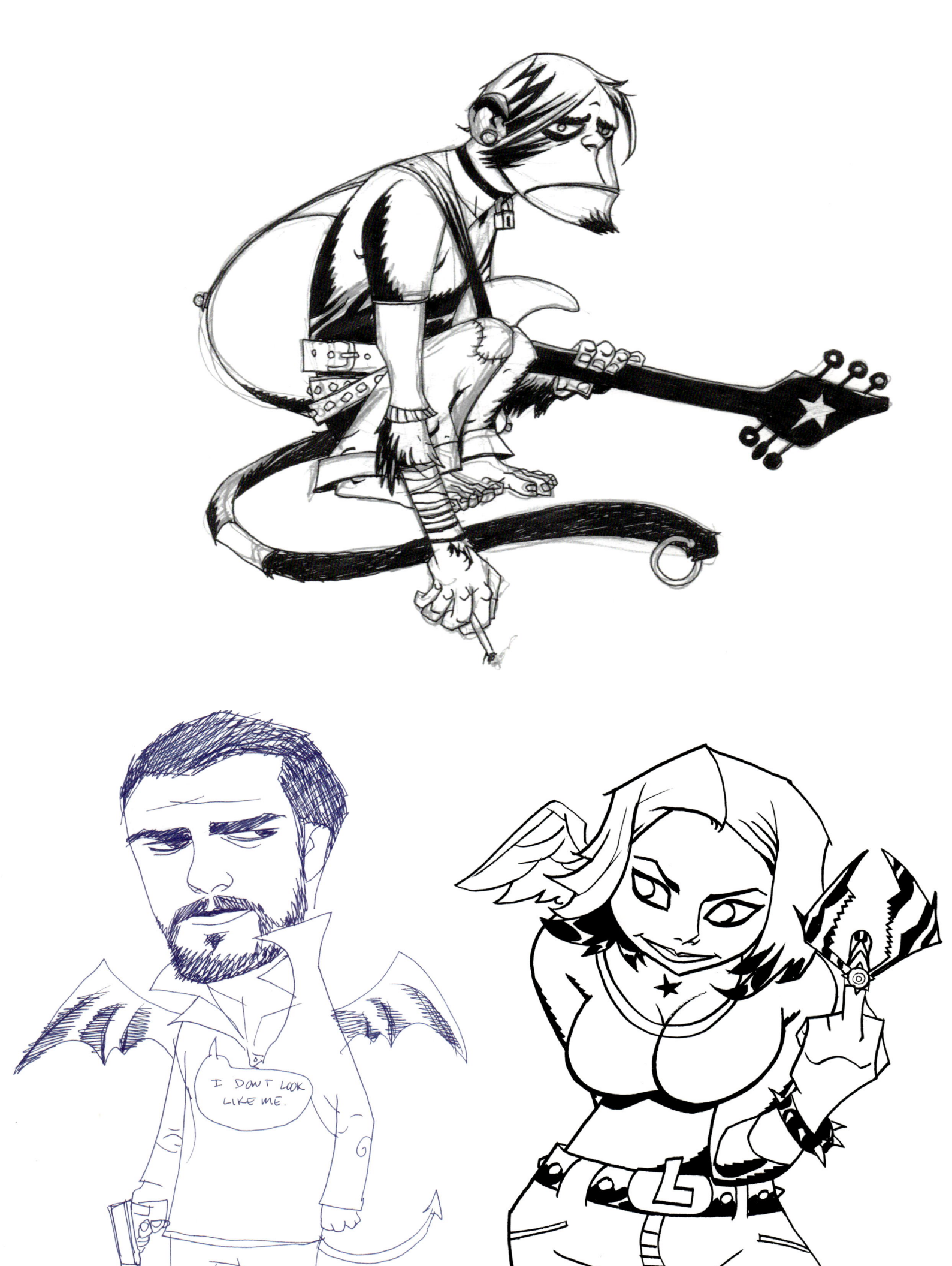

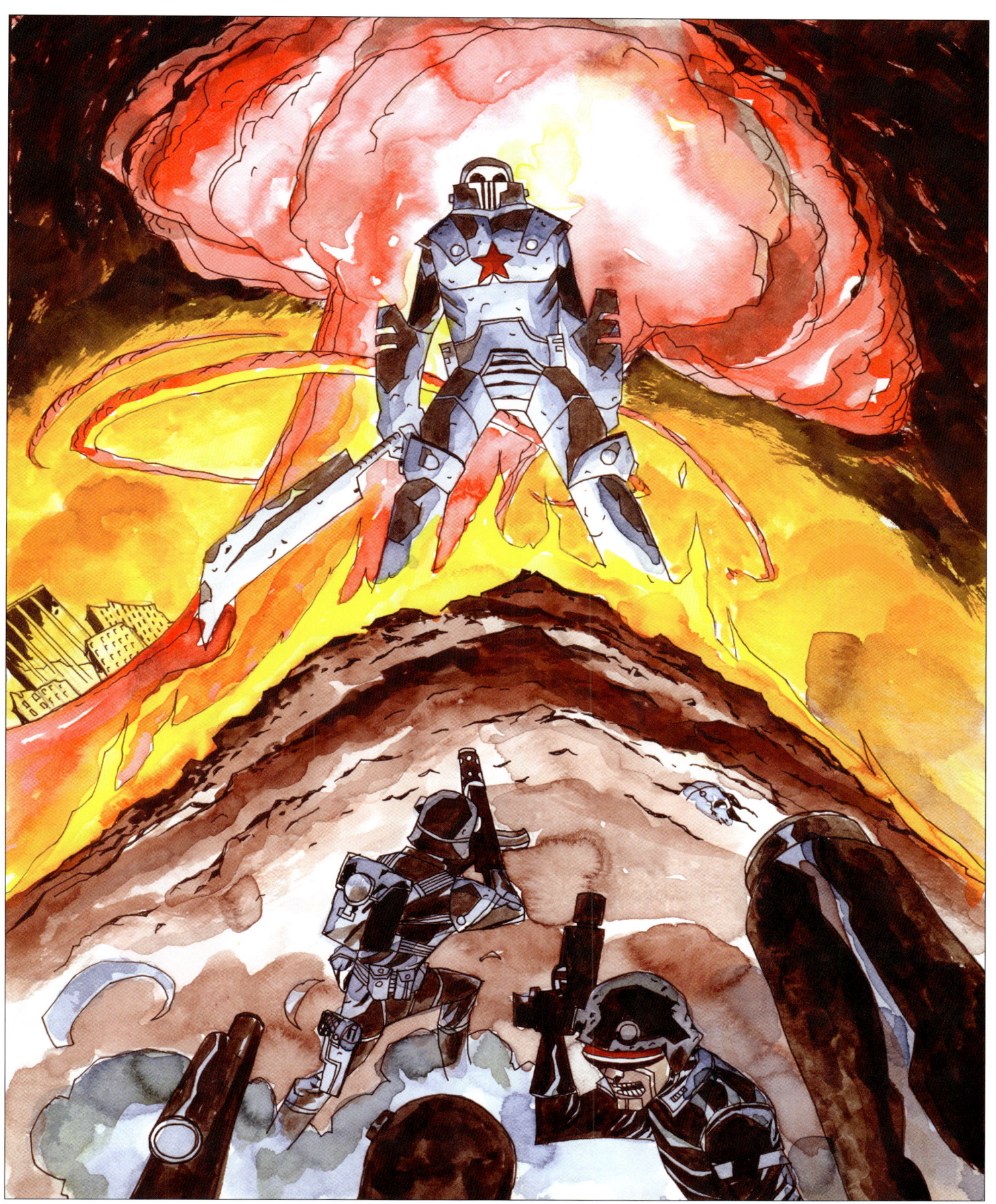
Interior page from Oeming's "7 Nation Army" in Ivan Brandon's anthology *24Seven Vol. 2*

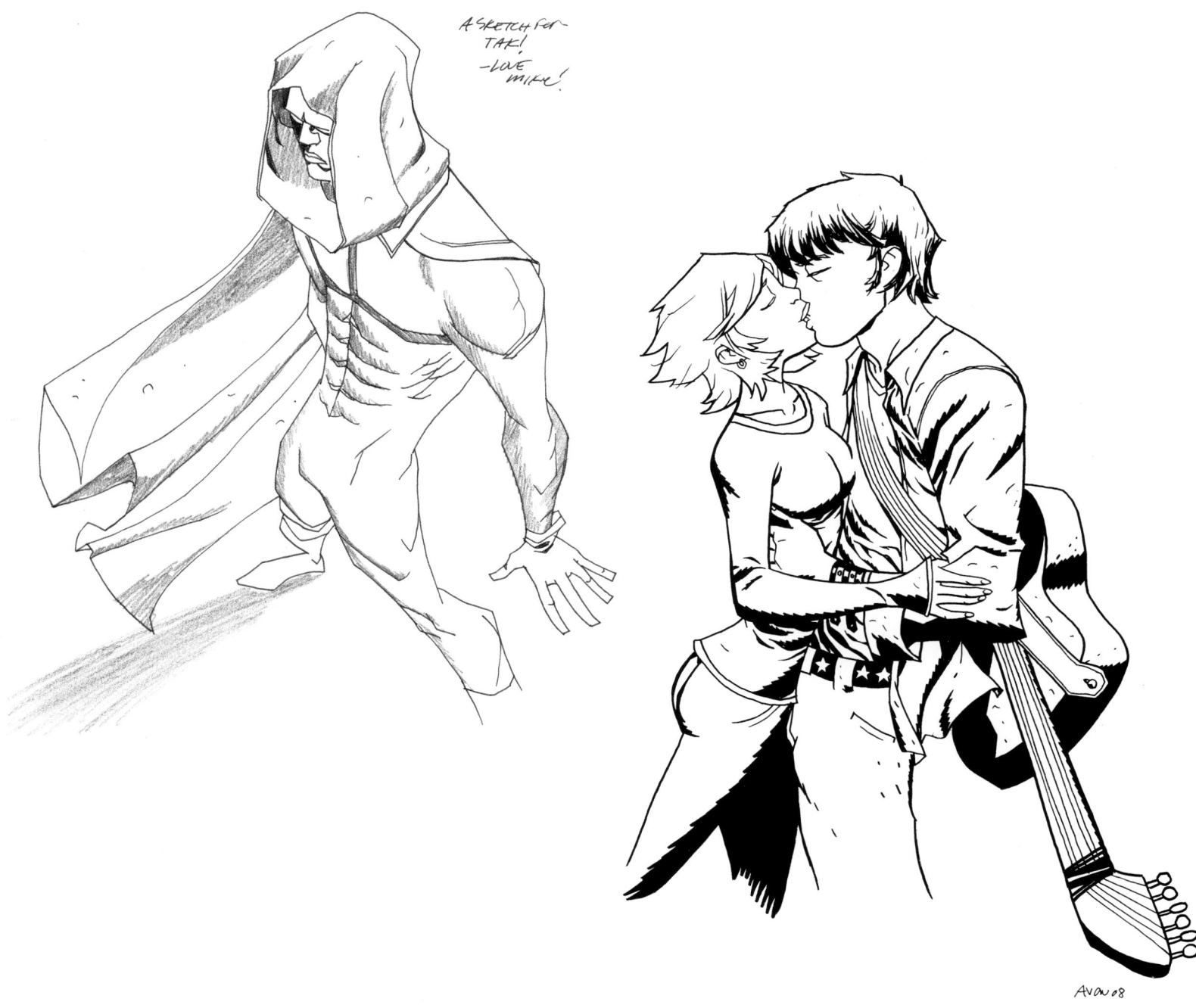

Rapture was the first thing Taki and I worked on and developed together early on in our relationship. I had come out of a divorce after a very long marriage and Taki had been through different relationships that were all really rough. We bonded over past relationship bullshit, talking about how breakups, even if they're for the best, always feel like the end of the world.

We talked about this as we moved her stuff from Minneapolis to New Jersey to be with me. A lot of the story was developed on the road. I'd had a general idea for a postapocalyptic superhero story, with the feeling of devastation and how you rebuild from it, but I didn't know how to put it together.

Rapture starts with a boy and a girl breaking up at an airport. In the early part of our relationship, when we were dating long distance, Taki and I often said goodbyes at airports. As the relationship ends in the story, all the superheroes leave the planet to fight in a universal-sized shootout, leaving the earth devastated. The main character gets called upon by a mysterious being called the Word, and she's granted powers to be earth's new protector. It's a postapocalyptic superhero story, but it's really about a breakup and the fallout from it.

Rapture was the first creator-owned book I'd done at Dark Horse. Taki and I switched off on the covers. It was her first cover assignment, and she kicked ass and had a really good time. It was published in 2009.

It was kind of scary to do a story about a breakup when we were at the beginning of a relationship while working out a creative partnership at the same time. If we'd broken up, as our characters did, at the beginning of our new relationship, we would have still had this comic to deal with. But we decided to be brave and jump into the deep end of this idea and go for it. It was a great experience.

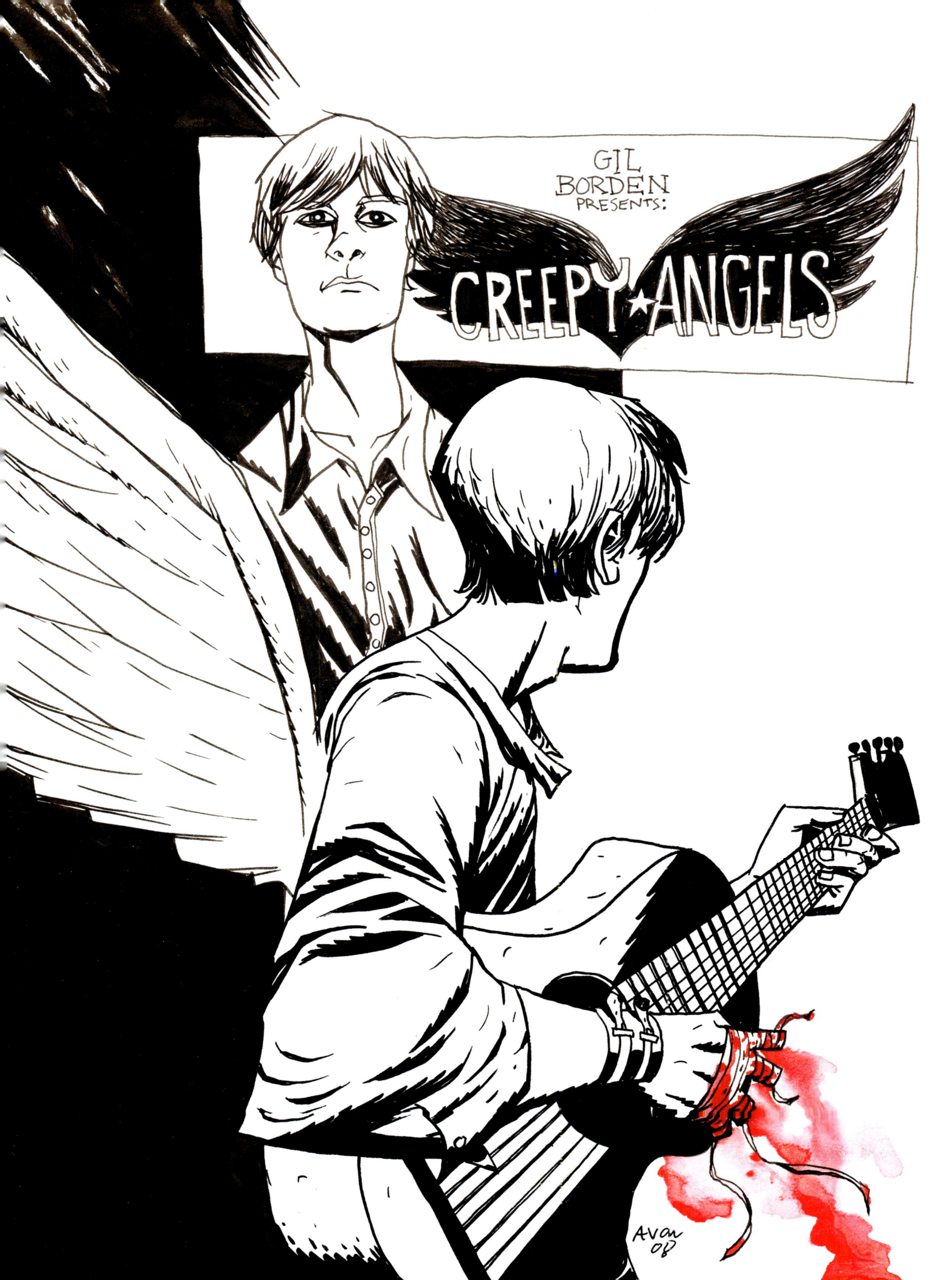

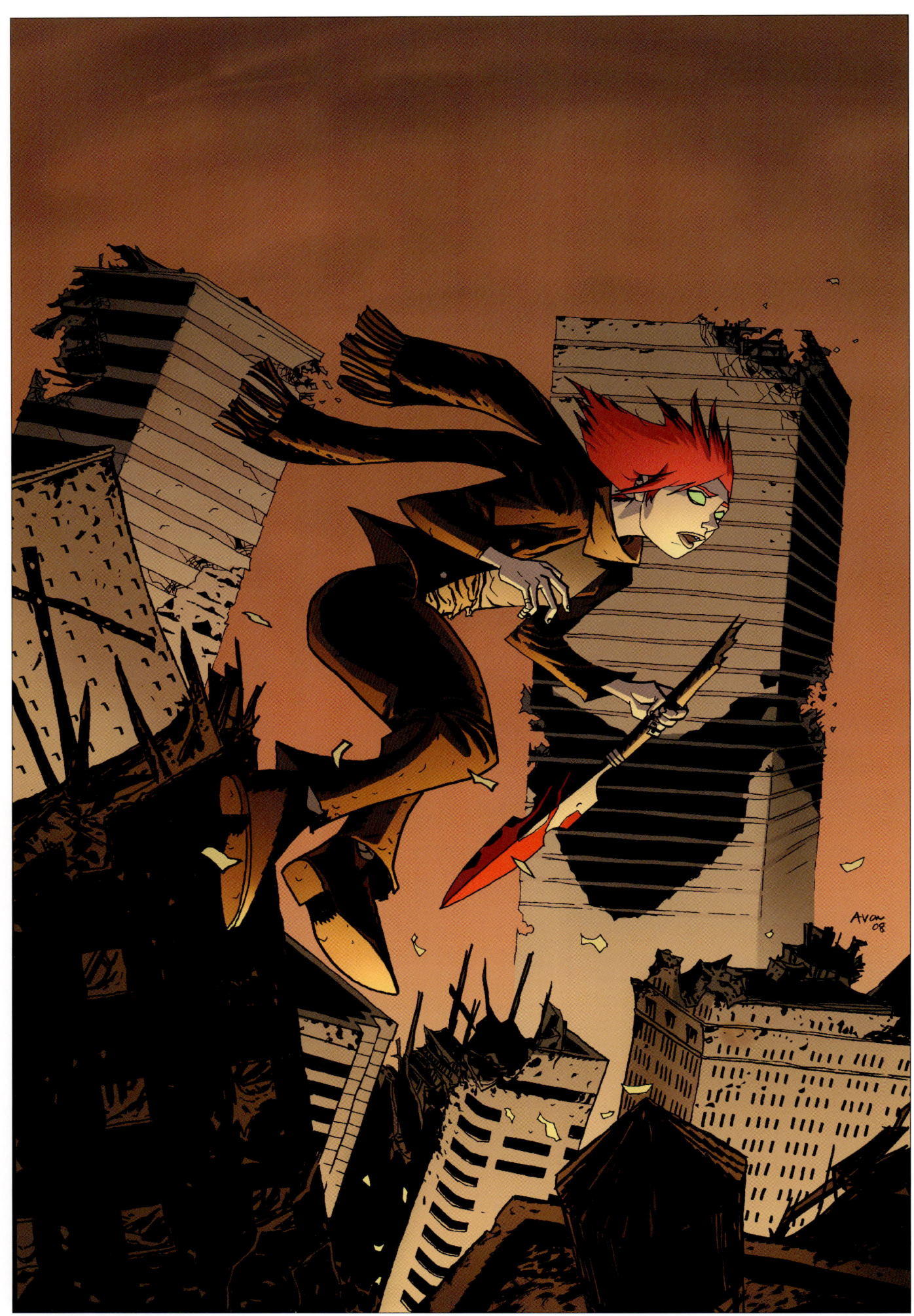

Rapture cover, colors by Val Staples

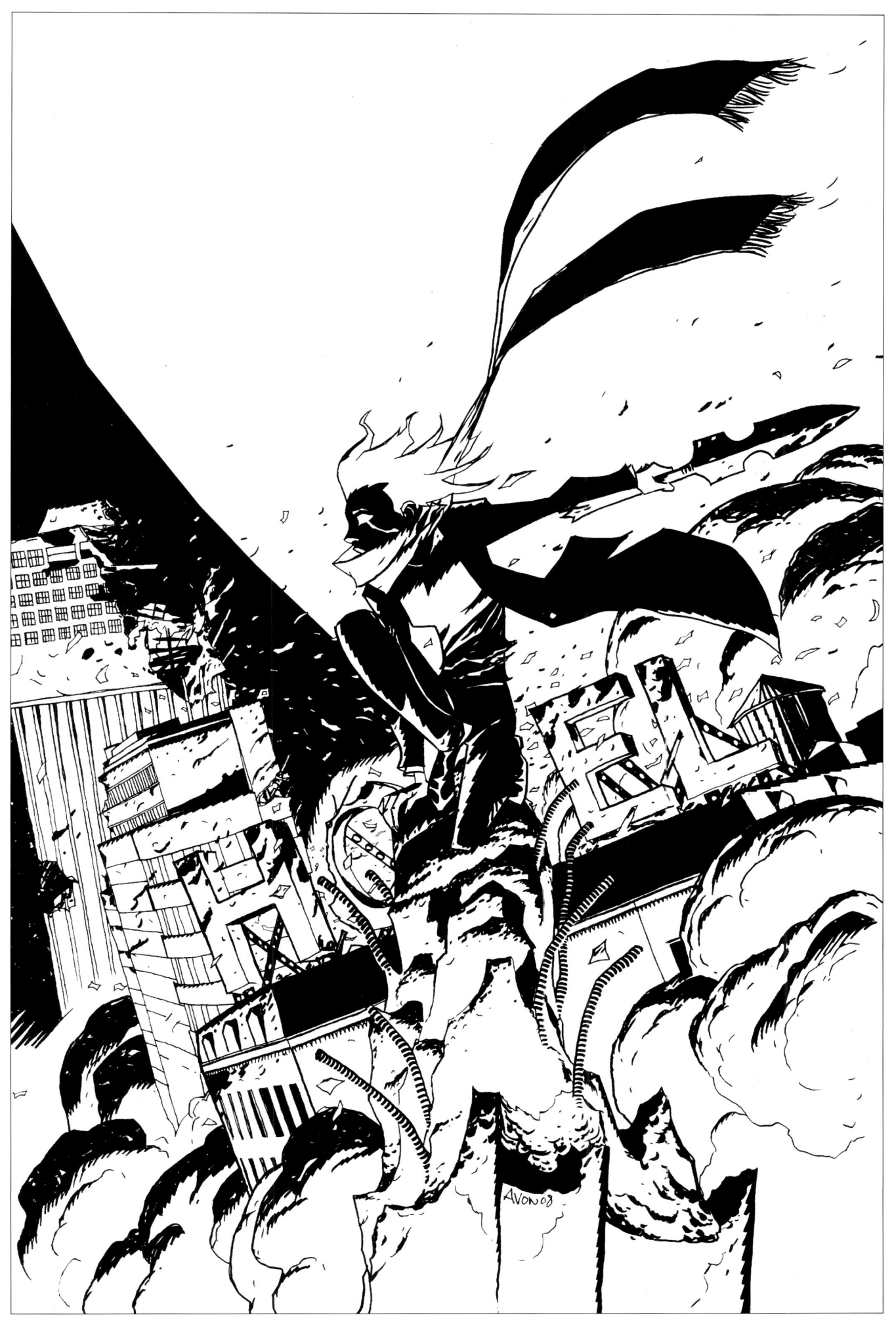

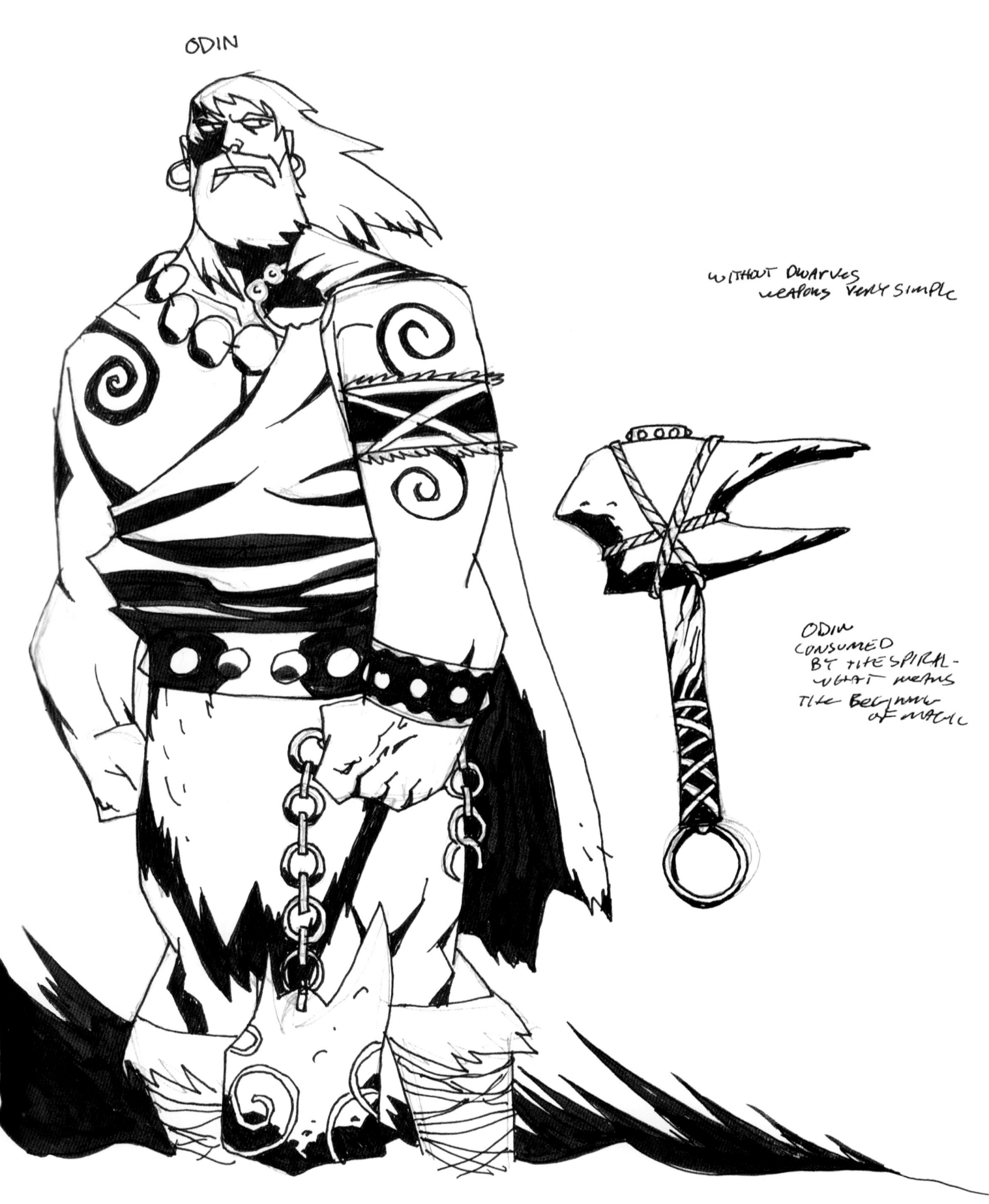

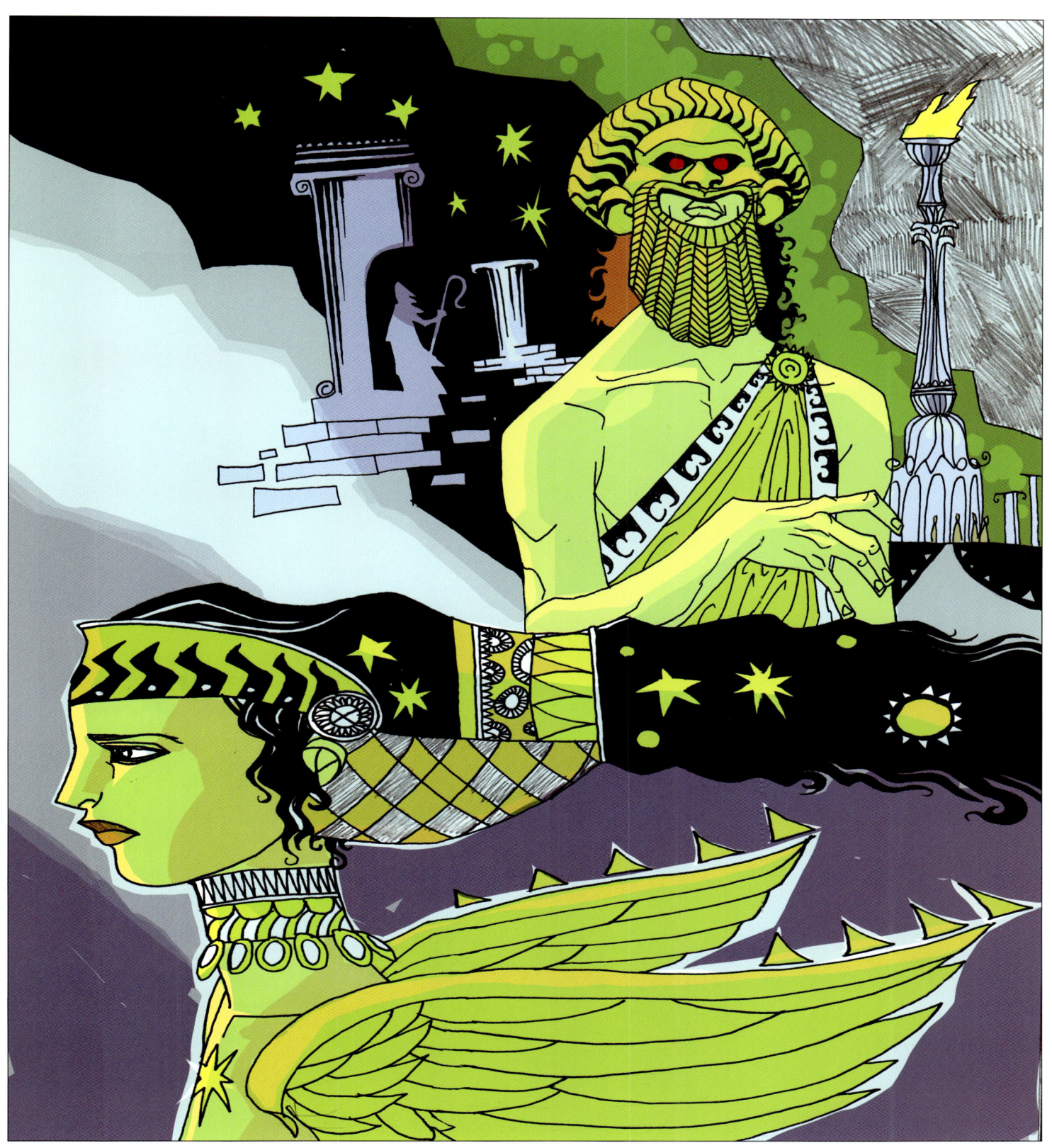
Oeming plays around with mythology and digital color

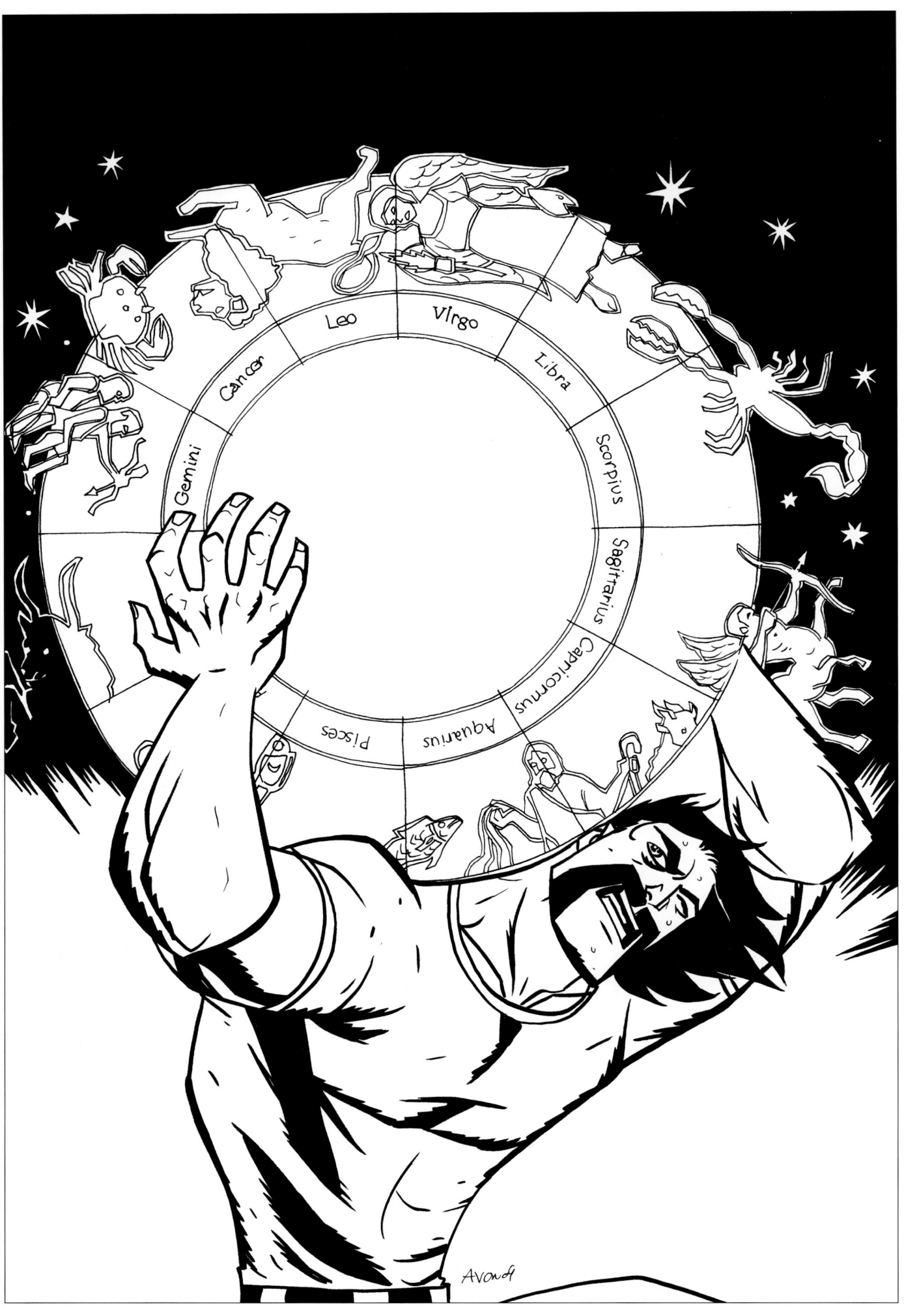

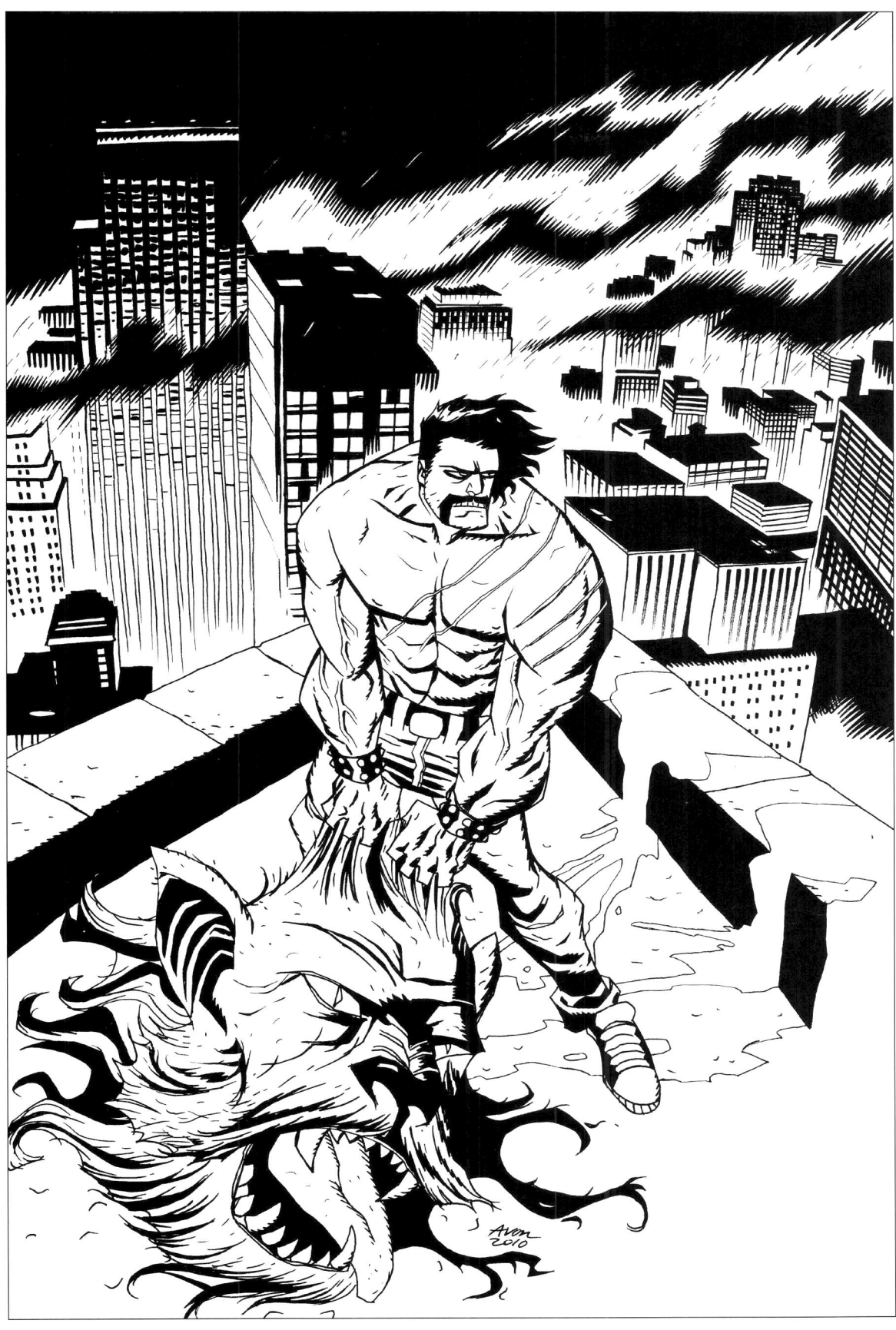

God Complex (Image Comics, 2009) was about an ancient god handling the problems of today's world, similar ideas to my work on *Ares: God of War* for Marvel Comics in 2006. *God Complex* was cowritten with Brian Bendis's brother-in-law Dan Berman. I was going to draw *God Complex*, but around this time I was invited to go work with video game studio Valve on the West Coast. Between moving to Washington, starting a new full-time job, drawing *Mice Templar* covers, and drawing *Powers*, I just couldn't do it. Still in Jersey, I'd gotten to know John Broglia at a local convention. He'd moved a couple towns over from me, and he was ready to be a pro, so passionate about his art I could sense how important it was for him to make comics. John pencilled and inked the book, and, surprisingly, Dan ended up doing colors.

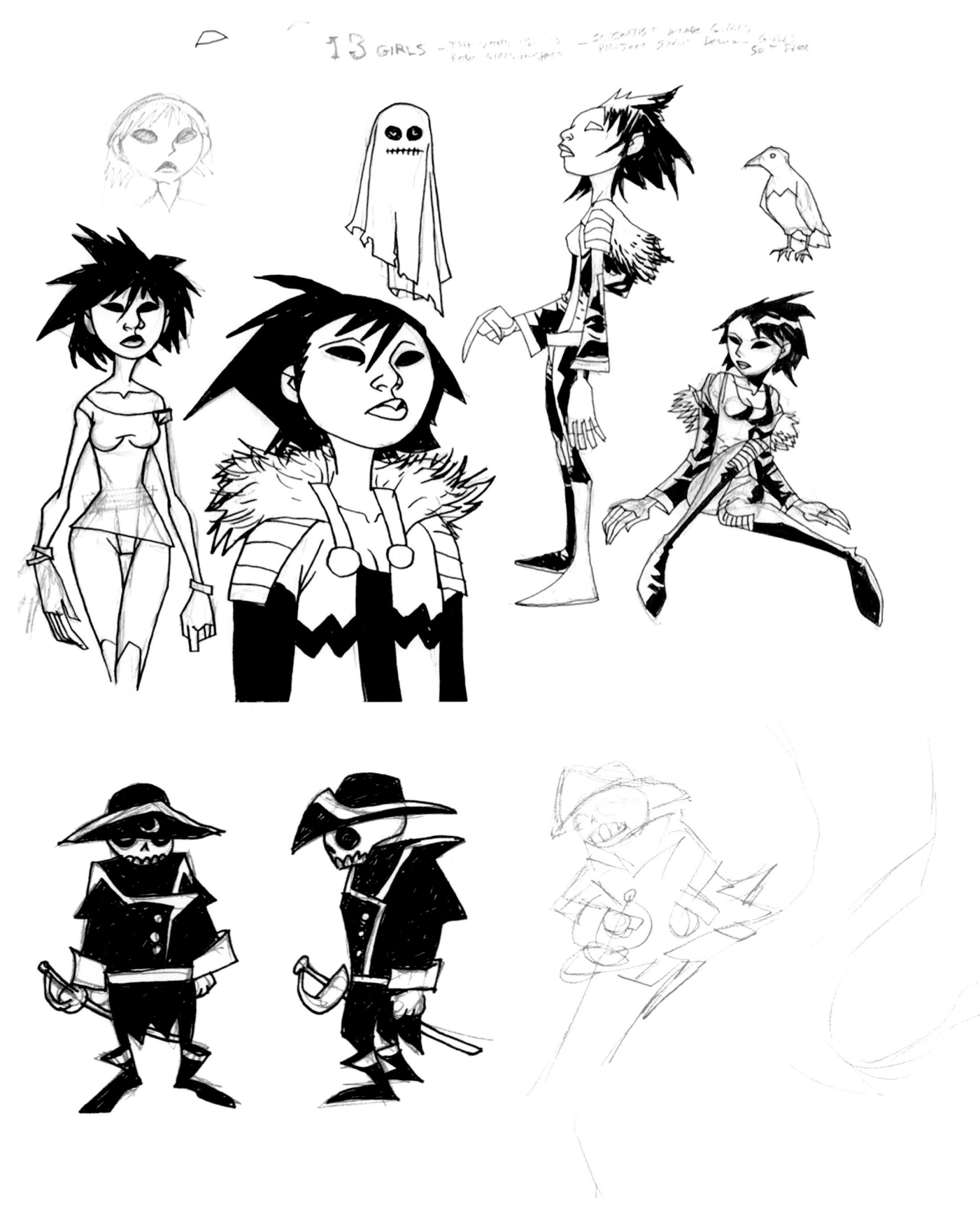

Following: *Mice Templar* covers

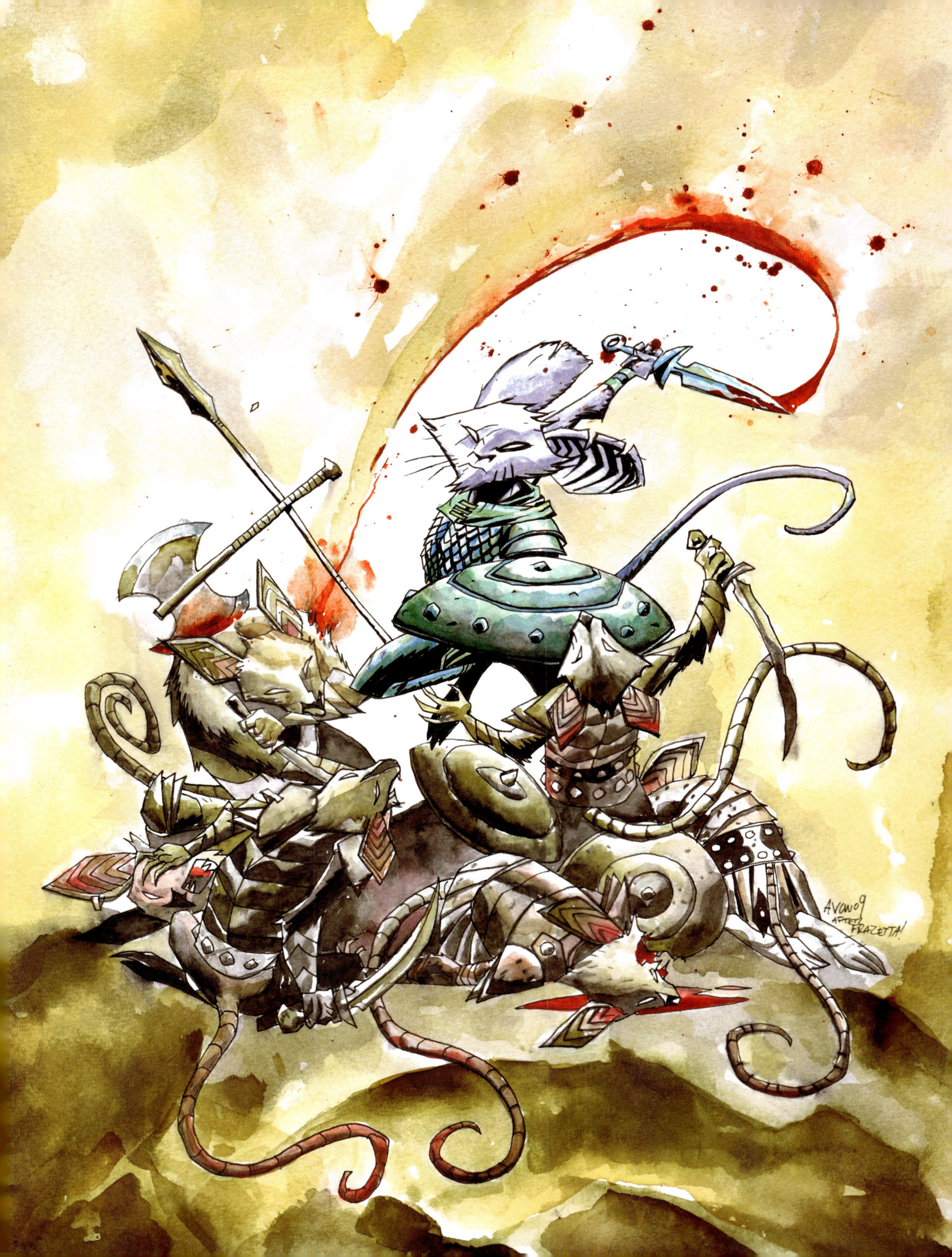

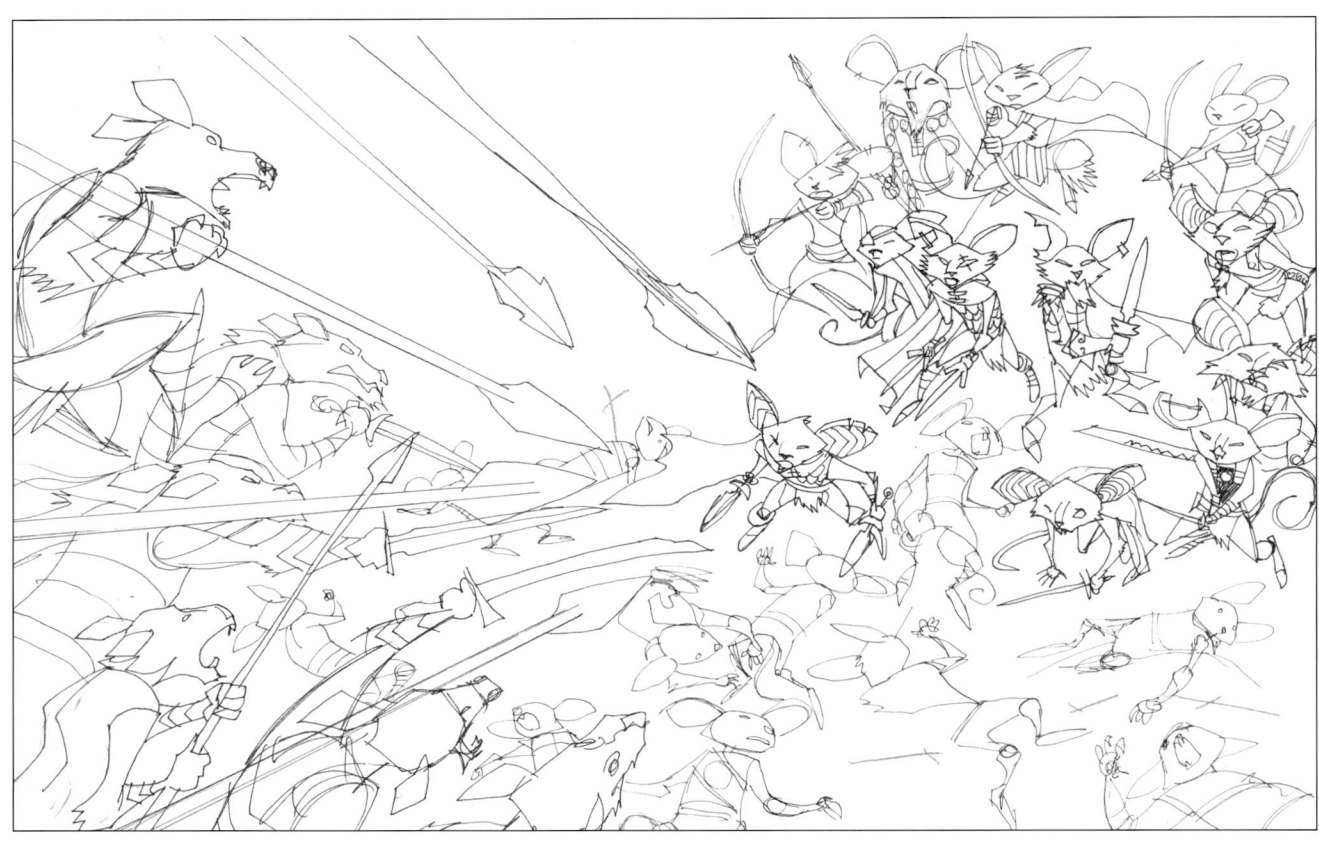
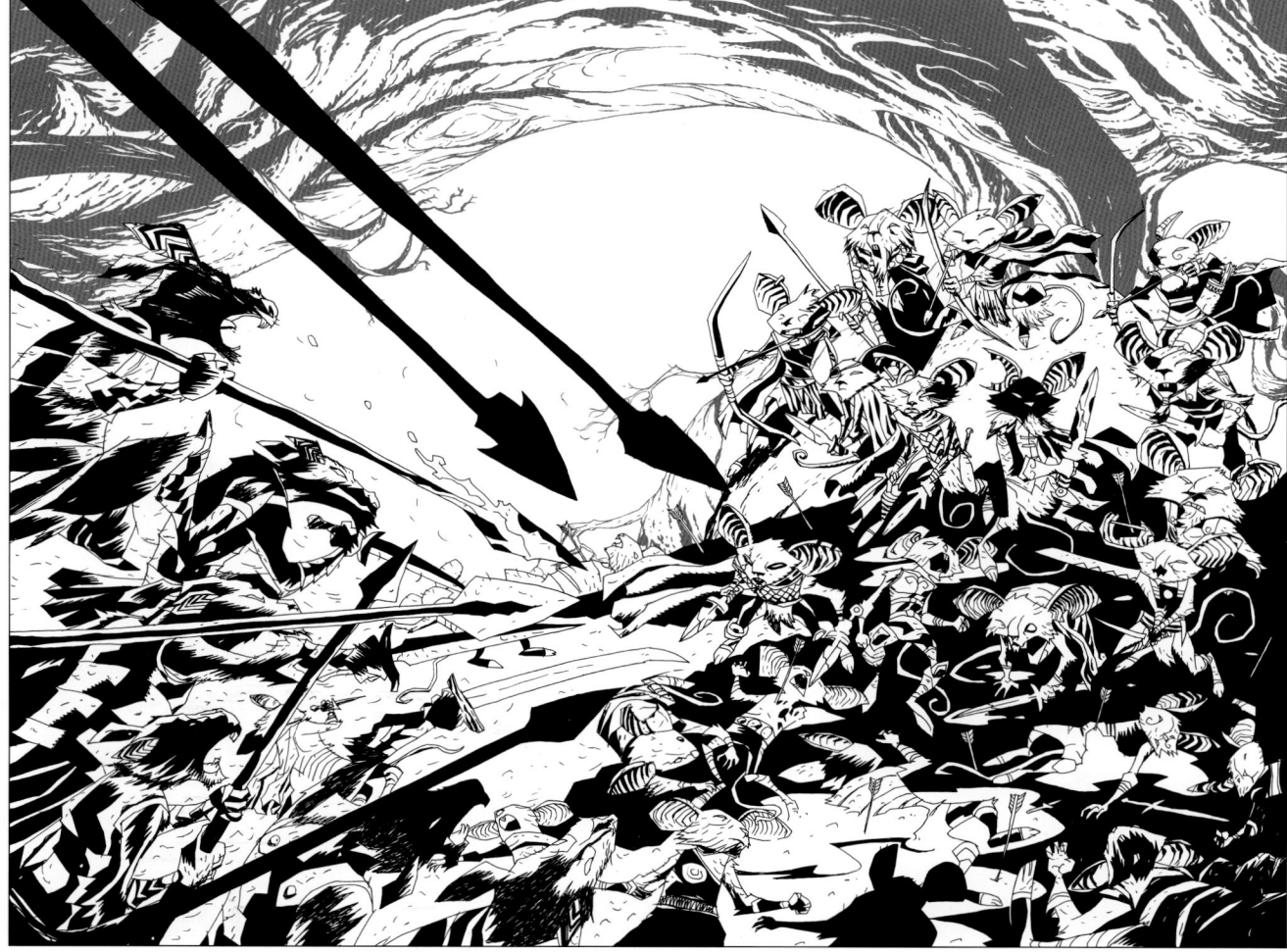

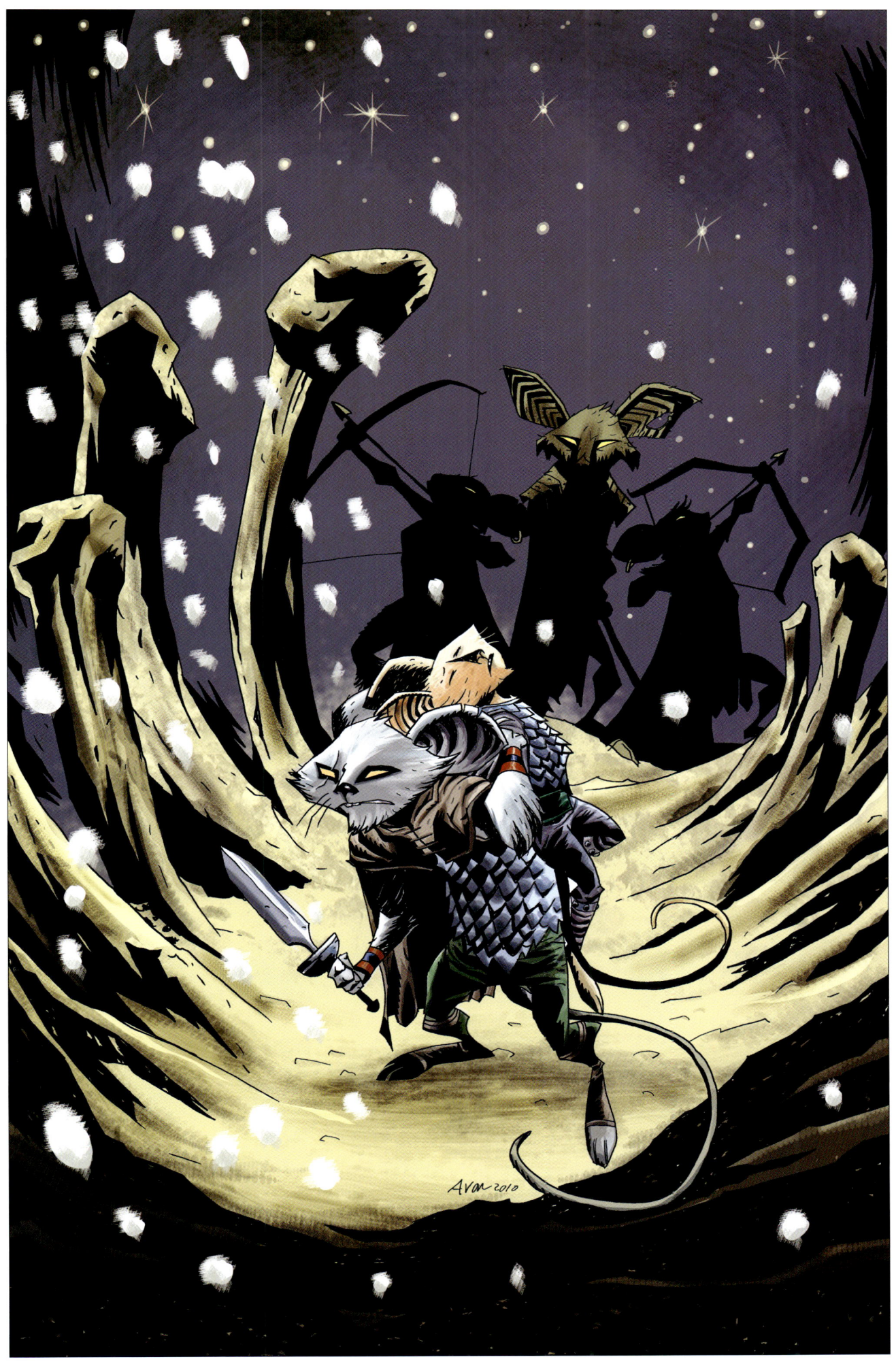

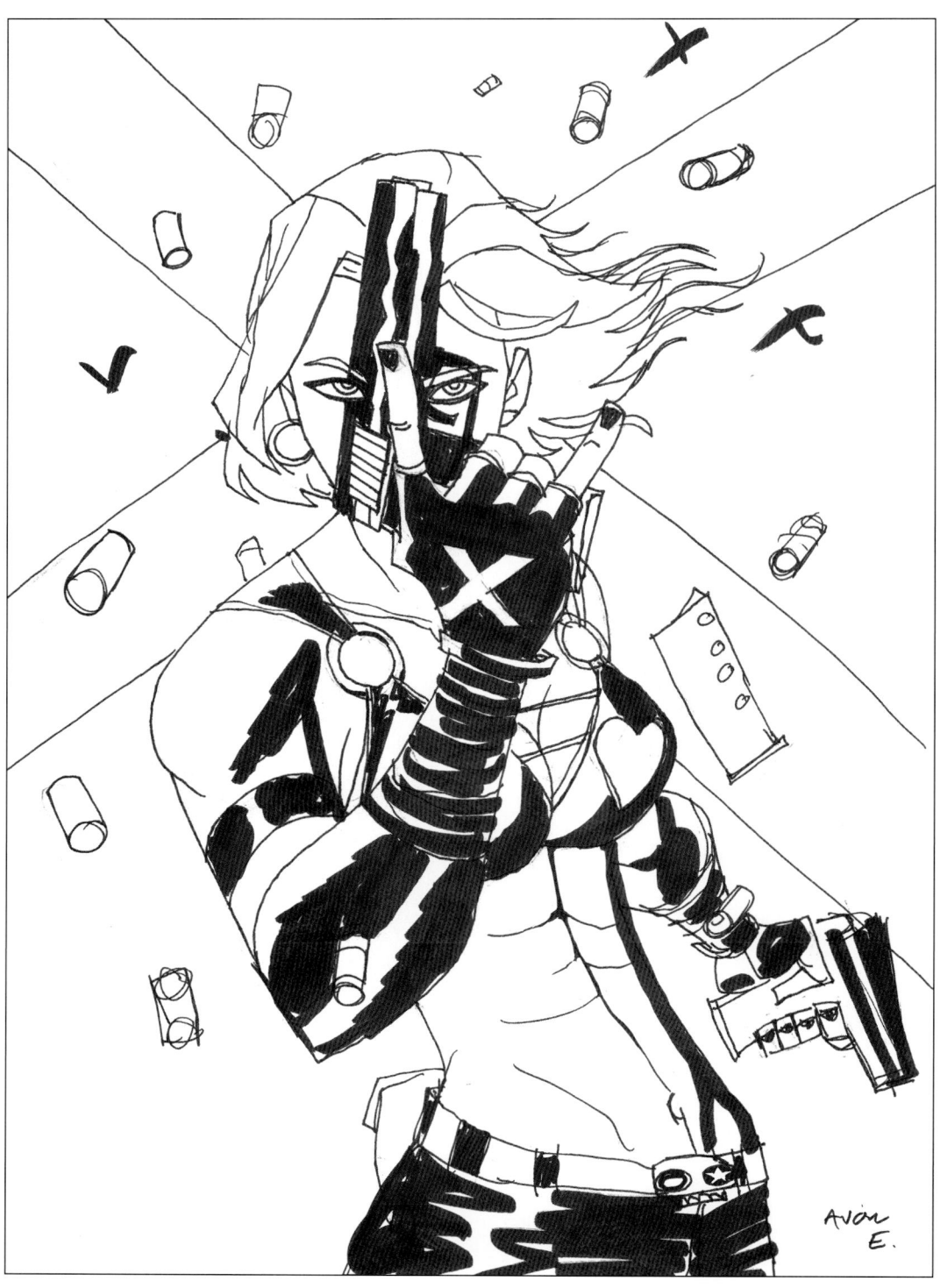

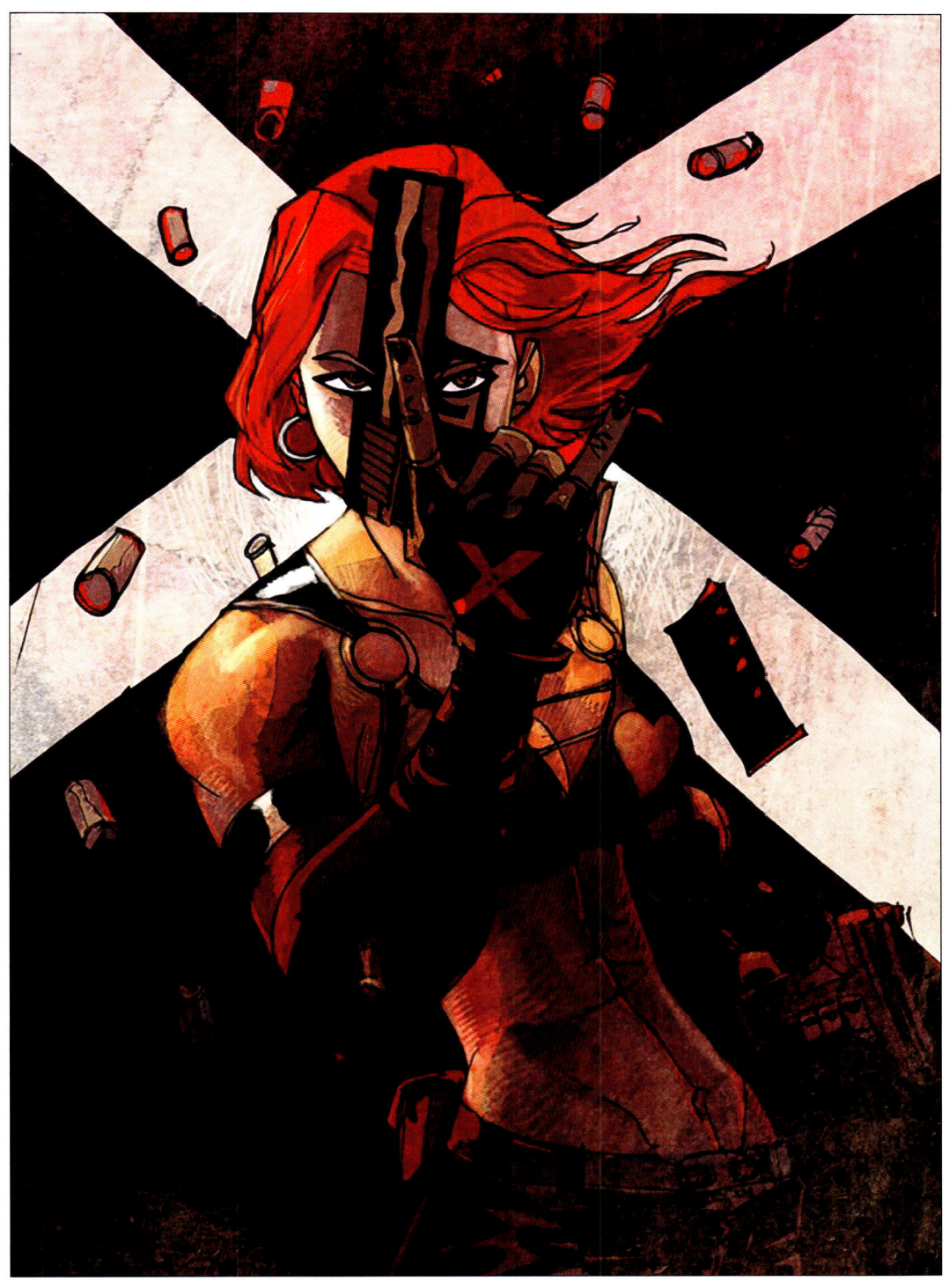

Cover for Brian Michael Bendis and Alex Maleev's *Scarlet*; facing, rough by Oeming; this page, finishes and colors by Maleev

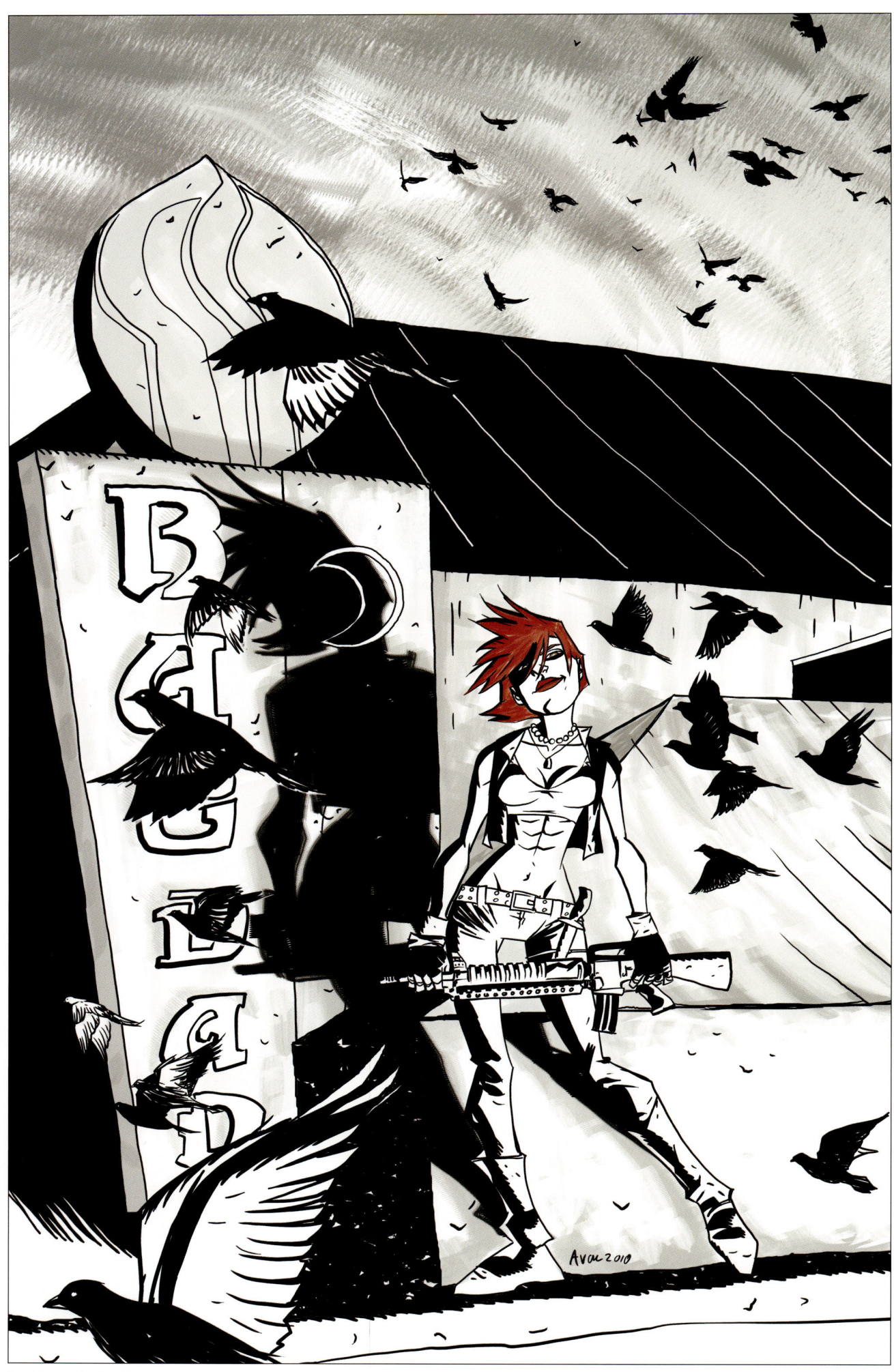

Scarlet cover by Oeming

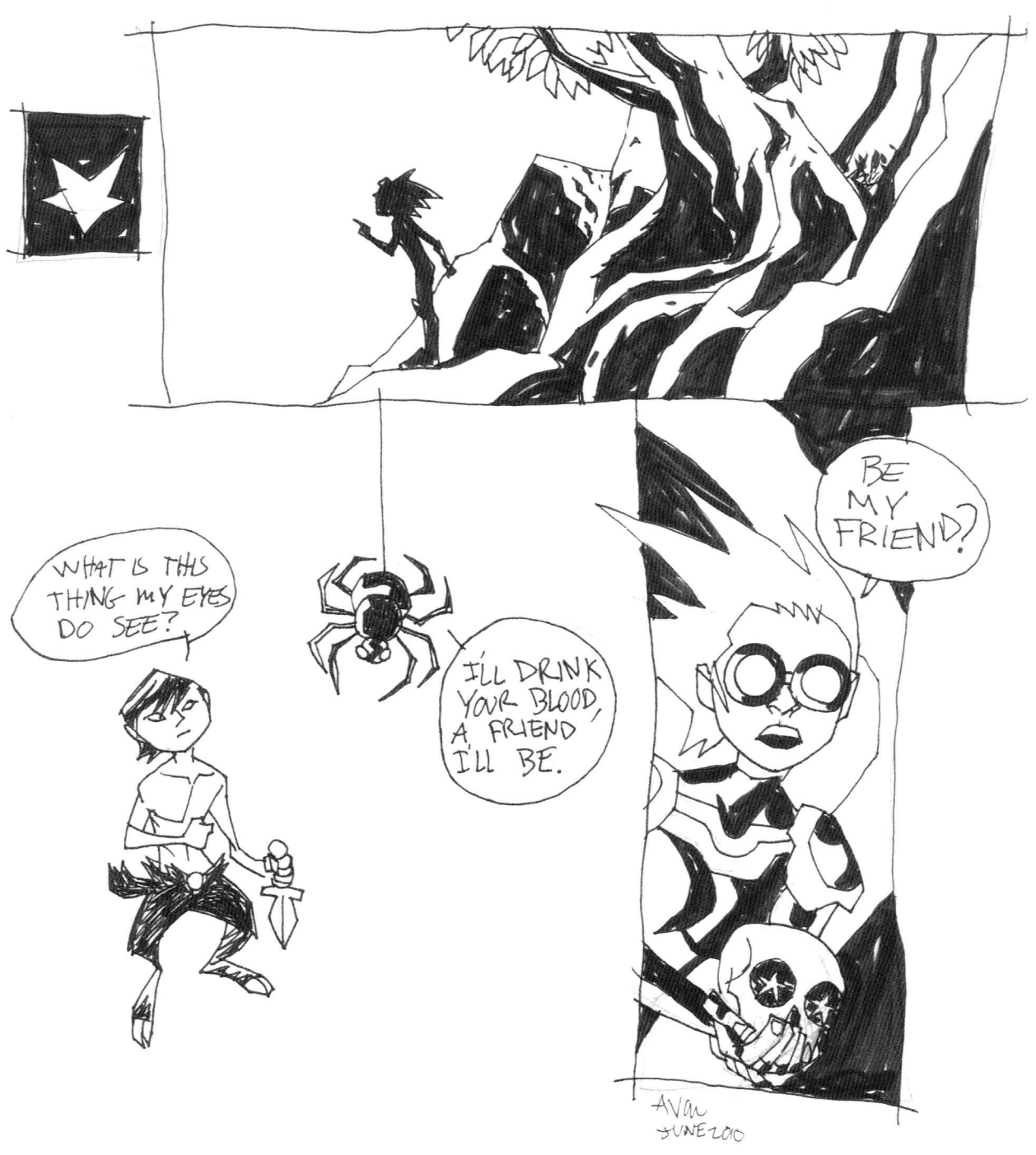

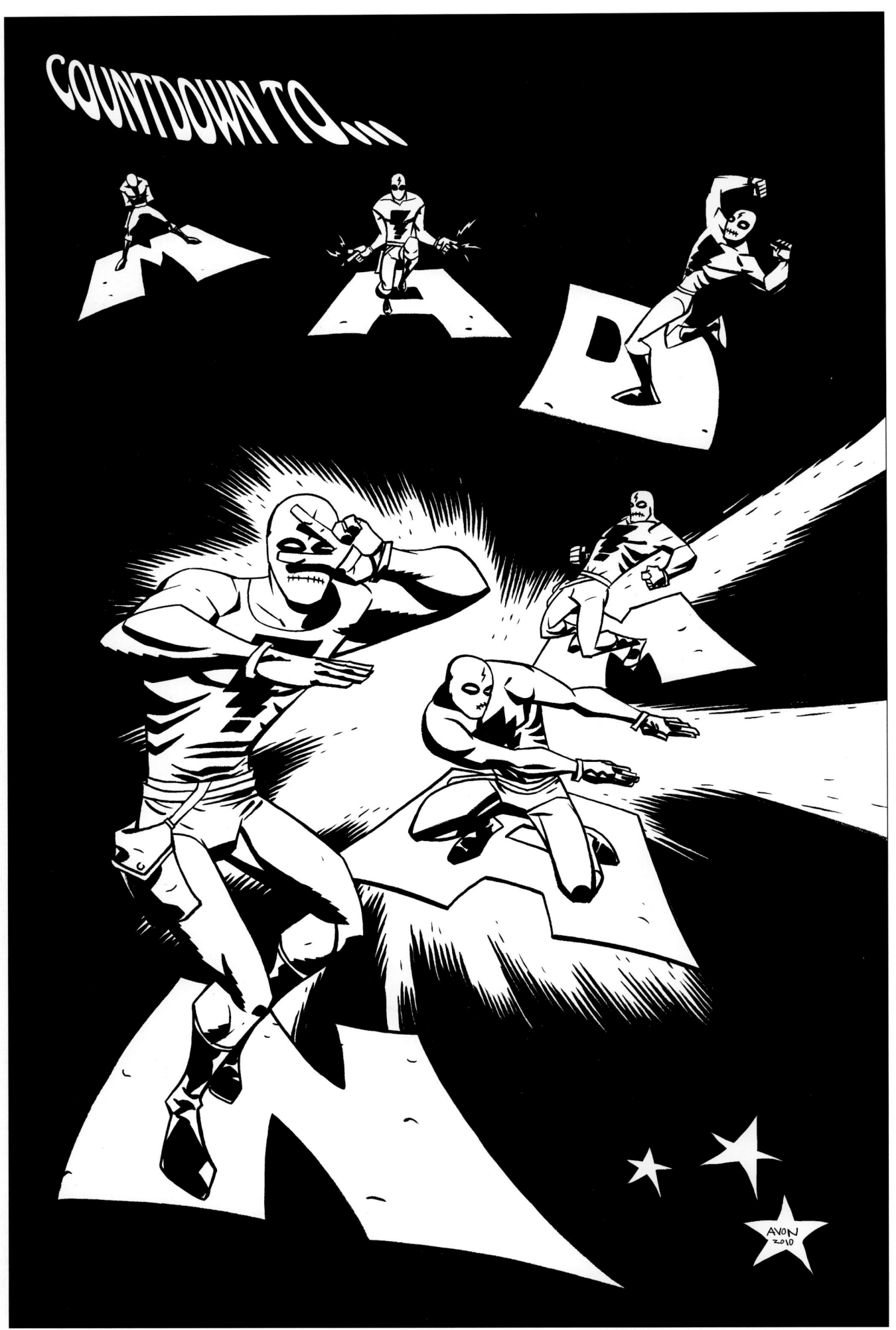

Pinup for Mike Allred's *Madman*

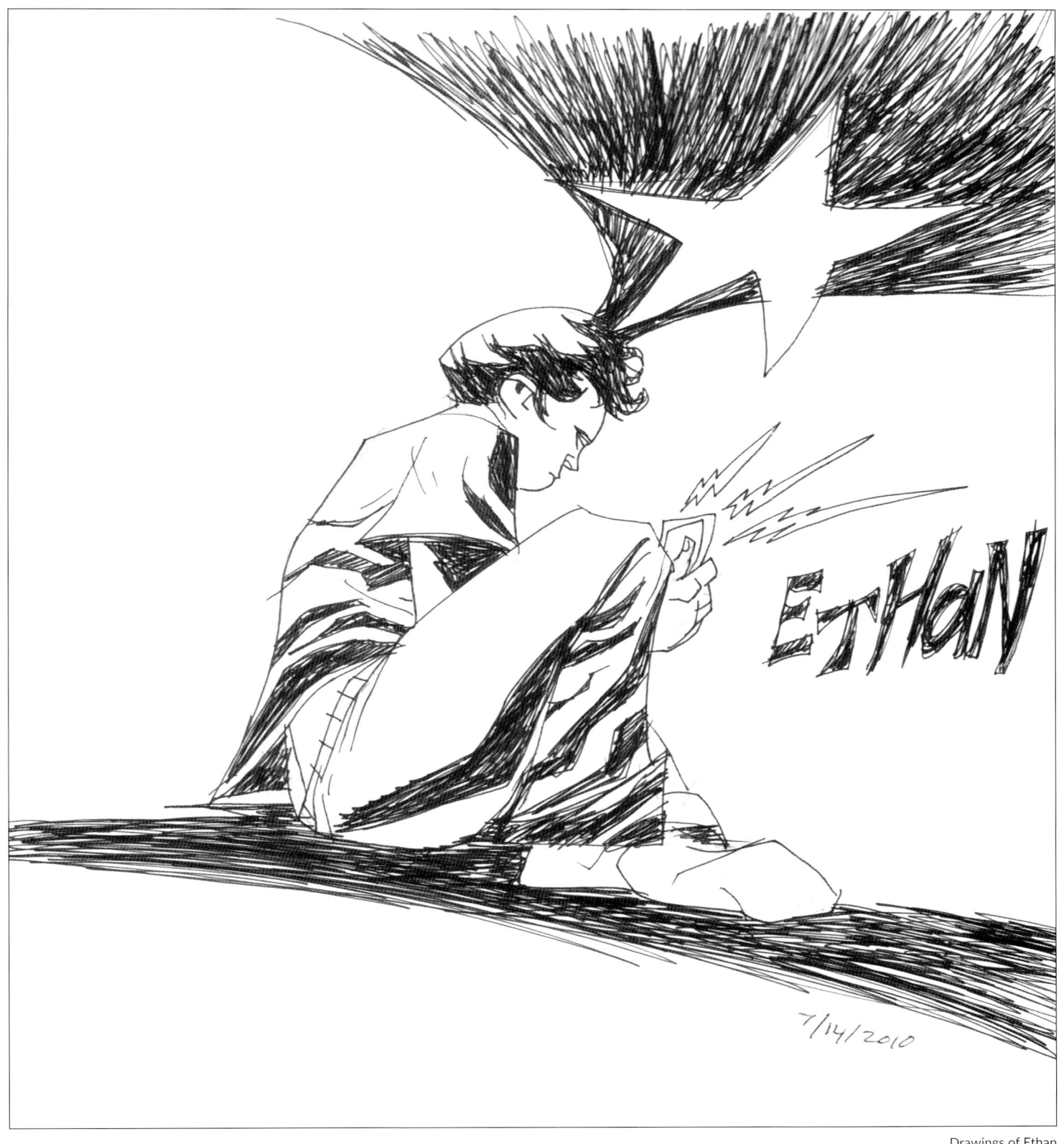

Drawings of Ethan

NO PLAN B: THE ART OF MICHAEL AVON OEMING

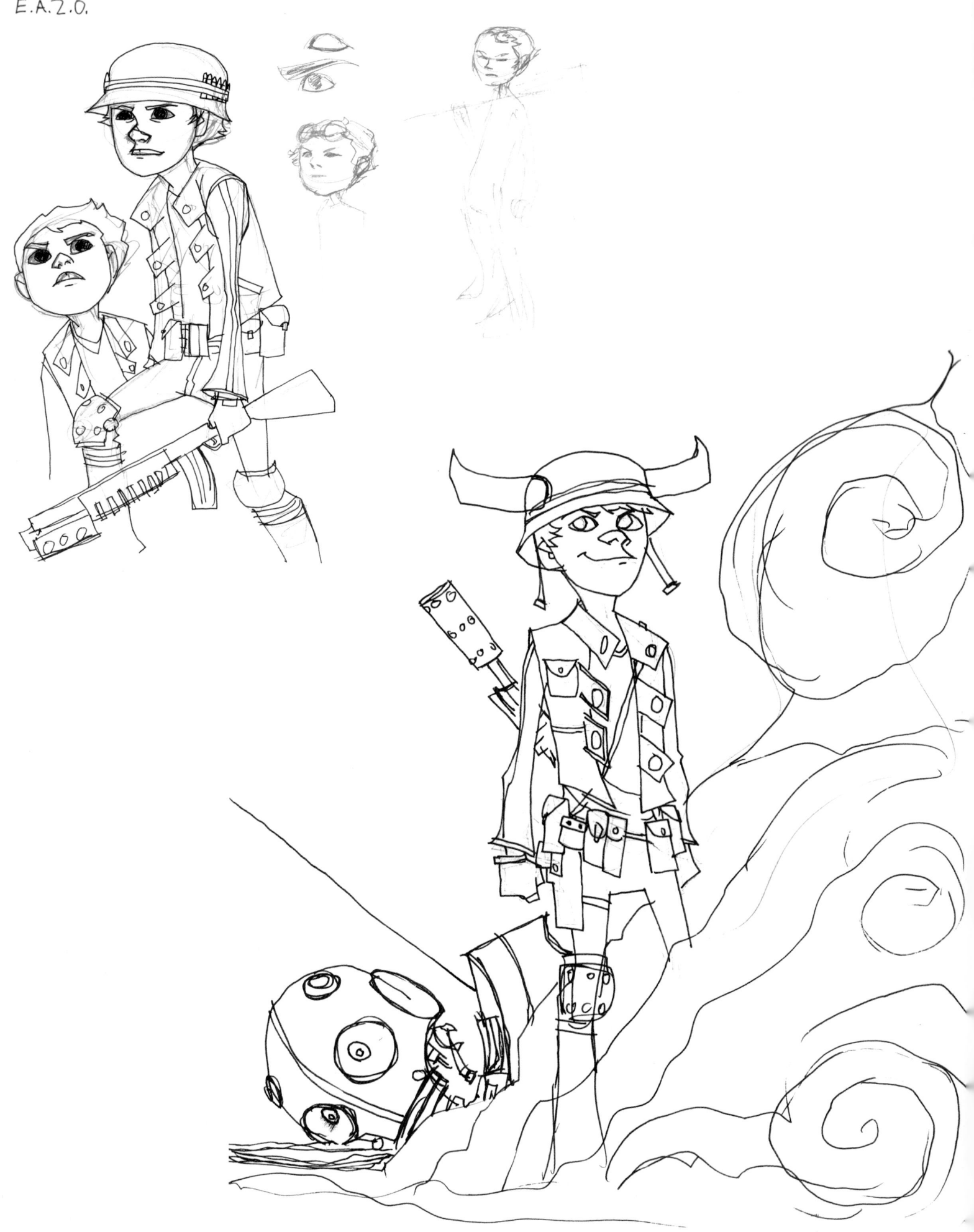

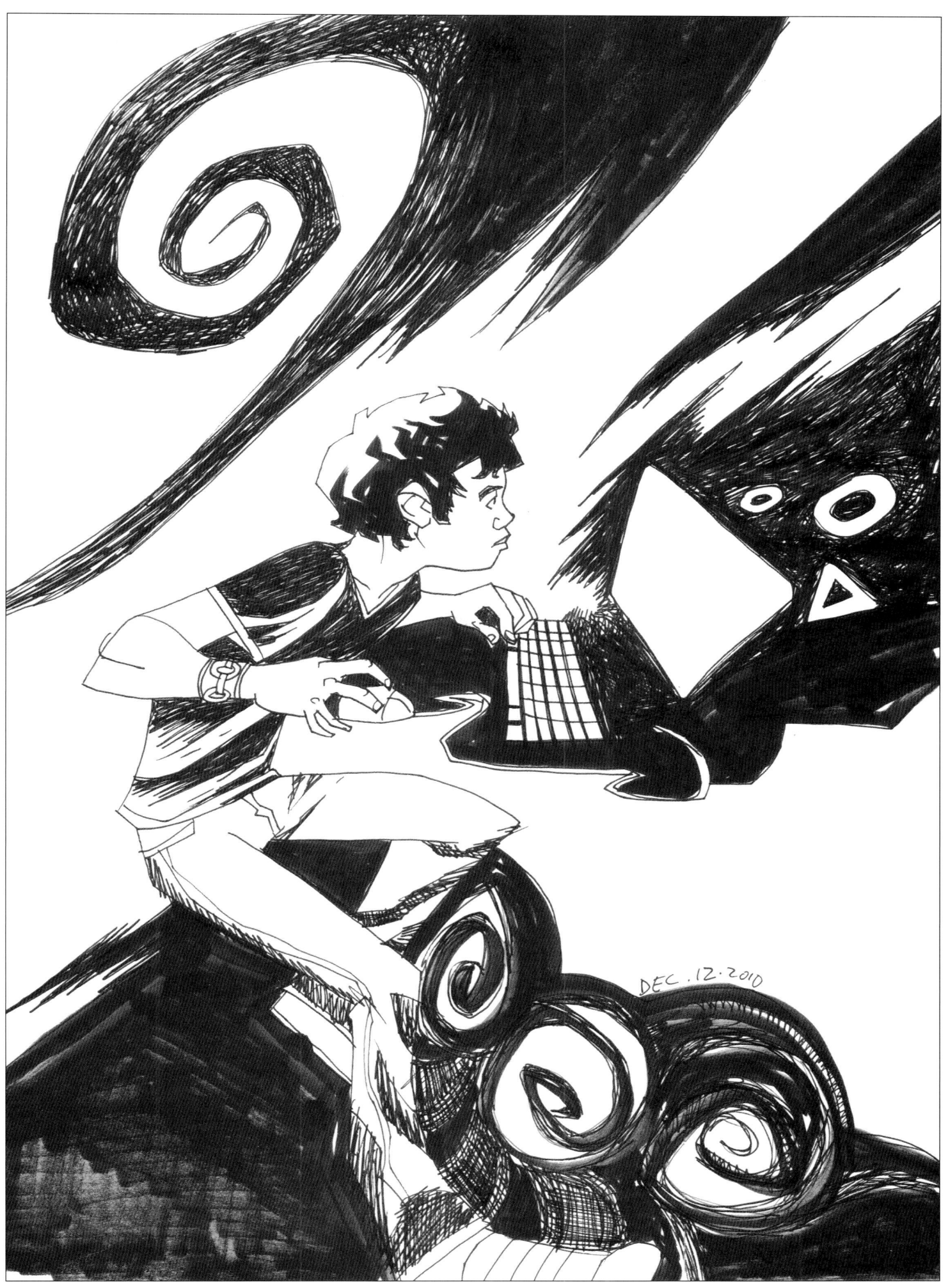

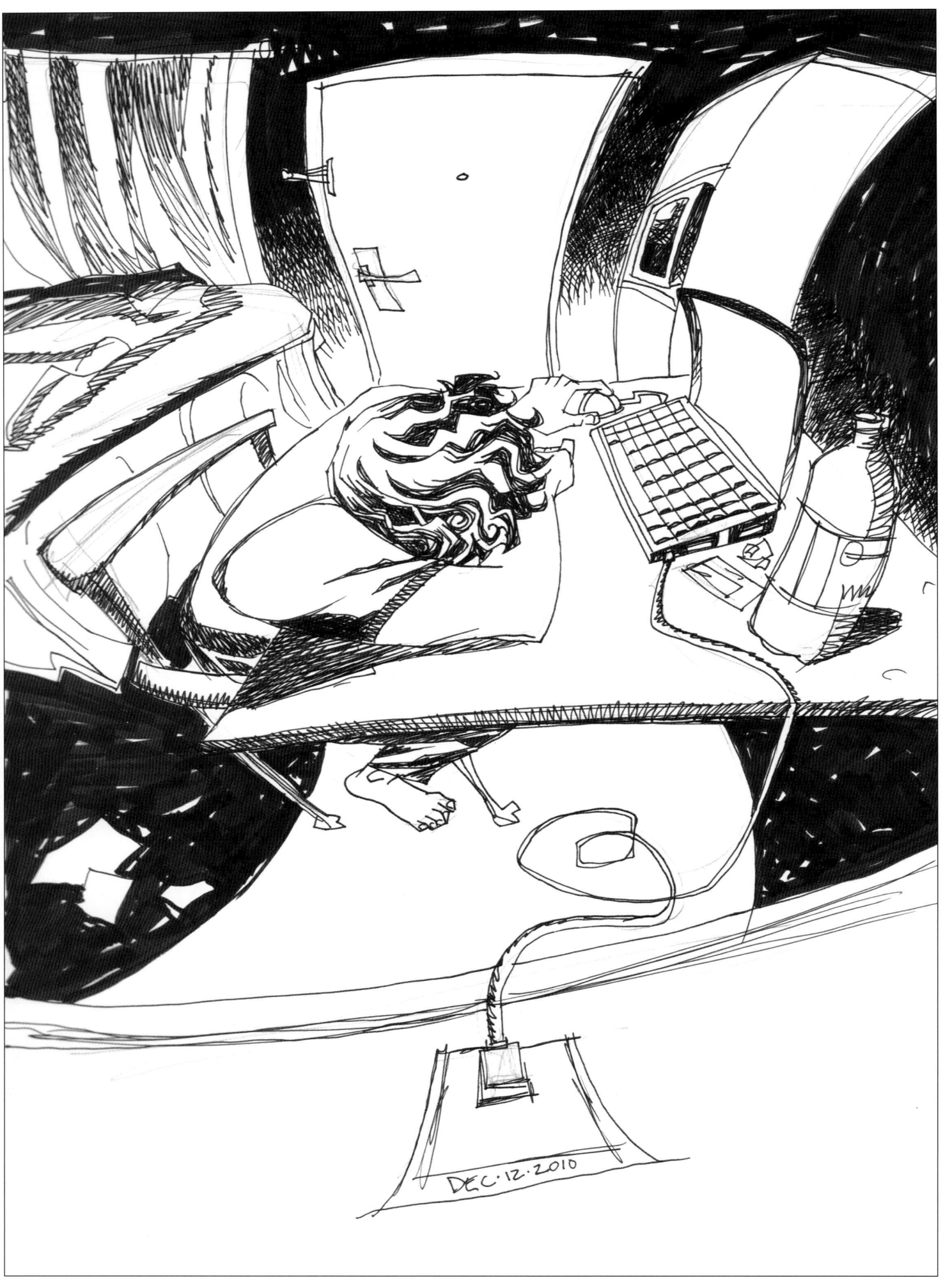

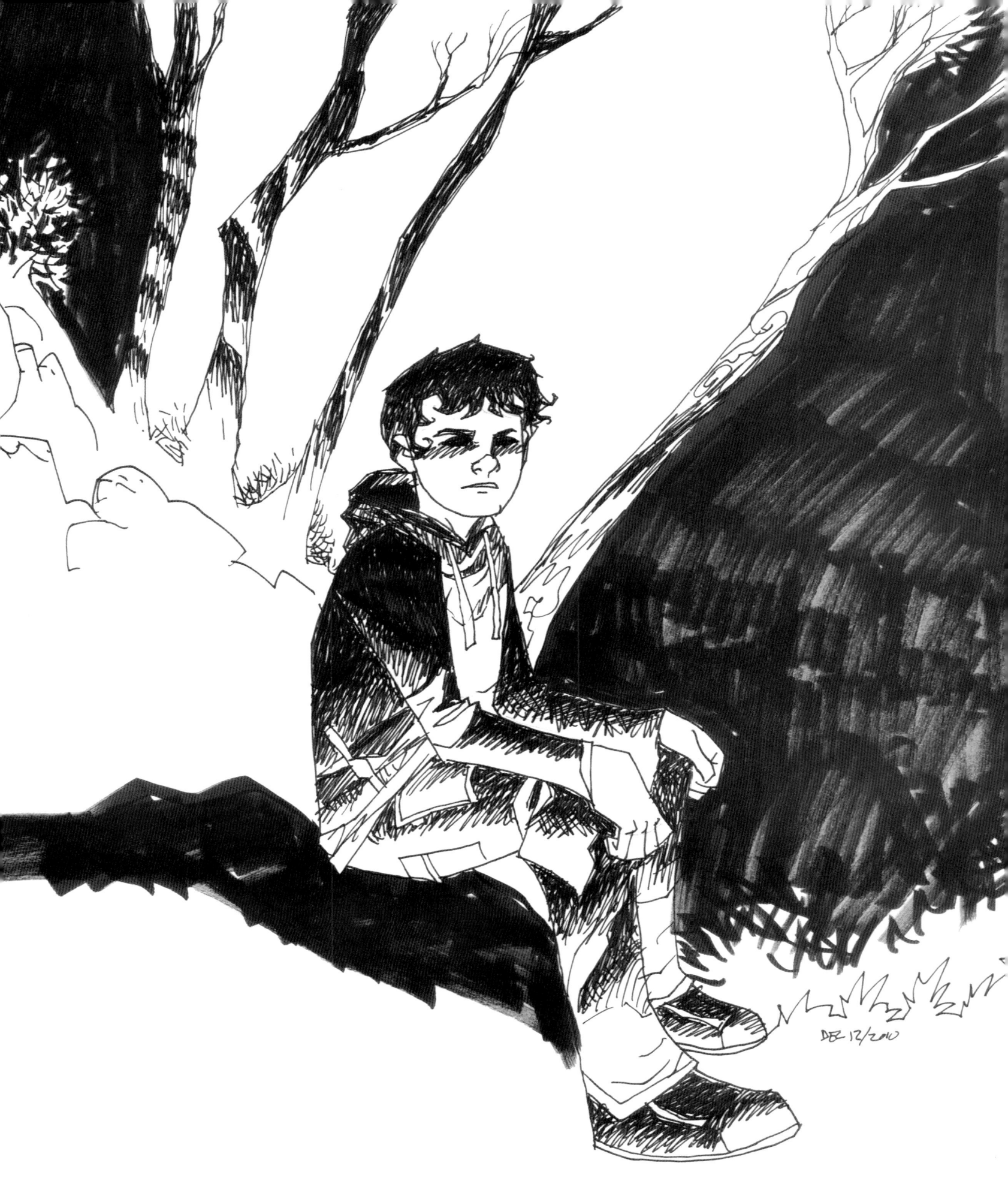

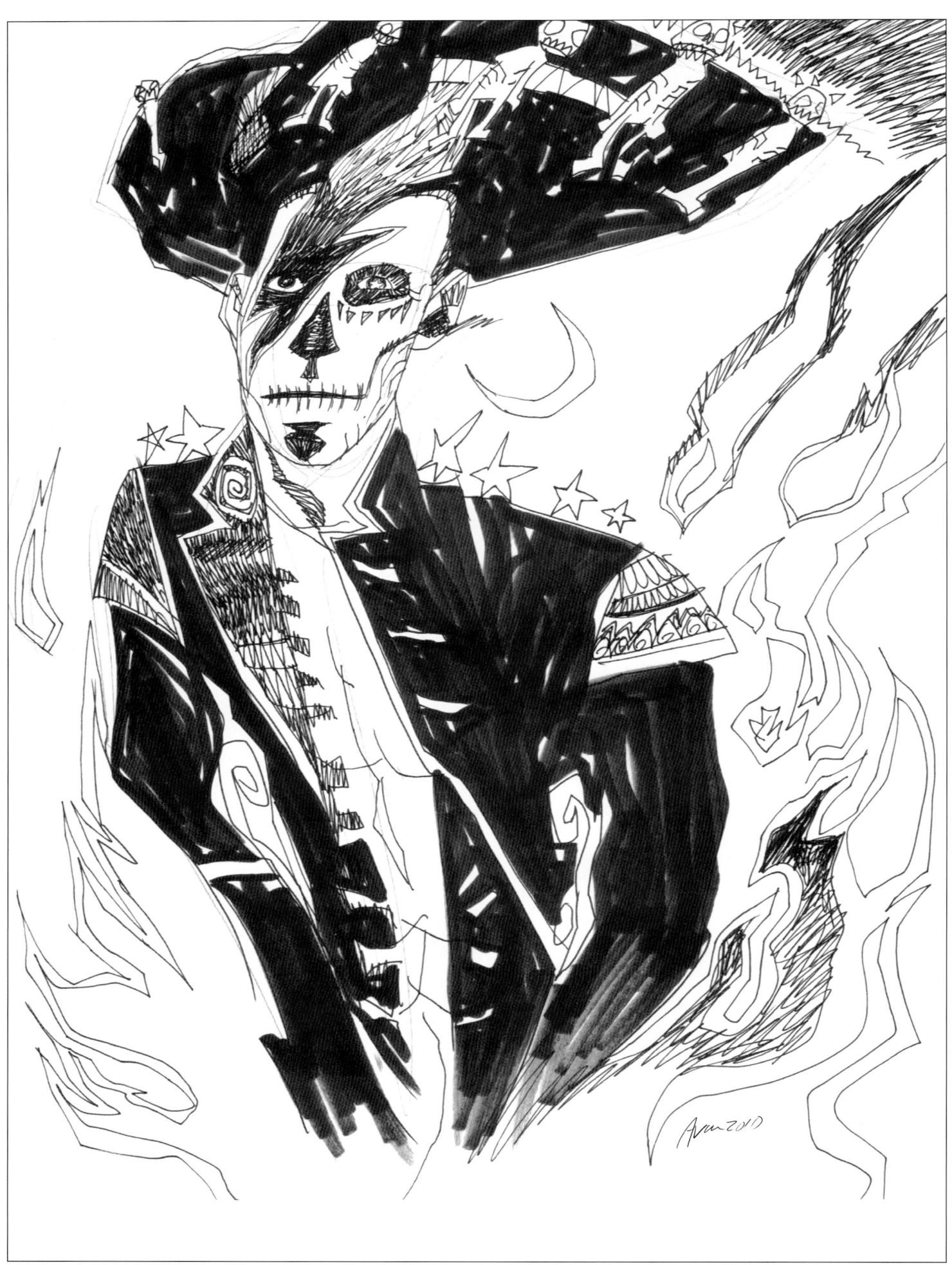

Portrait of Matt Fraction from a Halloween party, which led to Oeming and Bendis's *United States of Murder*

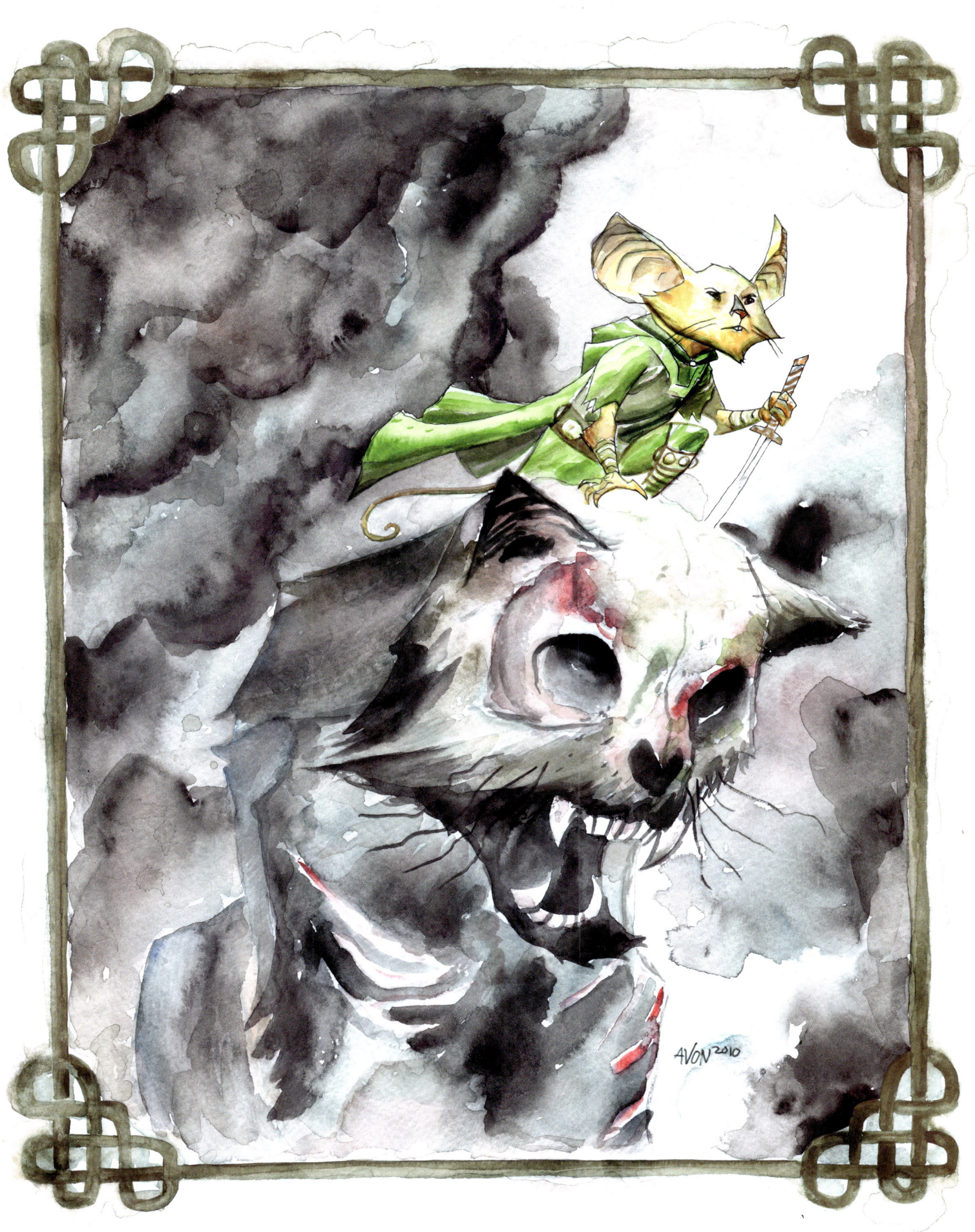
Mice Templar cover

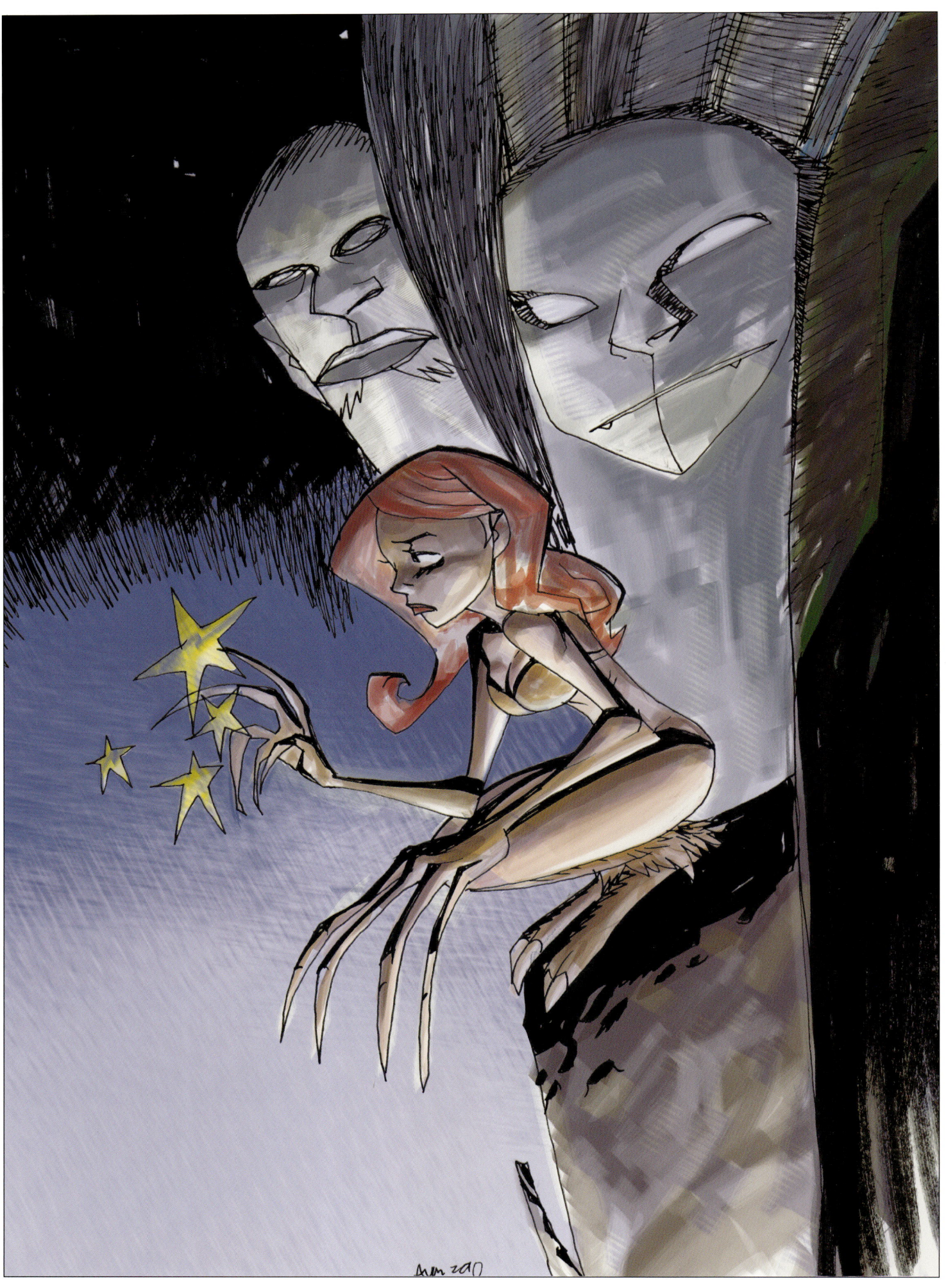

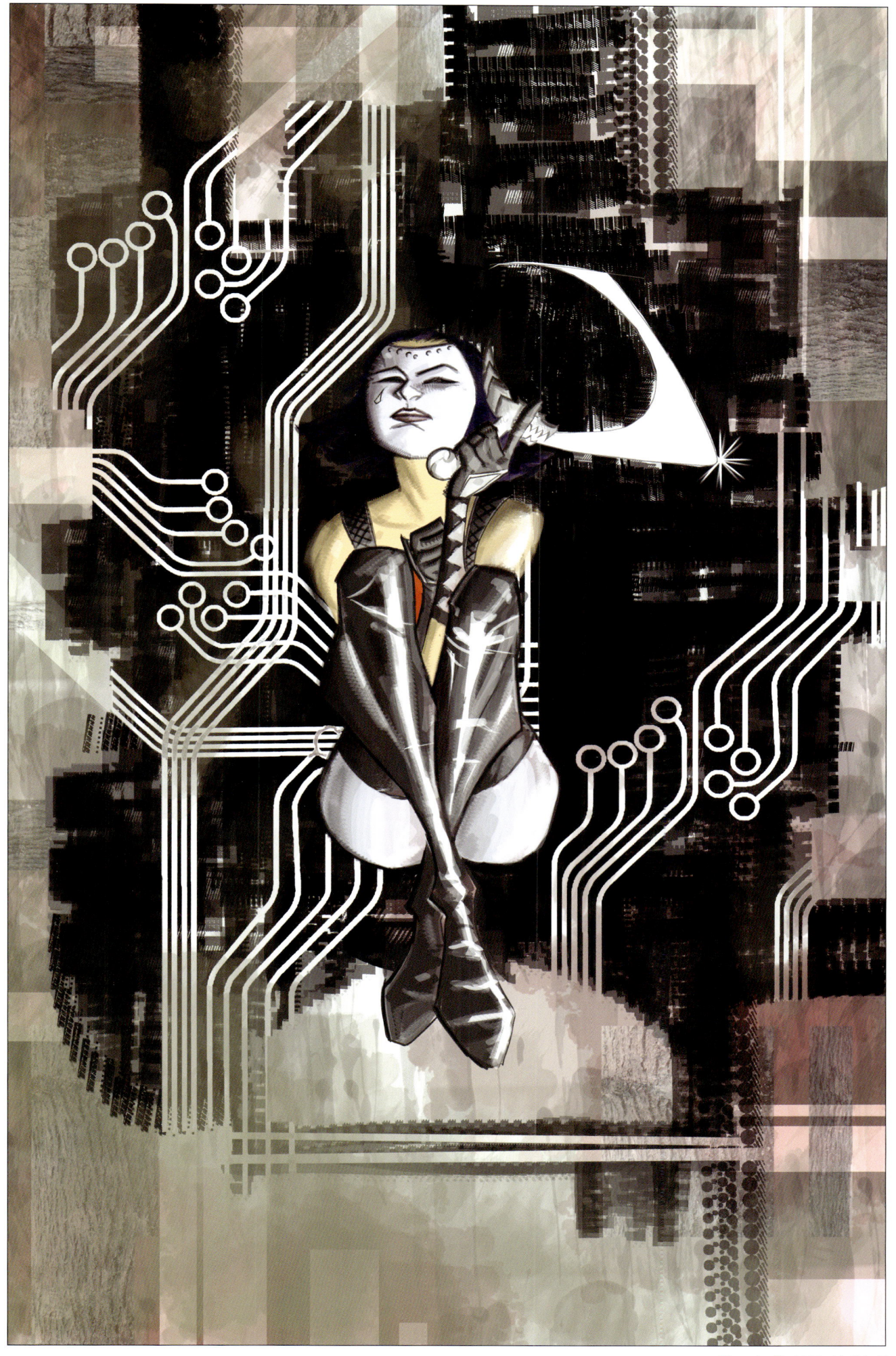

Pinup for David Mack's *Kabuki*

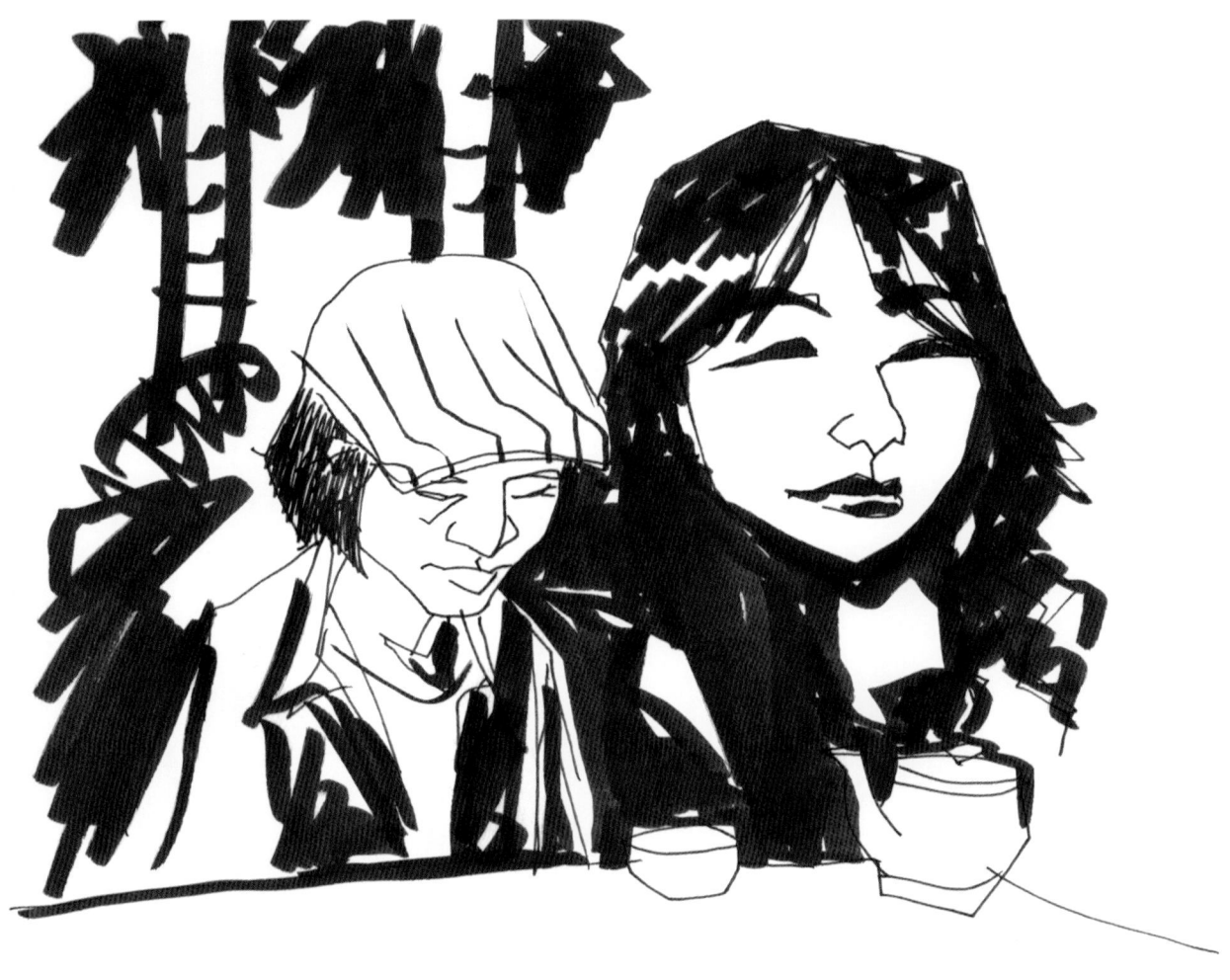

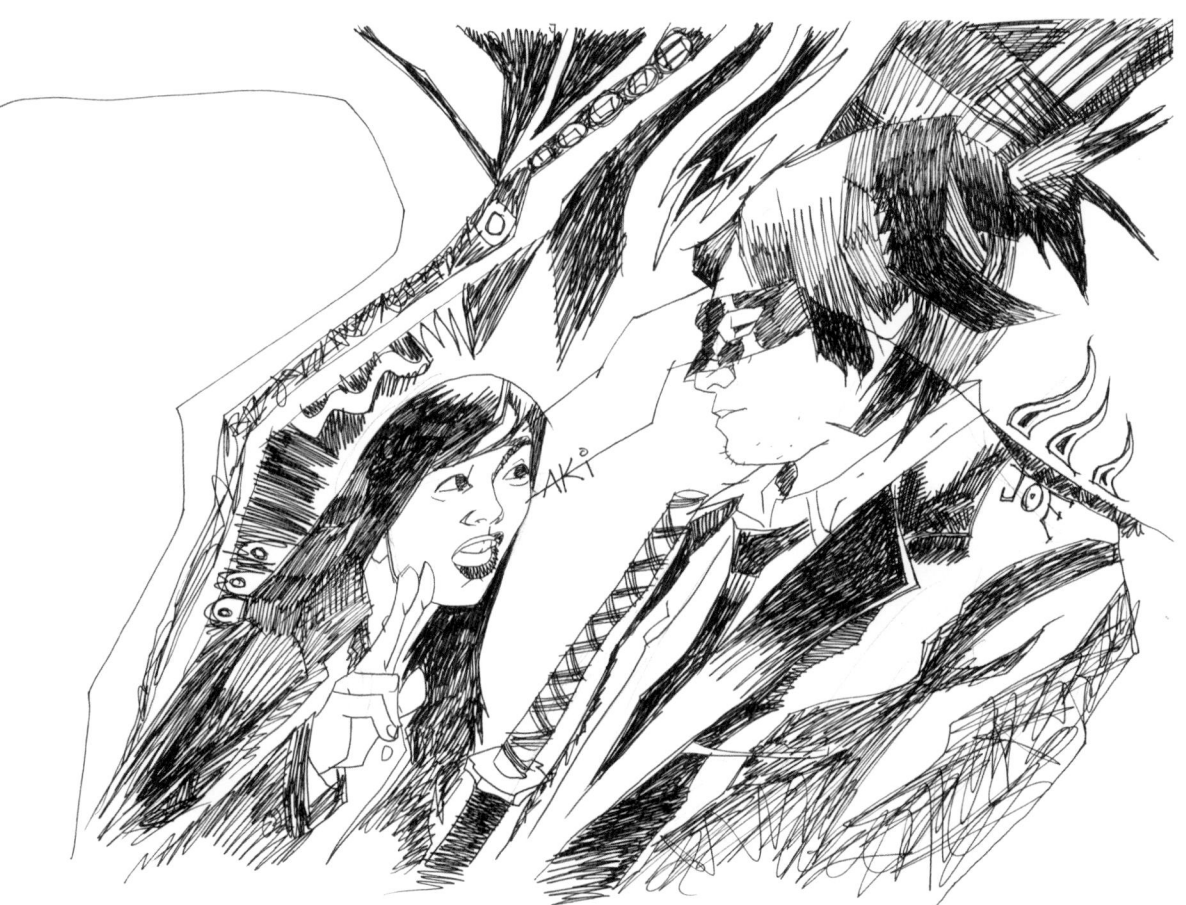

Friends Joe and Aki

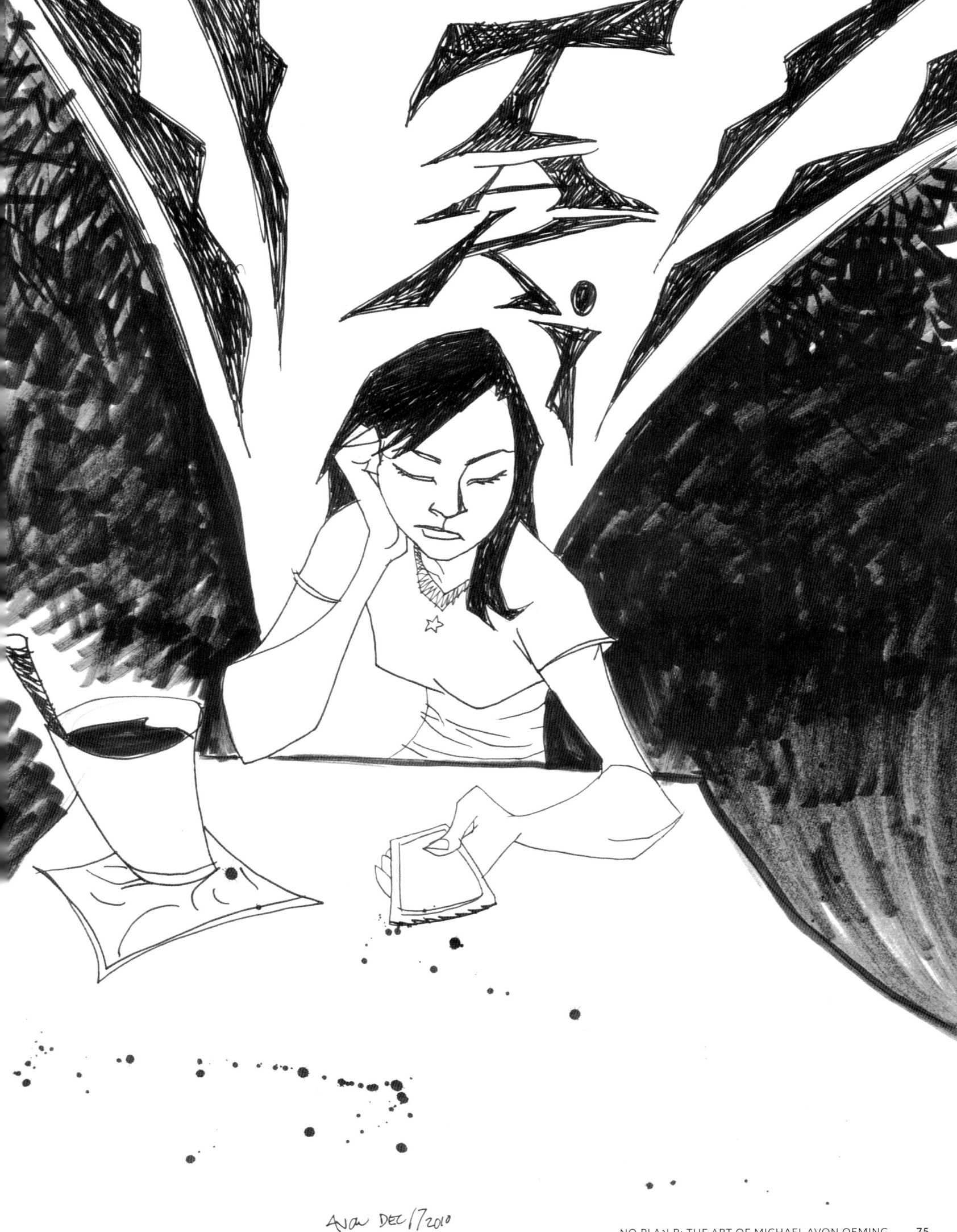

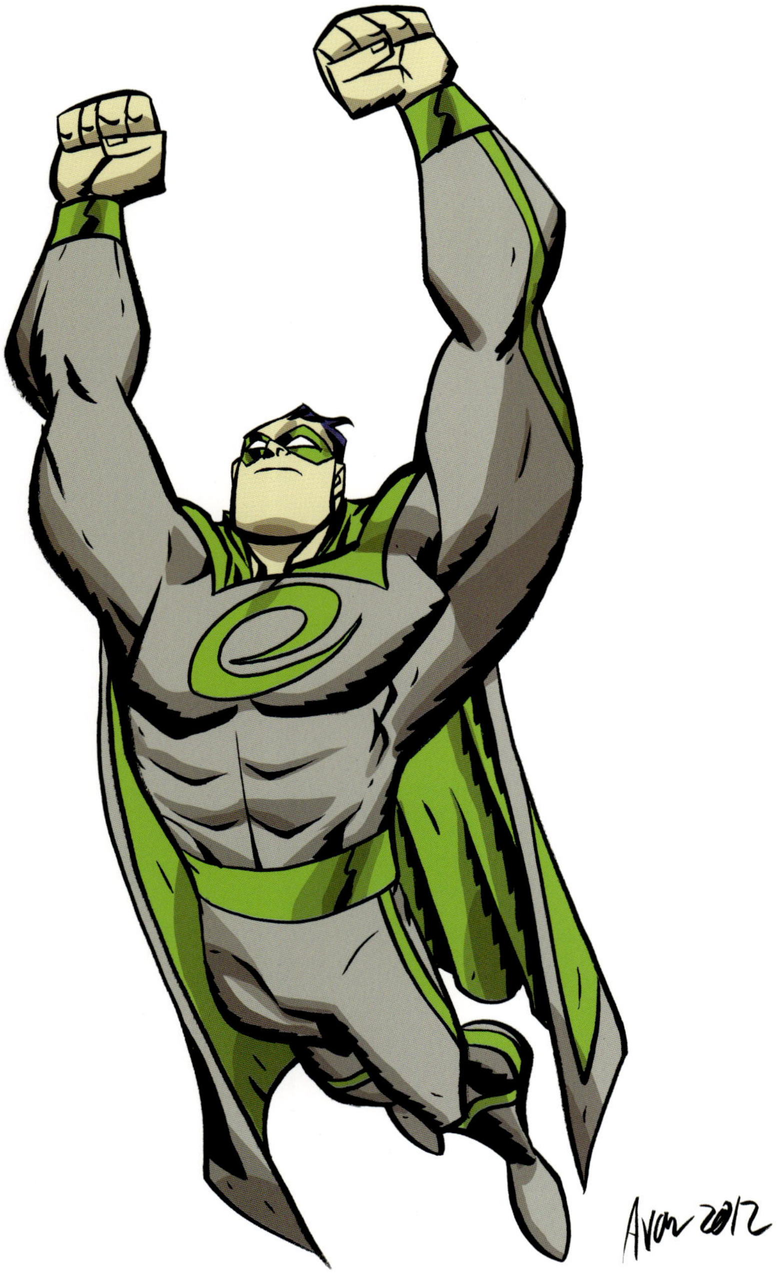

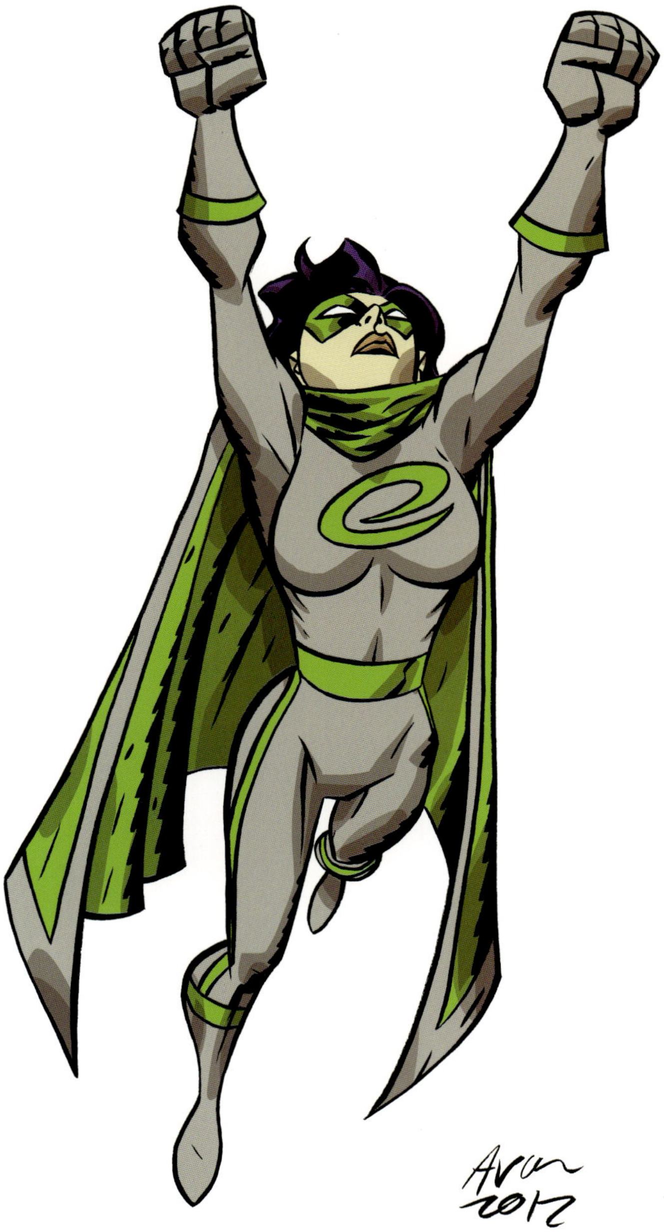

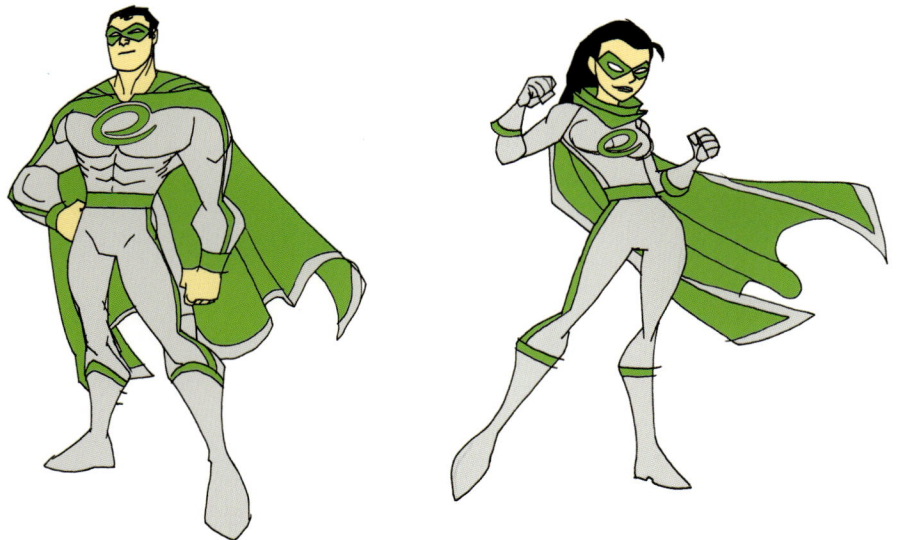

Wade Schwinn and Bay Raitt had worked at Valve for a long time, and had an interest in comics. When they first approached me to work at Valve, at San Diego Comic-Con in 2005, I turned them down. I was married with a kid in Jersey, and couldn't think about such a drastic move across country. But they approached me again at Emerald City Comicon in 2008, around the time Ethan's mom and I got divorced. I had to figure out a new way to support my family, and this was a creative job that offered things I wasn't used to, like health insurance.

One of the best things about working at Valve was being surrounded by amazing artists, many of whom were ex-Pixar and Disney animators, as well as traditional painters and programmers. As a freelancer, I'd never been exposed to working with creative people in this way. They introduced me to the Cintiq tablet, and I learned a little about animation. I never would have learned about digital coloring if not for them.

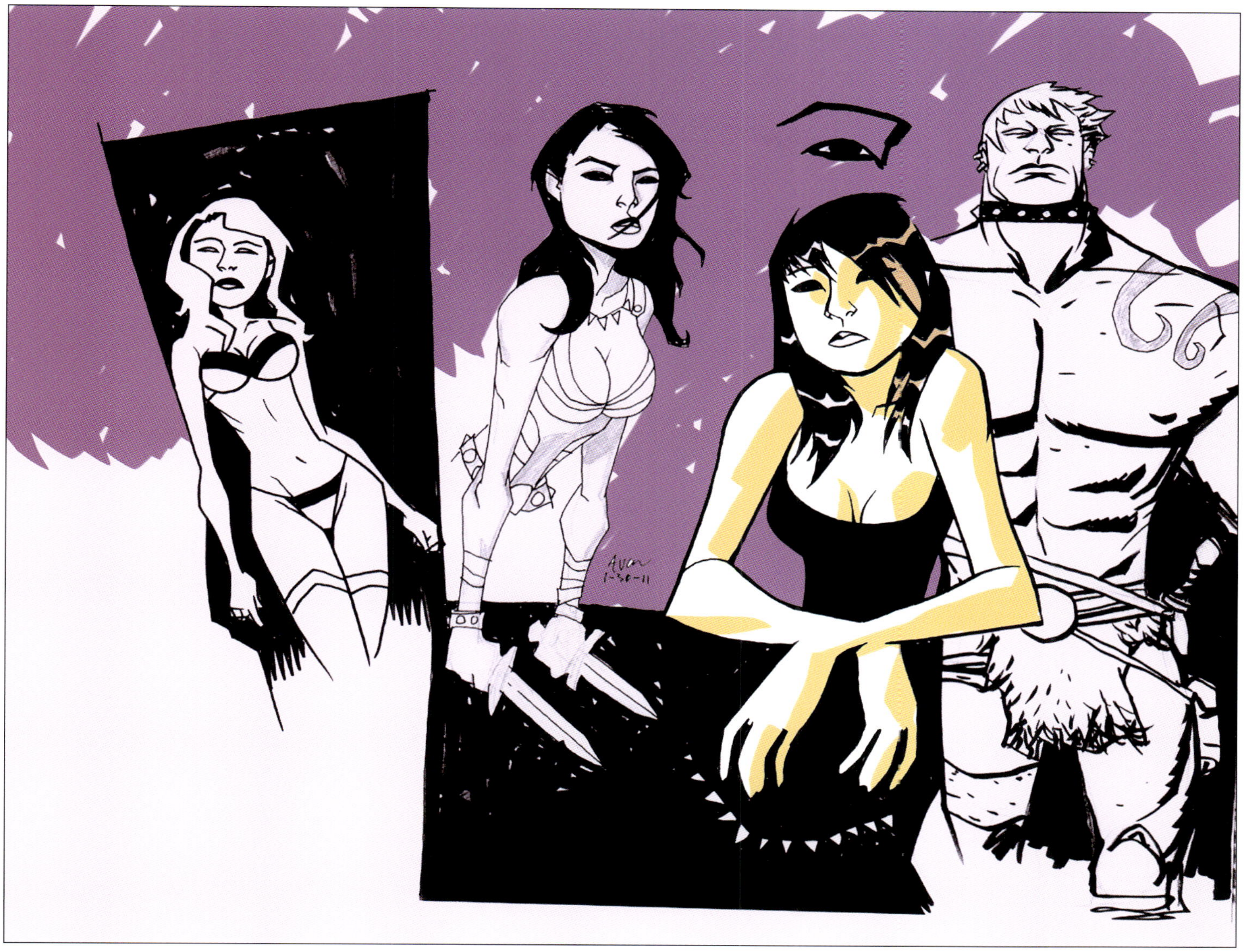

Gamers went to the Valve website to get news and updates on the games. They'd spend time on the computer playing the games, but Valve wanted another reason for fans to stay on the site. They decided to create web comics expanding on the stories of some of their biggest games, like *Left 4 Dead* and *Team Fortress*, comics that millions of people read online.

I helped design the cover for the *Portal 2* game. I did about a hundred different drawings, along with other employees, but the art director saw something I did and springboarded off that for the final cover design. I'm very proud of my contribution to *Portal 2*.

I left after three years because, as much as I learned and appreciated the security and the benefits, my heart wasn't in it, and I couldn't get used to the constraints of a regular job. It was an amazing experience, working with people who became good friends and taught me a lot. I can't put a price on what I learned at Valve.

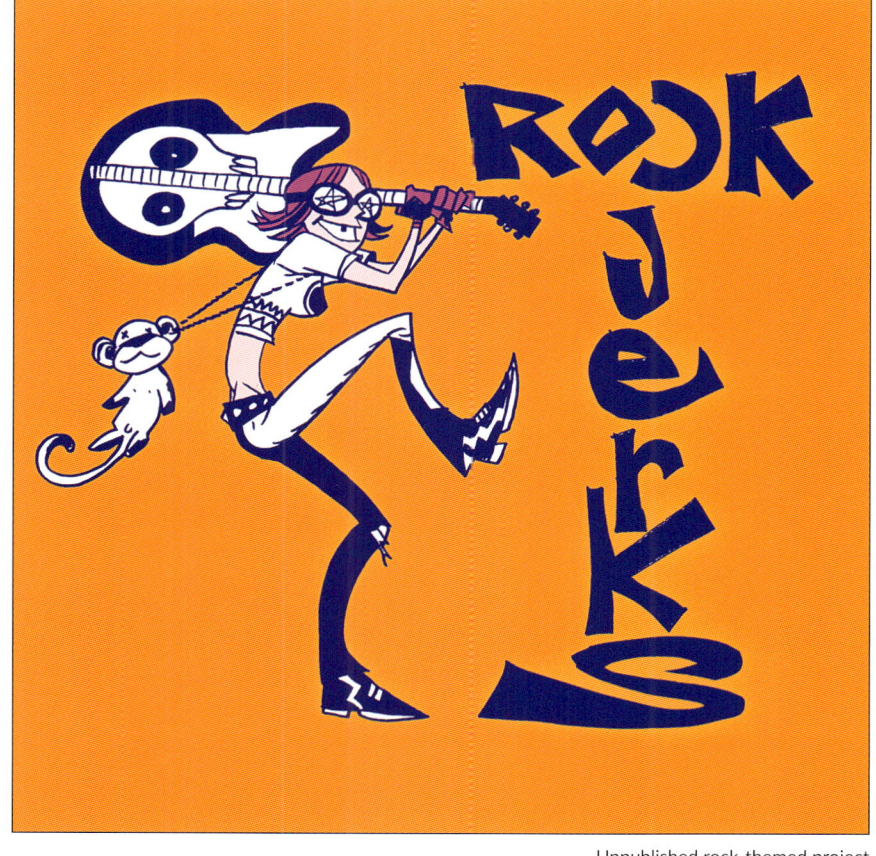

Unpublished rock-themed project

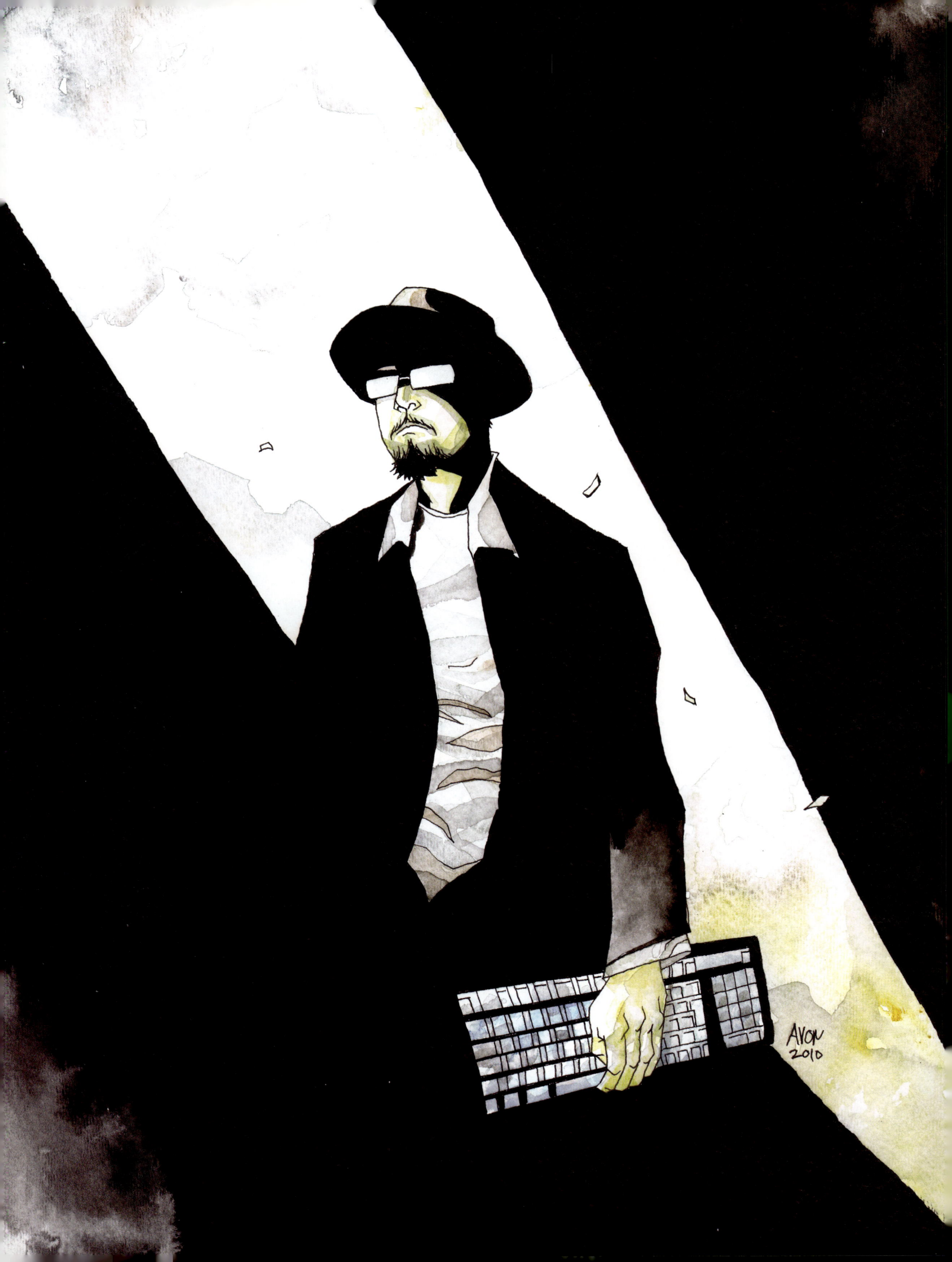

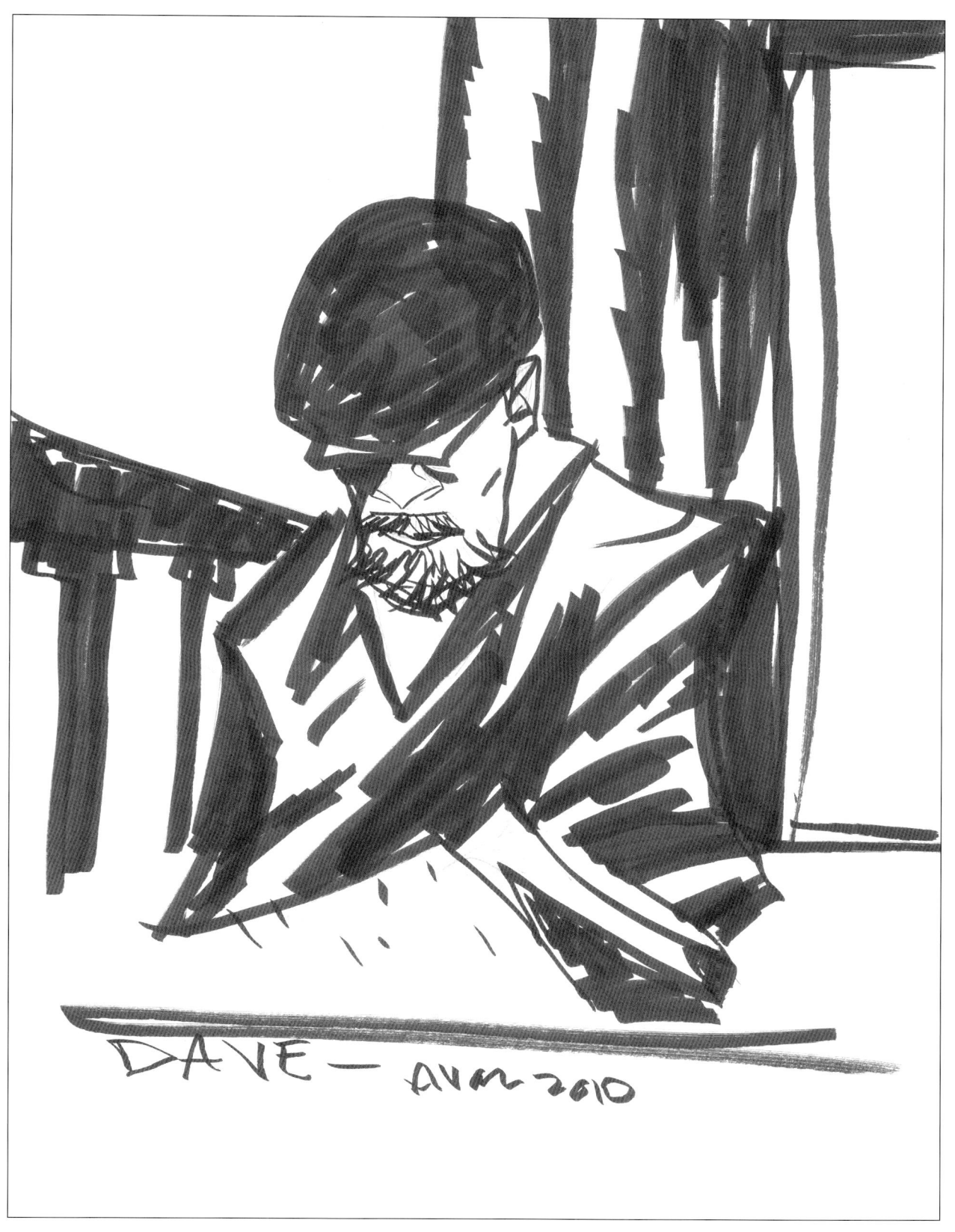

Facing, portrait of Ed Brubaker; above, bar sketch of Dave Johnson

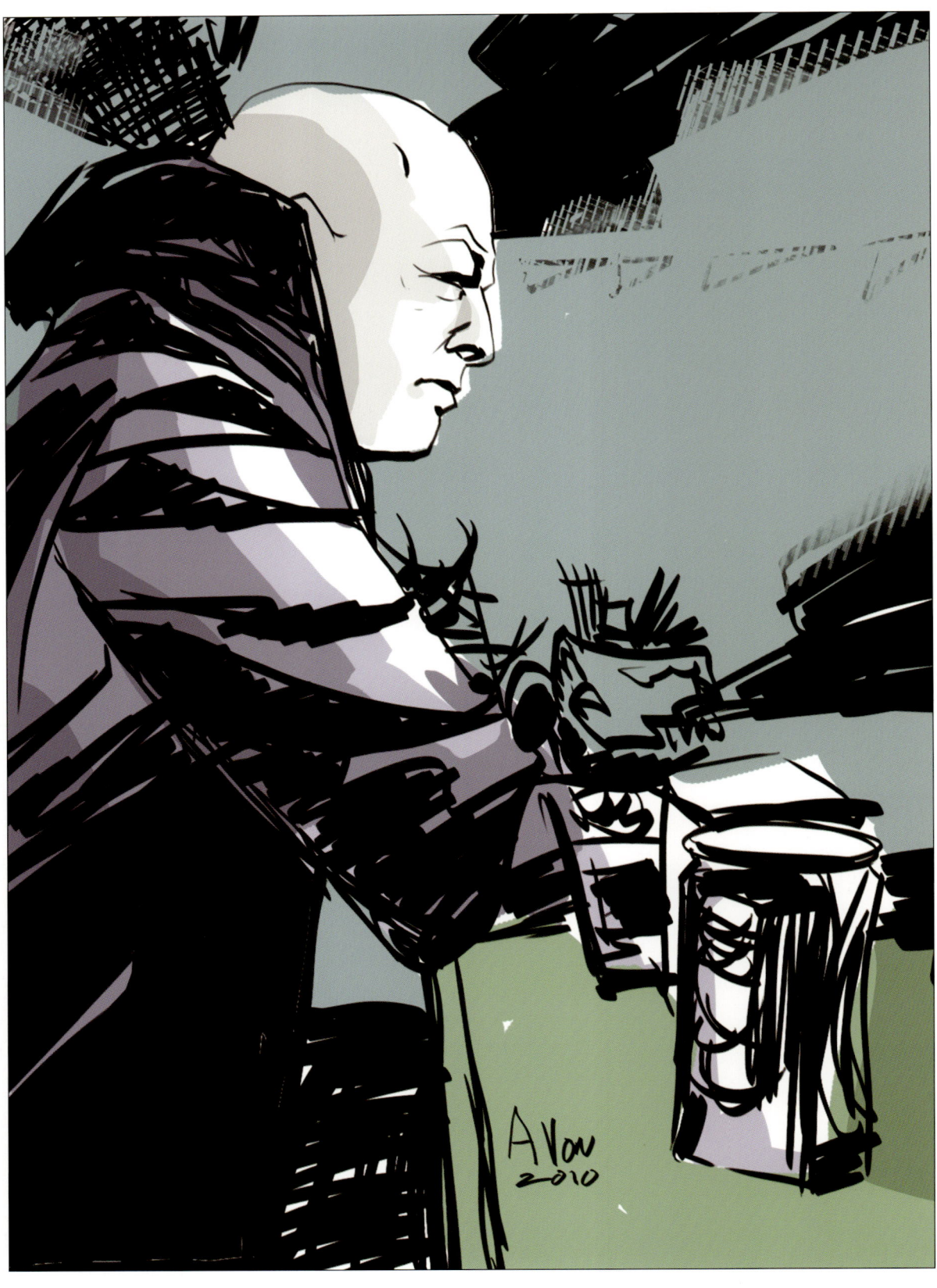

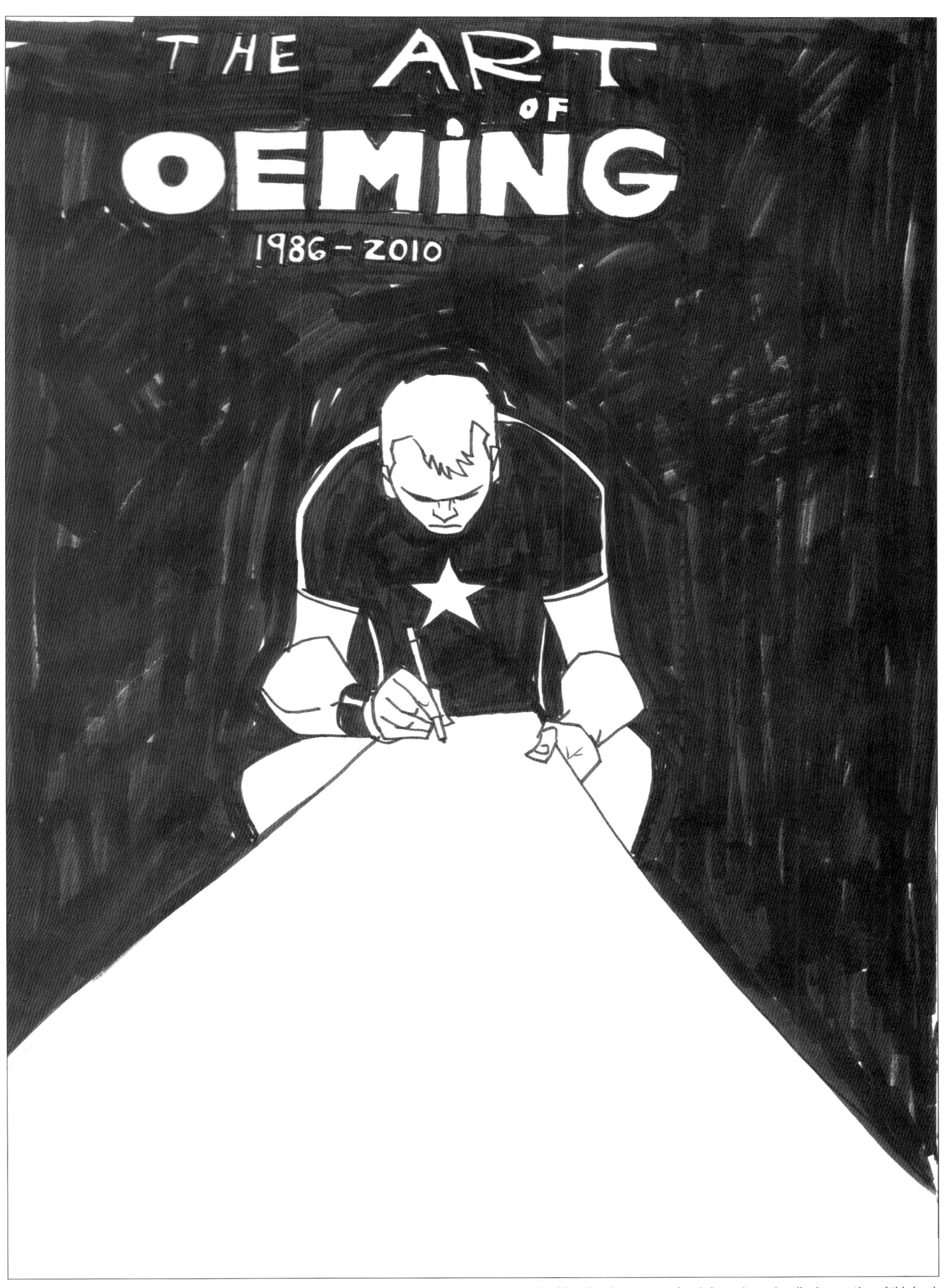

Facing, bar sketch of Bendis; above, cover sketch for a planned earlier incarnation of this book

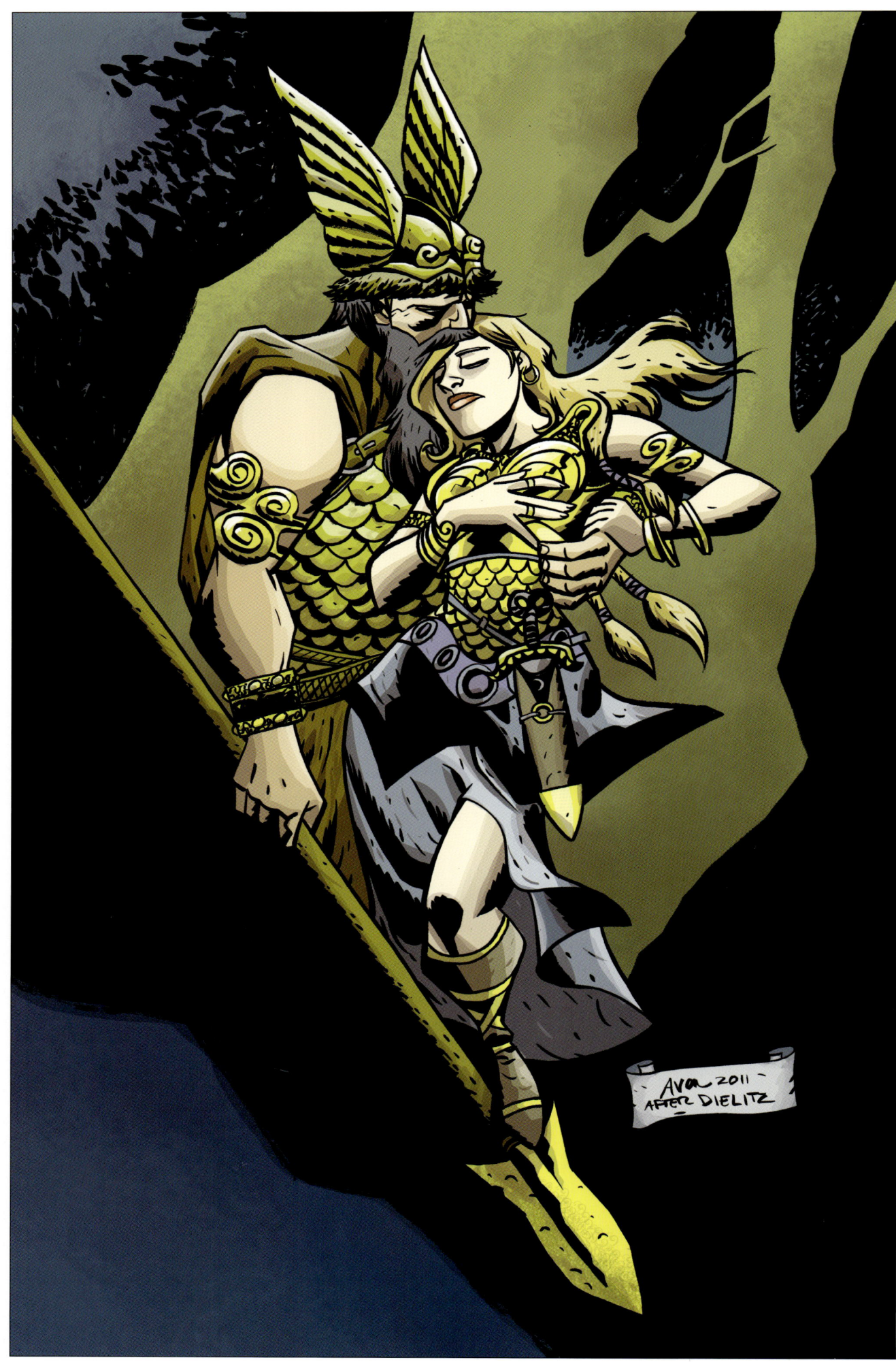

Mice Templar pinup

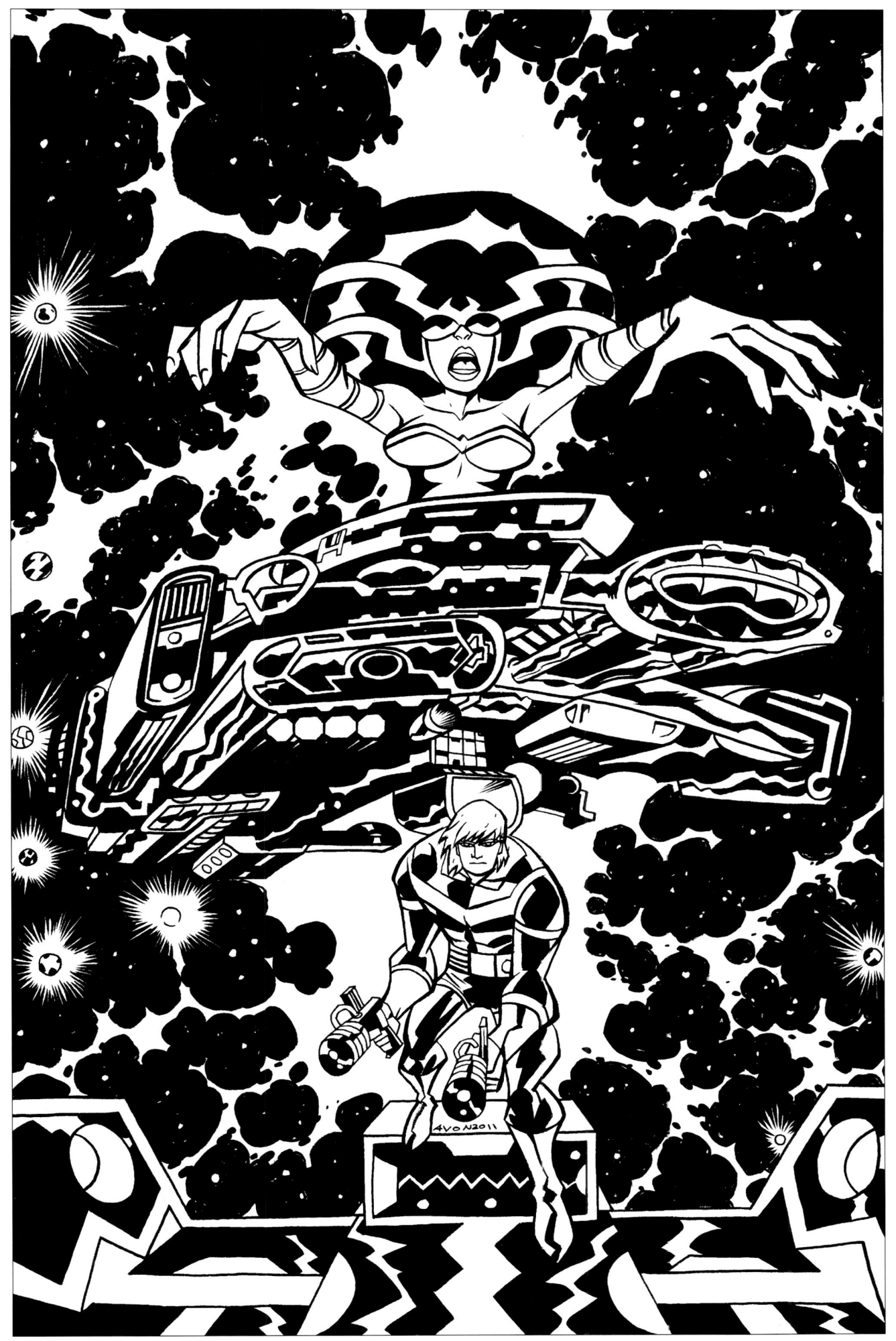
Cover for Jack Kirby's *Captain Victory*

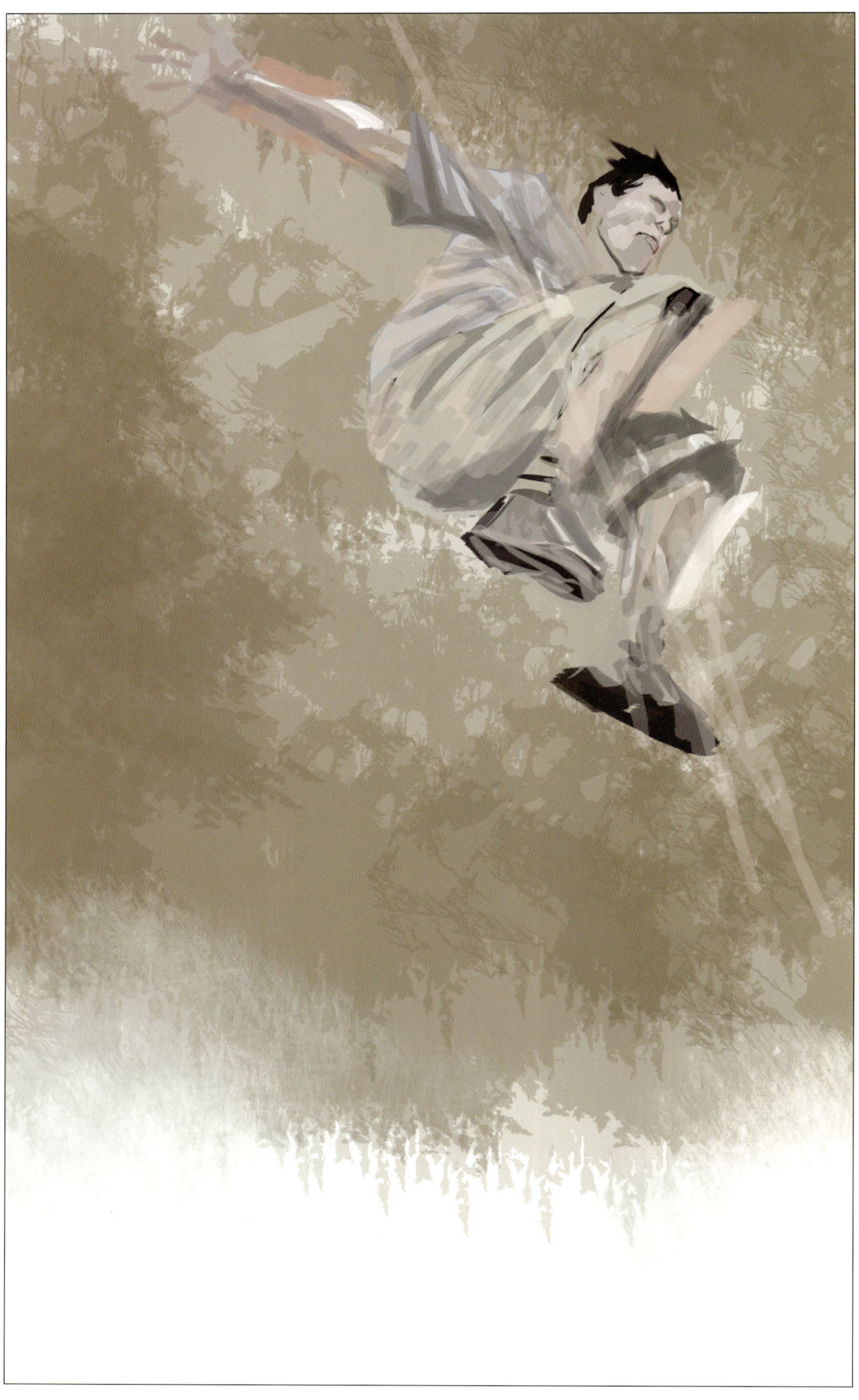

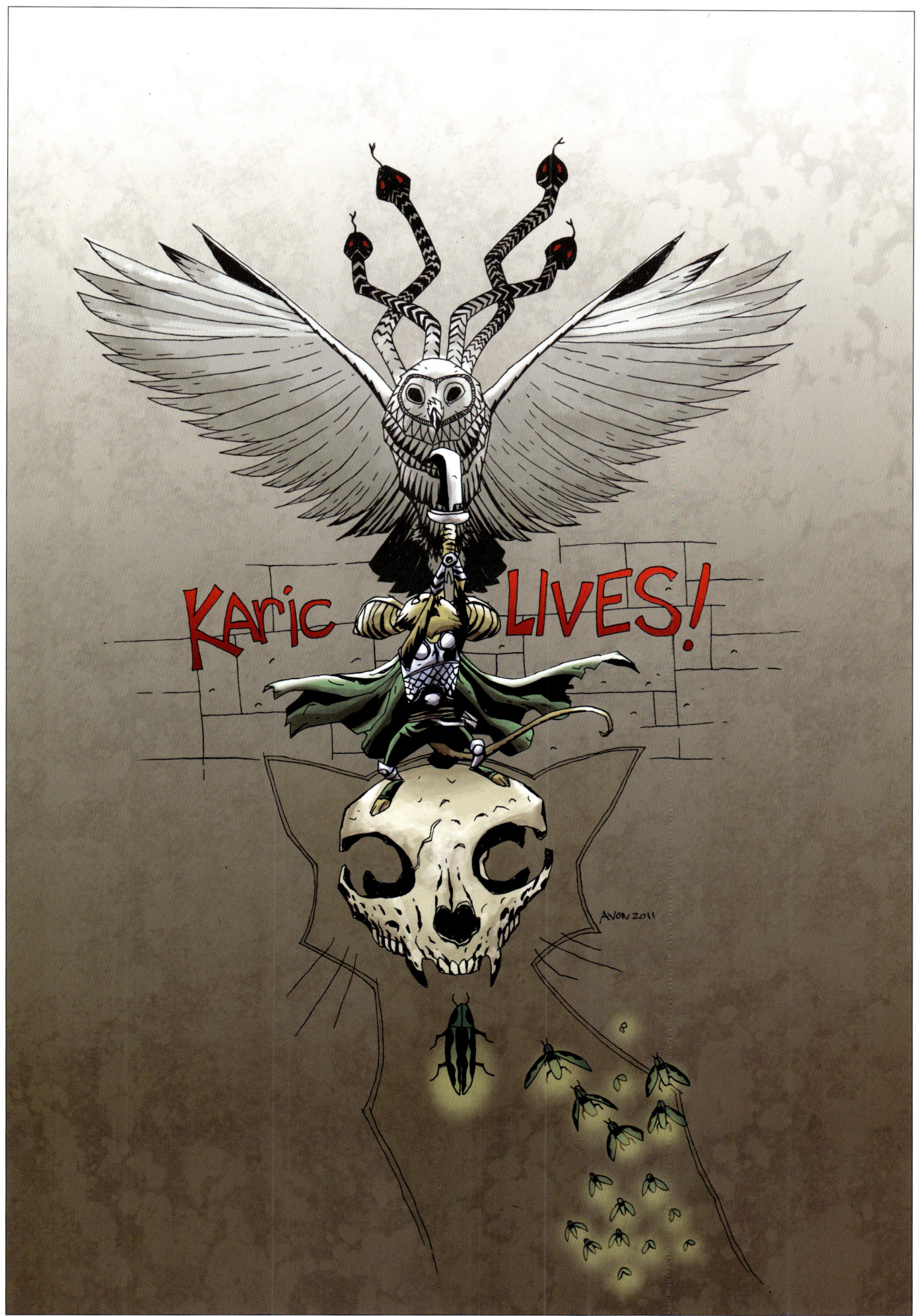

Mice Templar cover

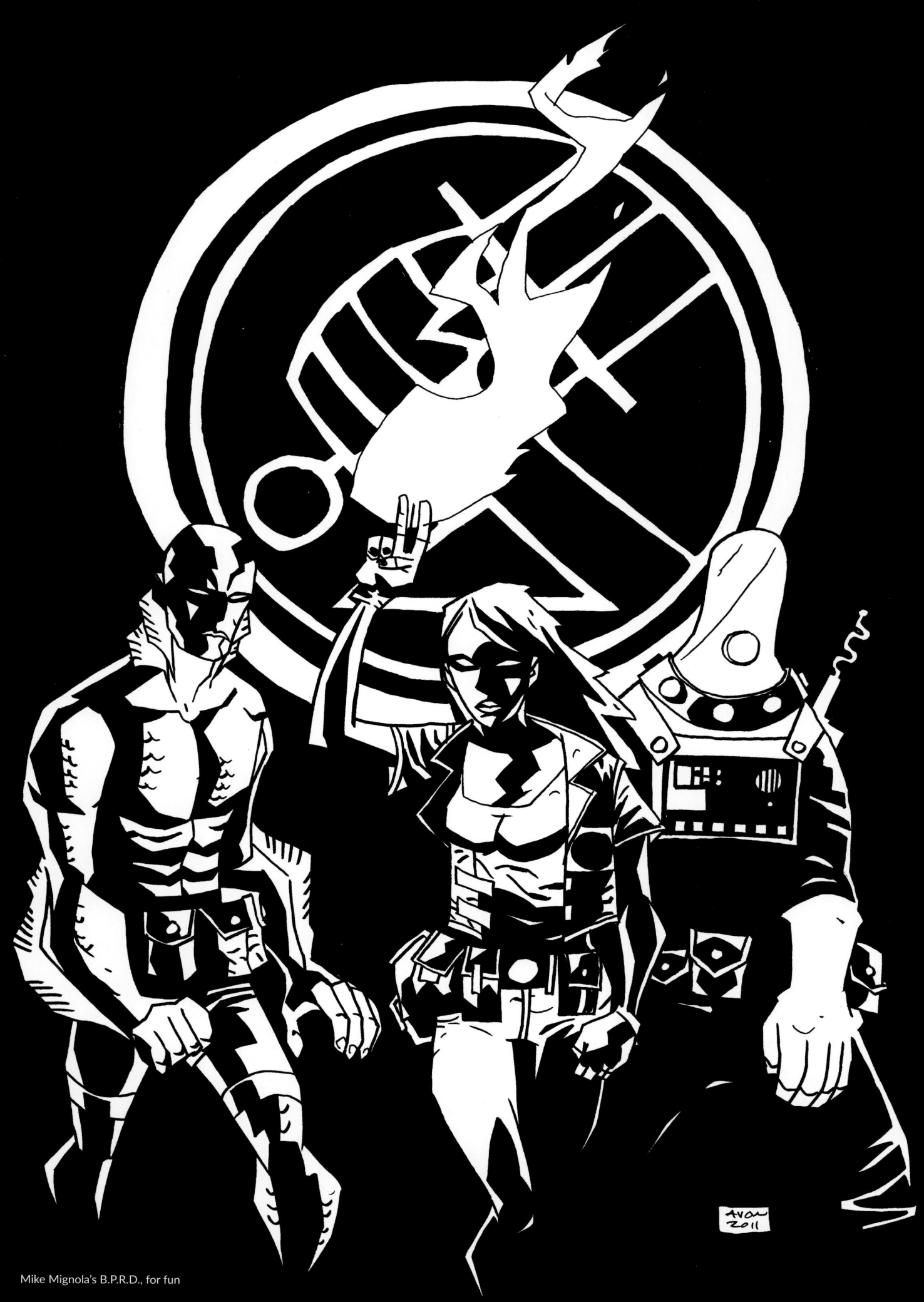

Mike Mignola's B.P.R.D., for fun

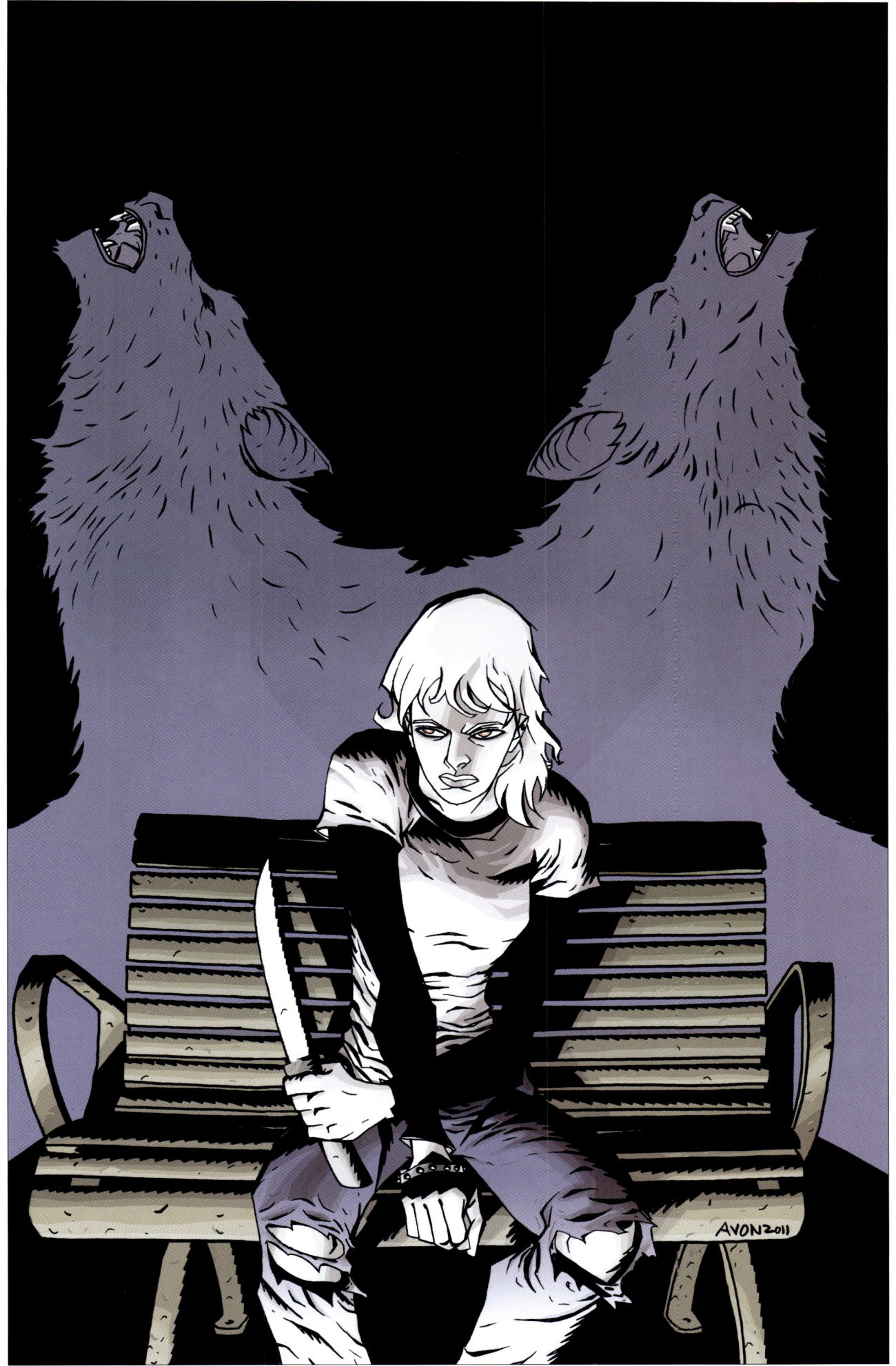

Cover for Caitlín Kiernan's *Alabaster*

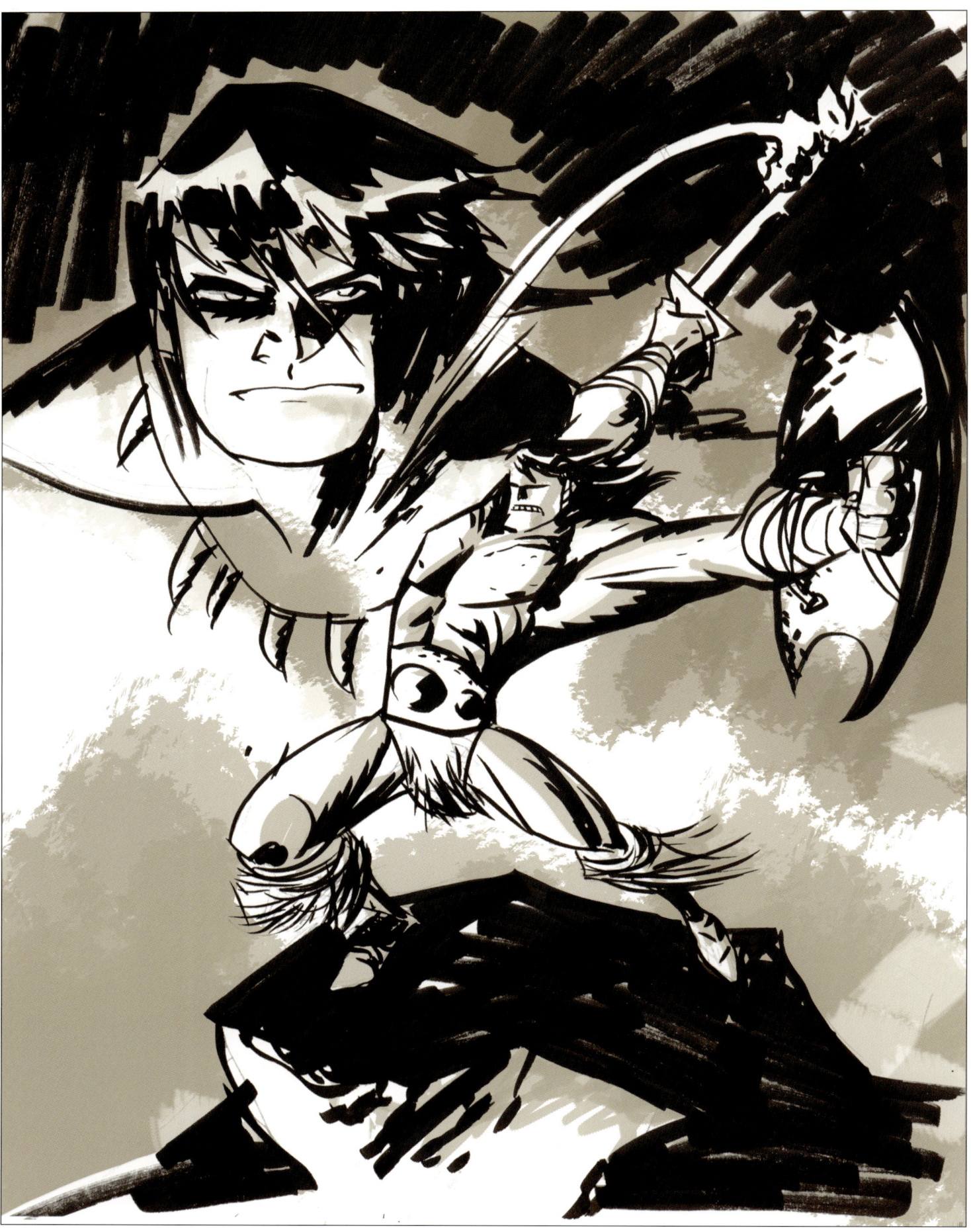
Conan, for fun

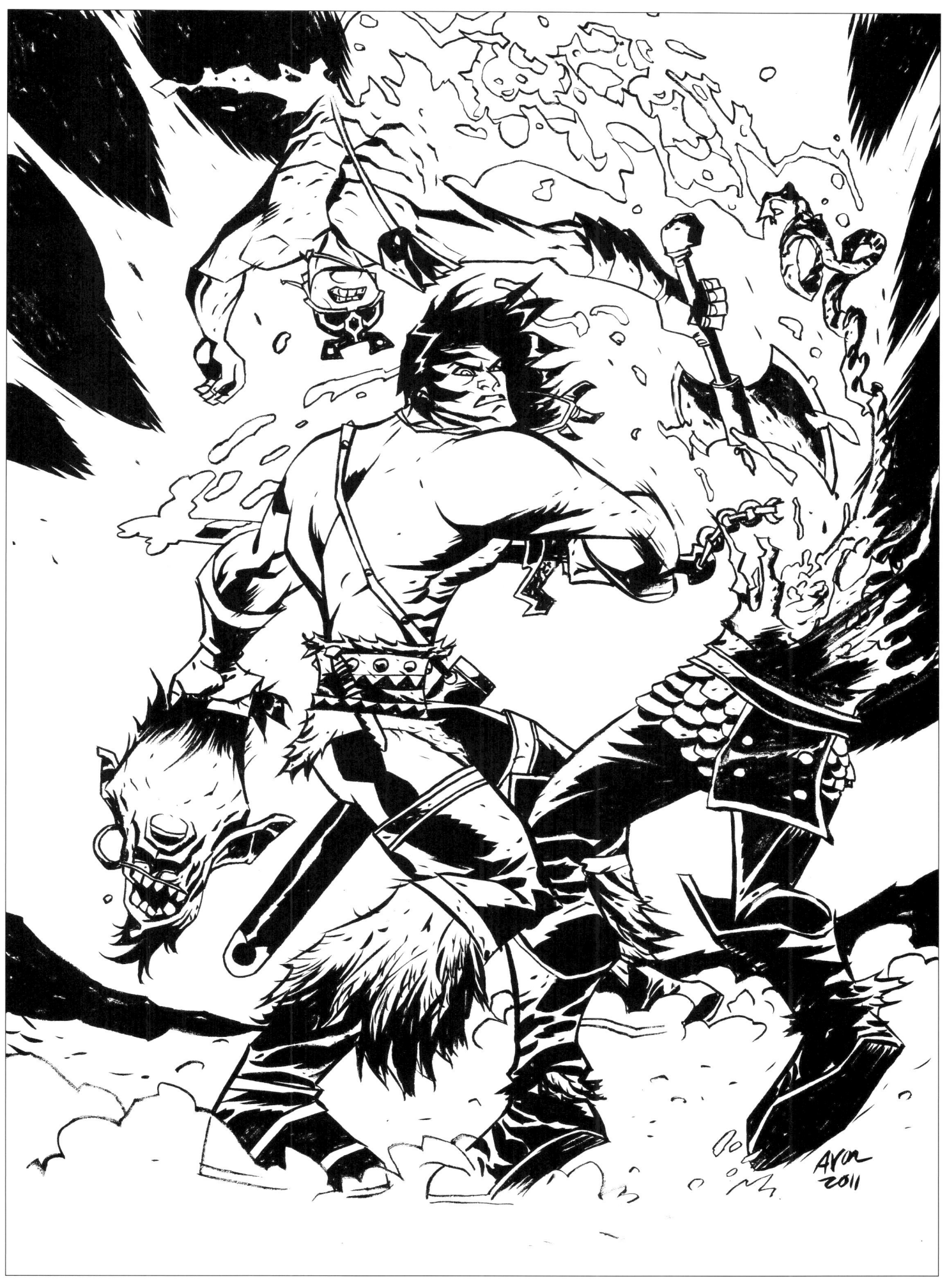

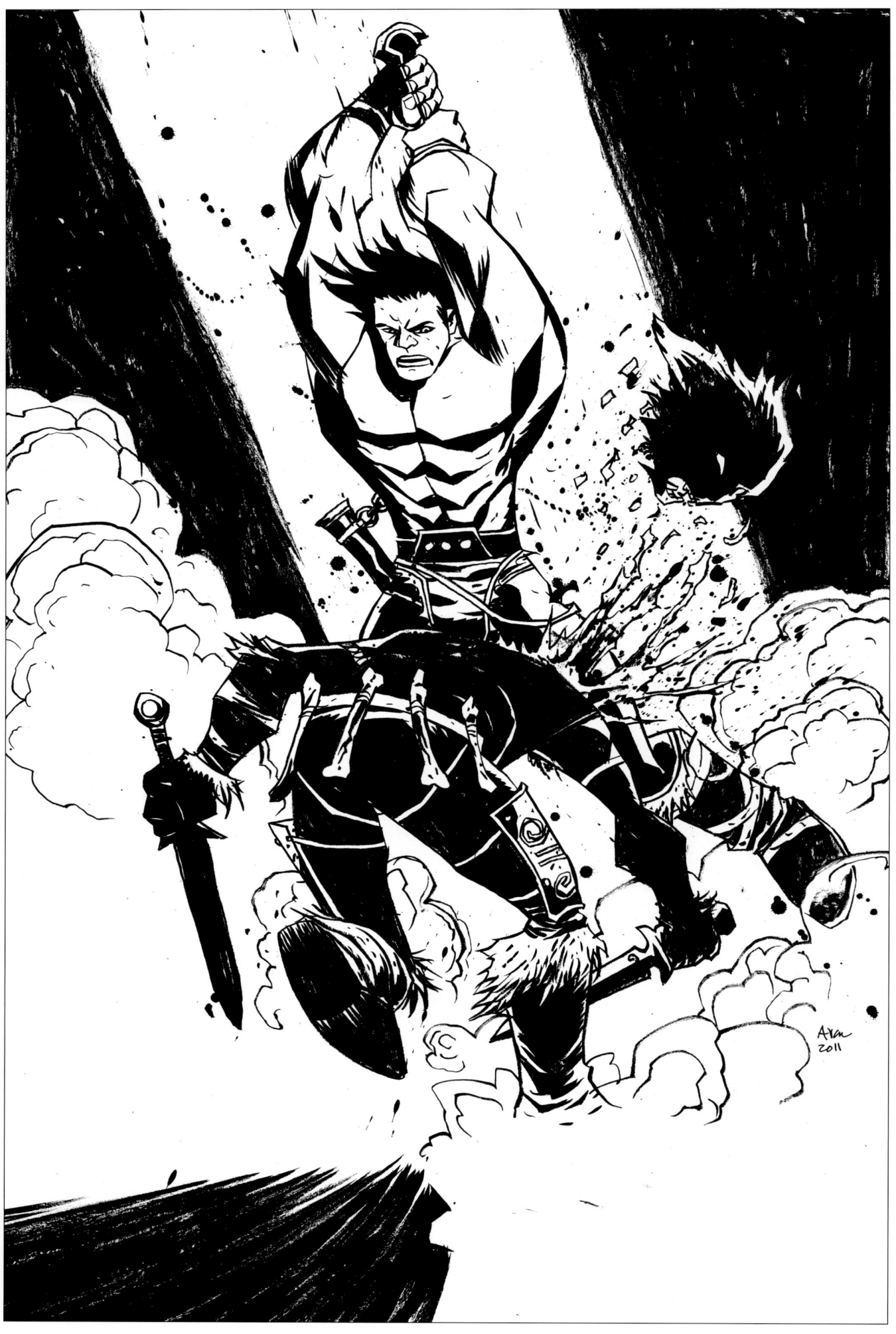

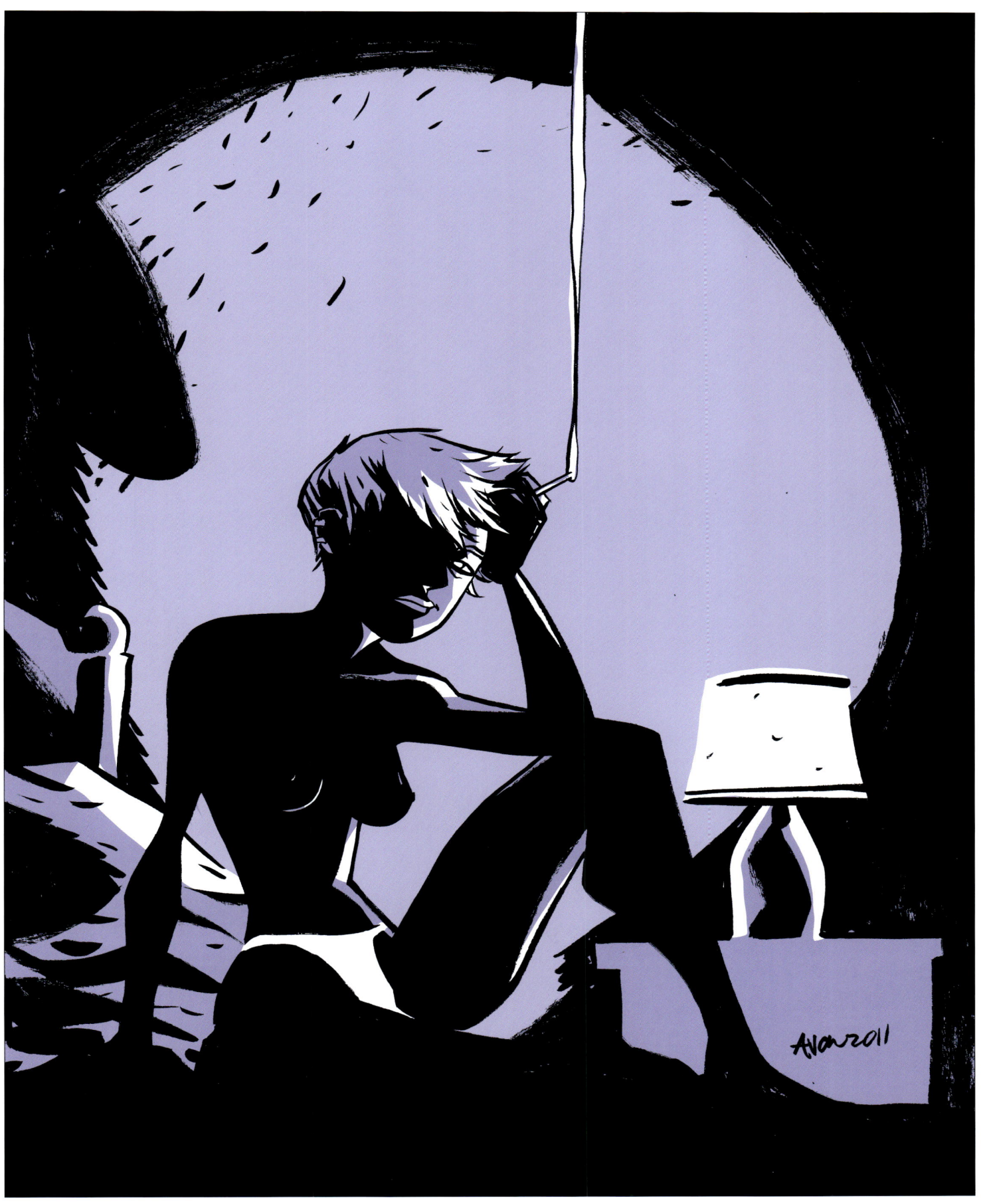

Deena from *Powers*

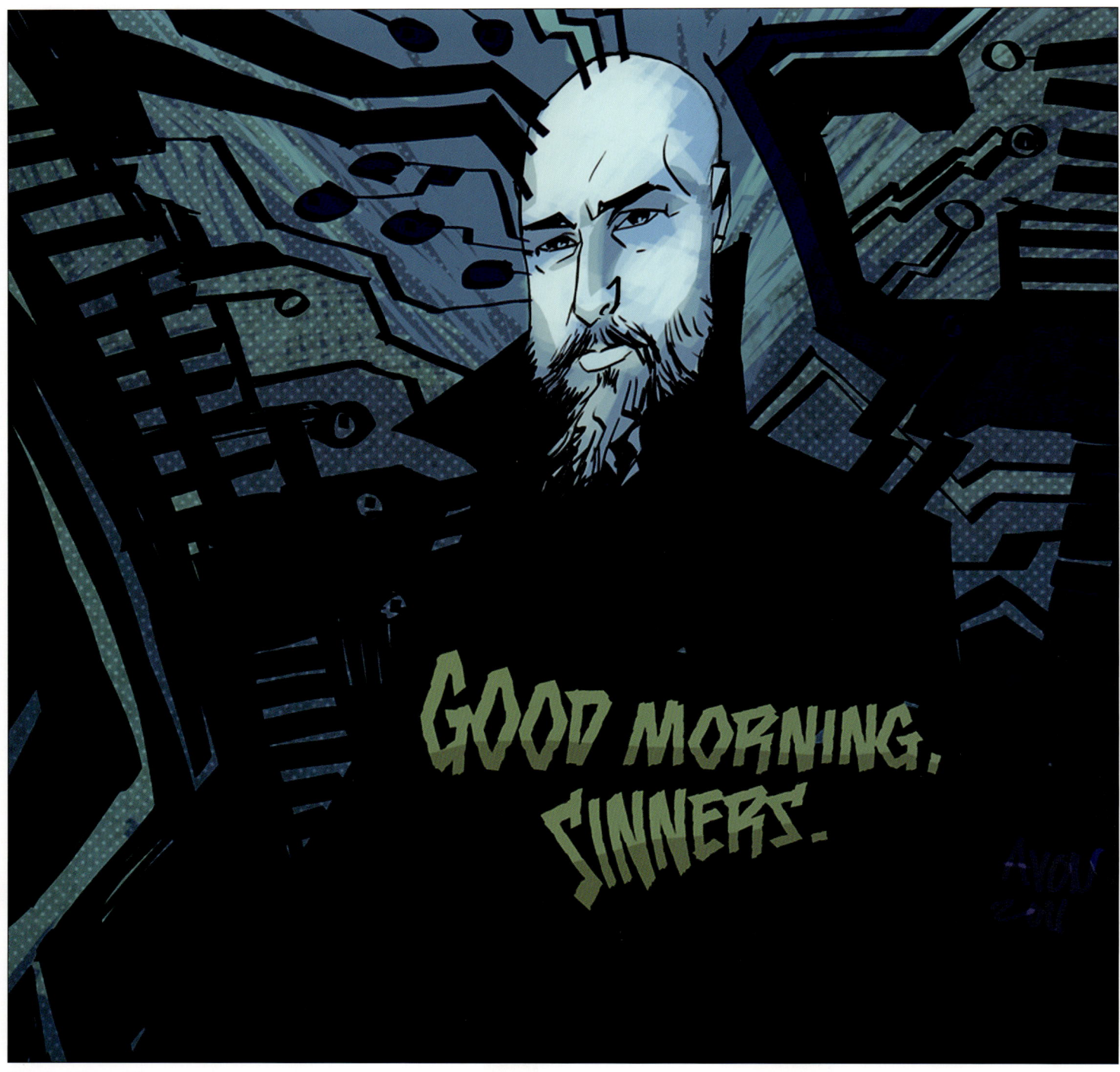

Portrait of Warren Ellis

I'm a big Warren Ellis fan. His Vertigo series *Transmetropolitan* was mind blowing, and I loved his Image book *Fell* with Ben Templesmith. I first became aware of Warren through *Powers* #7, in a story called "Ride Along."

Ride alongs are of course when police officers let citizens join them in squad cars to observe. Lots of writers do it. Brian Bendis did it to research his crime comics, and I've done it too. For *Powers* #7, Bendis asked Warren if he wouldn't mind being a character in the book, doing an eventful ride along with Walker and Deena. It was an early favorite story with *Powers* fans.

After I started at Valve, I approached Warren about doing an experimental short digital comic that would break the rules. We could post the story online and let people pay what they want, or nothing at all.

Warren live blogged the process of the project and posted sketches and pages on his website. Because the whole thing was experimental, I tried out a more rendered, abstract style of art. Unfortunately we both got sidetracked with other projects and never finished it, but maybe we can go back to it one day.

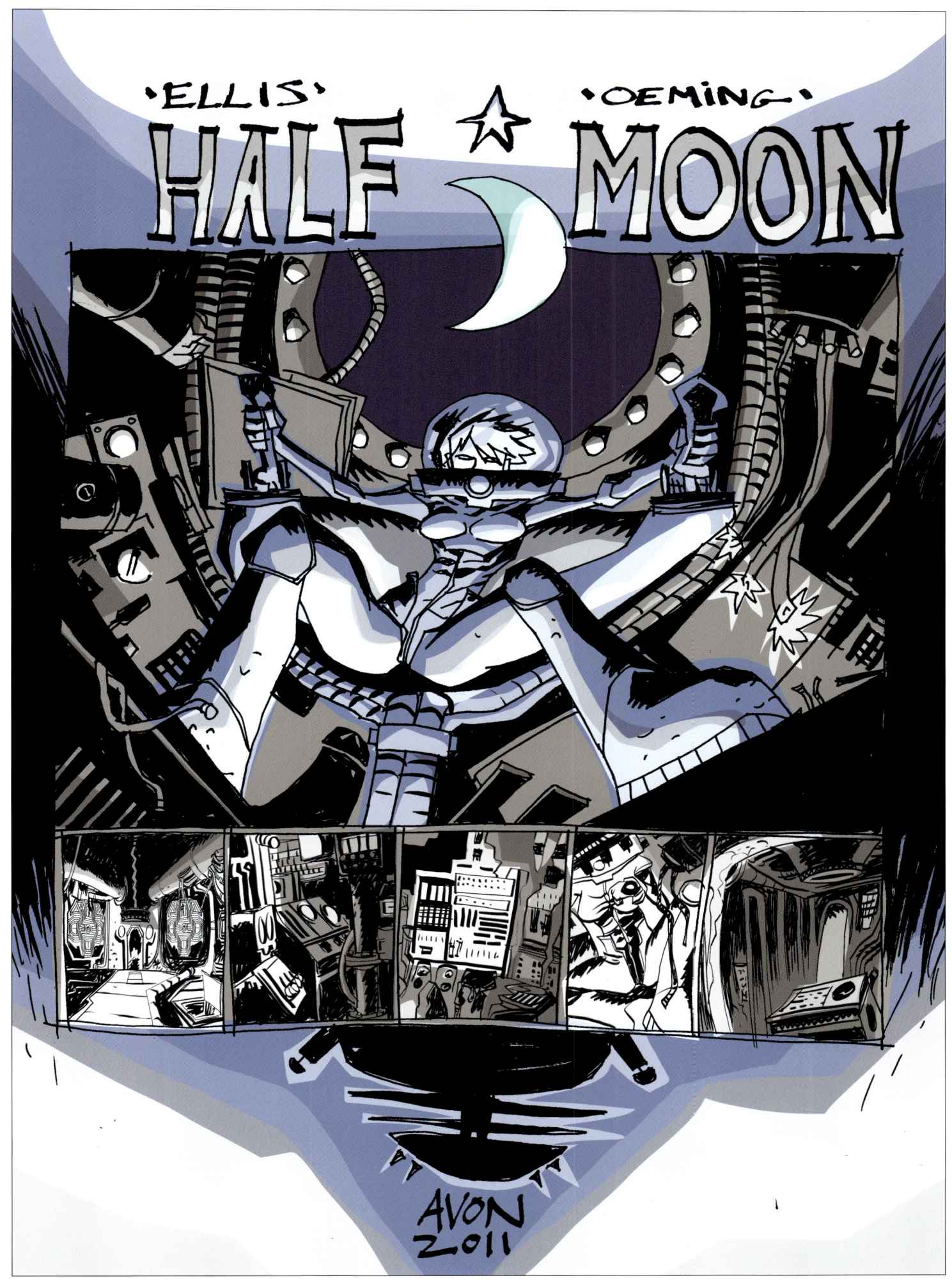

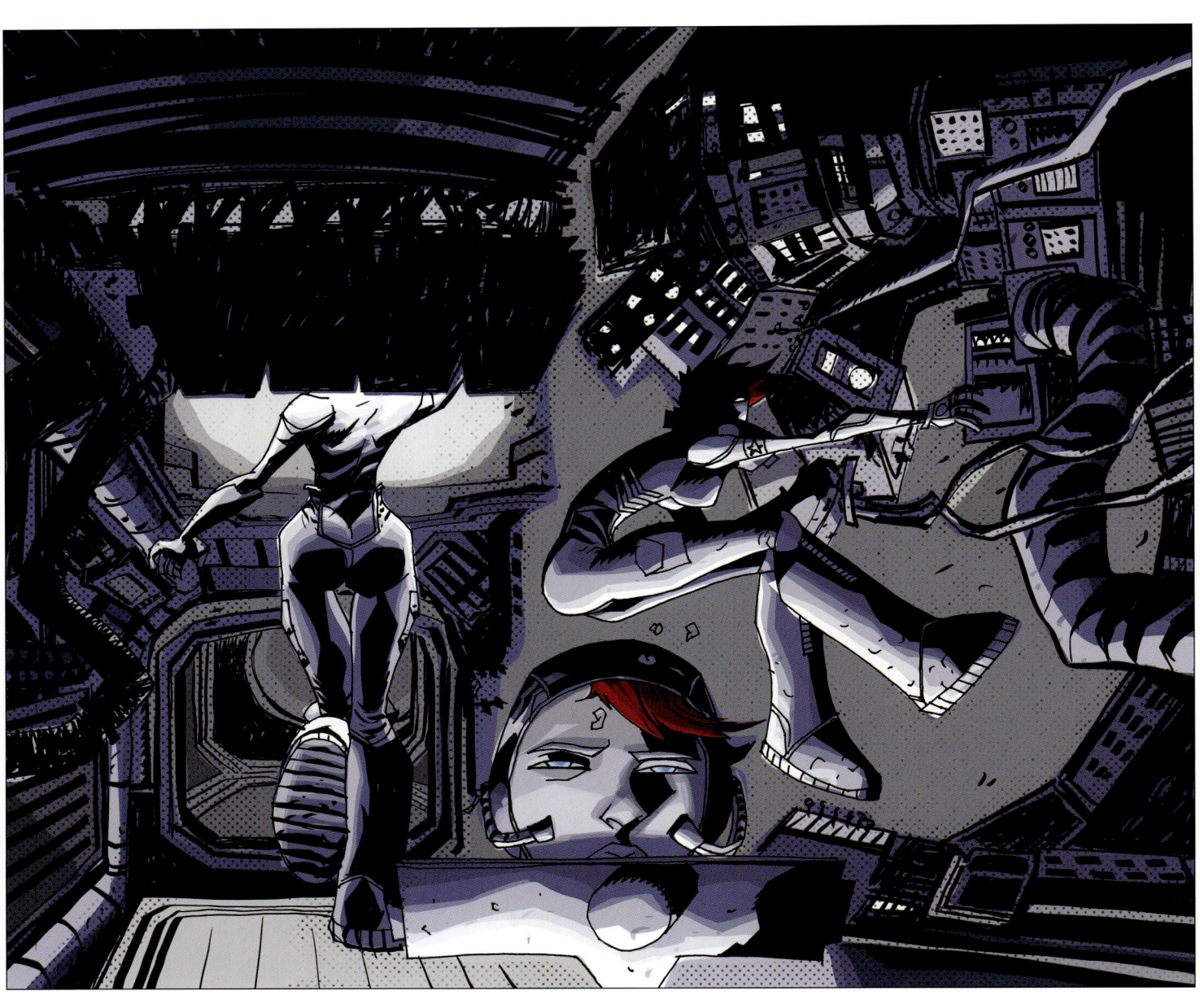

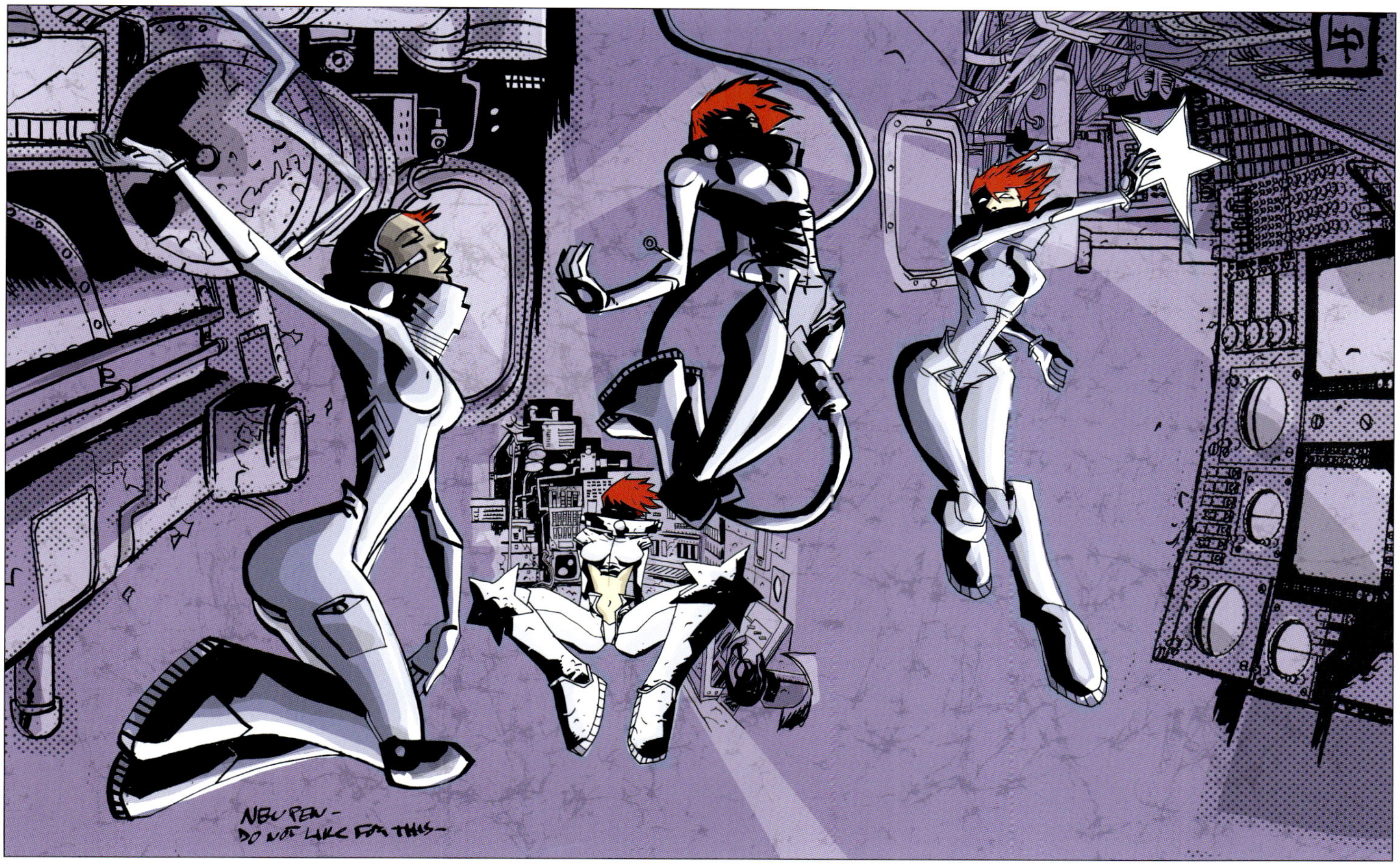

NO PLAN B: THE ART OF MICHAEL AVON OEMING 95

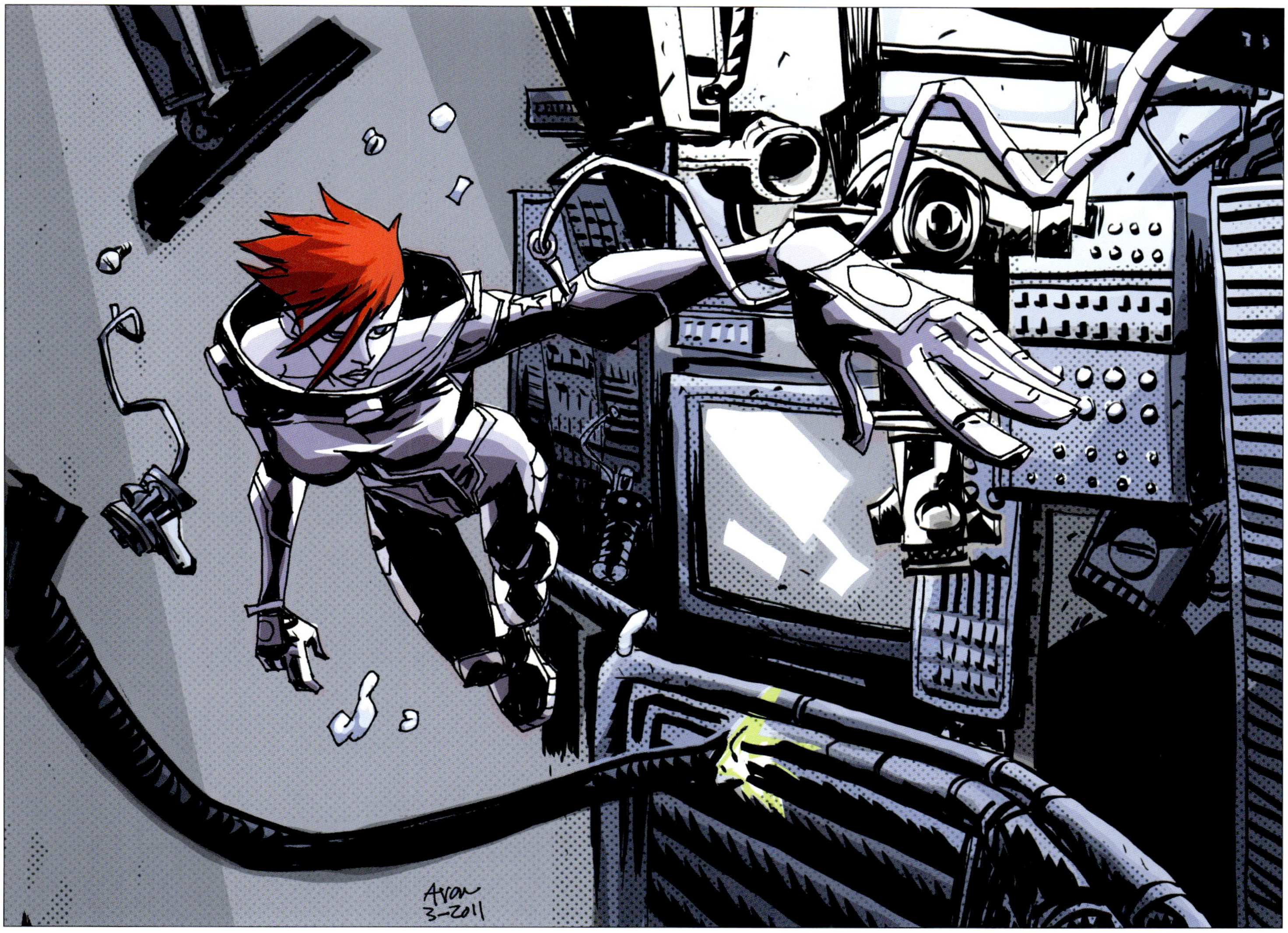

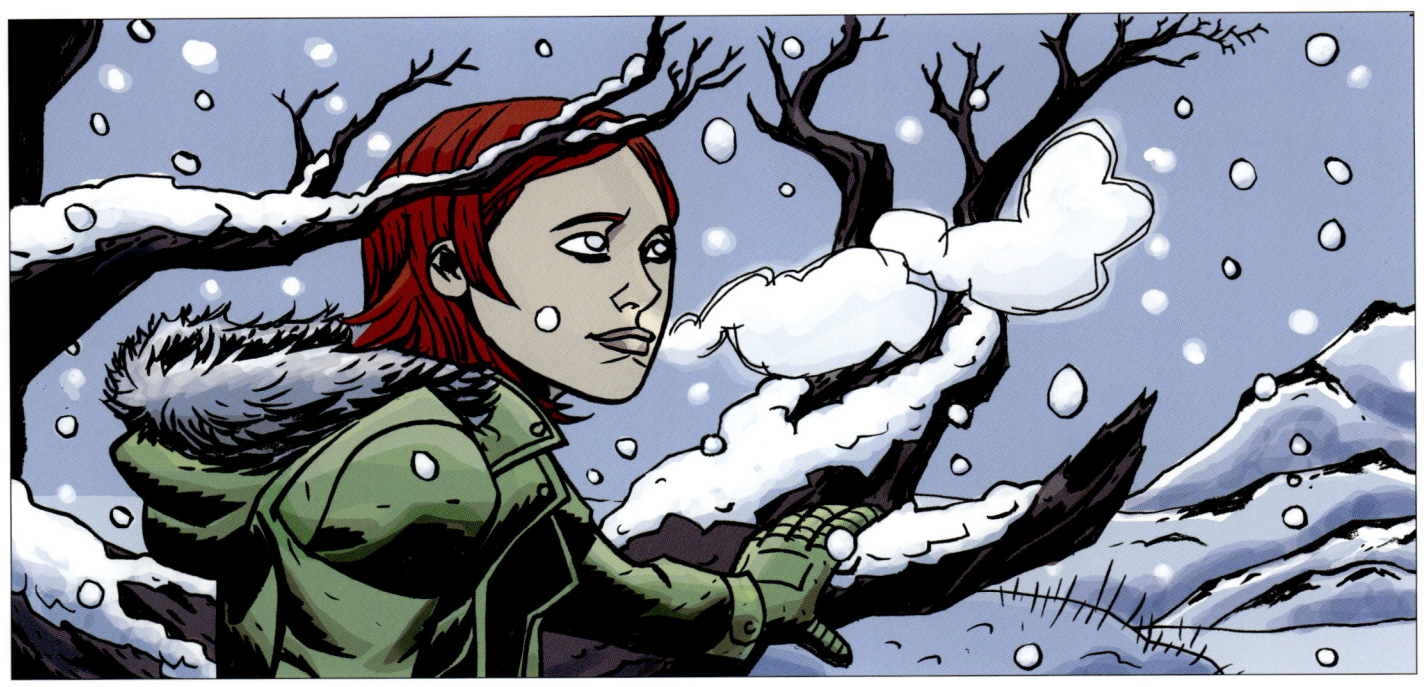
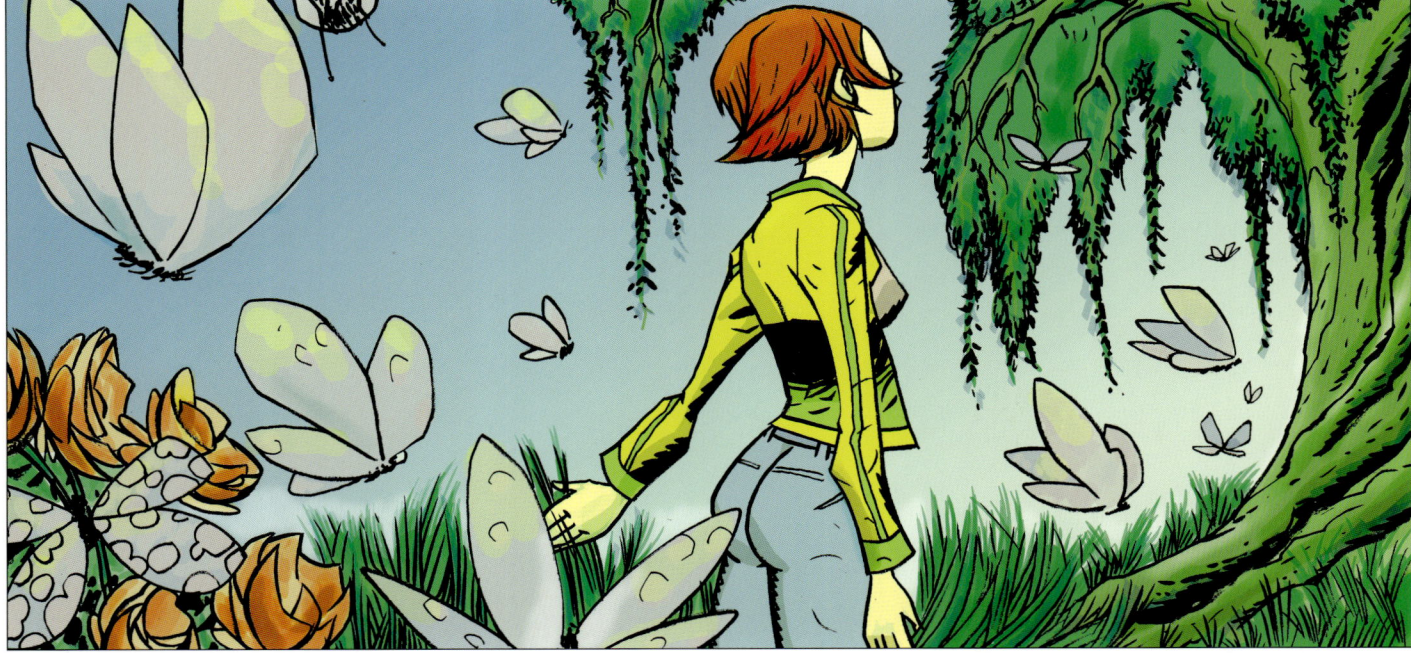
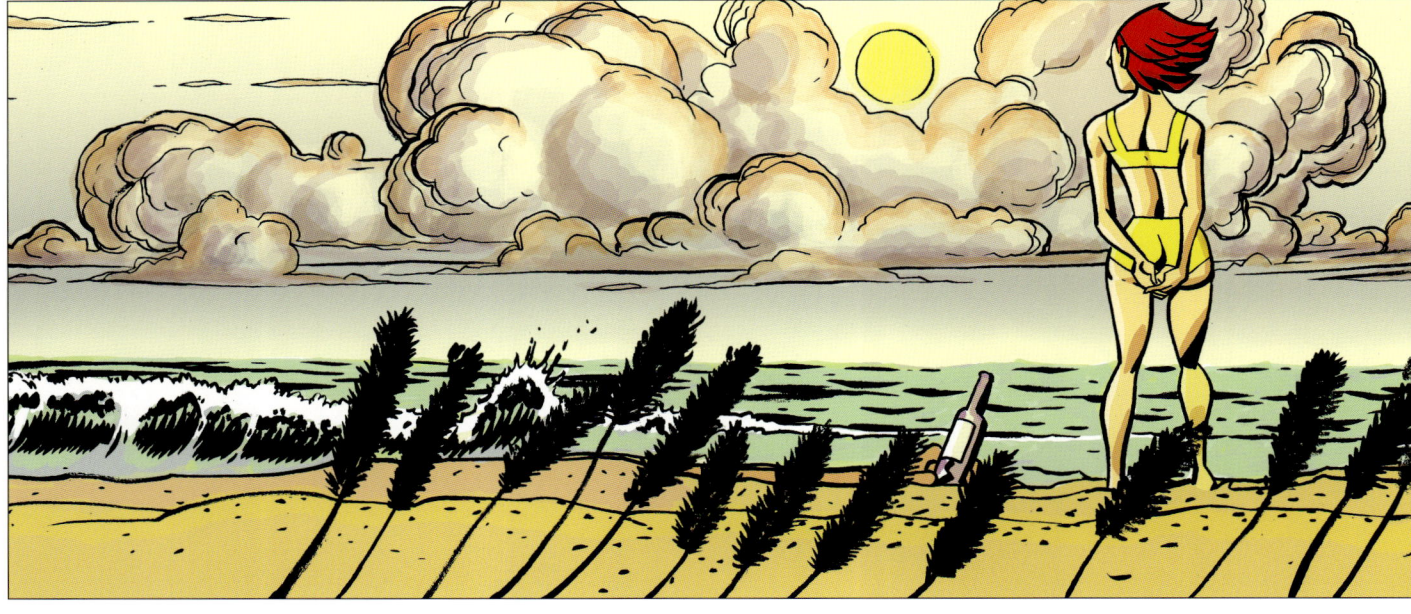

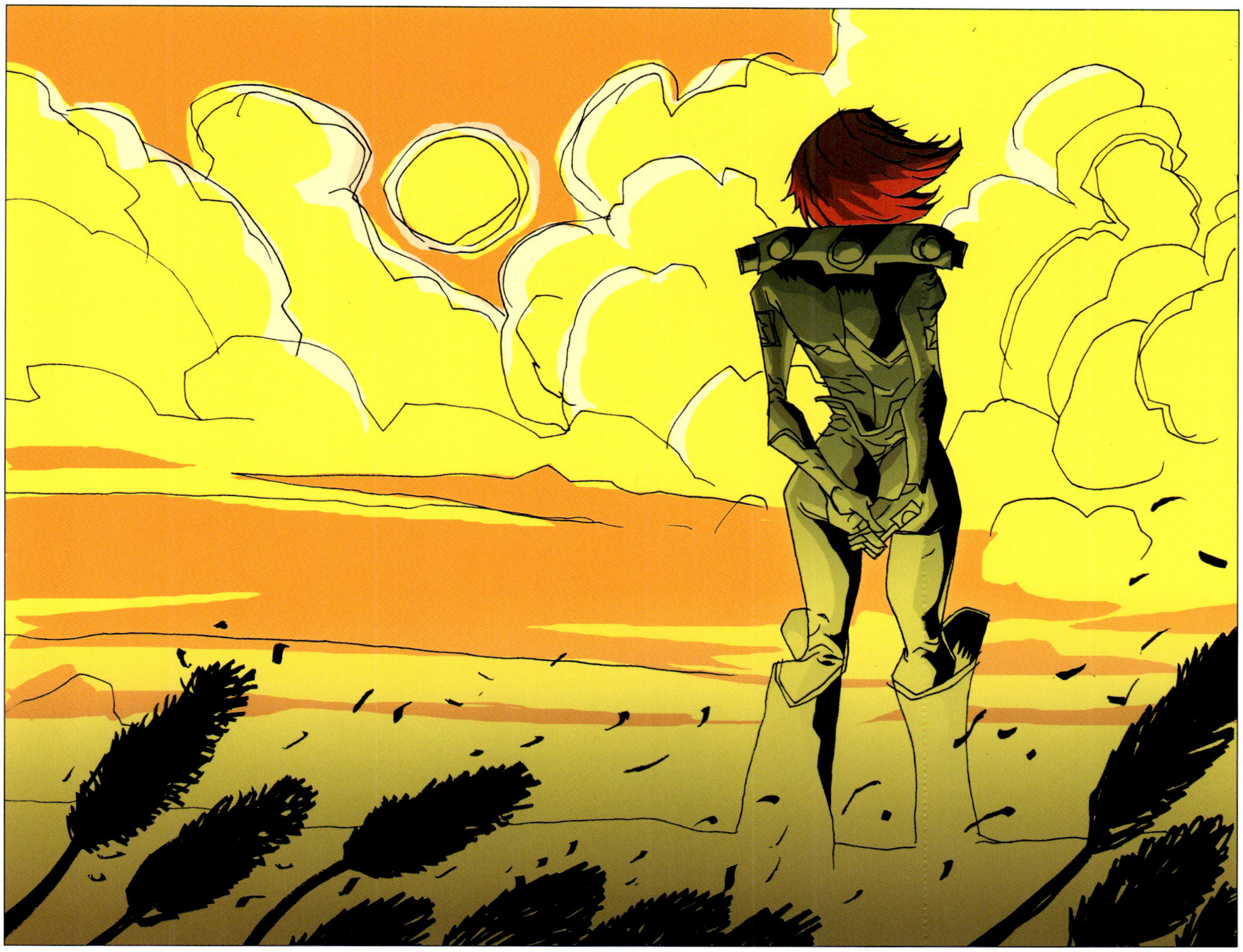

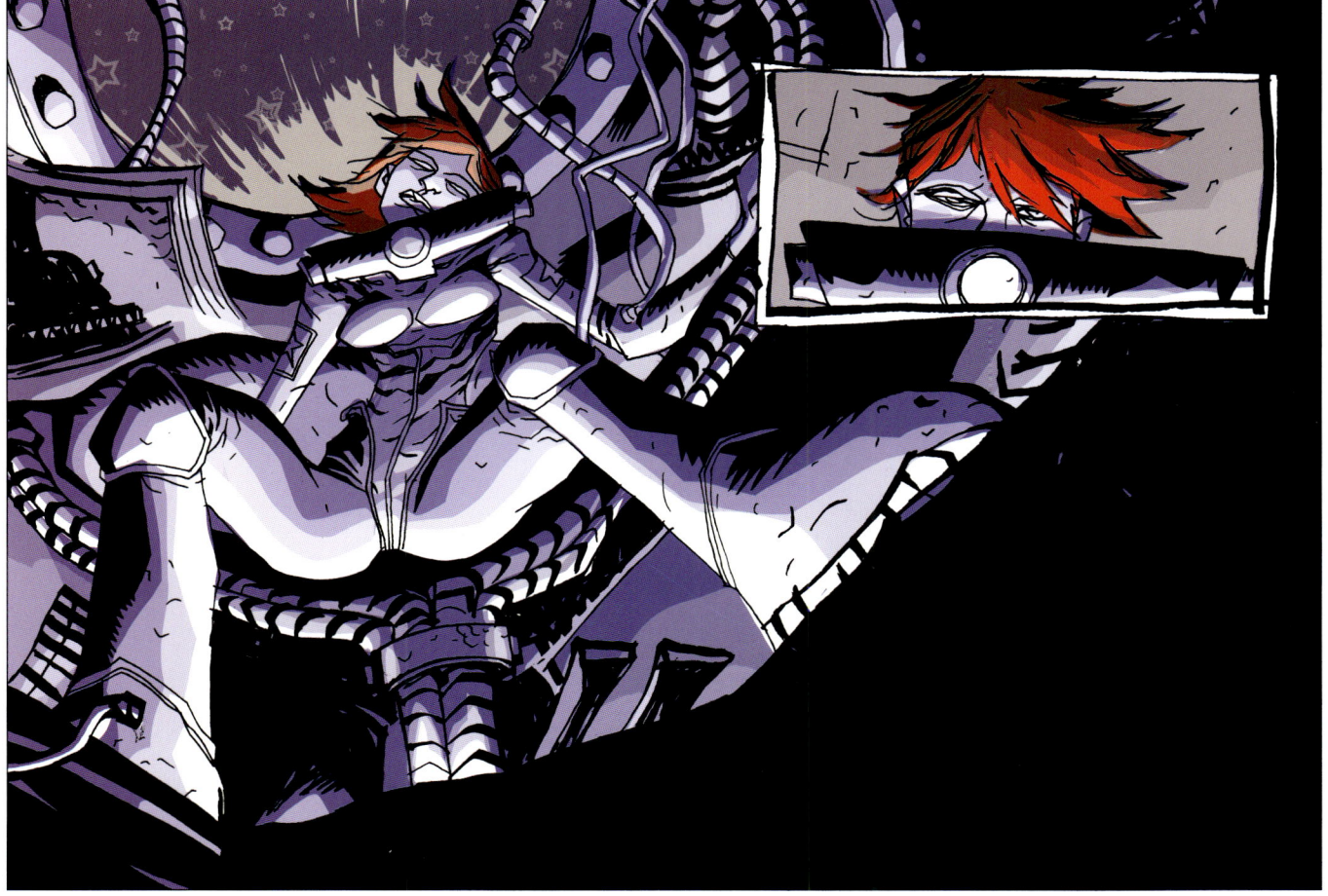

When Taki and I relocated to the West Coast we saw the Bendis family more often, and Brian's oldest daughter, Olivia, just fell in love with Taki. It didn't surprise me. Taki is super cute, fun, and huggable.

Growing up with a father like Brian, Olivia started having her own story ideas. One day she asked Brian, "What if Taki was my sister and we had superpowers?" and she and Brian started working out the basic idea. Initially she'd pitch Brian stories she'd seen on *Wizards of Waverly Place*, but he'd say, "How can you make this more of your story? What would life with Taki as your sister be like?" That's when Olivia started coming up with her own ideas, like having their powers work through kung fu telekinesis—perfect for a kids' book. Violence and action without having to punch anybody. To get their looks right, I had Olivia and Taki go to the park and do lots of action poses for me. This evolved into the book Brian and I did for Marvel's Icon imprint, *Takio*, in 2011.

The family inspiration for *Takio* characters continued. Brian brought my son Ethan in, along with our friend and comics writer Kelly Sue DeConnick. Nick Filardi was our colorist, and the whole book became an all-ages project about family inspired by our real family and friends.

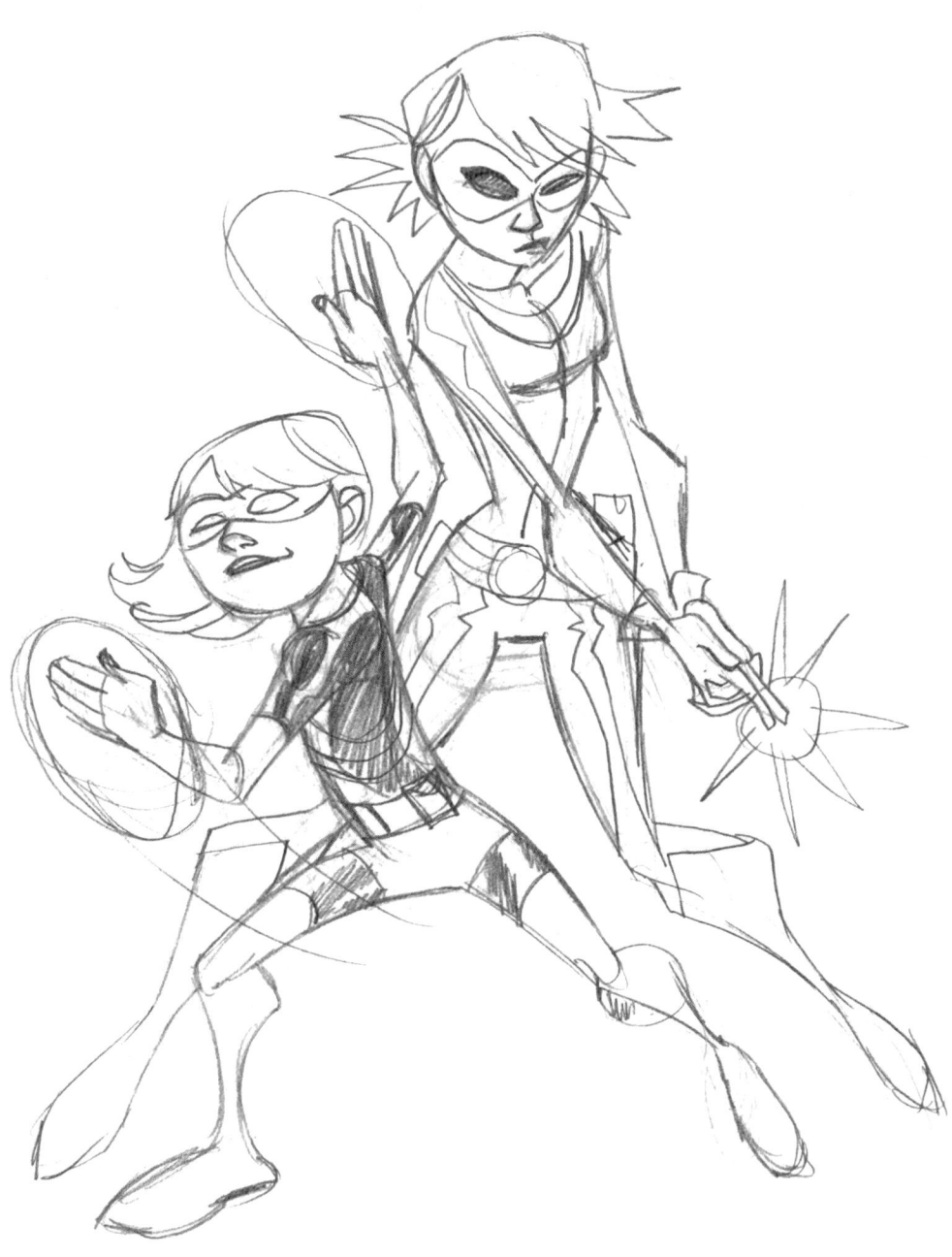

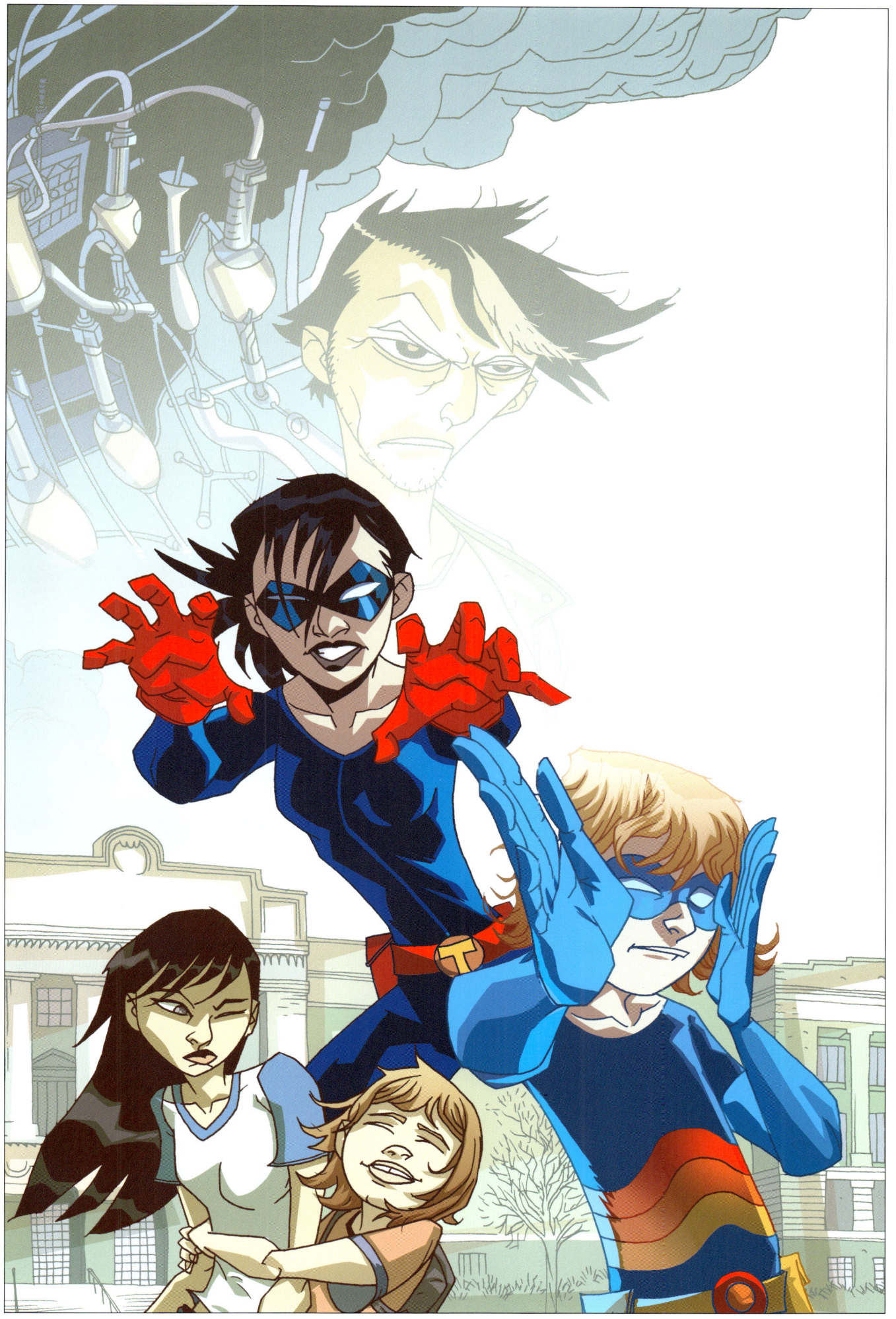

Takio cover, colors by Nick Filardi

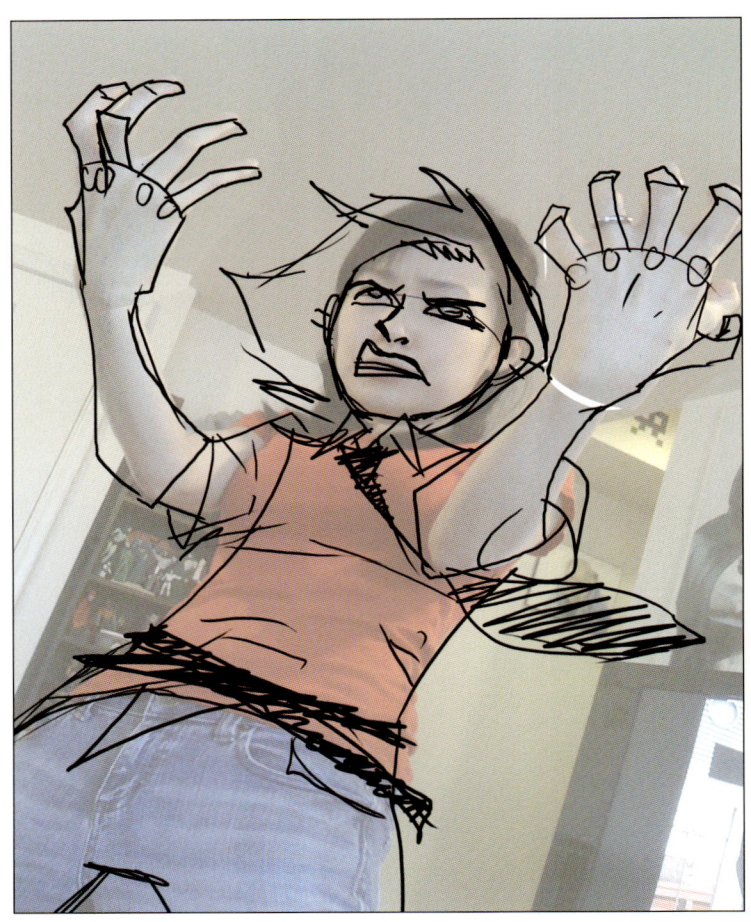
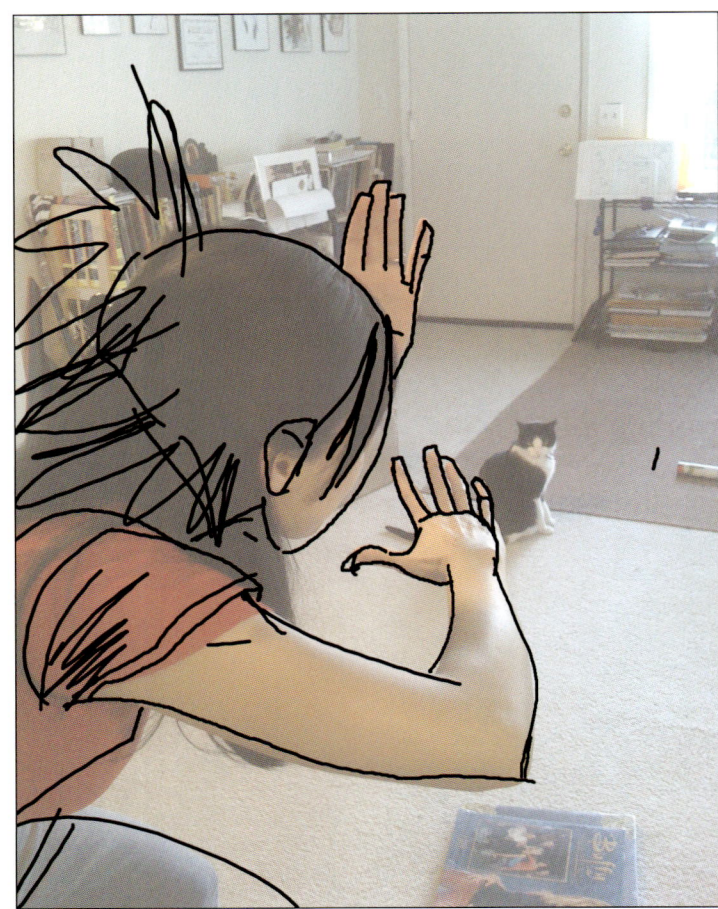
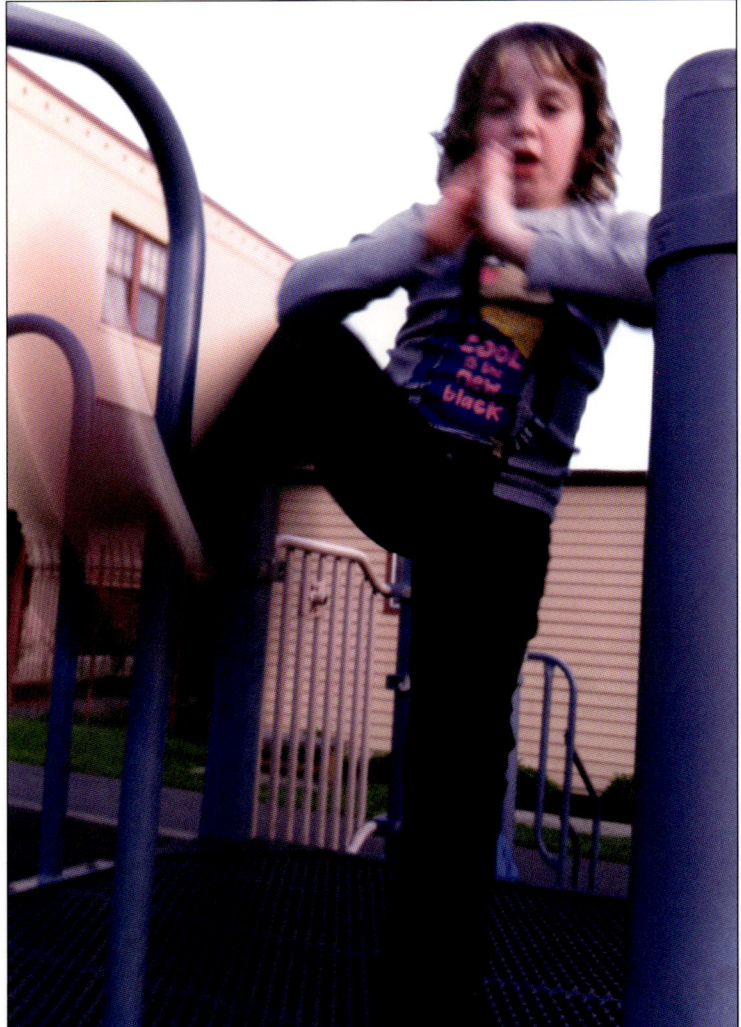
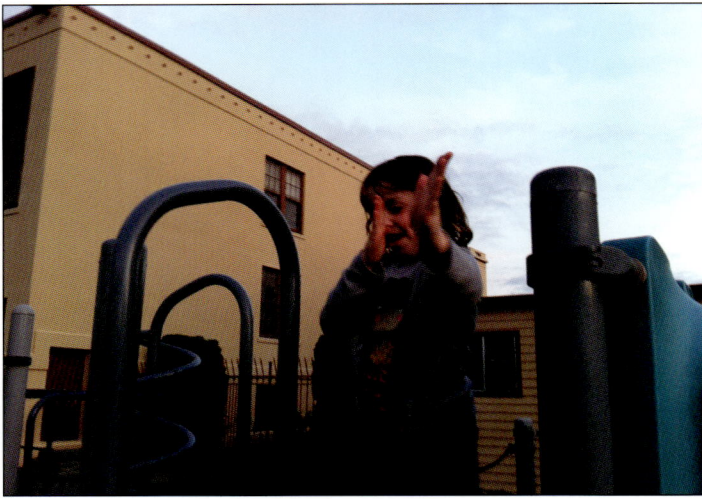
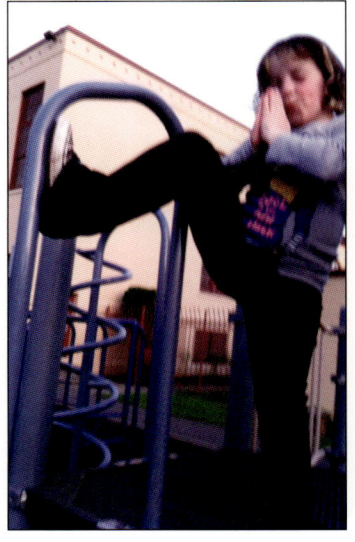
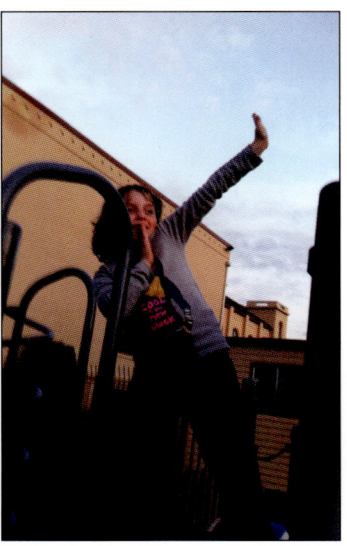

Reference photos of Taki and Olivia Bendis

100 NO PLAN B: THE ART OF MICHAEL AVON OEMING

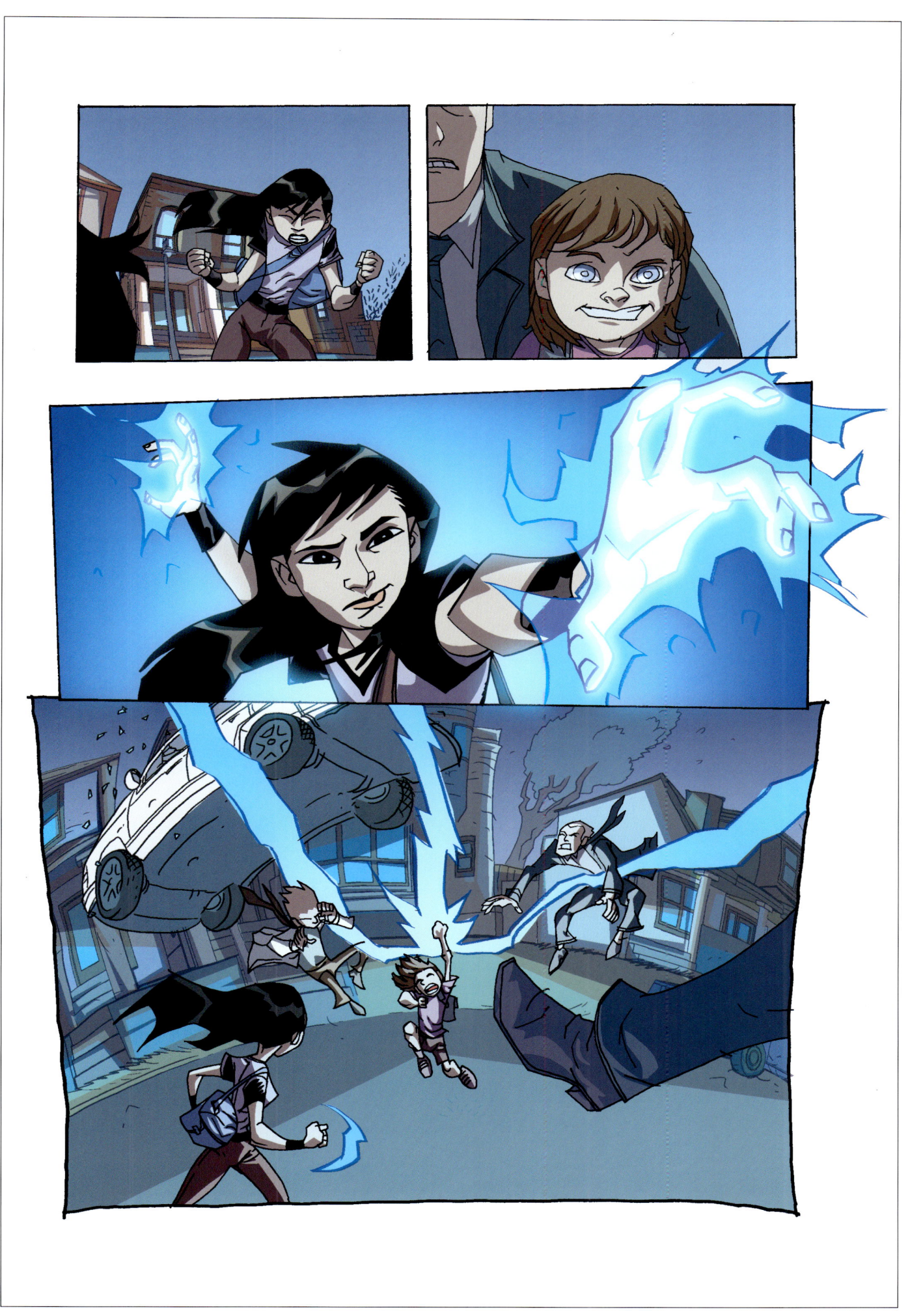

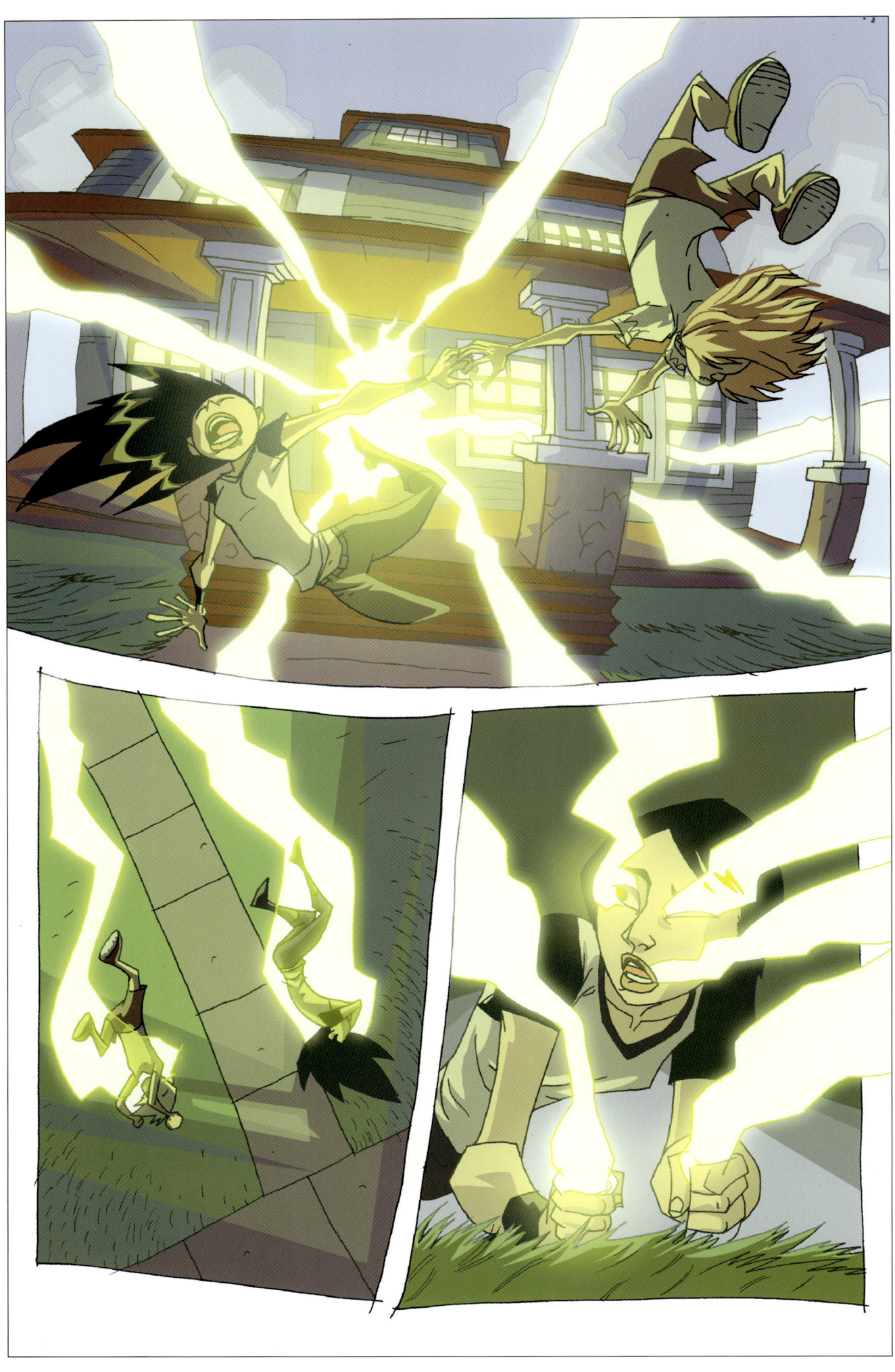

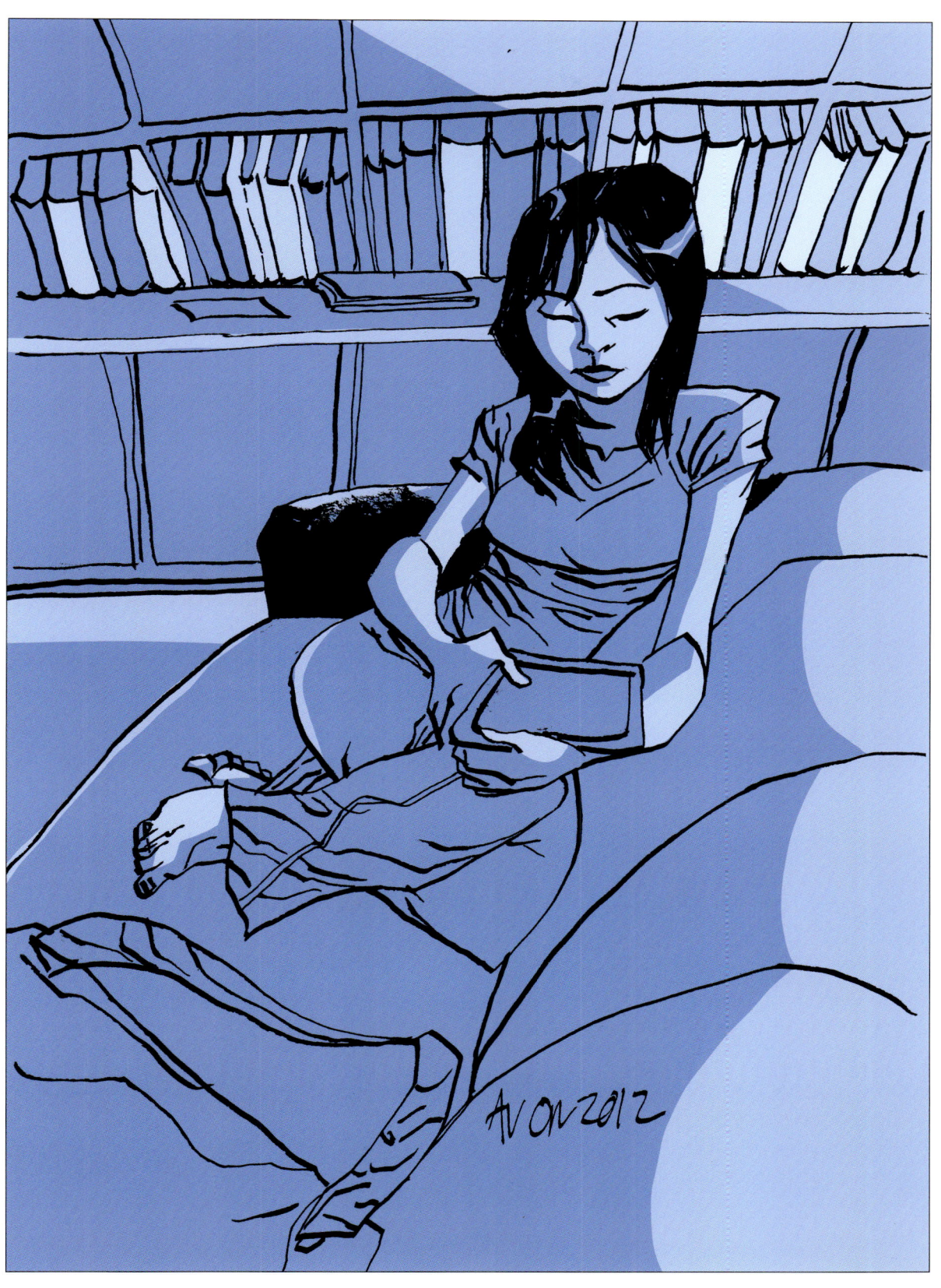

NO PLAN B: THE ART OF MICHAEL AVON OEMING   103

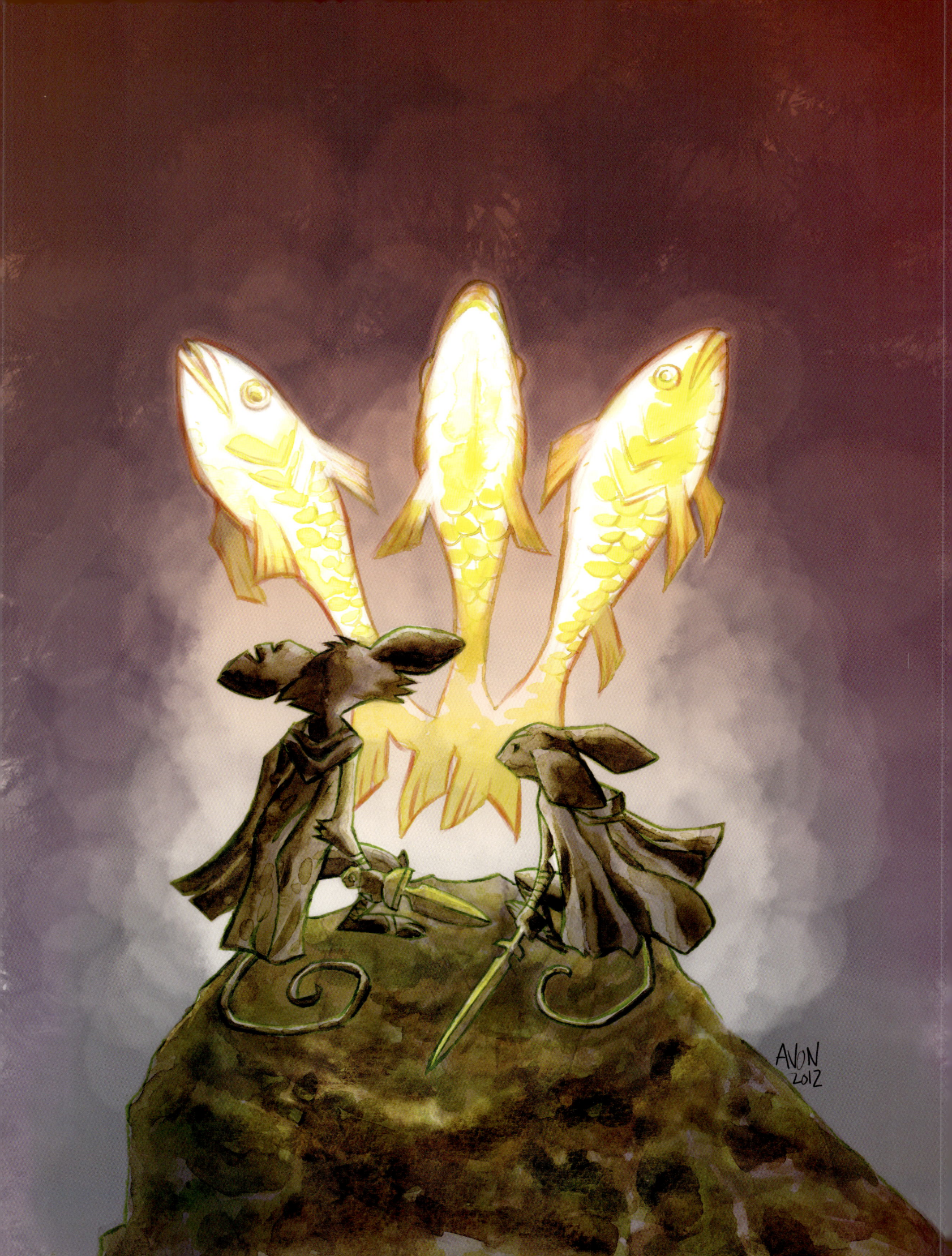

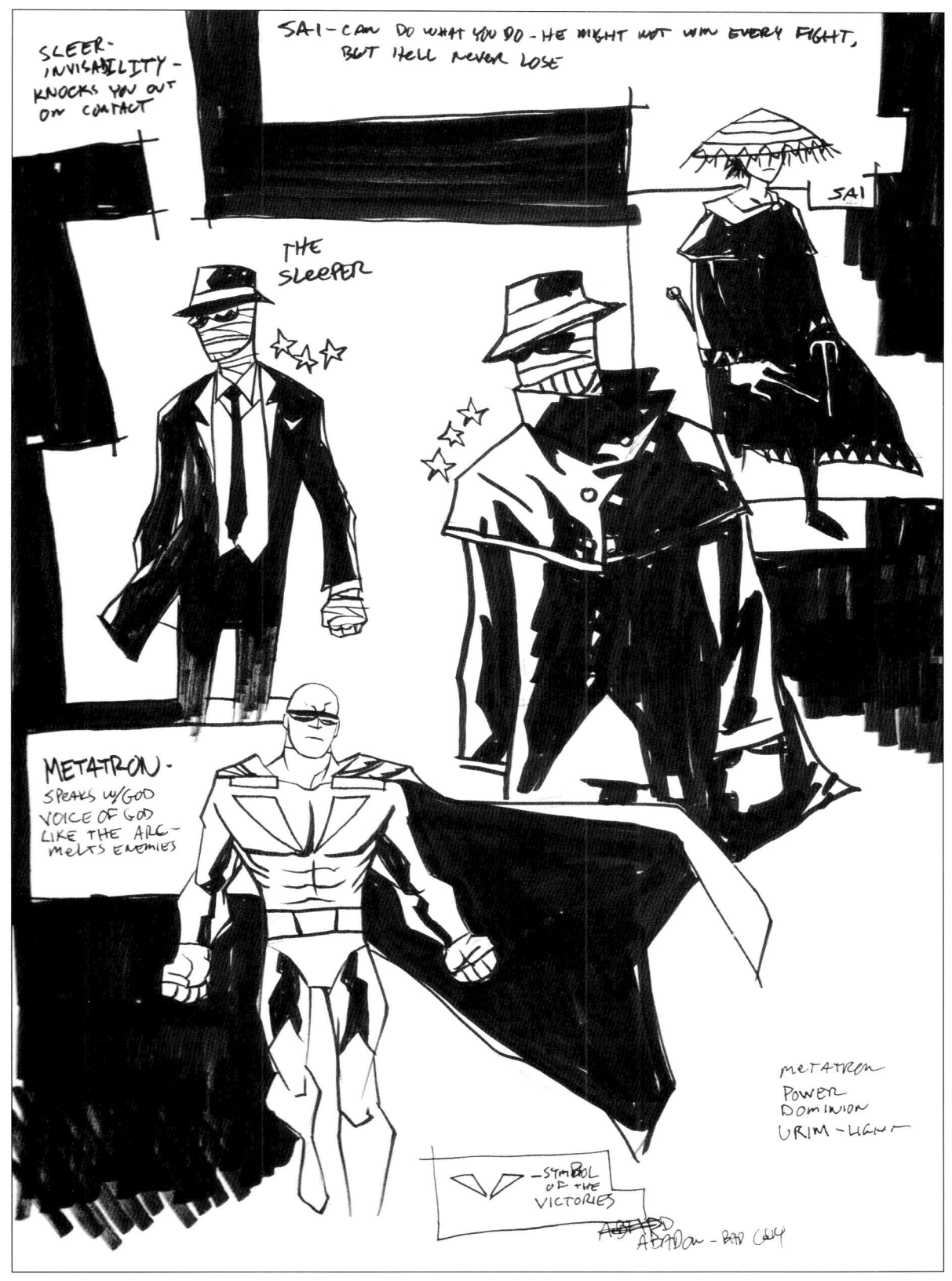

Facing, *Mice Templar* cover; above, *The Victories* character designs

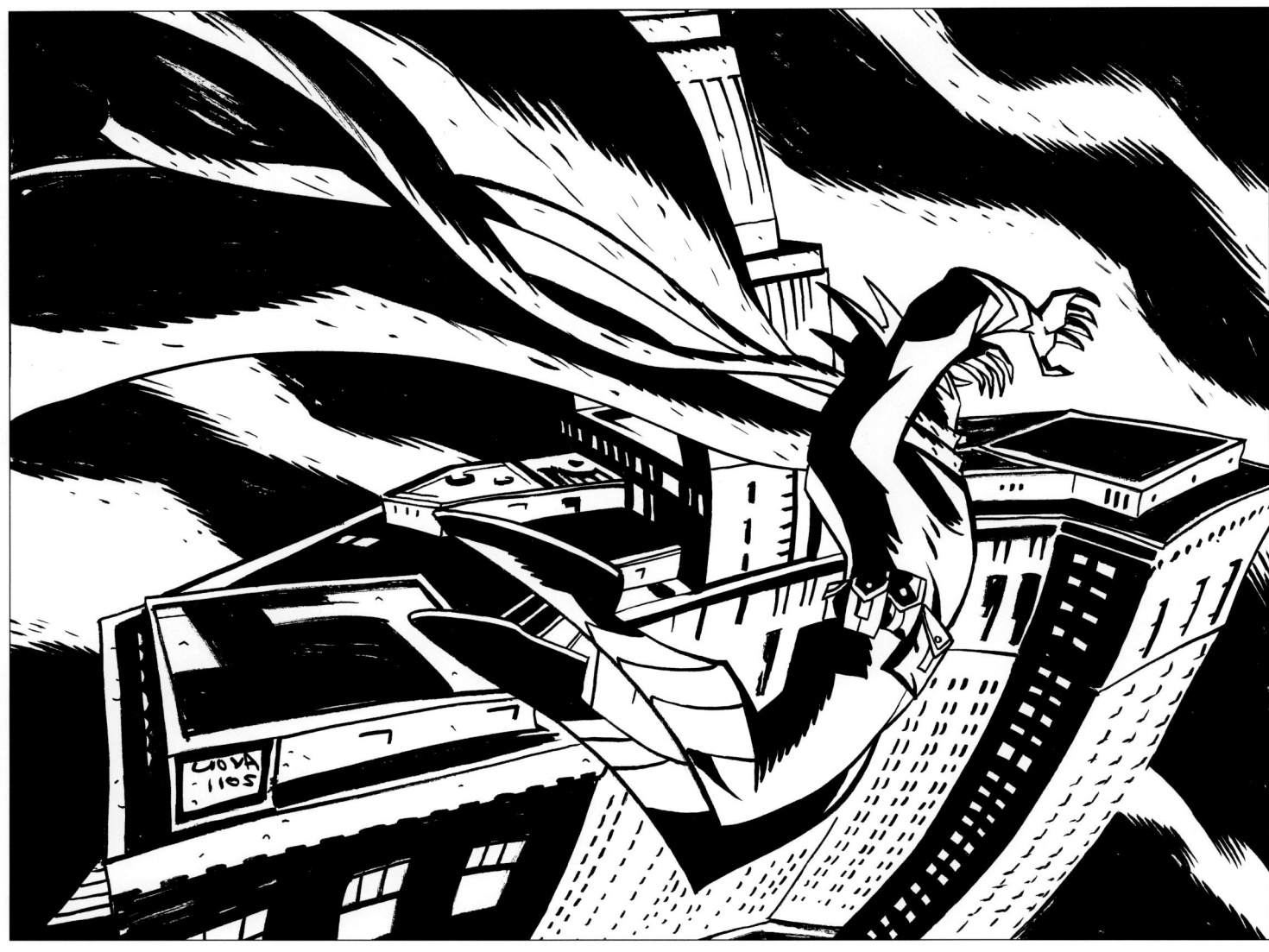

The Victories (Dark Horse, 2012–2014) was a result of getting into therapy. I'd been through horrible shit as a kid, my mom being an alcoholic, living in a broken home. I'd also experienced sexual abuse as a kid. I haven't spoken much about it because my uncle who raised me was like a father to me. He just passed away in December 2016. If he'd ever heard this had happened to me, he'd blame himself for not protecting us. Now that he's passed, I think it's okay and important to talk about this kind of stuff.

In therapy I looked at my compulsion to always be drawing. Most artists constantly draw. If I was in meetings or at dinner with friends, I was always drawing in my sketchbook. My therapist said, "Your compulsive drawing is a control mechanism in reaction to the things you went through in your life."

It's ironic the thing that I do for joy, drawing, also protects me from the worst things in my life. I realized that's my own personal superhero origin story. I never thought I'd have something like that. So how could I put this into a story?

What if the thing that gives a superhero powers also brings him the most pain? In *The Victories* I posed the question "What if a superpowered martial artist 'mentors' two children to give them powers through a ceremony that also gives the teacher the opportunity to molest them?" The boys grow up and discover their mentor is still taking advantage of kids. They have to decide whether to bring him to justice or to be vigilantes and take the ultimate revenge.

Facing: *The Victories* covers, colors by Nick Filardi

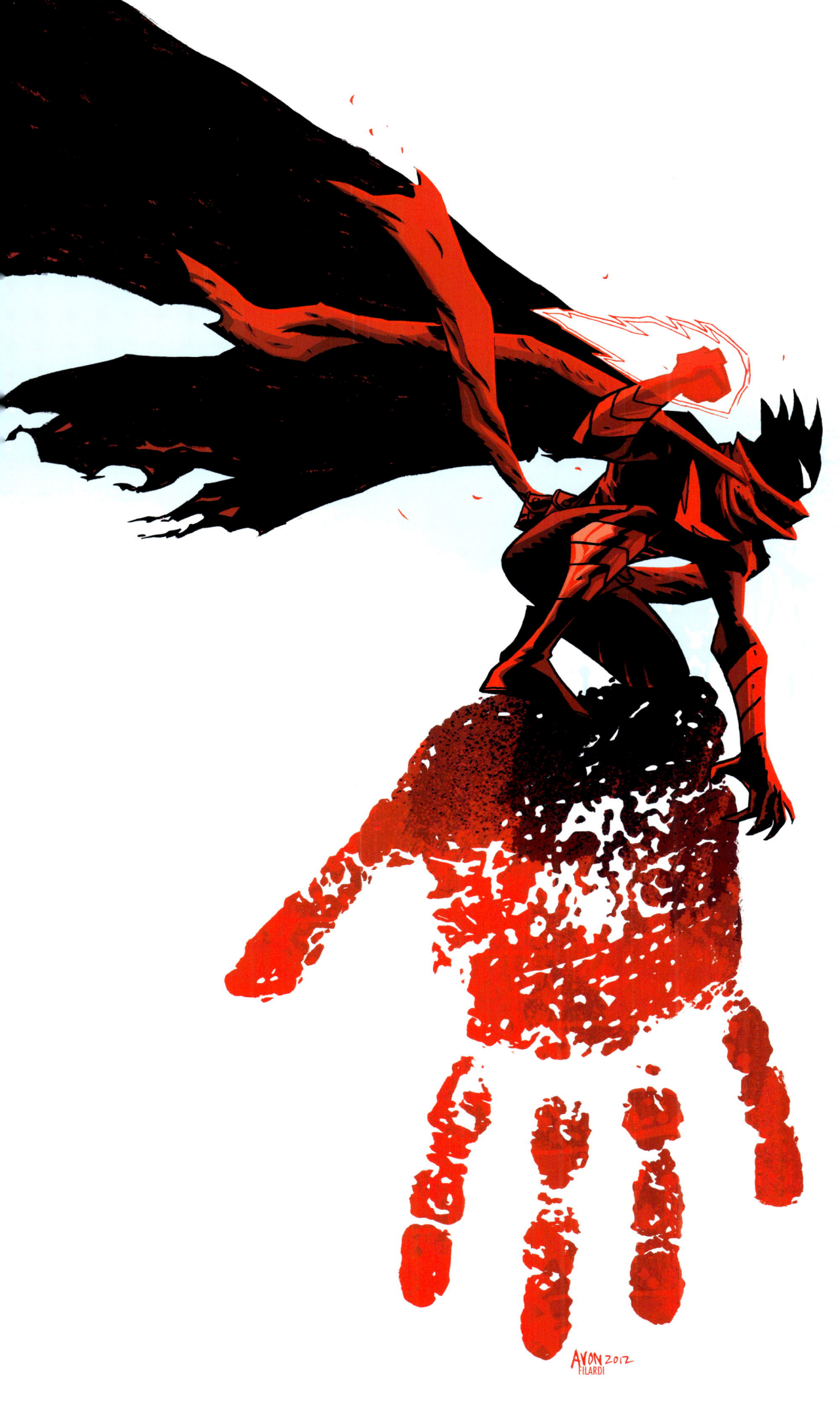

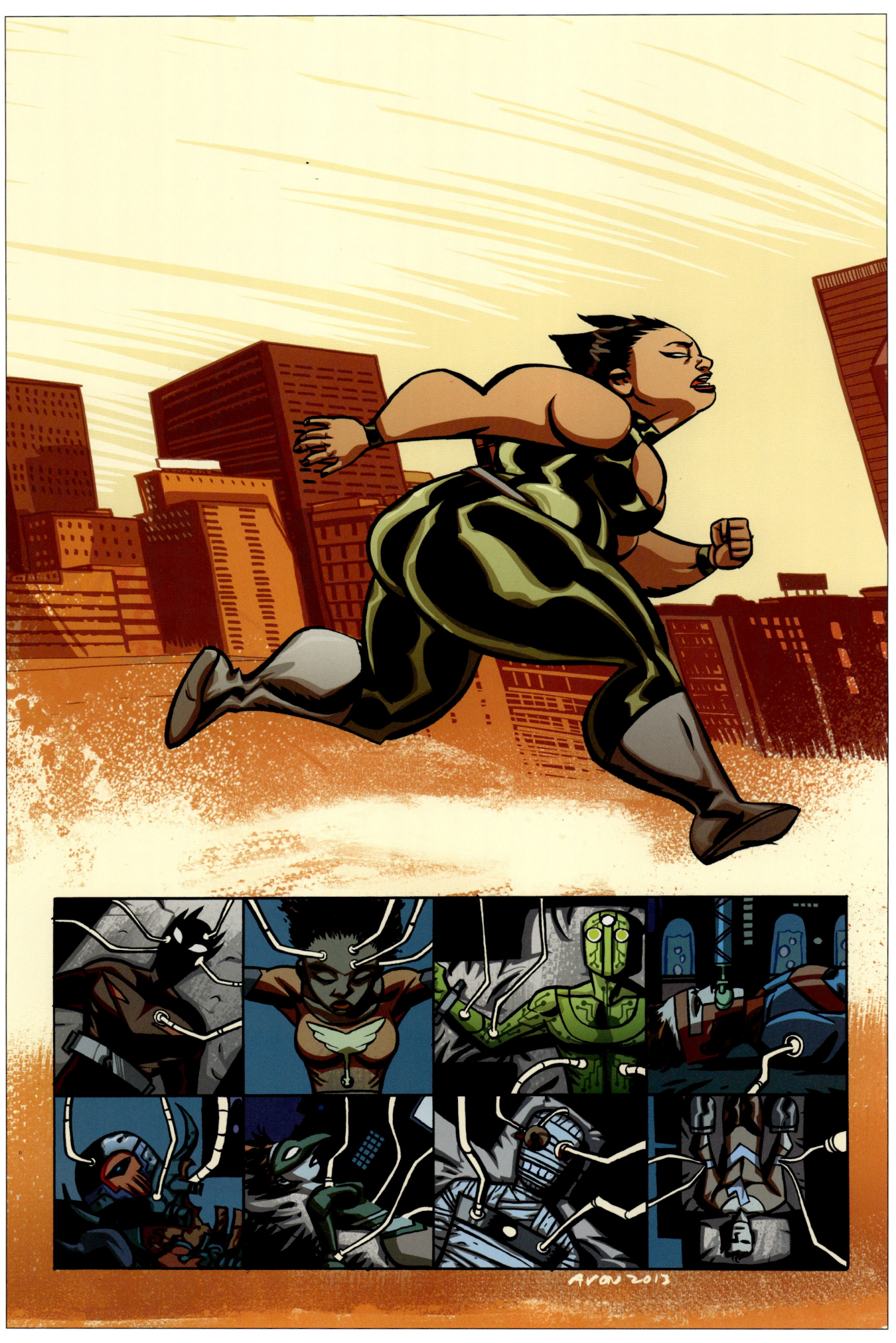

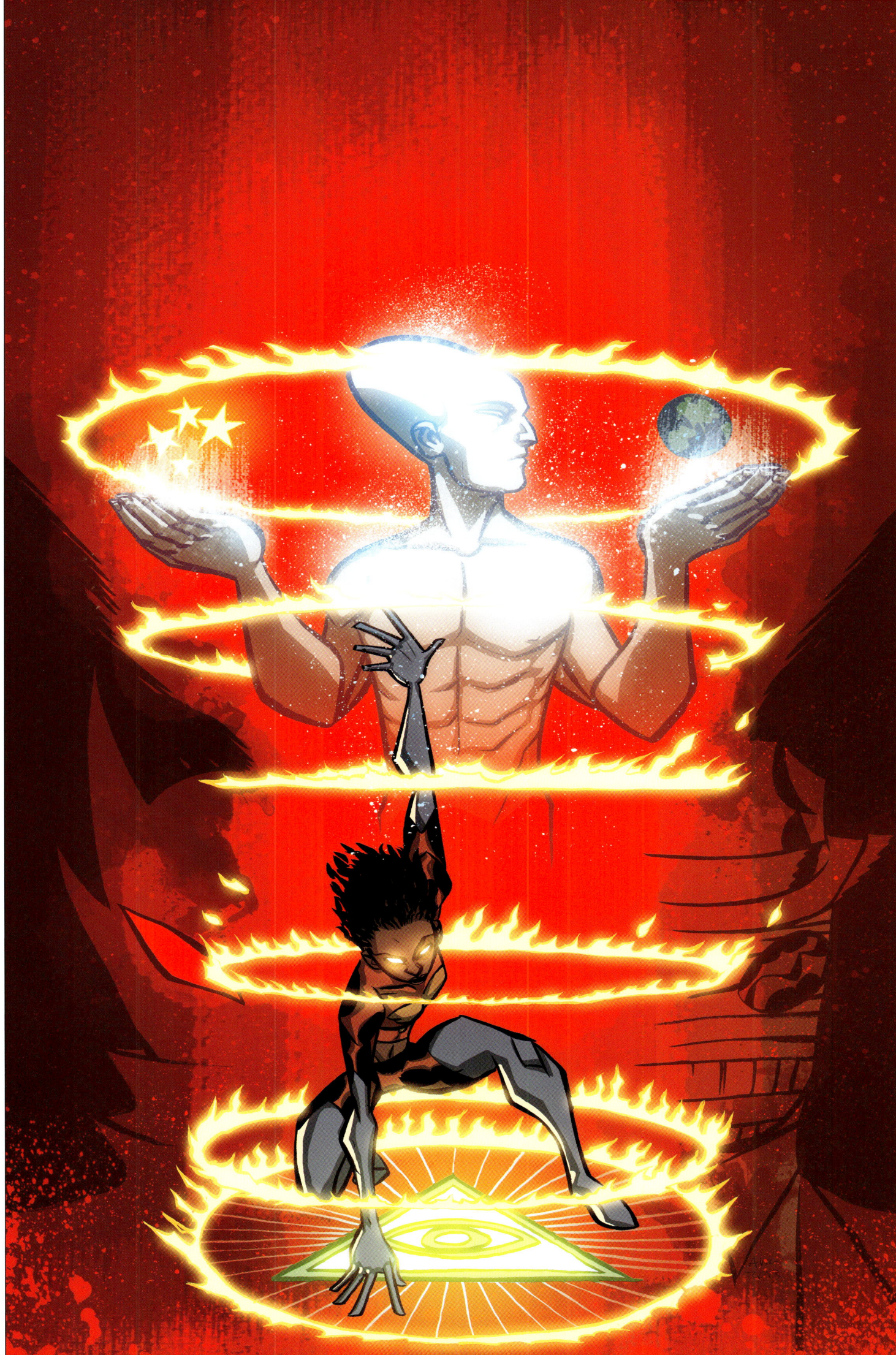

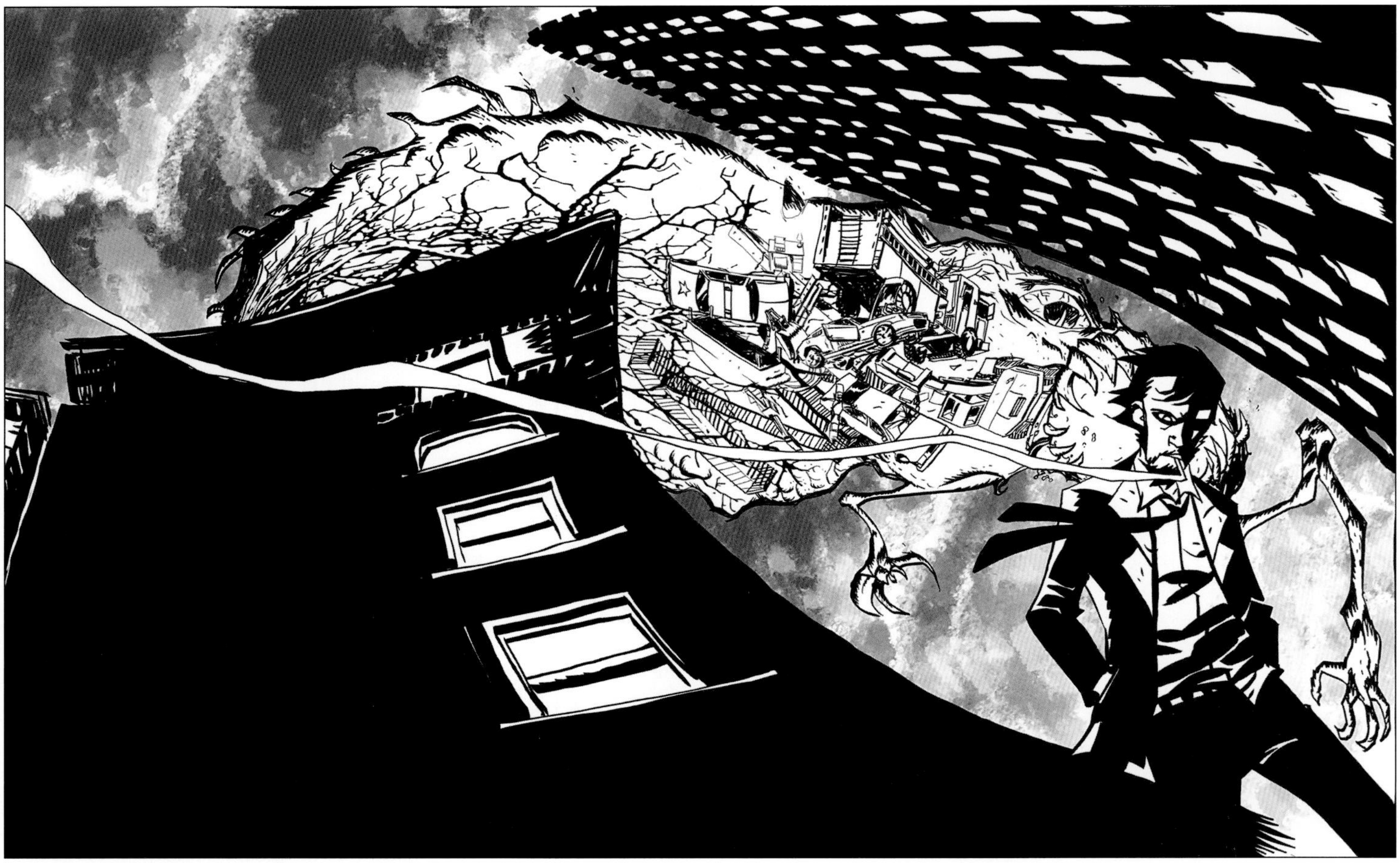

Wild Rover, which I did in *Dark Horse Presents* in 2012, also came about during my Valve days, when my life was really stressful. I'd moved from the East to the West Coast and become a bicoastal father. With *Powers* still going, I was basically working two full-time jobs, learning all this new digital stuff, and adjusting to late hours and different kinds of deadlines. There was a lot of pressure.

I was drinking a lot, and of course there's a history of alcoholism in my family. I became a functioning alcoholic, to the point that I was drinking privately. I had put the brakes on, to stop drinking to figure out if I was an alcoholic or not. This brought back lots of memories of my mother's drinking, which led to her losing custody of me during most of my childhood.

Wild Rover is about an alcoholic hero who battles demons manifested through drinking and alcohol. He has to get drunk to fight the demons, can only see them when he's drunk. I'm a big fan of the band the Pogues, and I based my main character on their brilliant singer Shane MacGowan, who's publicly known as an alcoholic, and whose songs are so sad and full of pain.

The existing *Wild Rover* story ends with a cliffhanger, but I hope to get back to it. I'm going to have the hero travel the world to fight alcoholic demons of different countries. When I wrote it I was in the throes of recovery, so it'll be interesting to return to it from a better place, to see if I can balance the emotional stress of that experience with exploring the psychological angle.

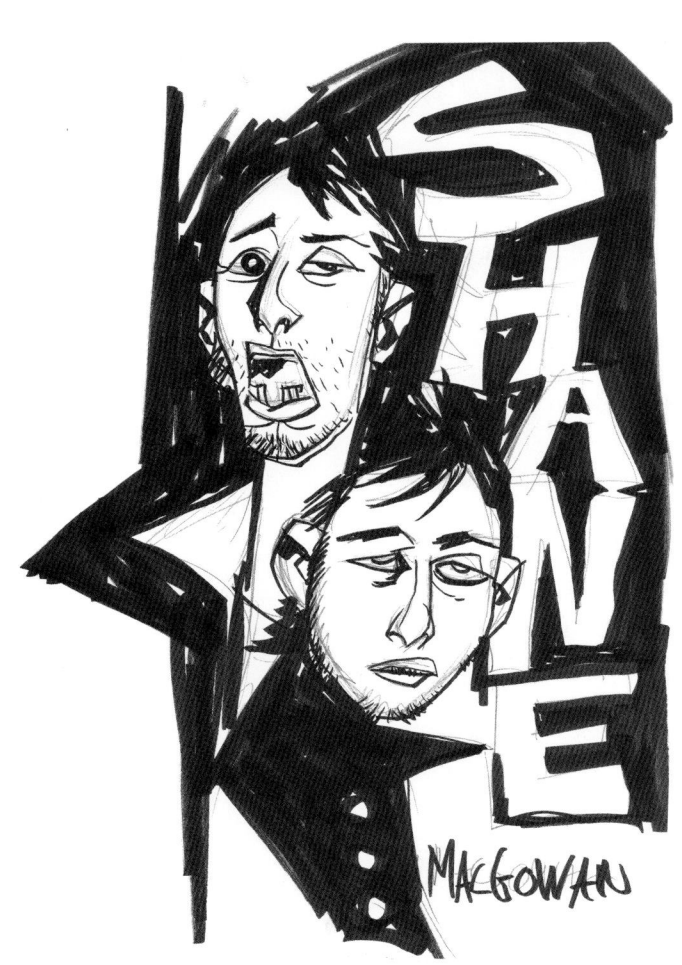

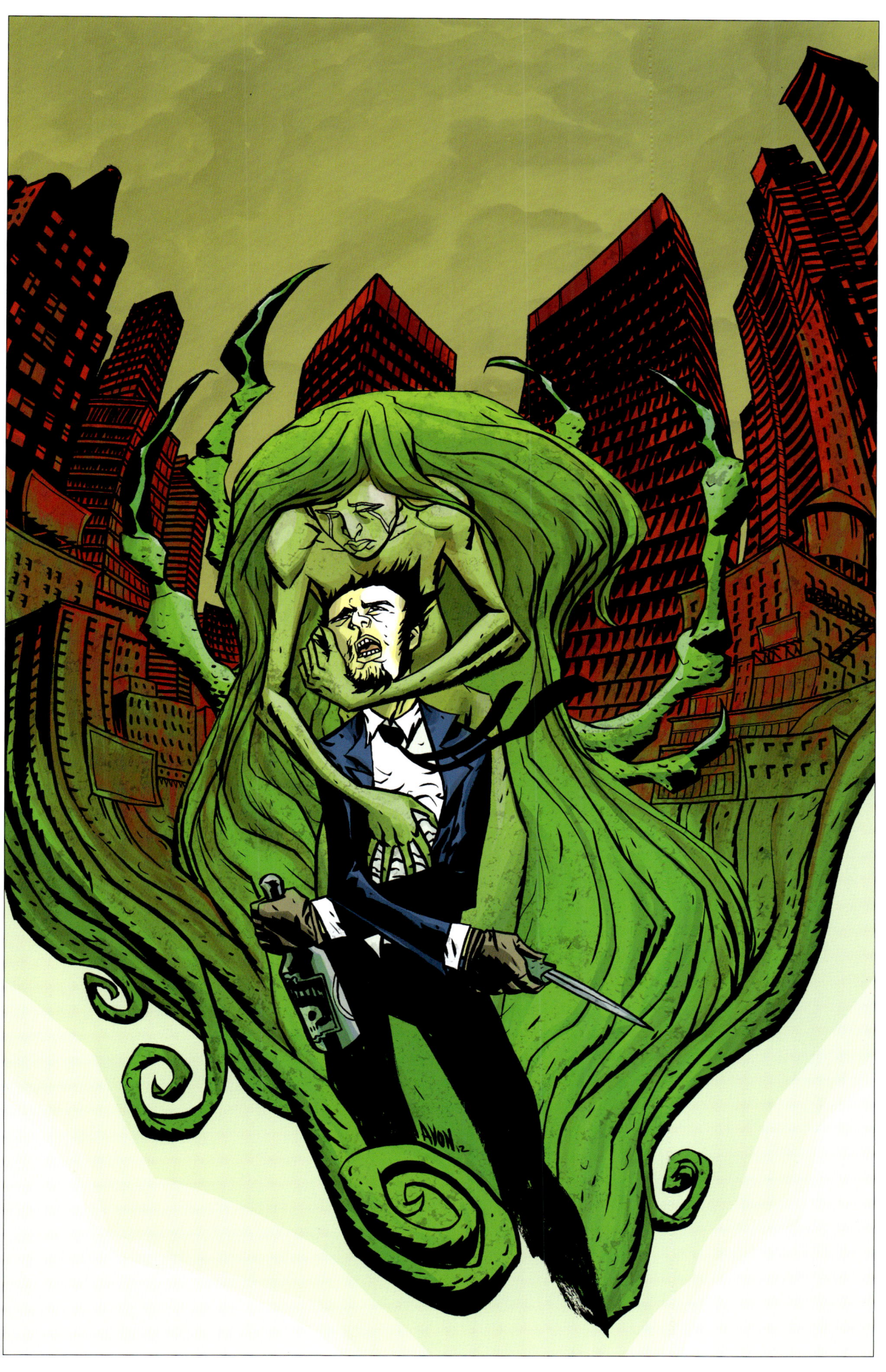

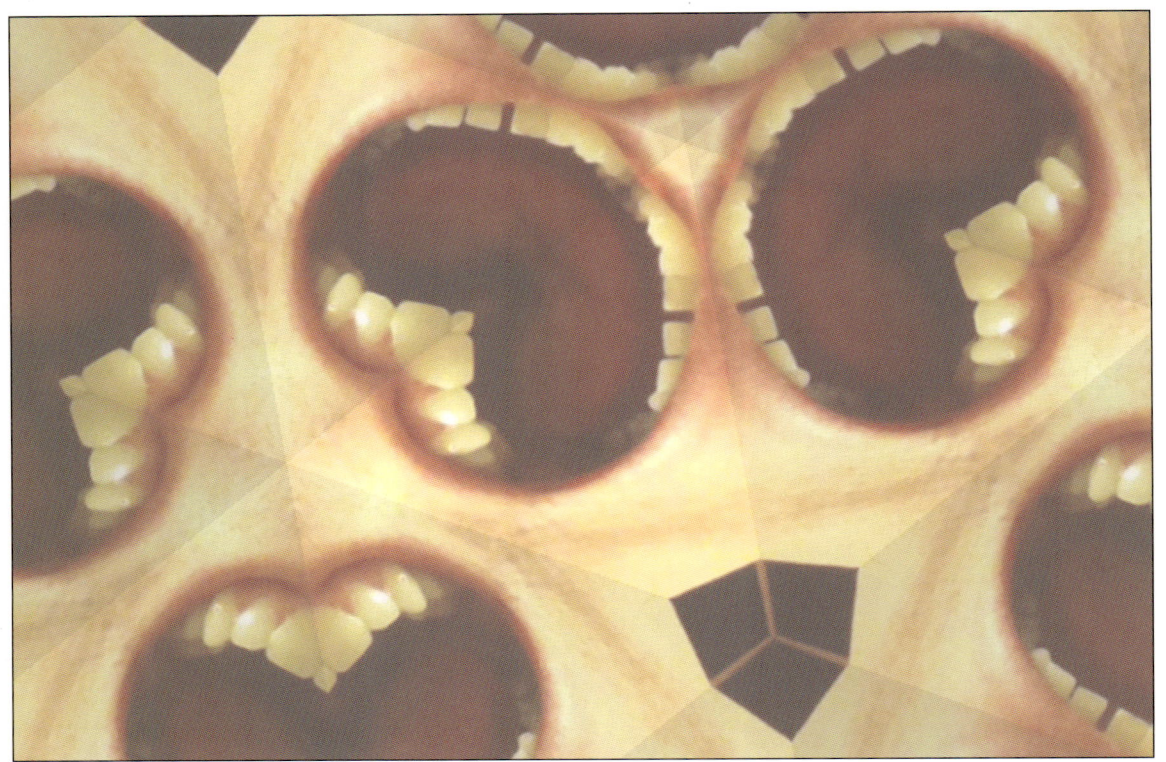

Wild Rover studies and photos; facing, interior page

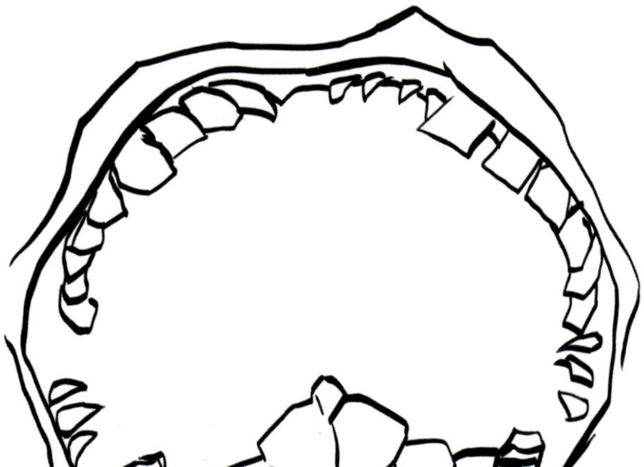

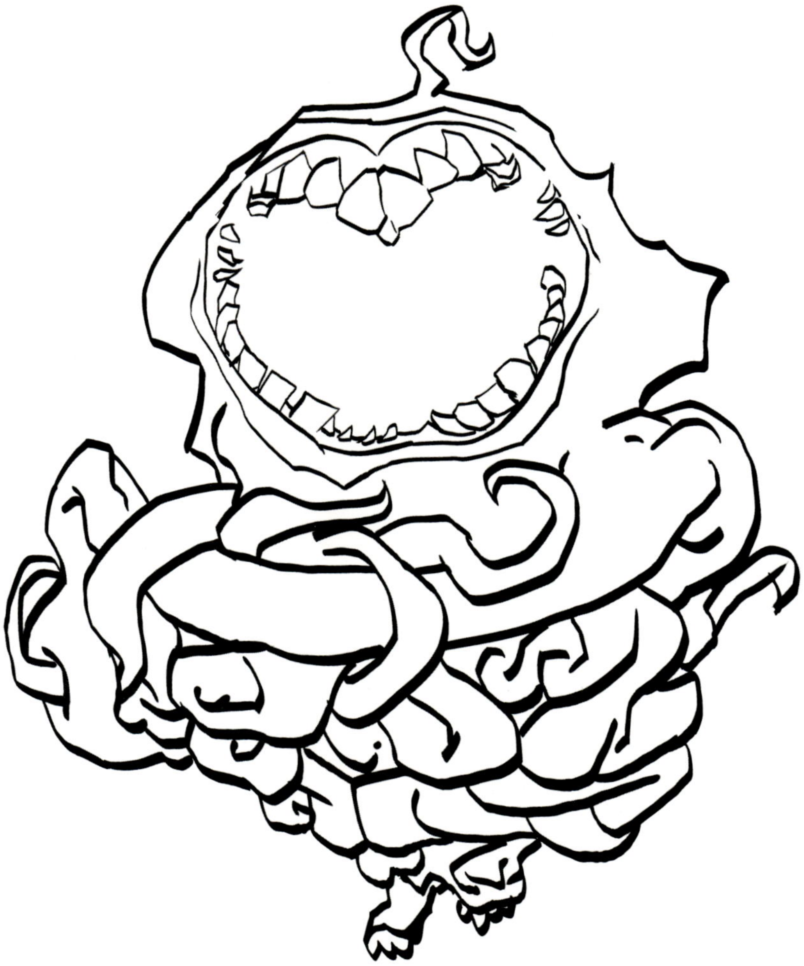

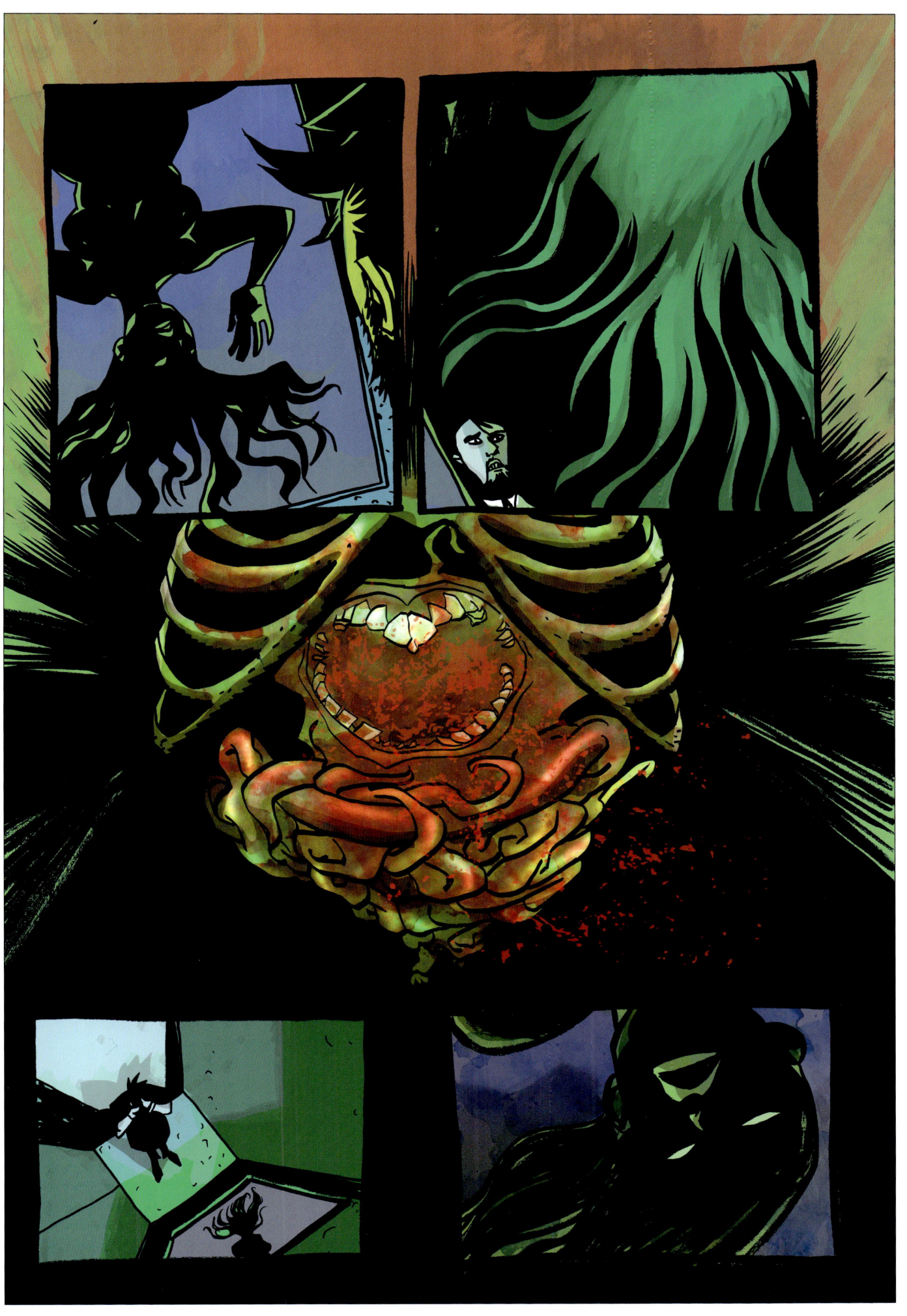

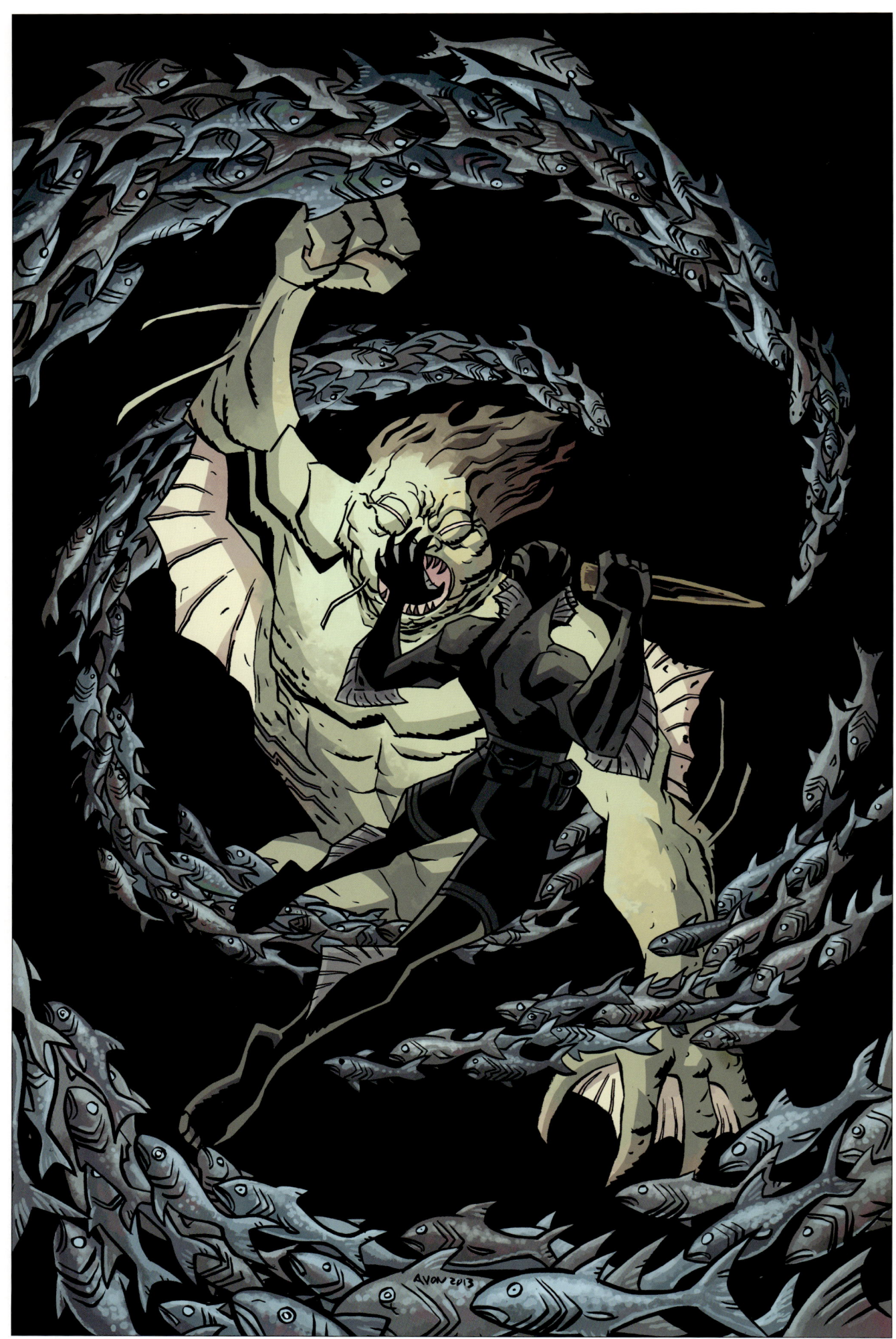

Cover for Mike Mignola's *Abe Sapien*, colored by Dave Stewart; facing, *Abe* pinup drawn and colored by Oeming

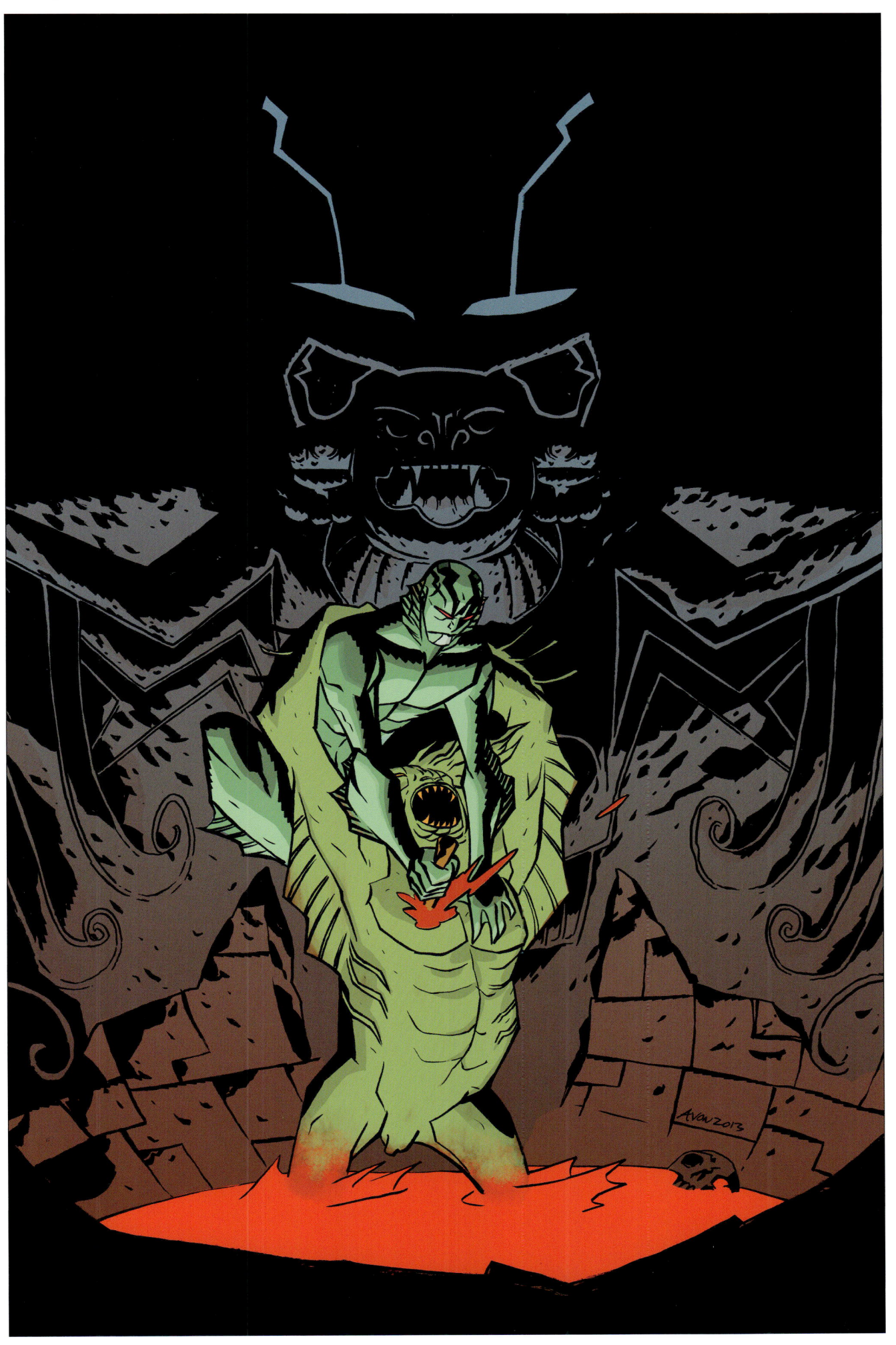

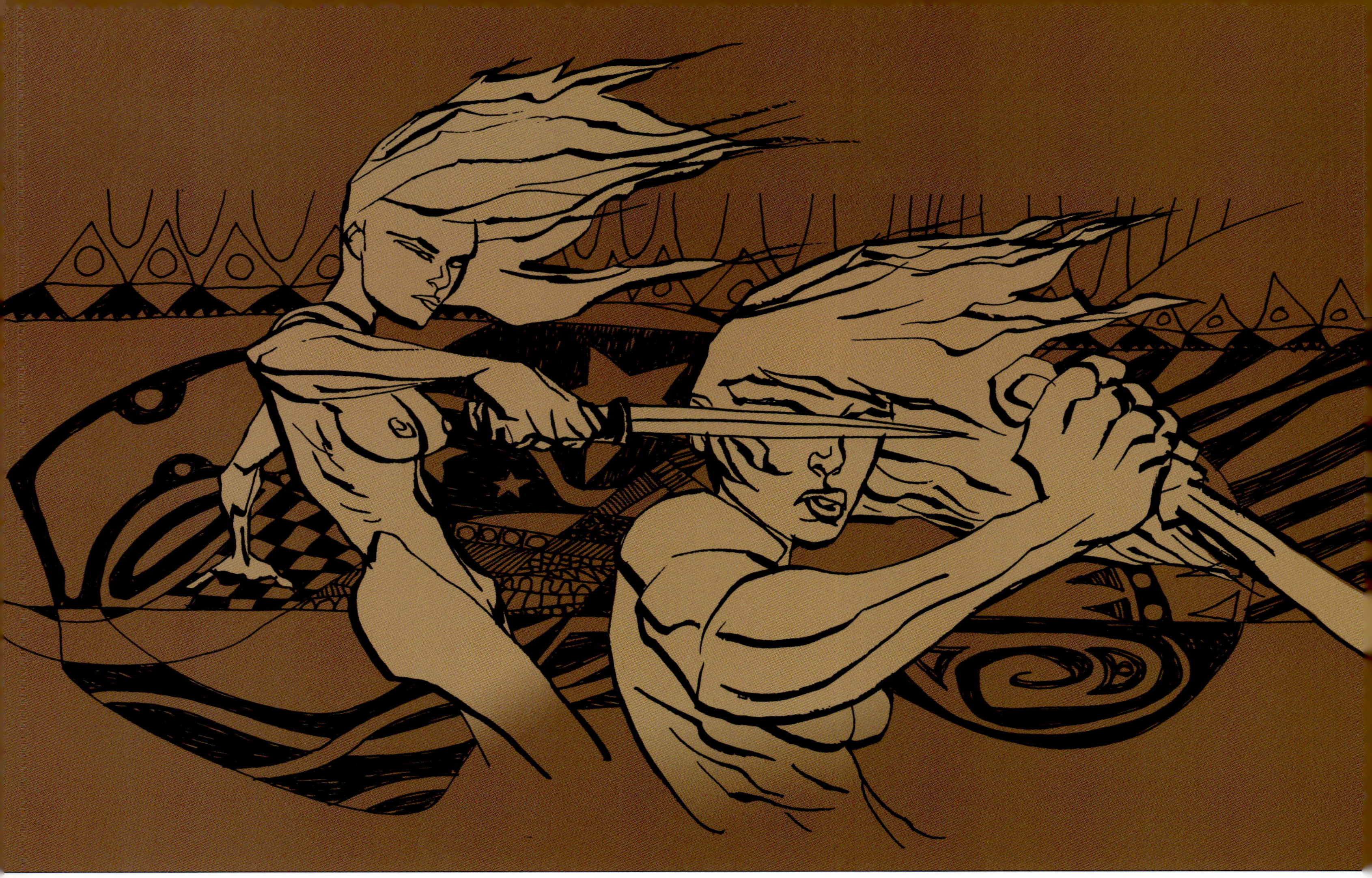

I love sketchbooks, just working out ideas, mood, and inspirations.

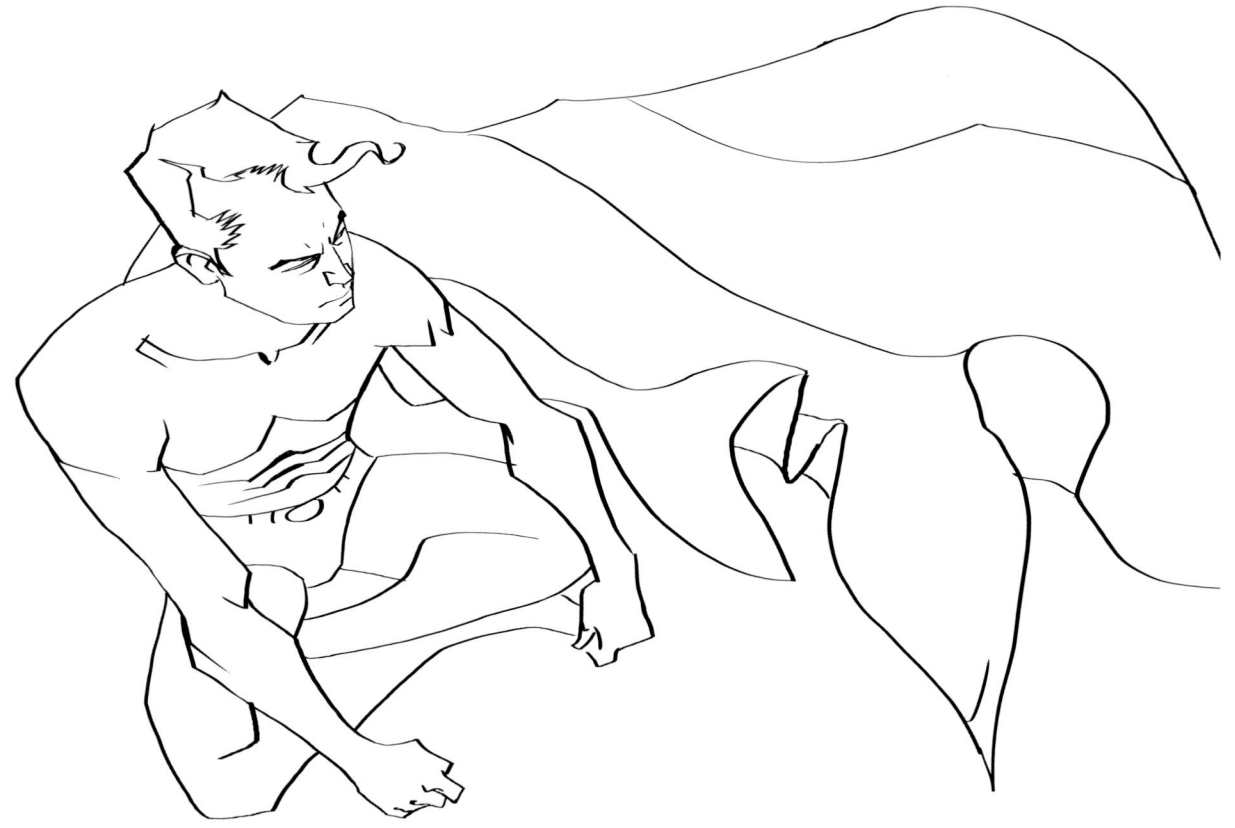

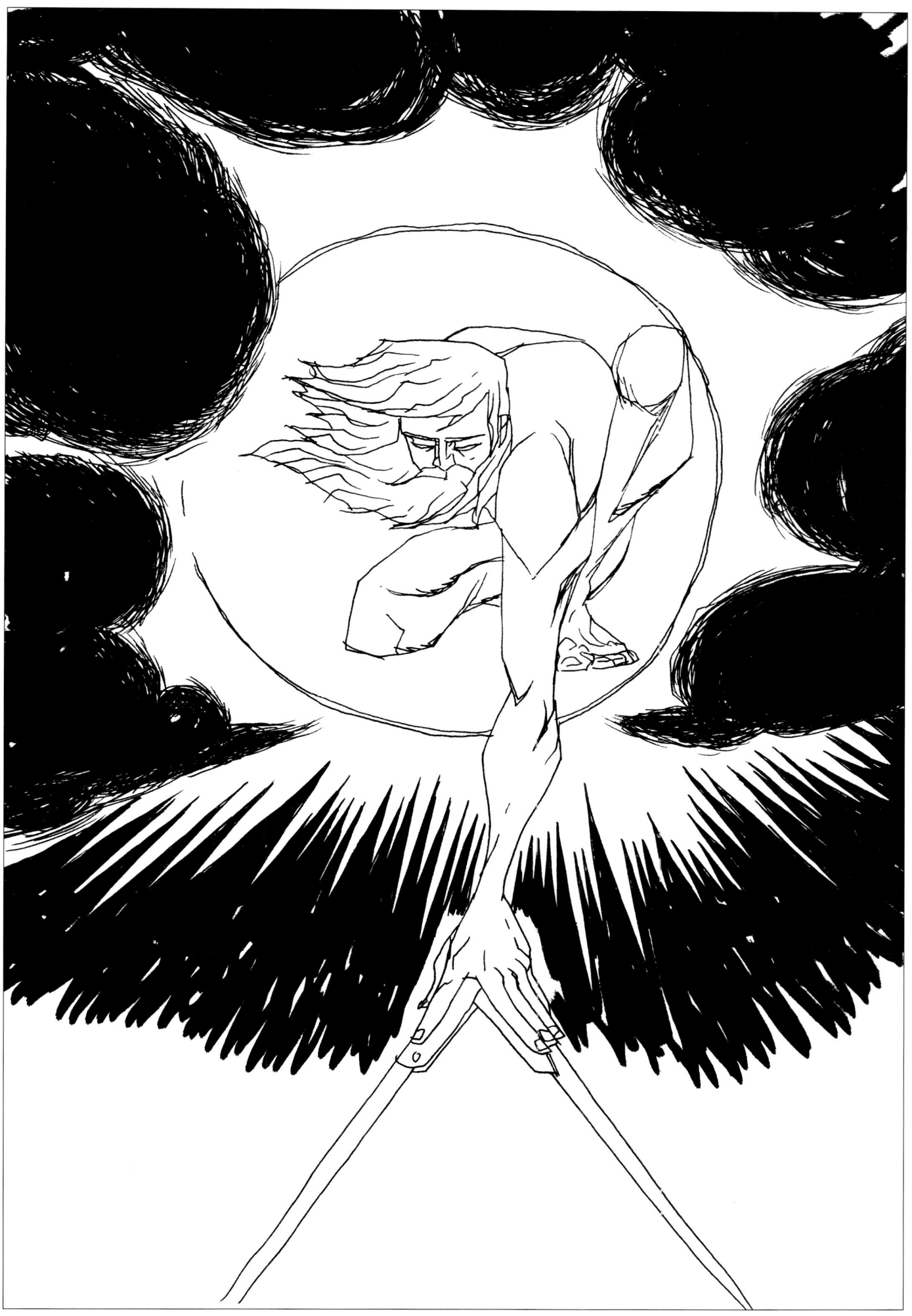

After William Blake

NO PLAN B: THE ART OF MICHAEL AVON OEMING

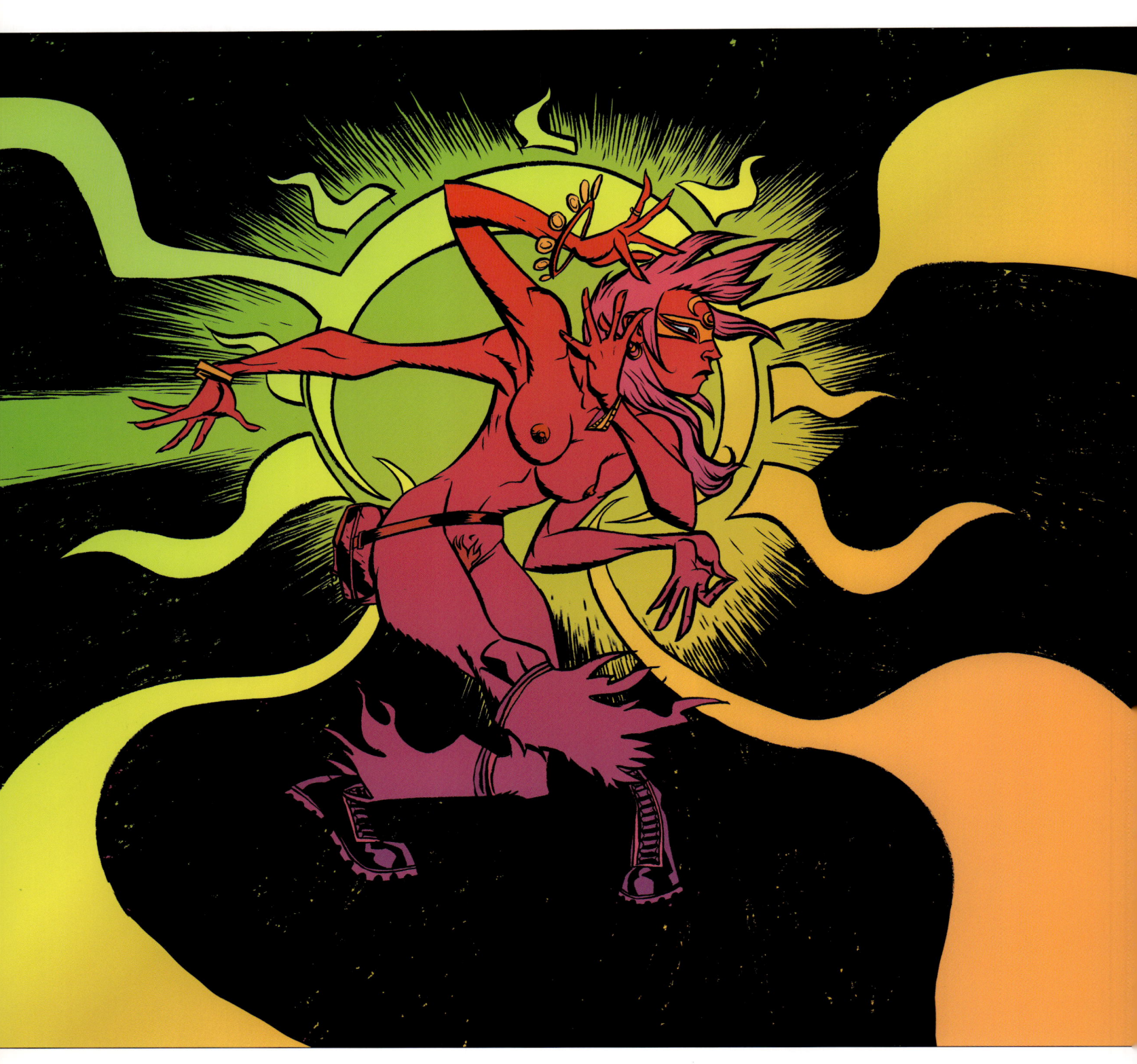

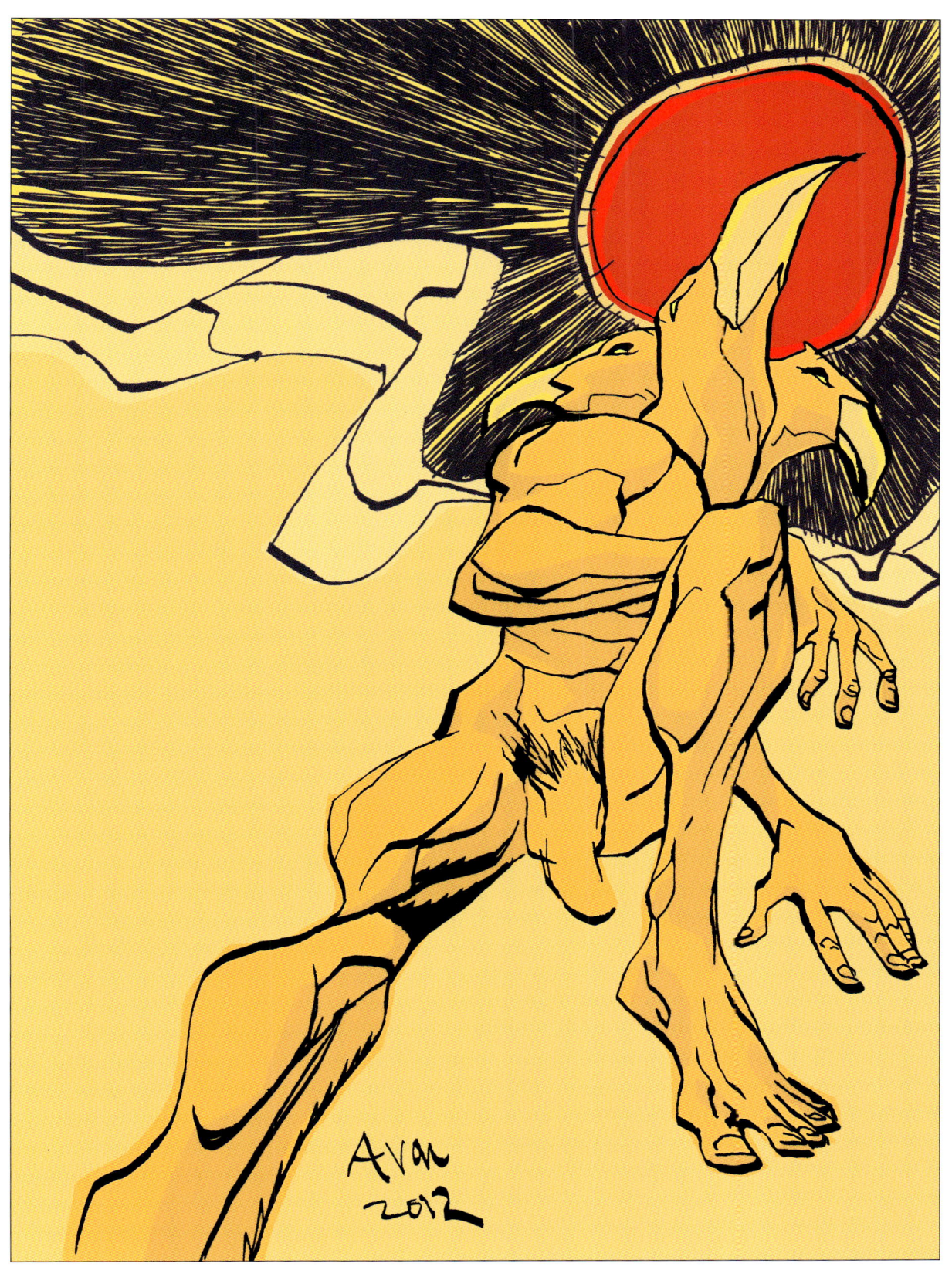

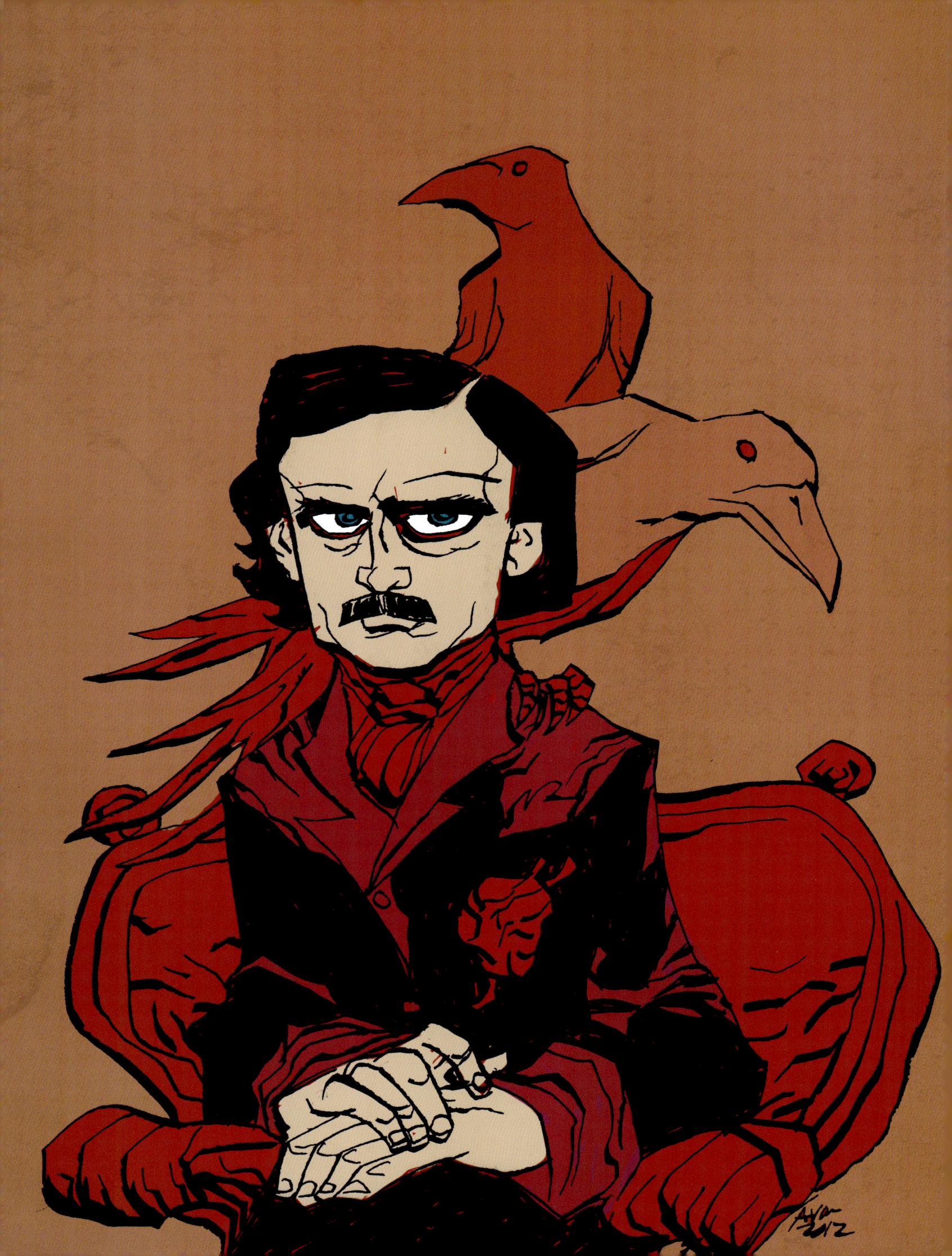

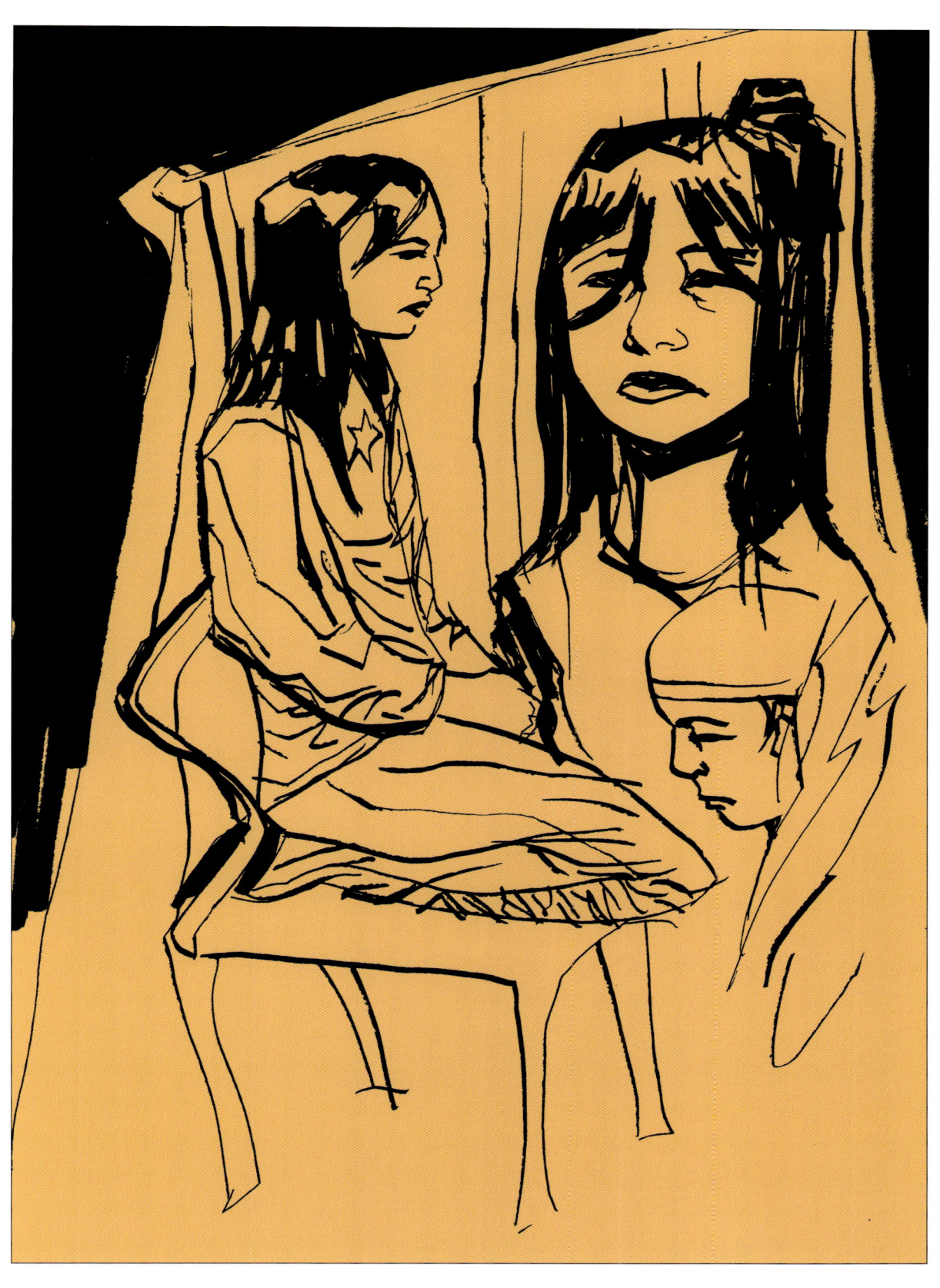

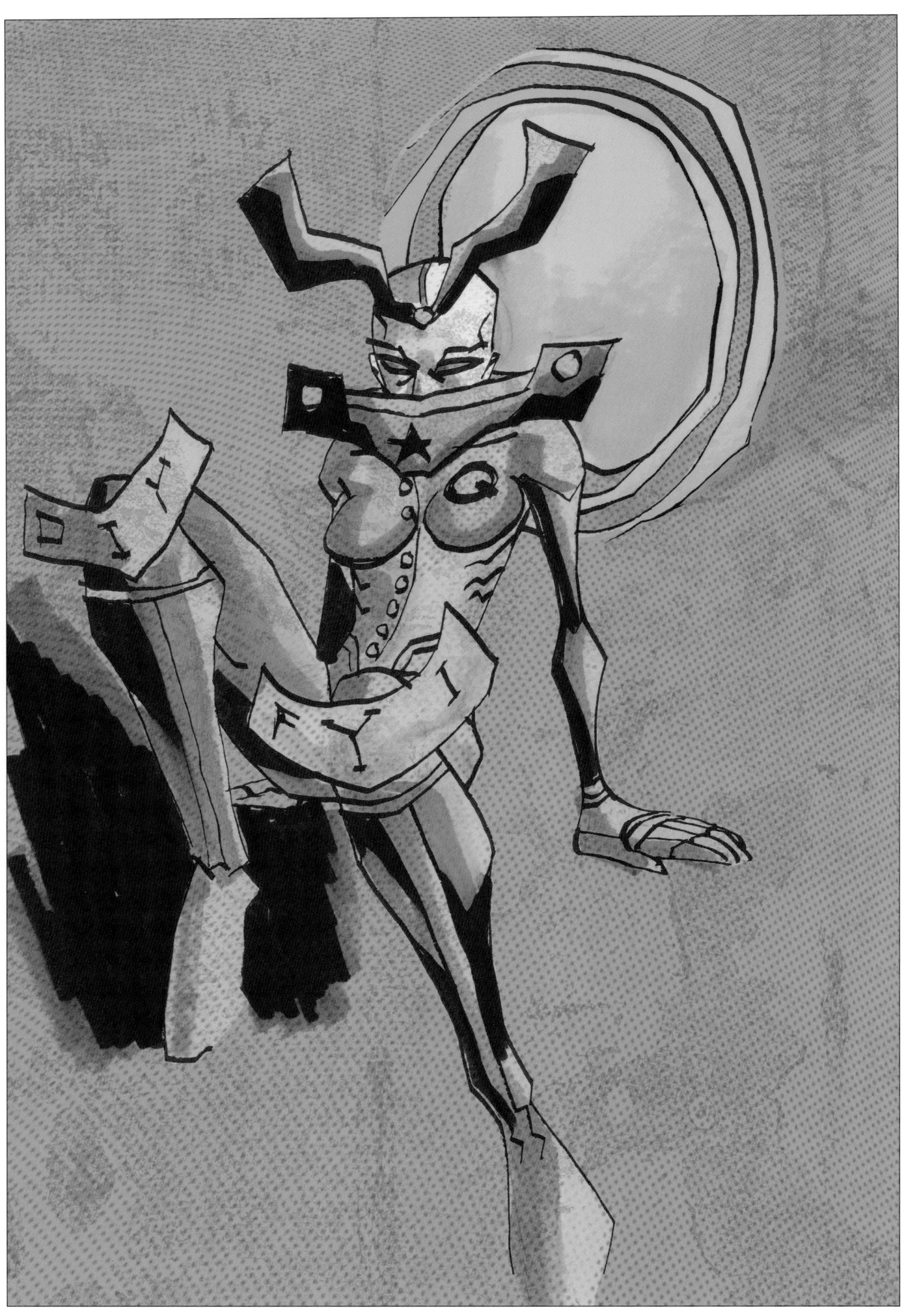

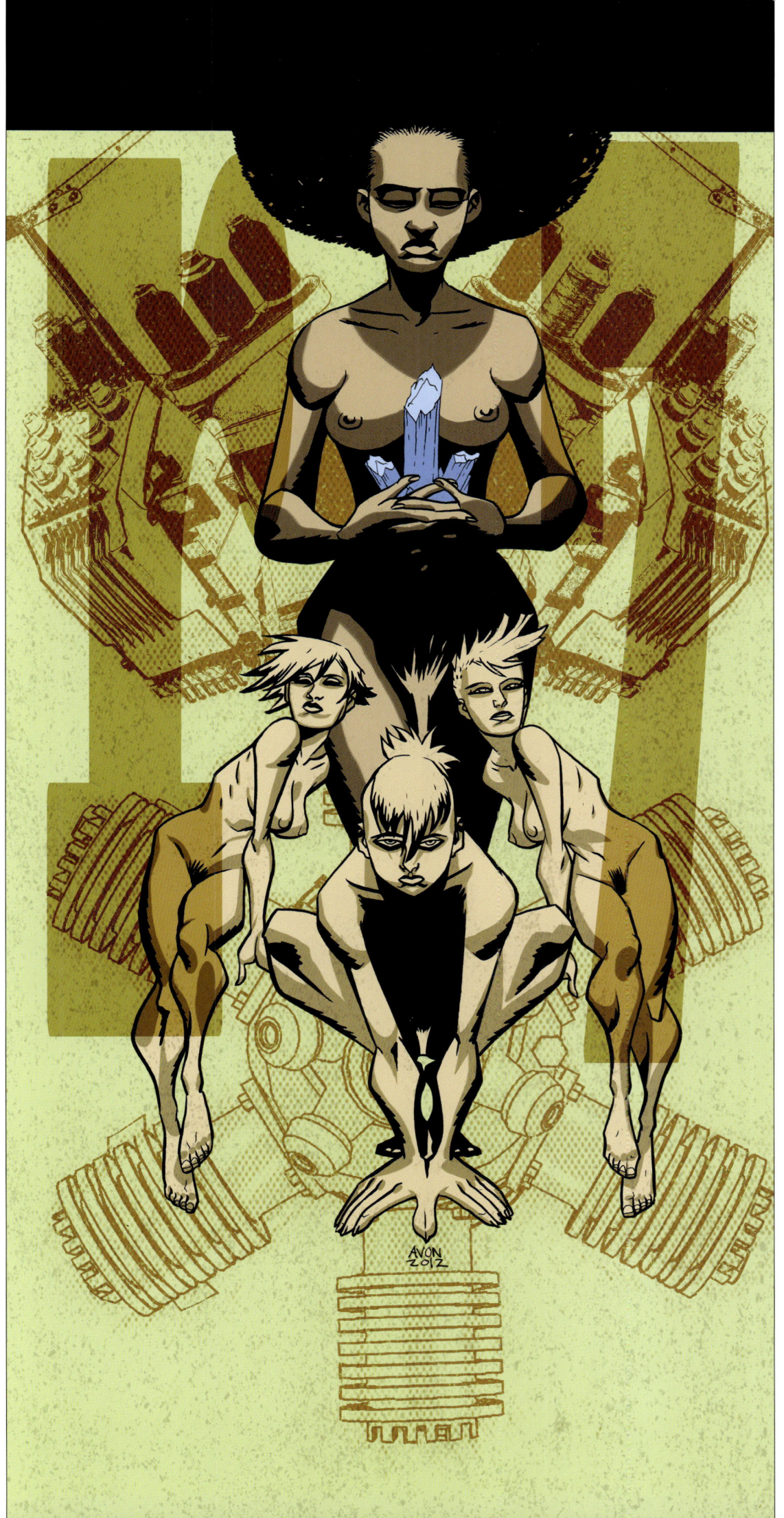

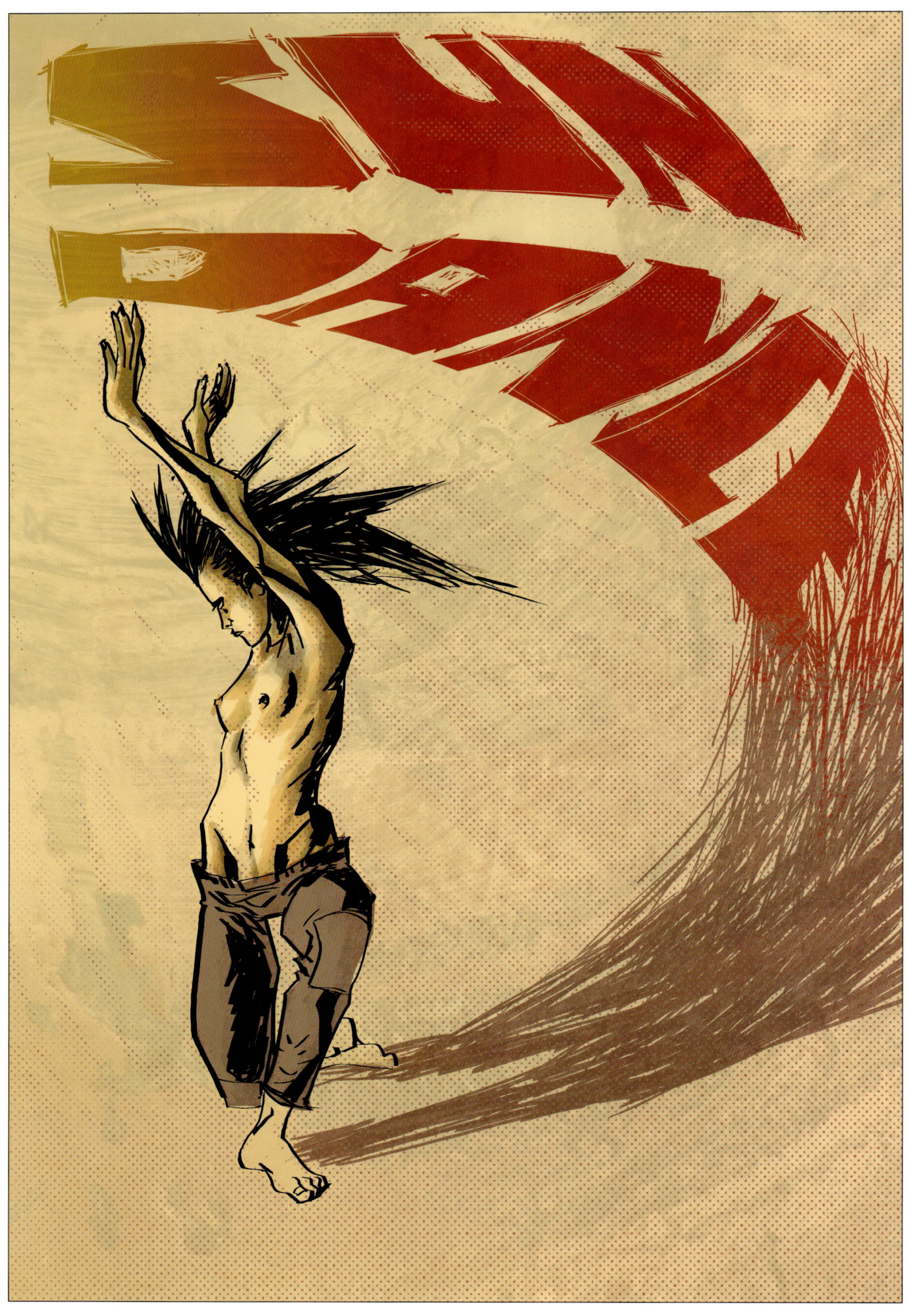

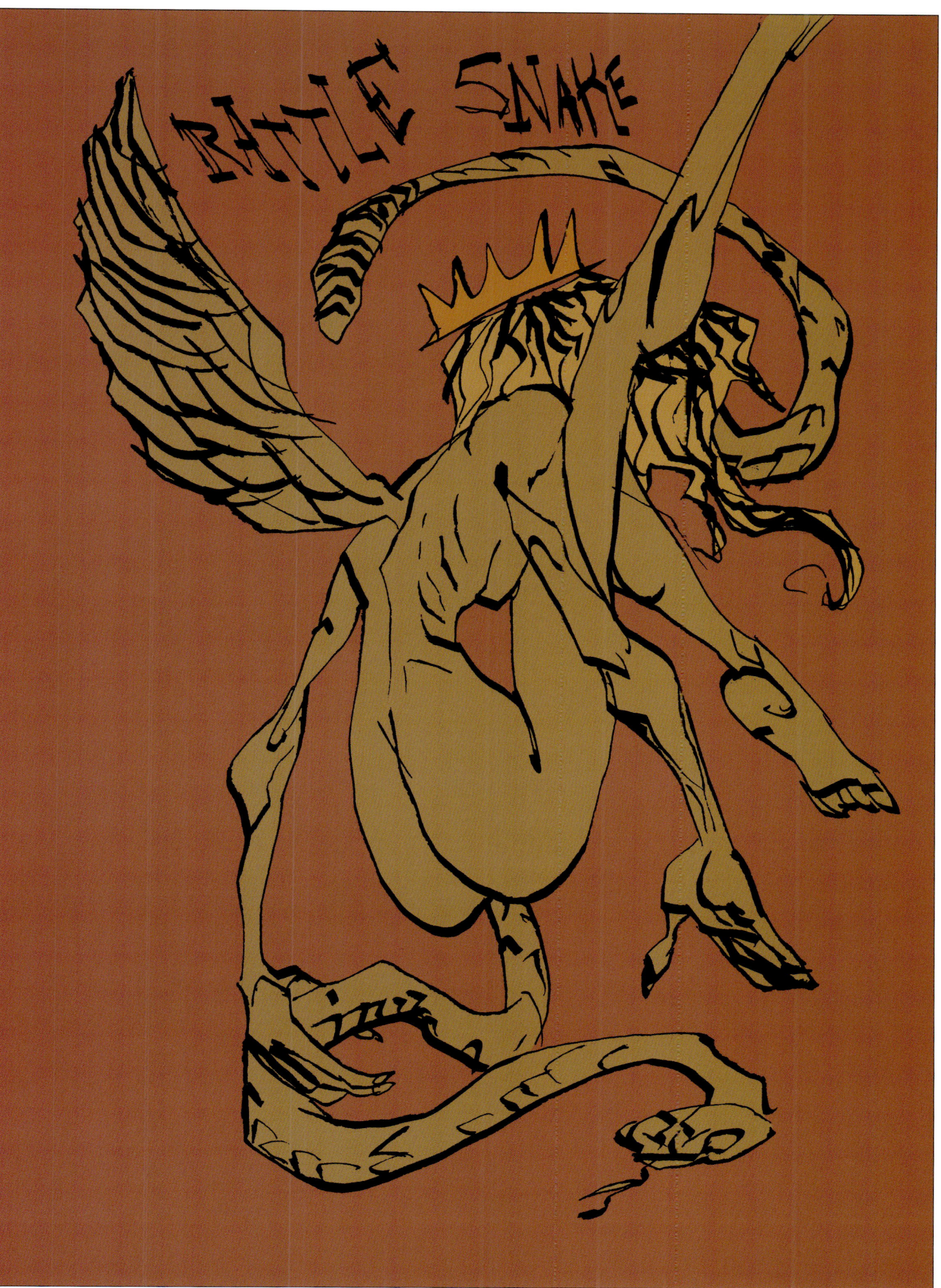

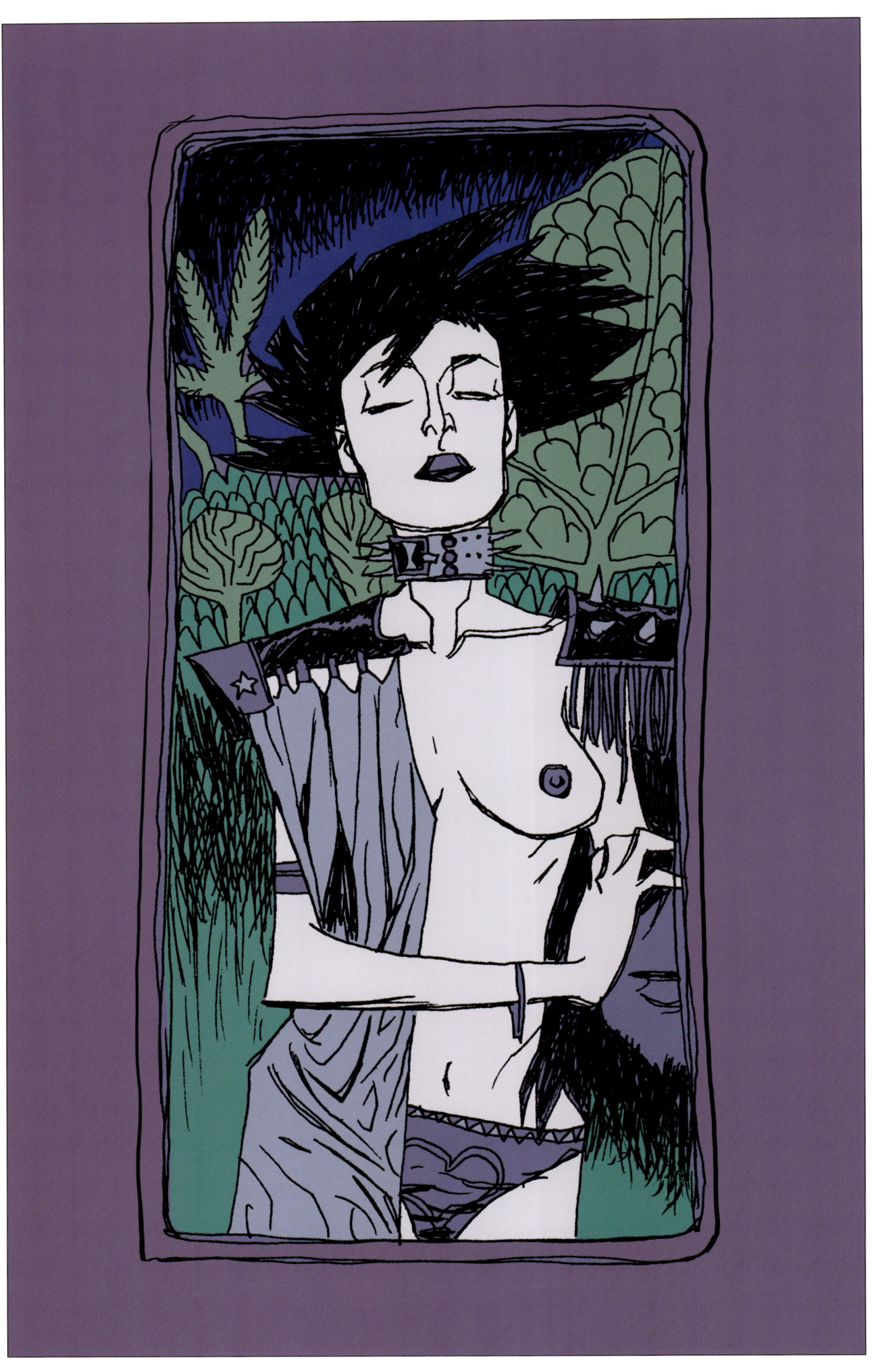

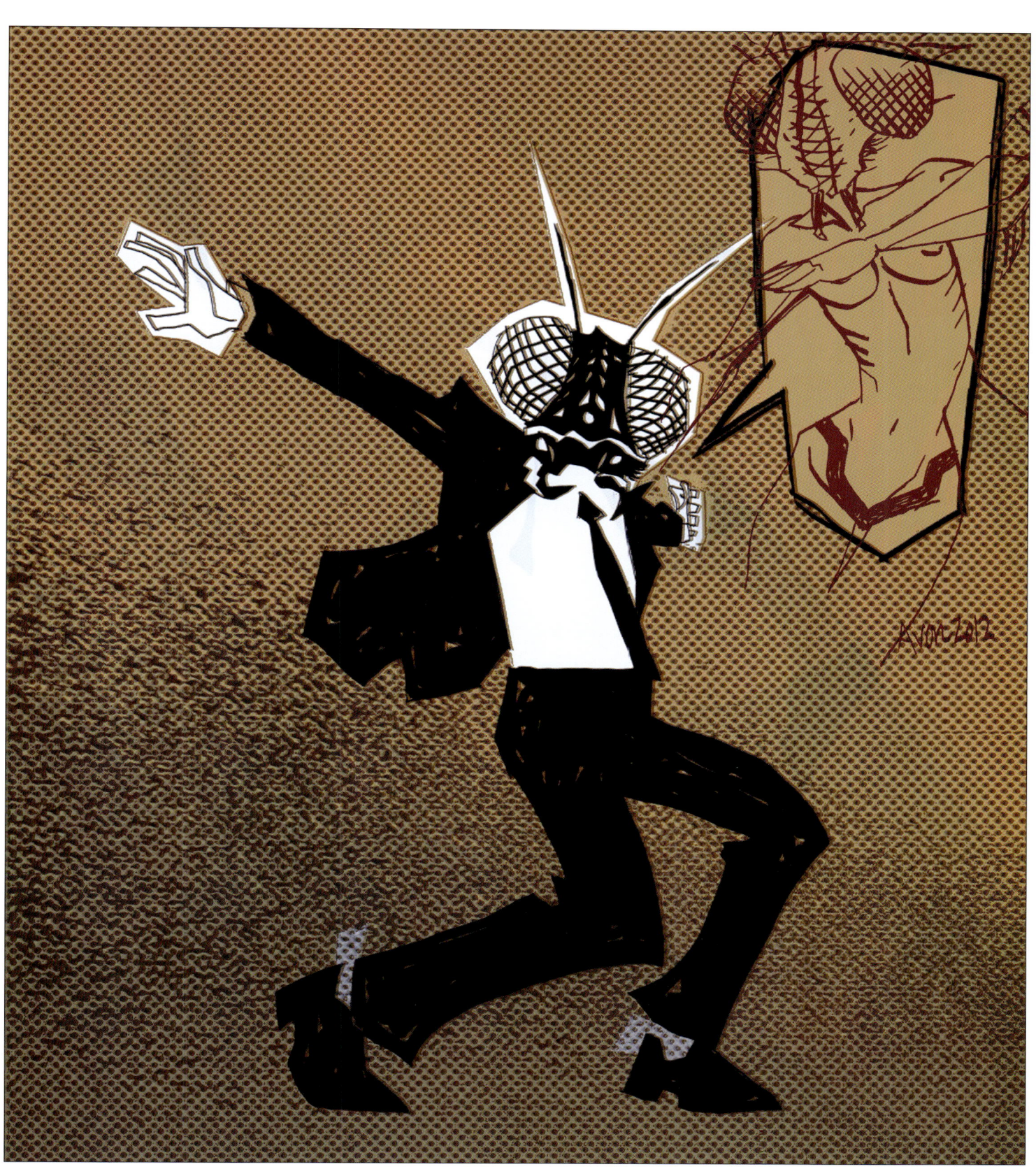

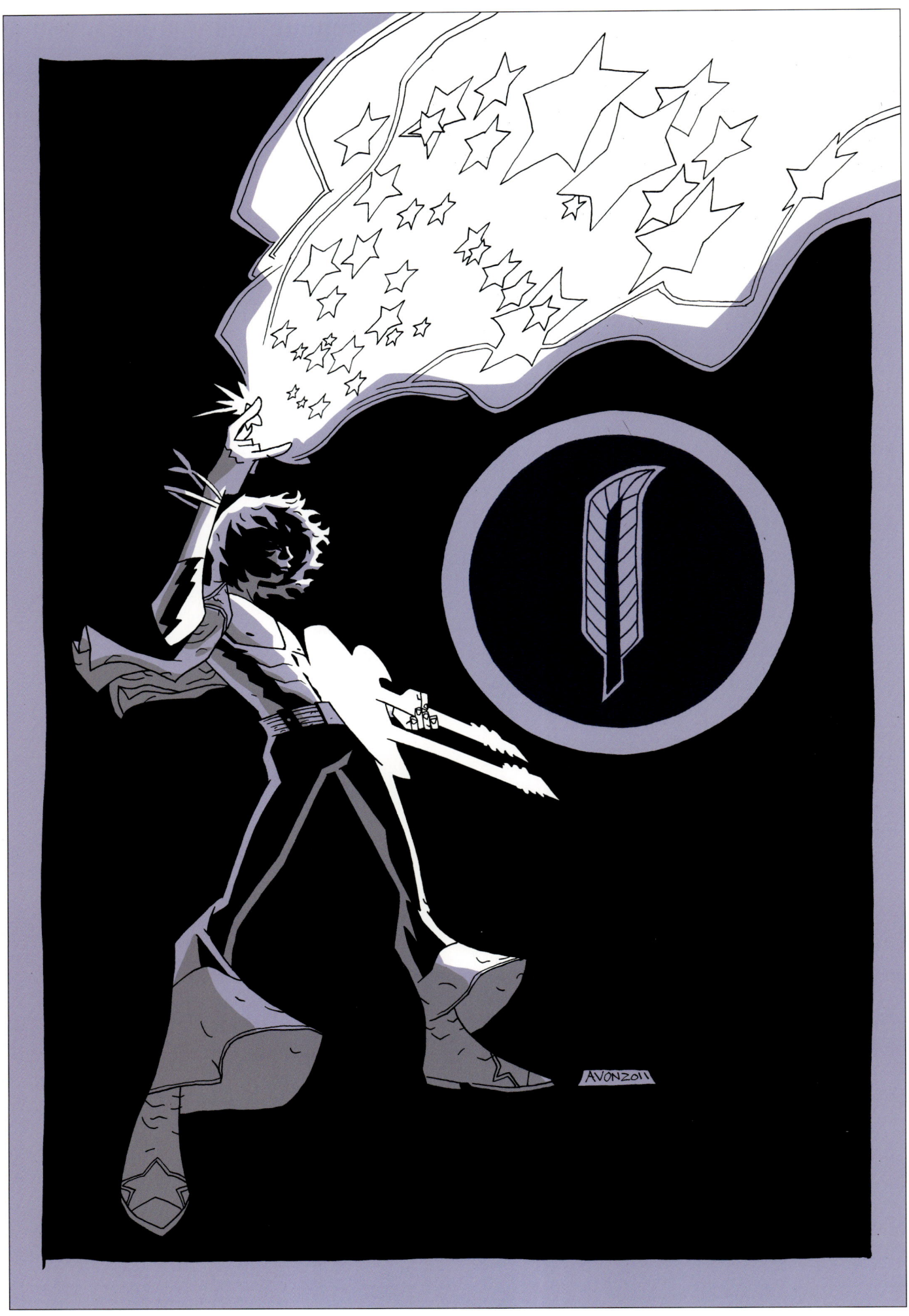
Jimmy Page

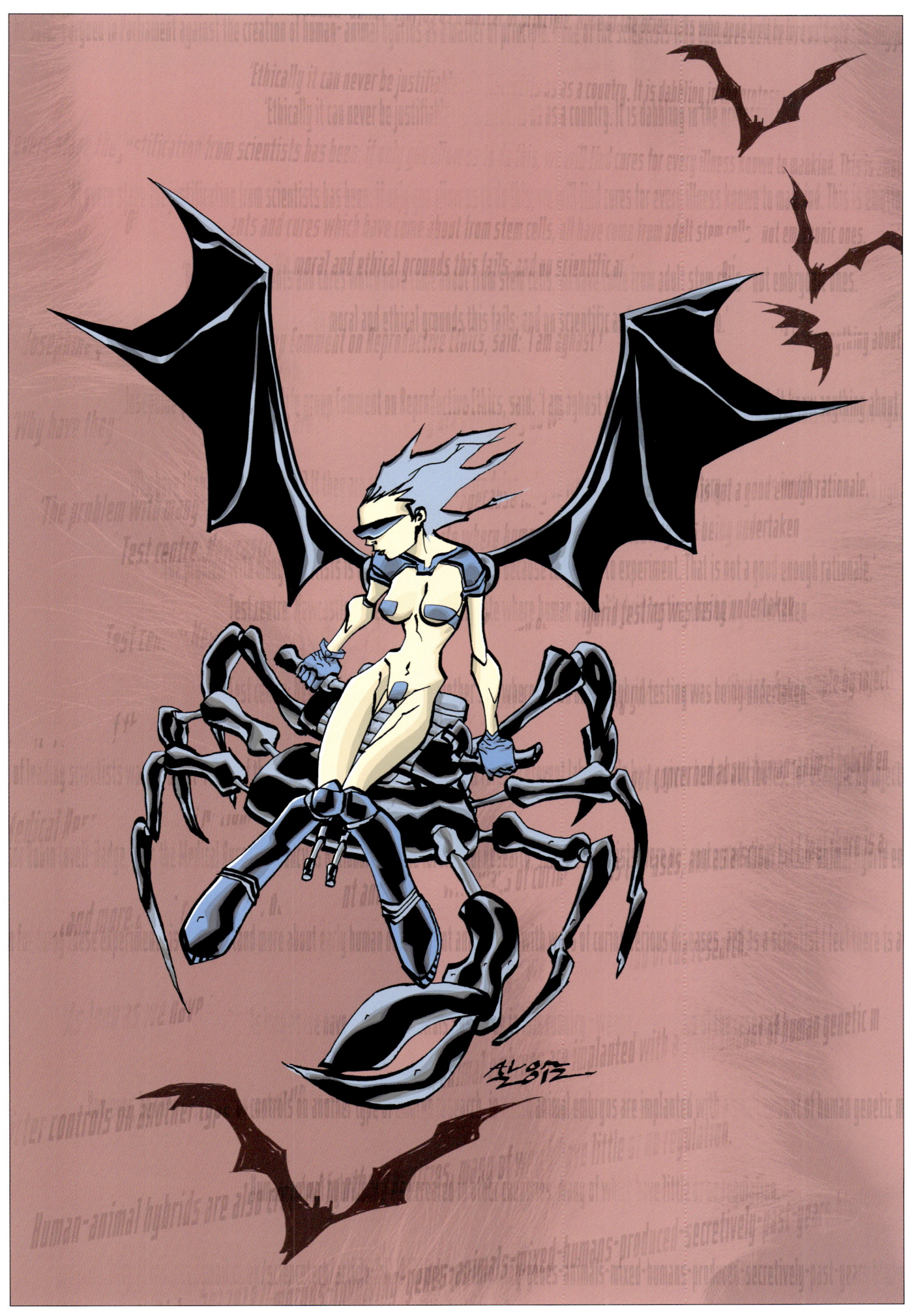

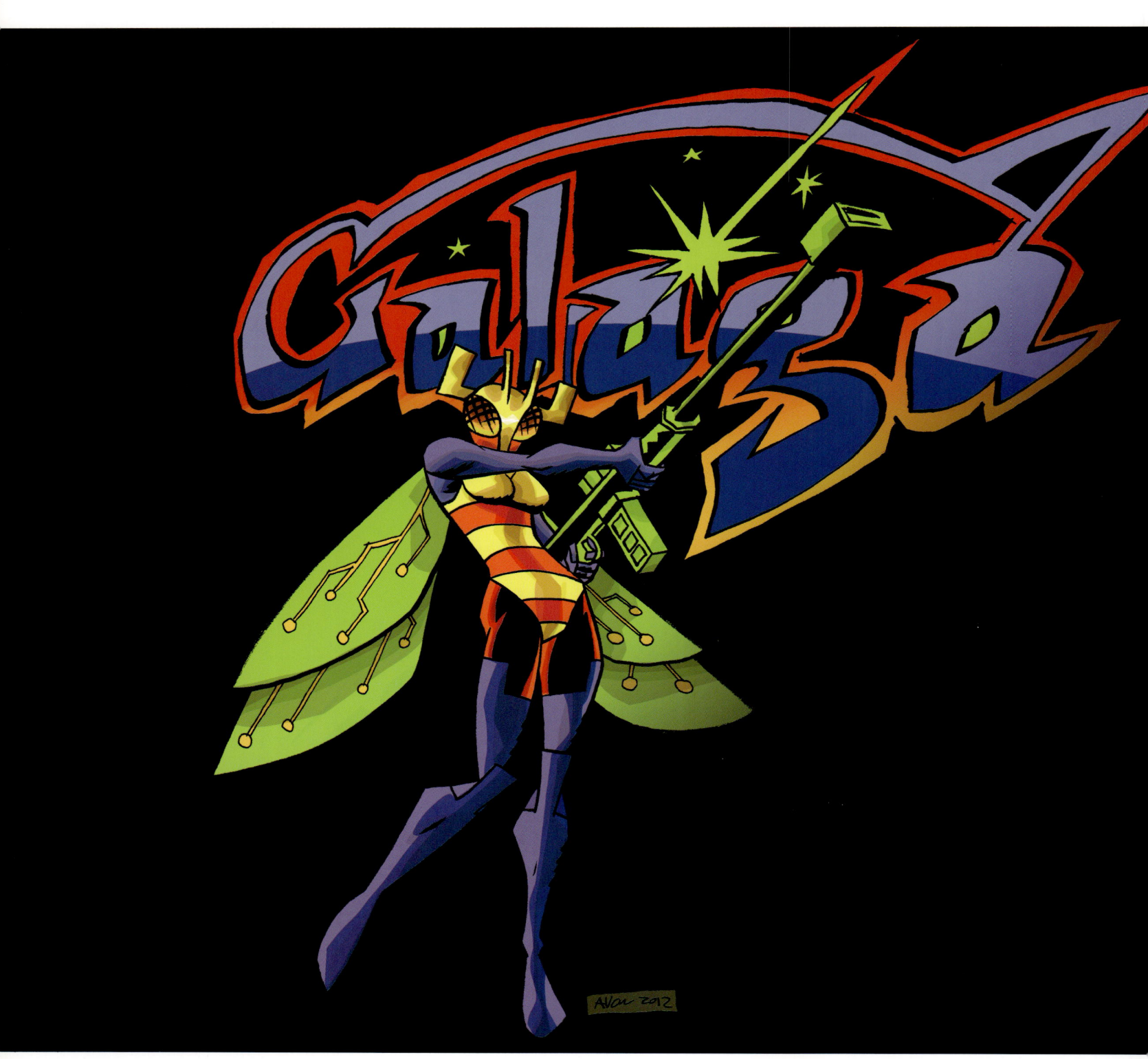

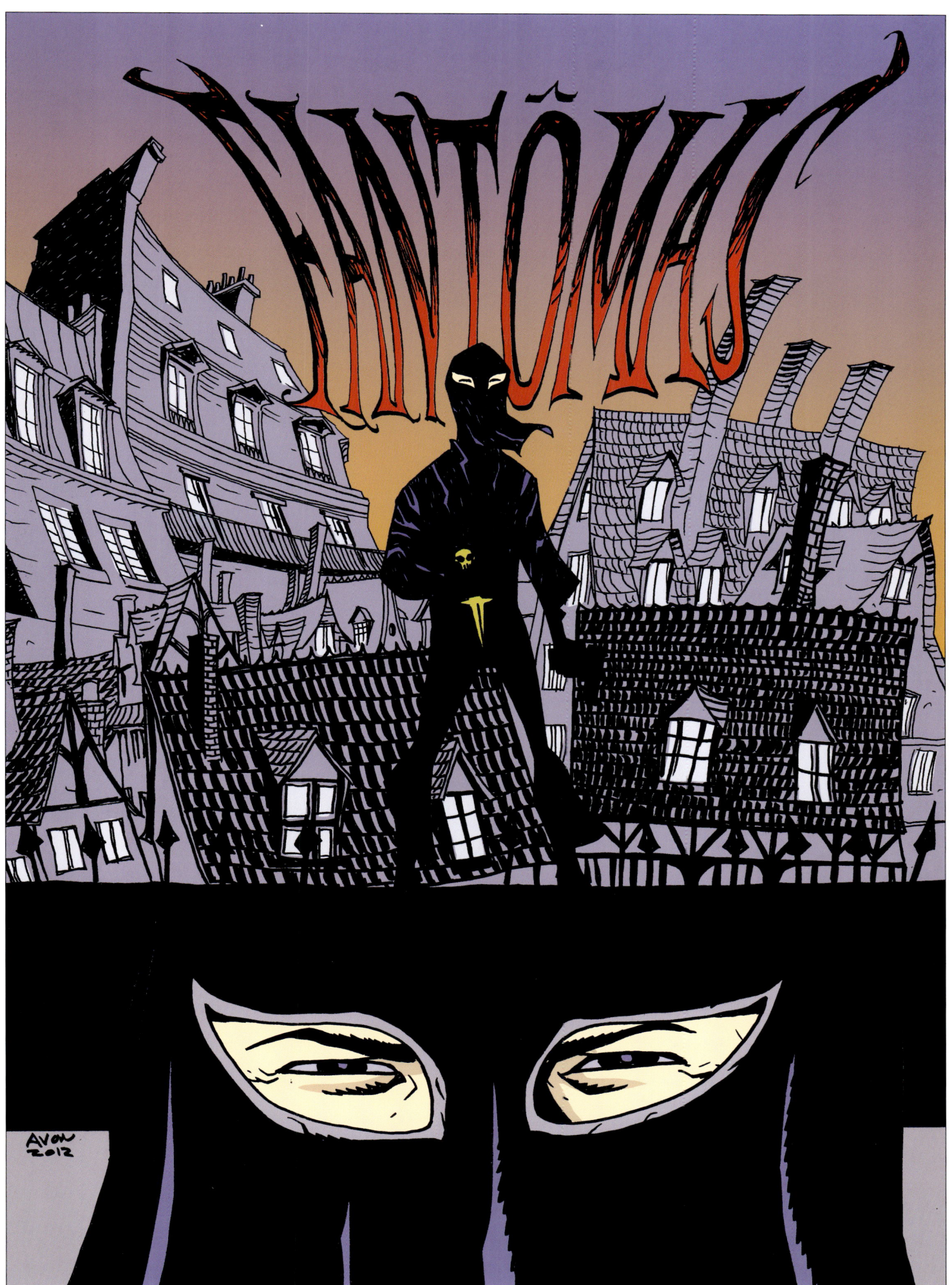

Pinup for Emerald City Comicon's annual *Monsters and Dames* portfolio

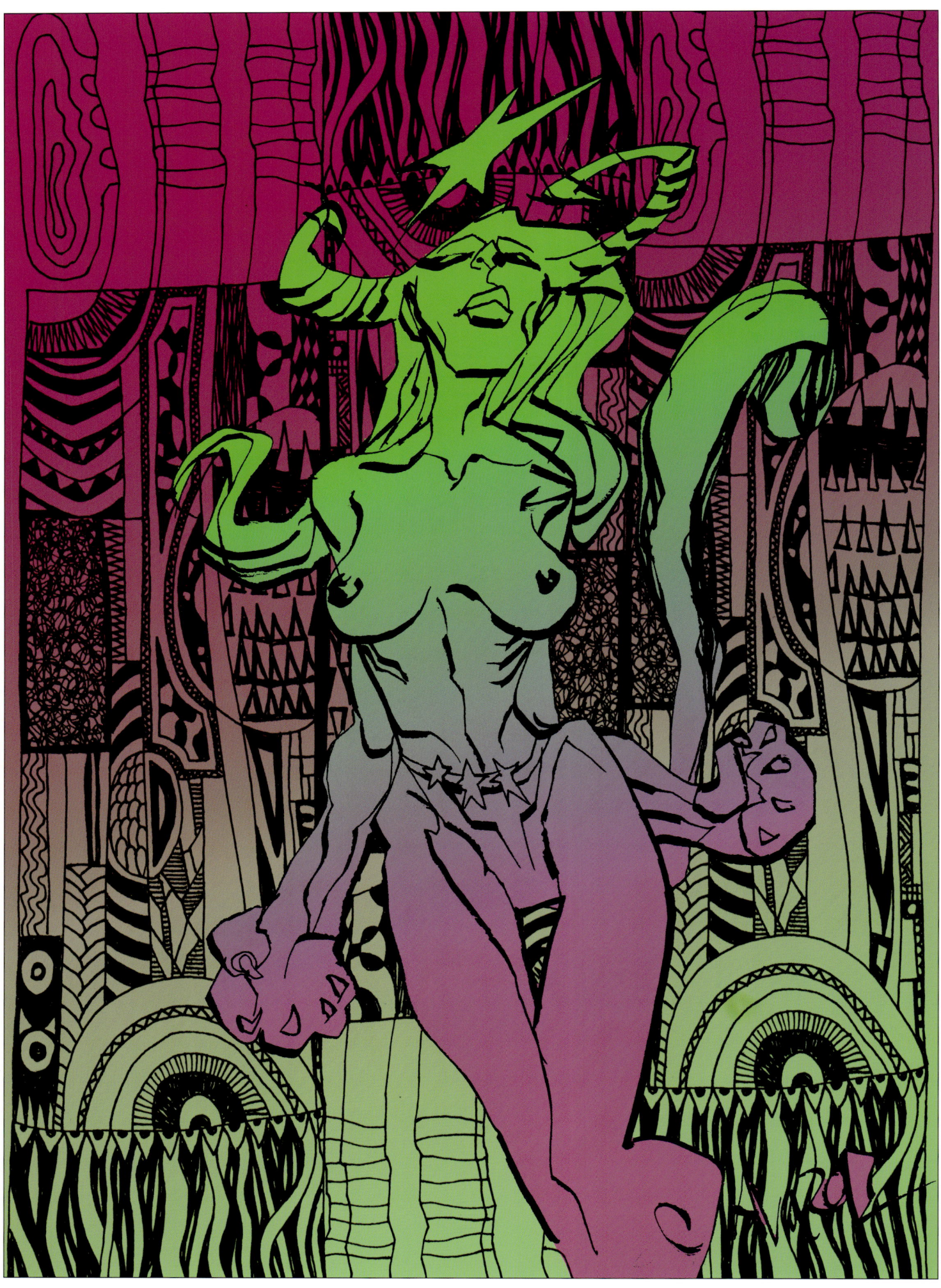

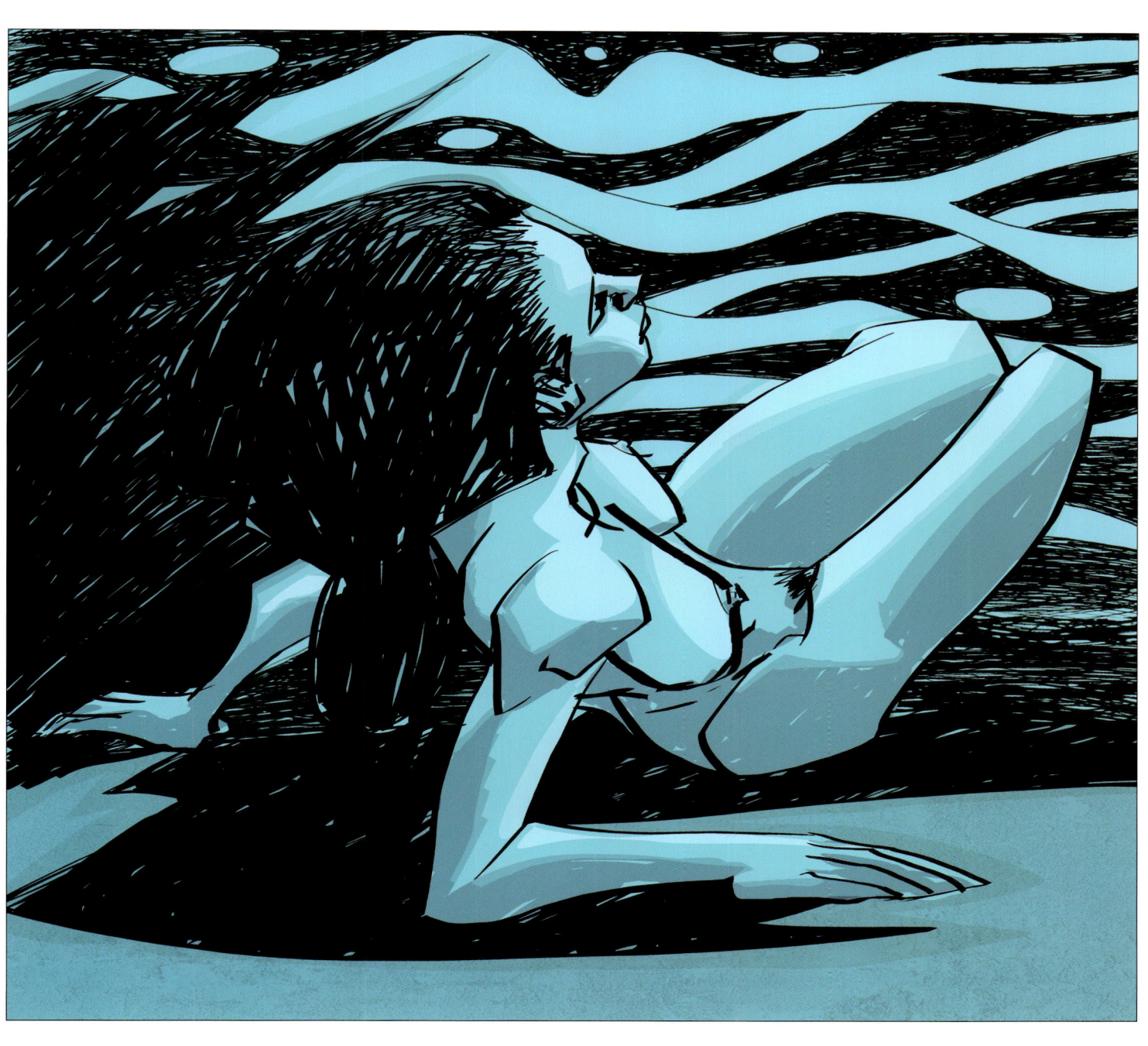

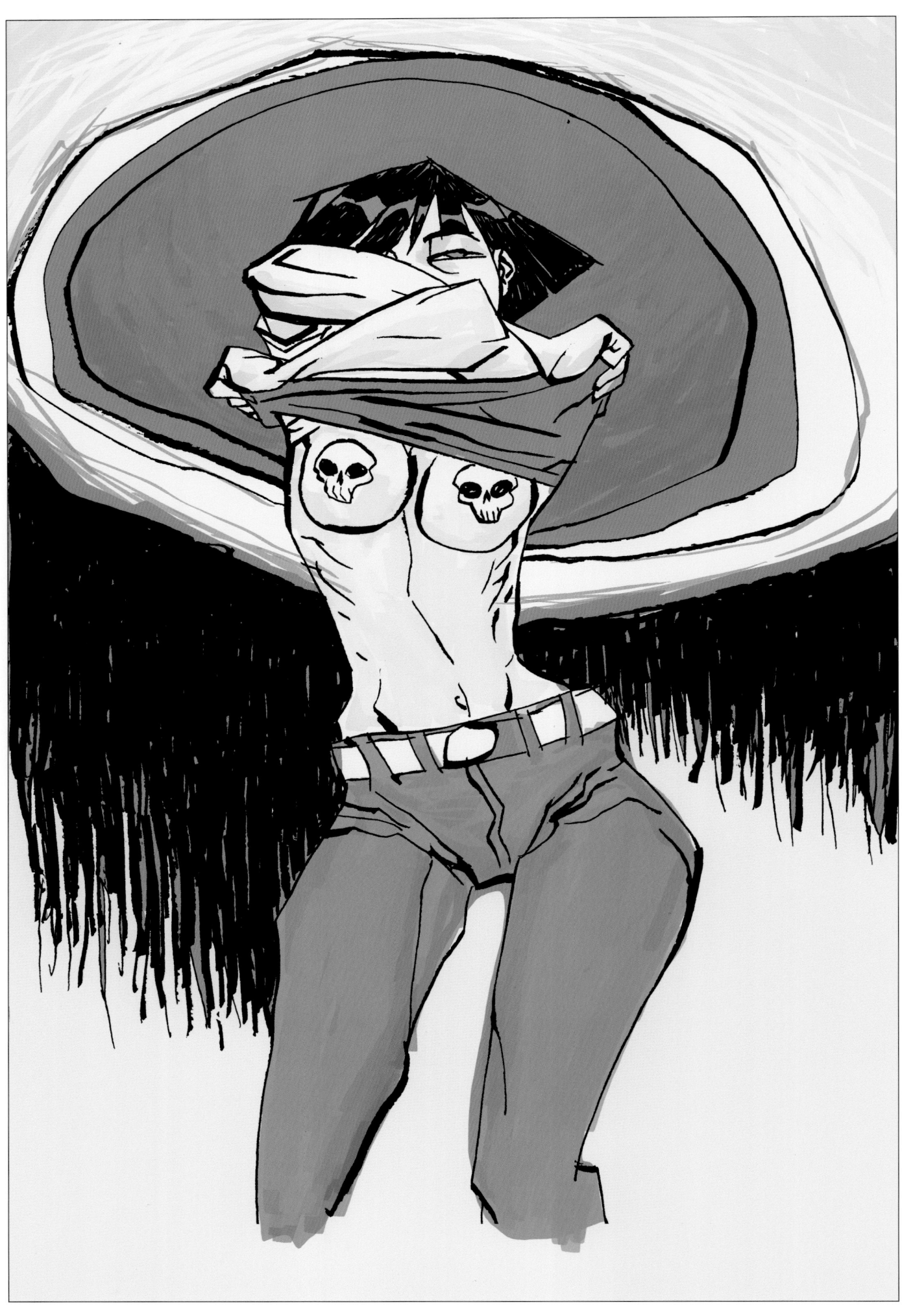

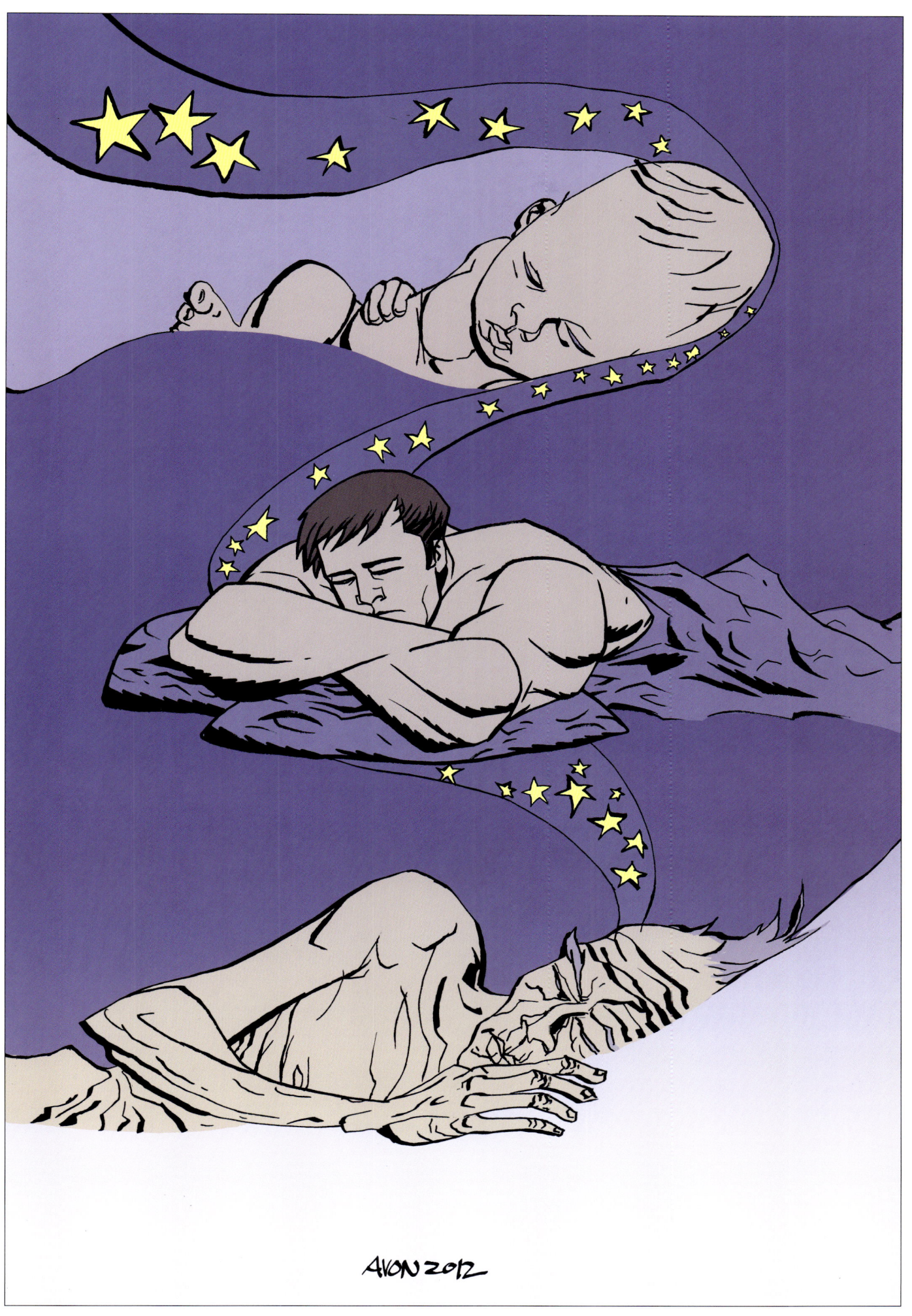

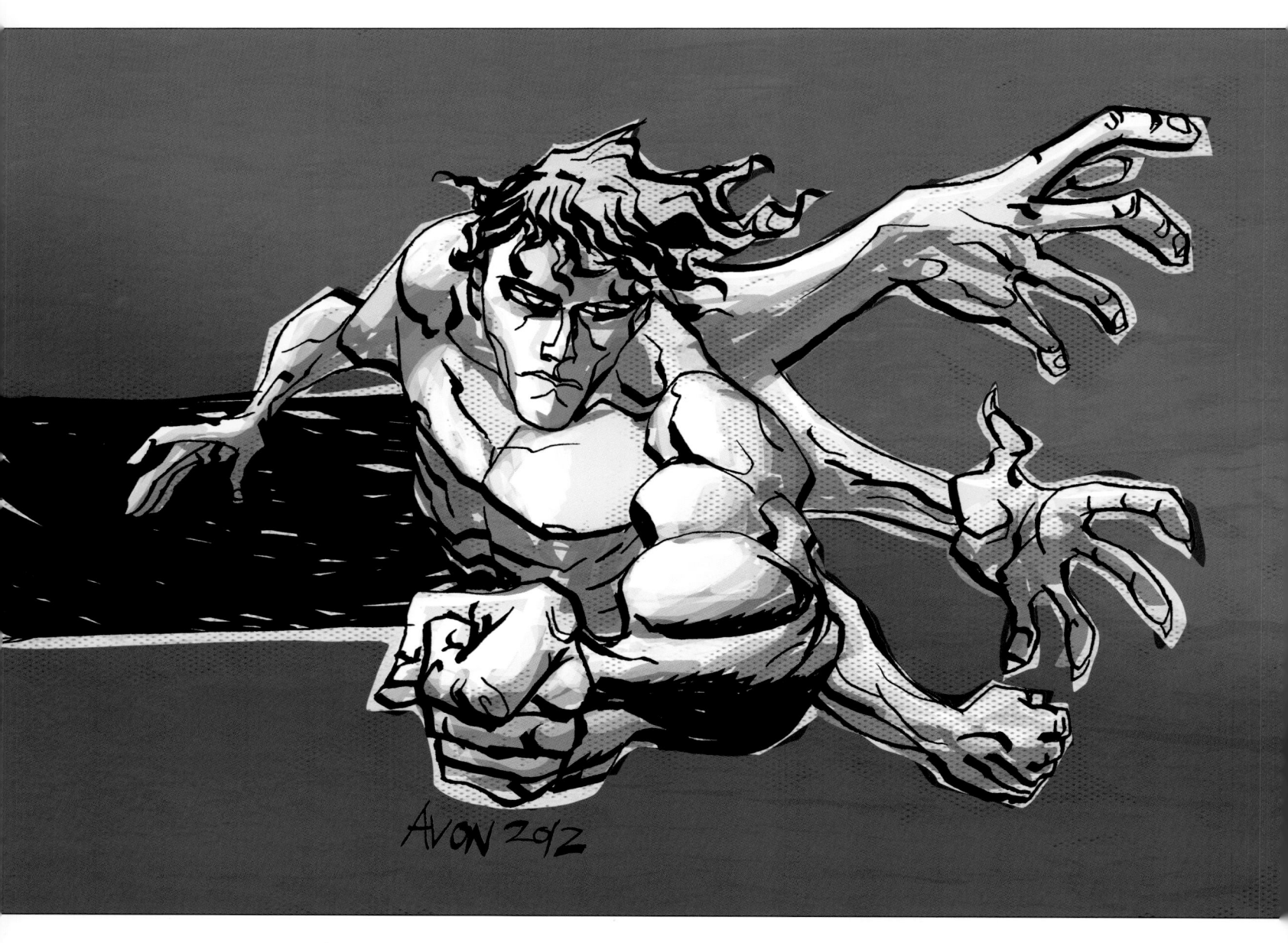

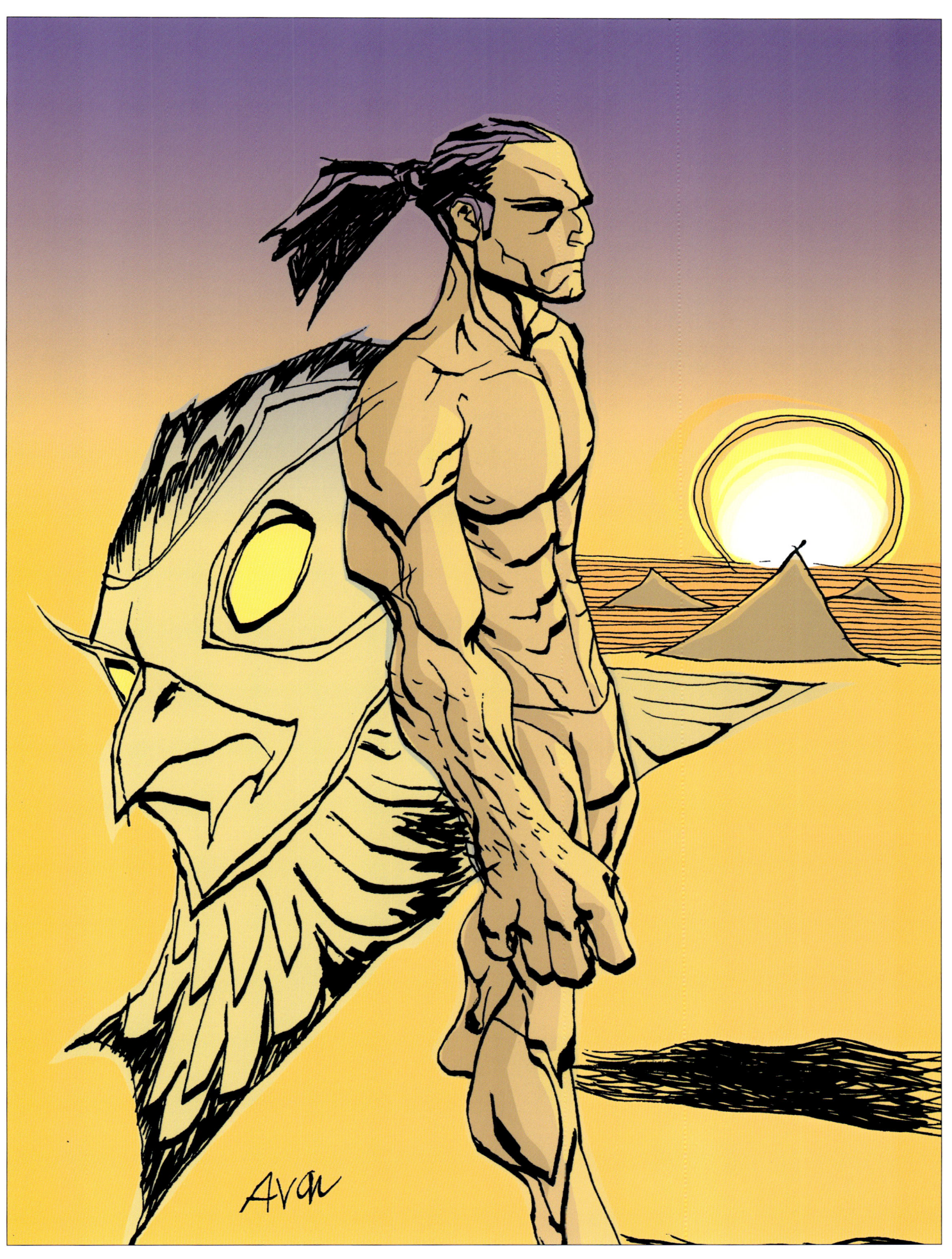

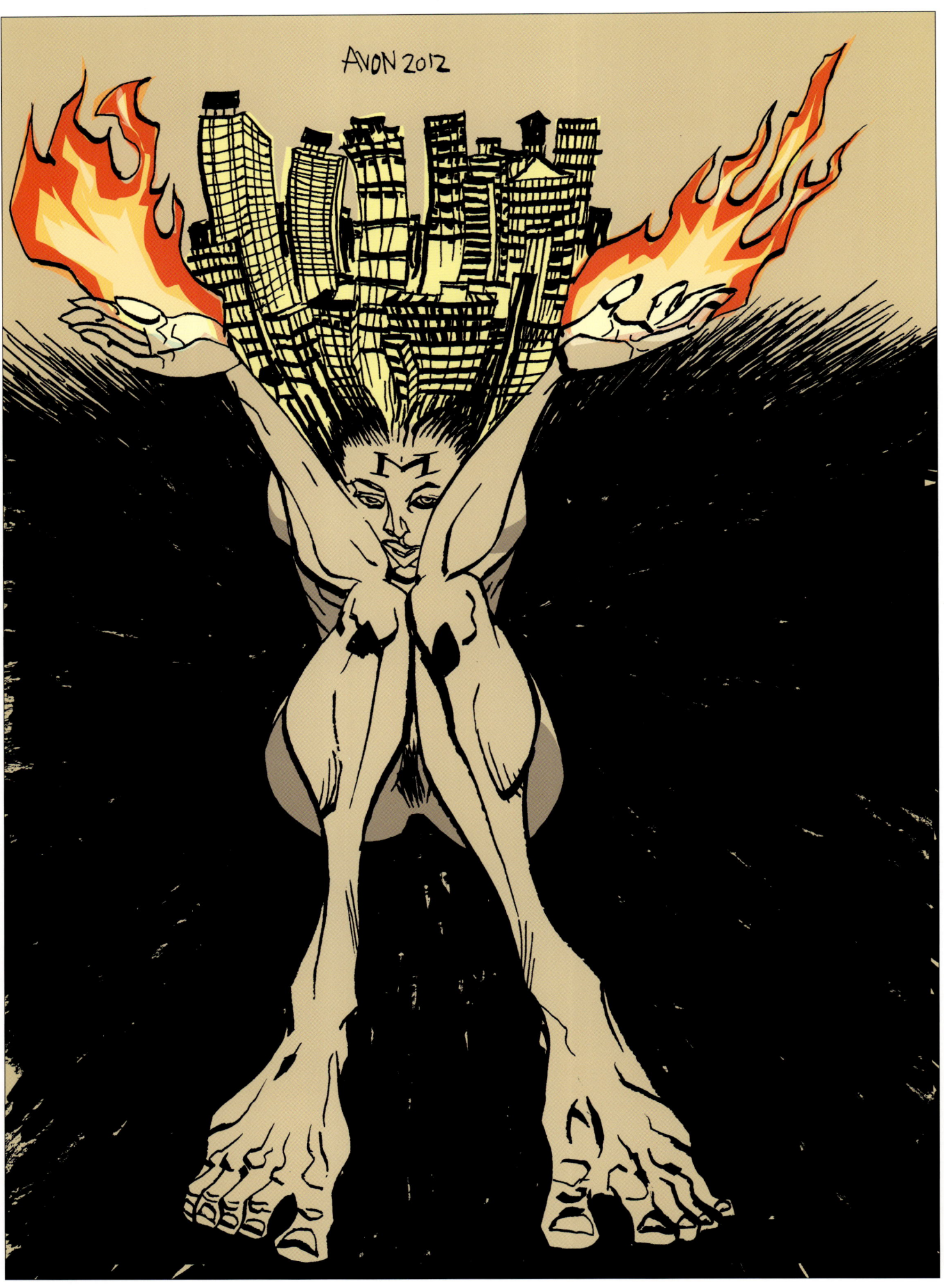

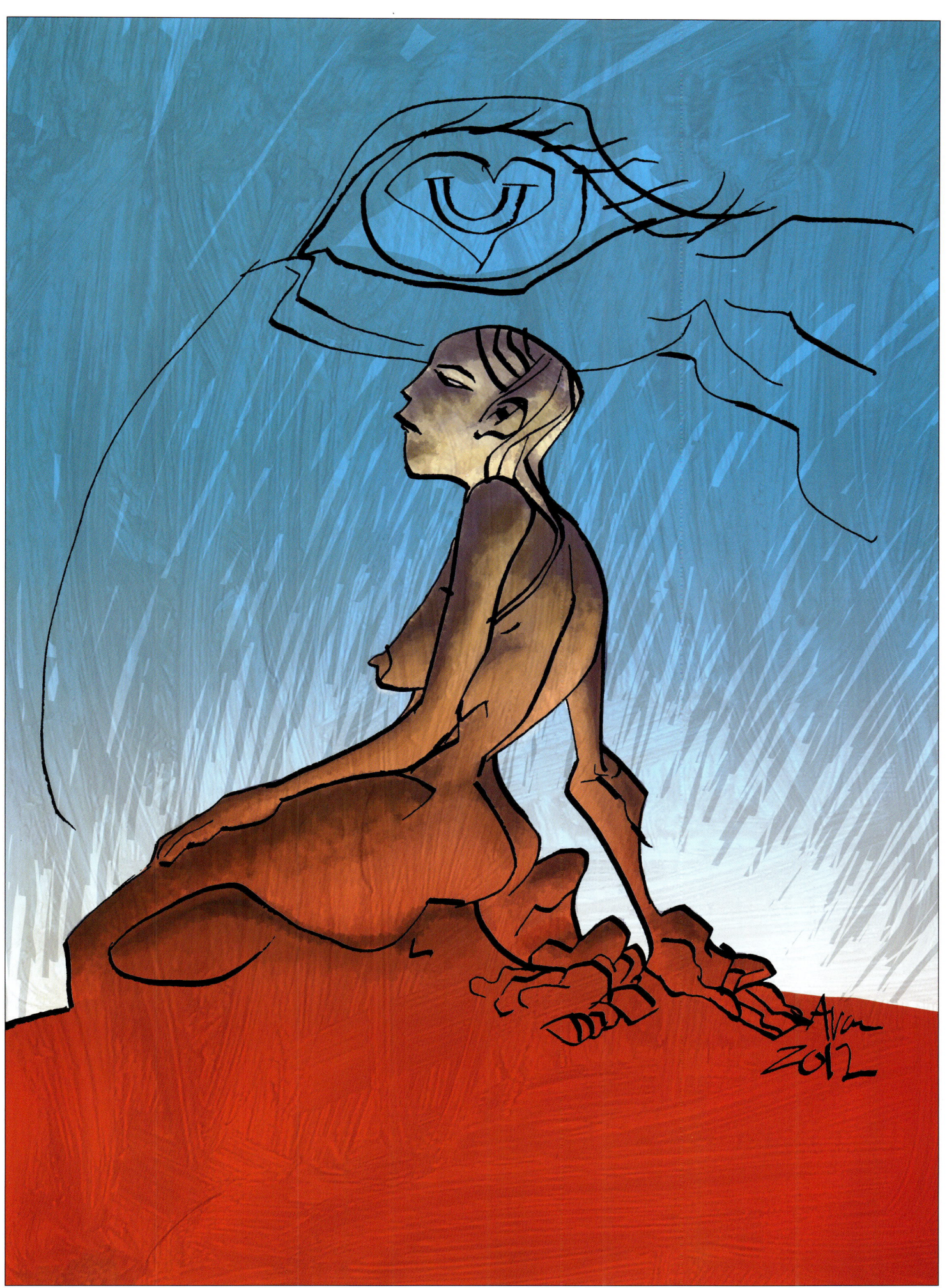

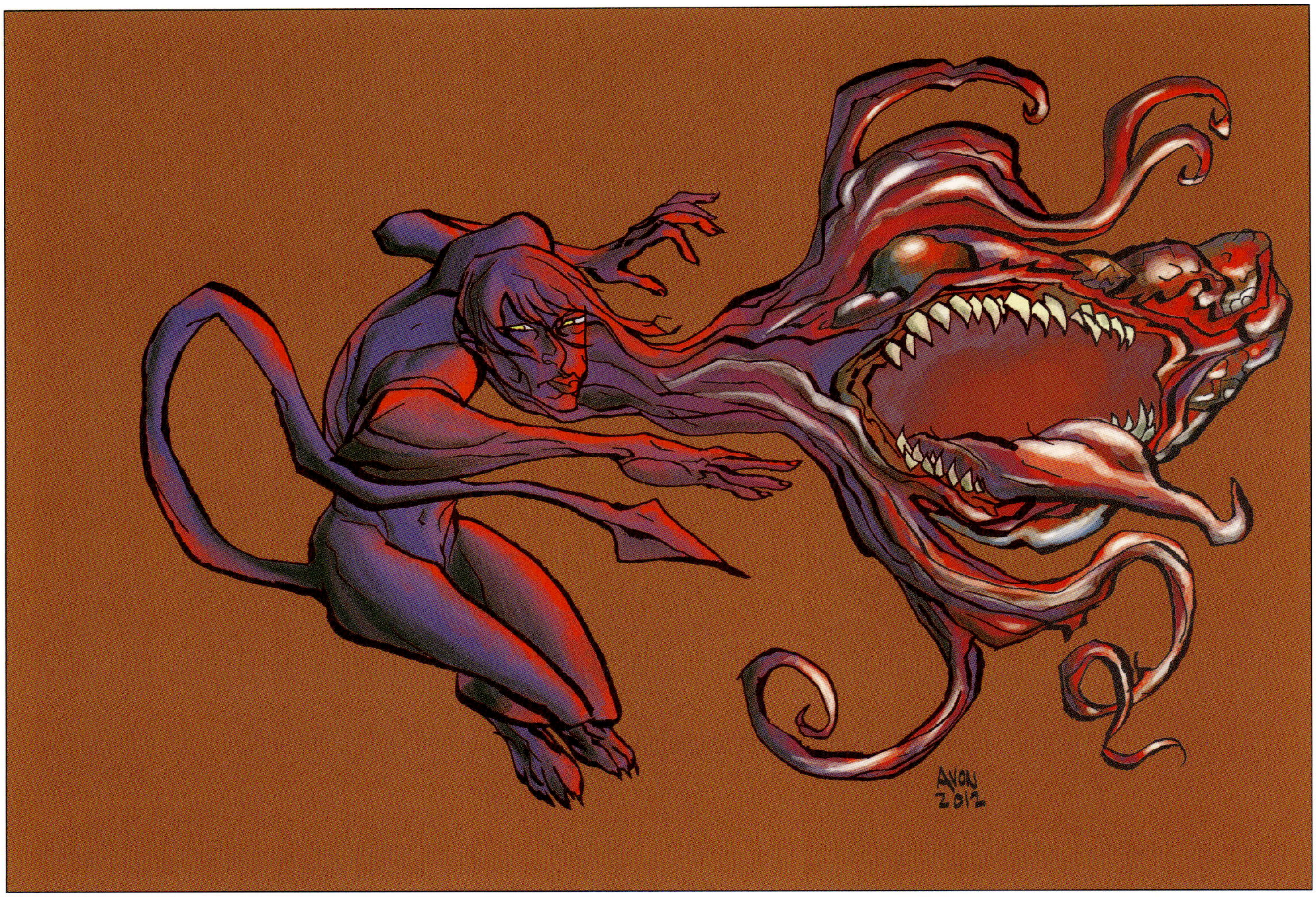

140 NO PLAN B: THE ART OF MICHAEL AVON OEMING

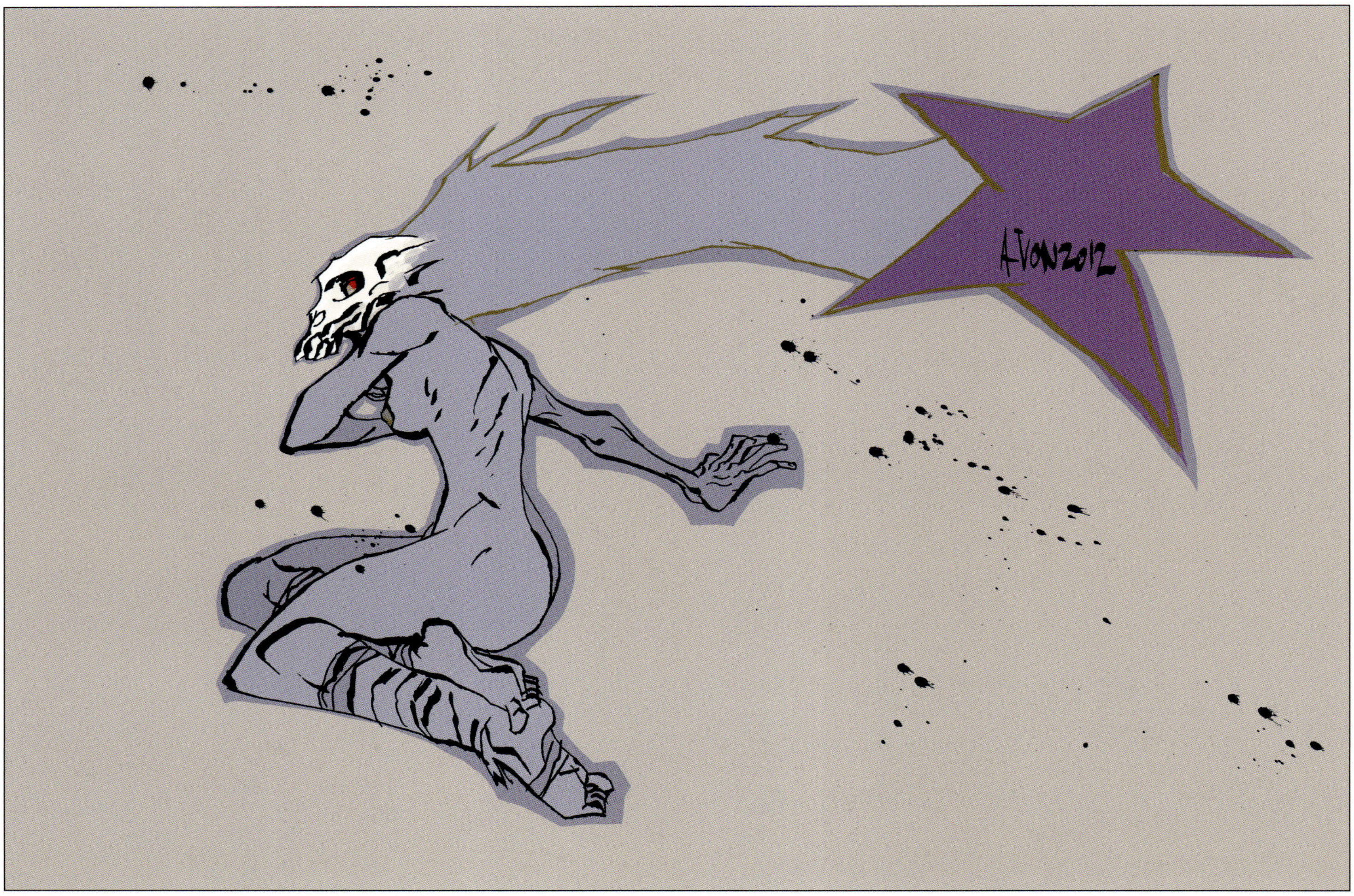

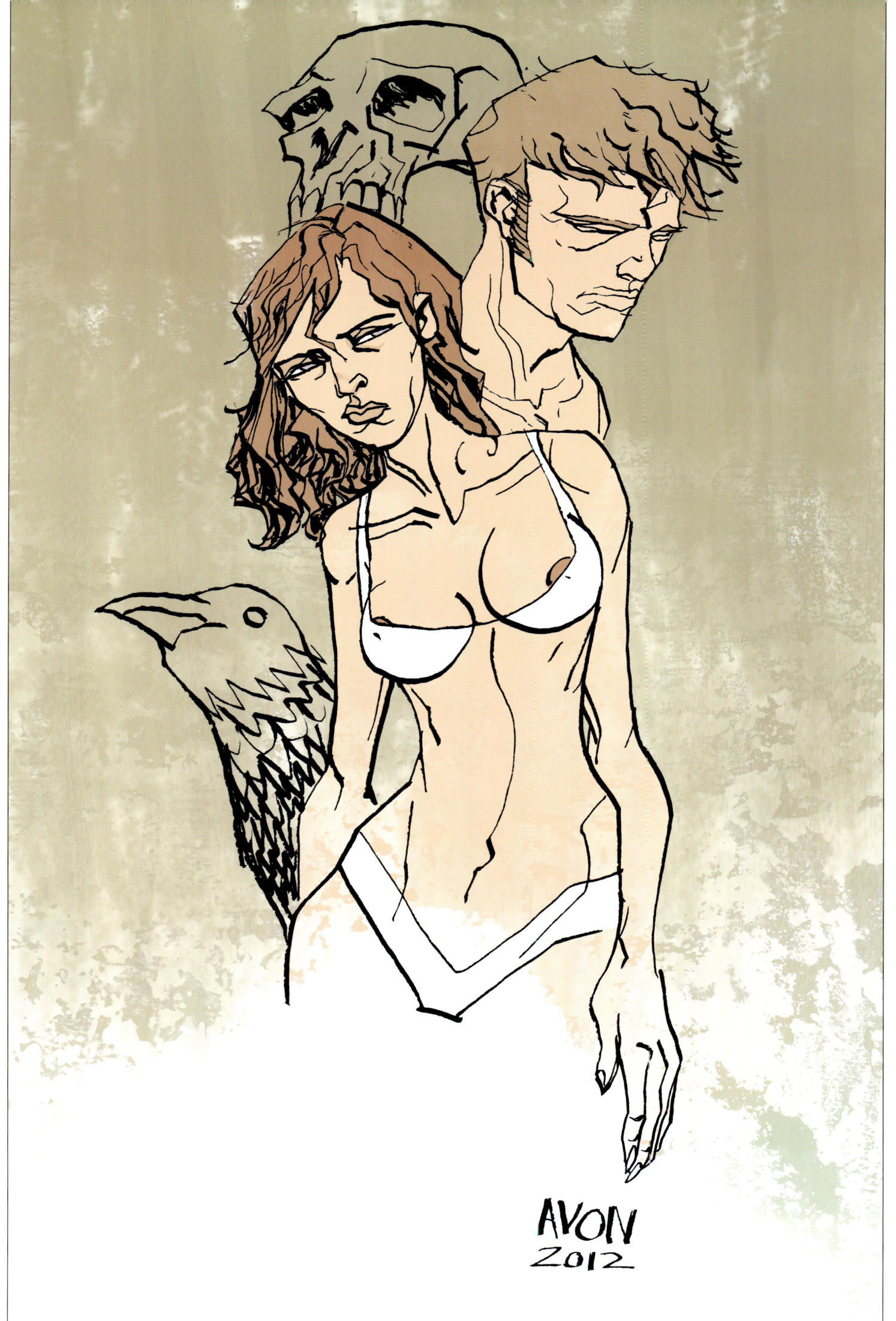

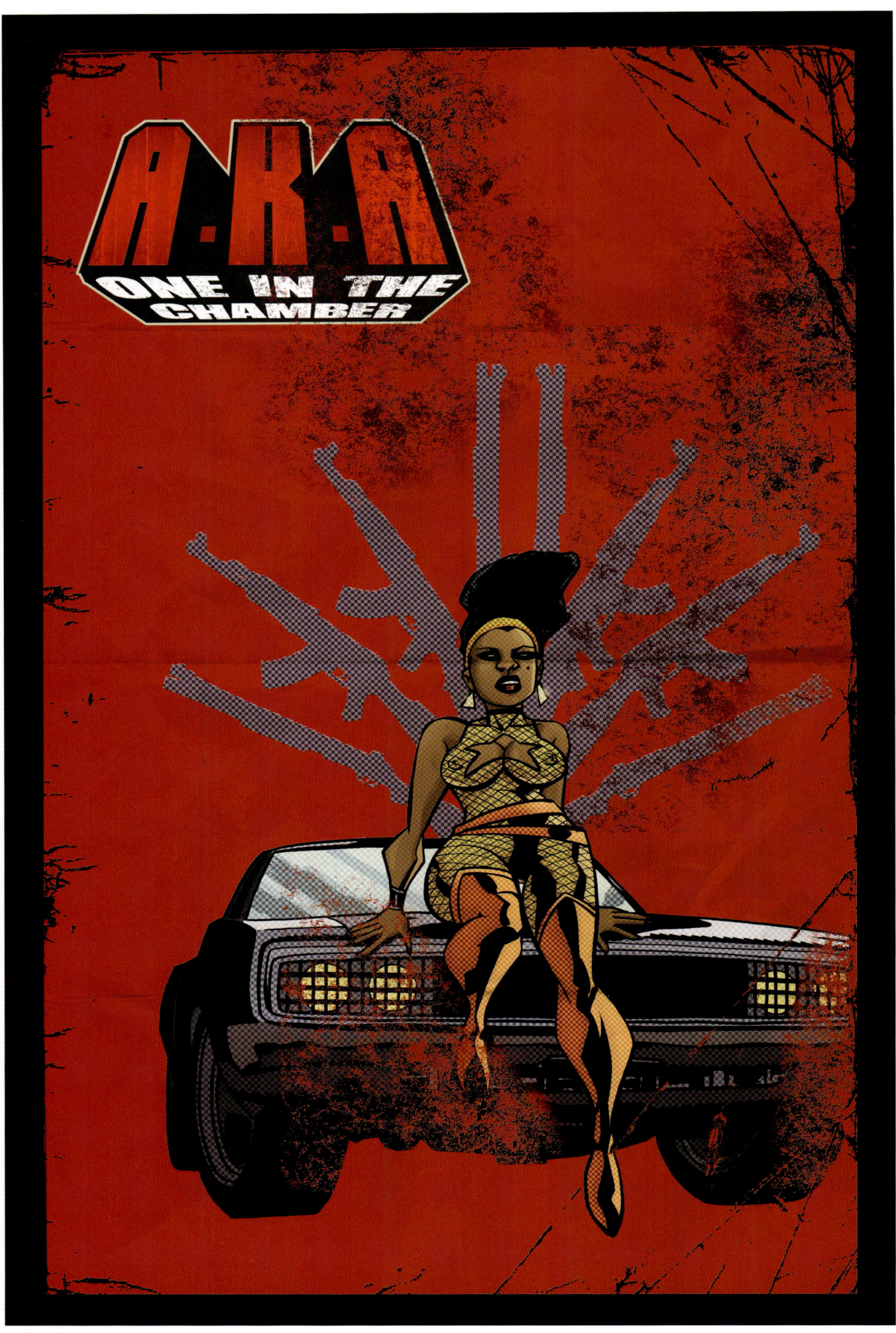

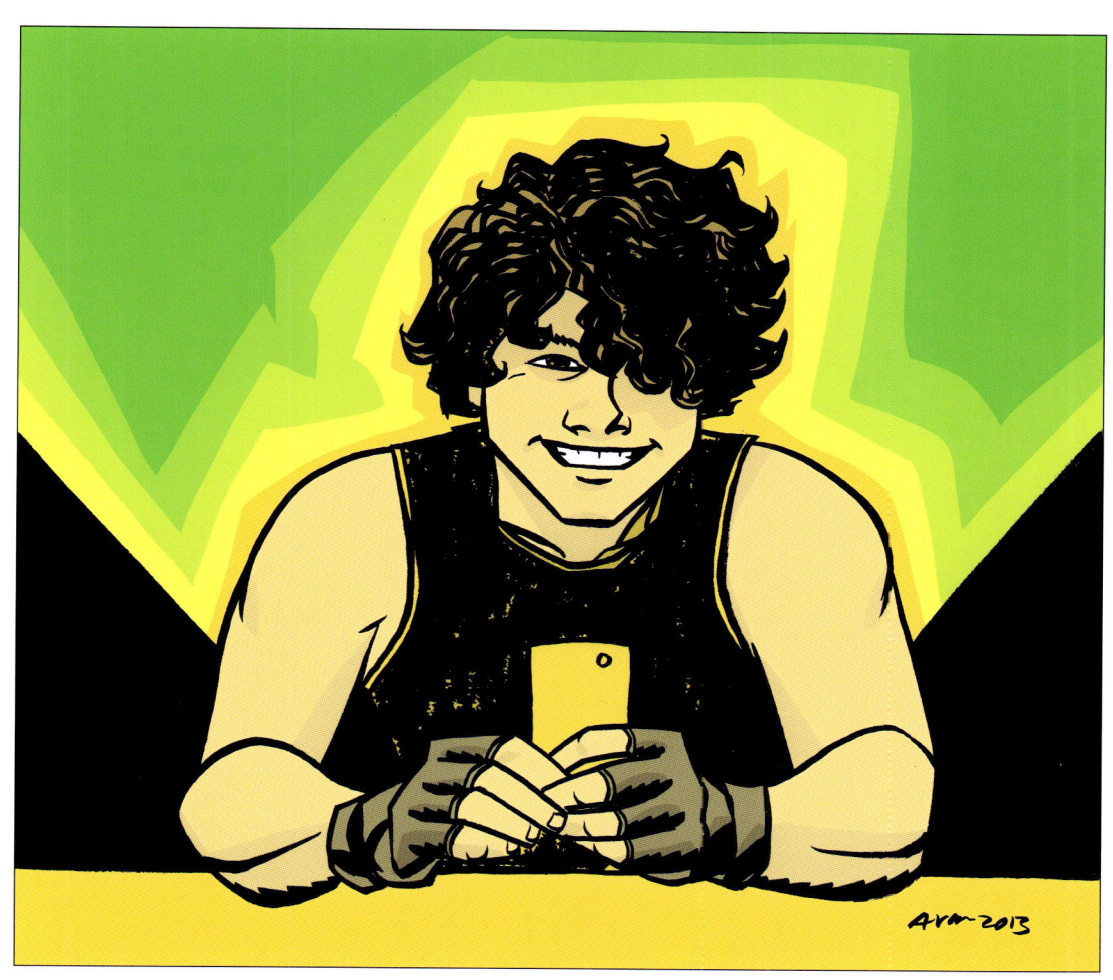

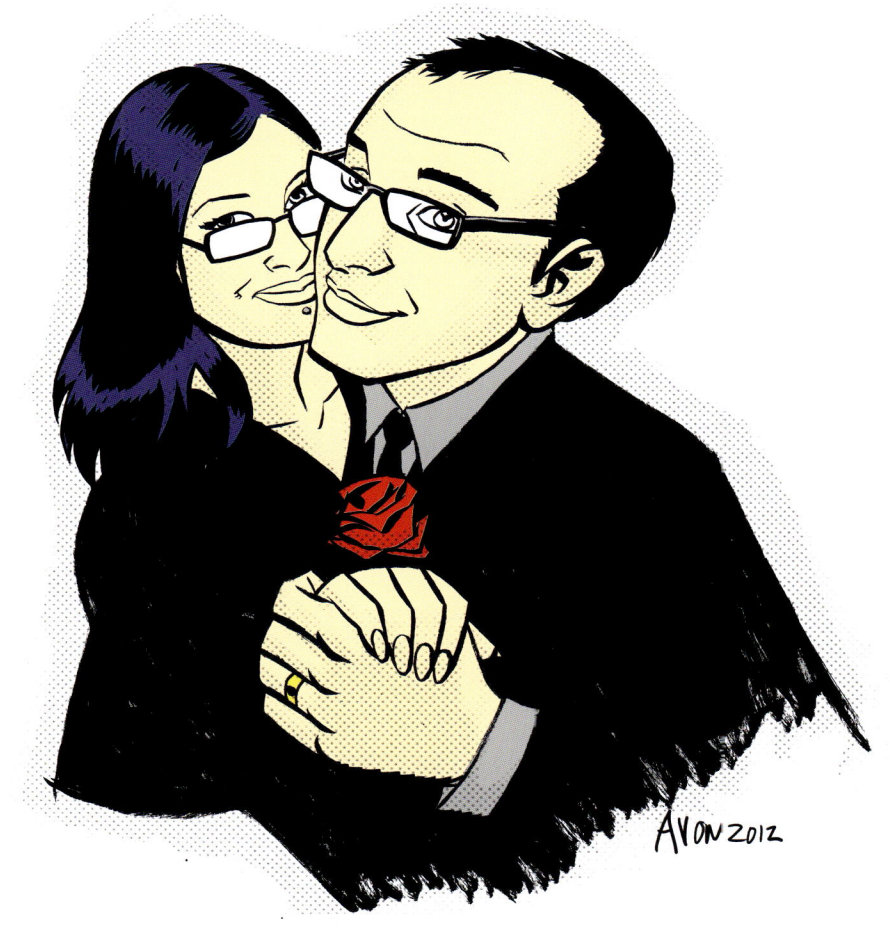

Facing, for Rob Reilly's *A.K.A. One in the Chamber*;
above, top, Ethan; bottom, Joe and Aki

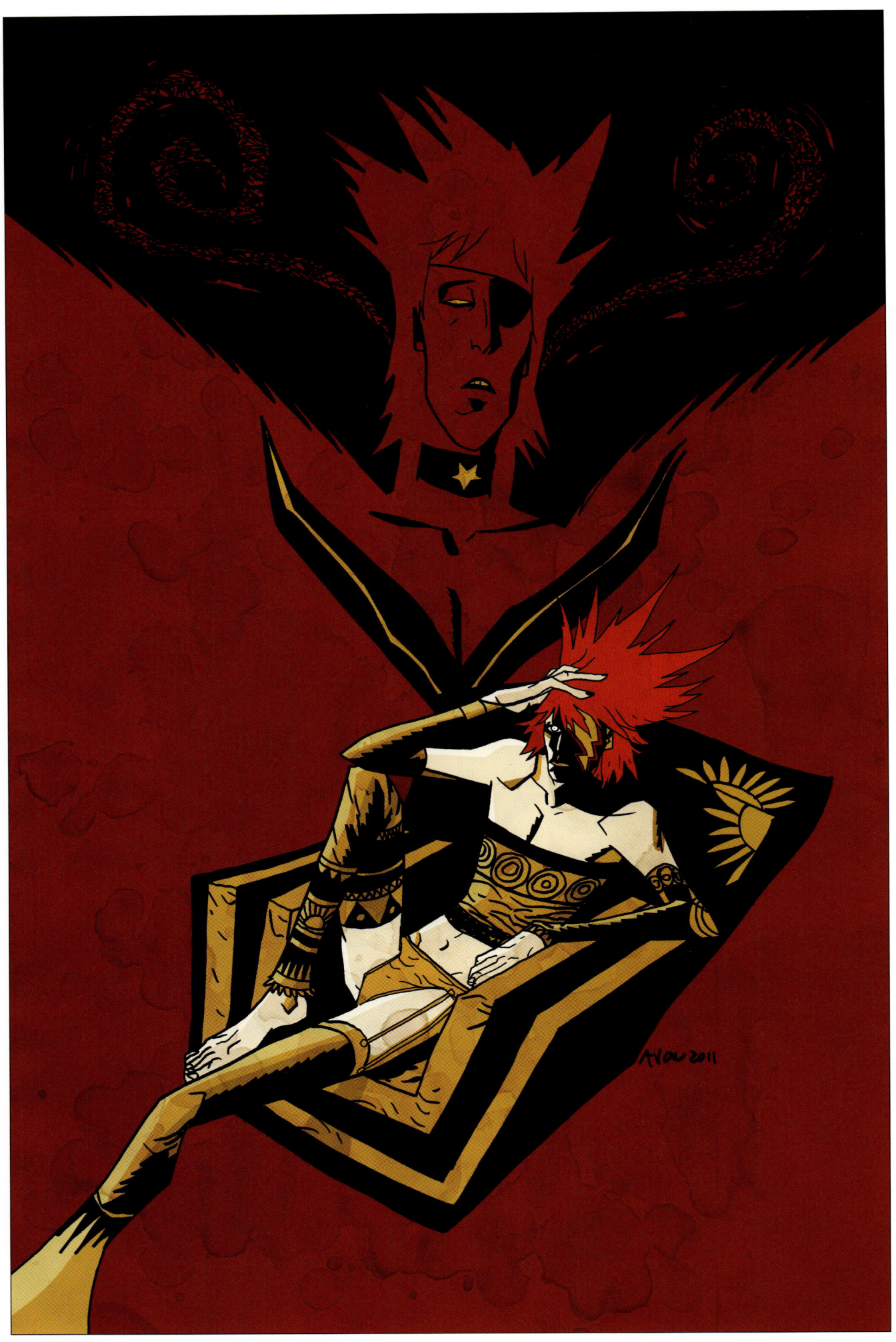

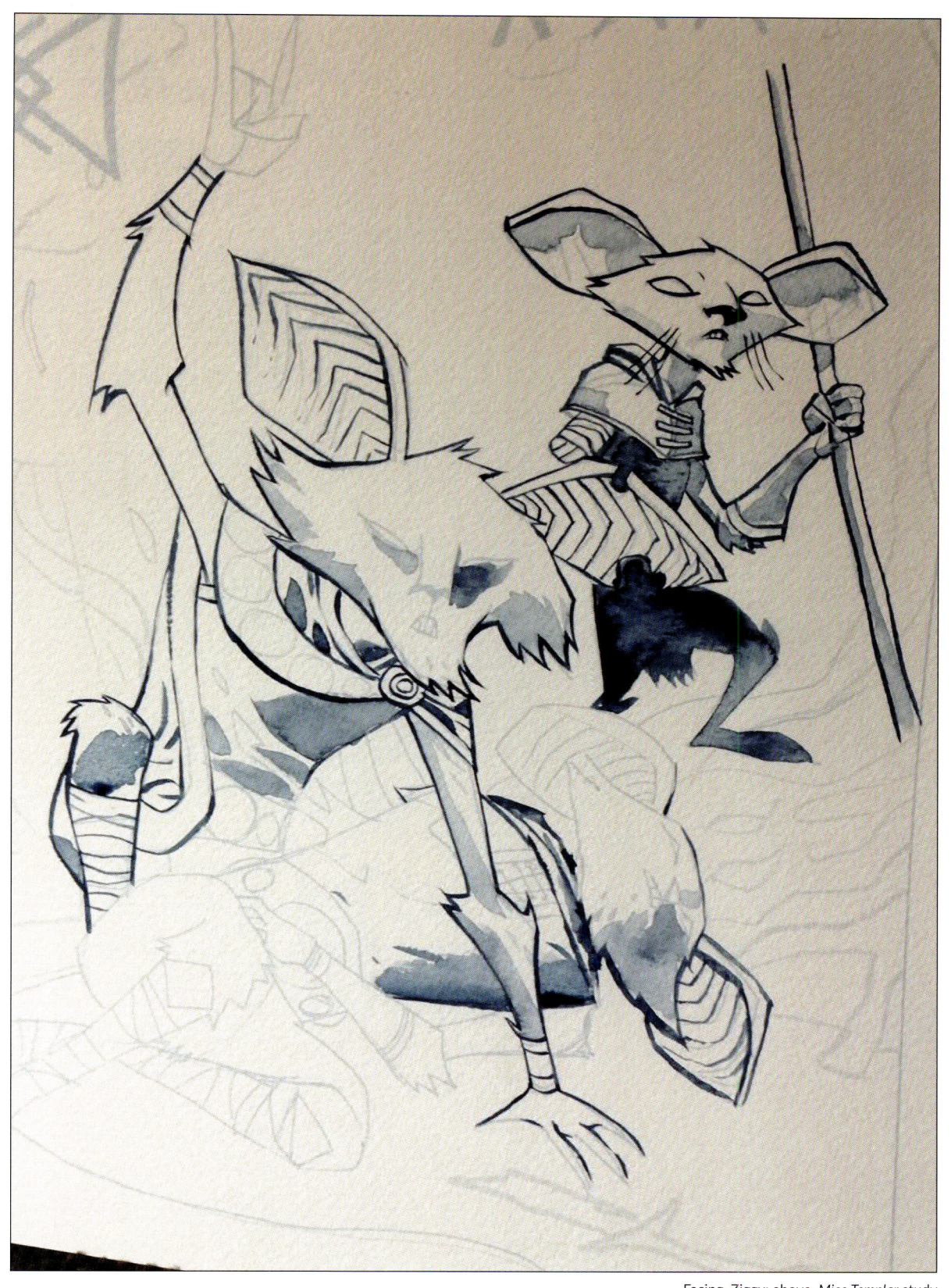

Facing, Ziggy; above, *Mice Templar* study

NO PLAN B: THE ART OF MICHAEL AVON OEMING 145

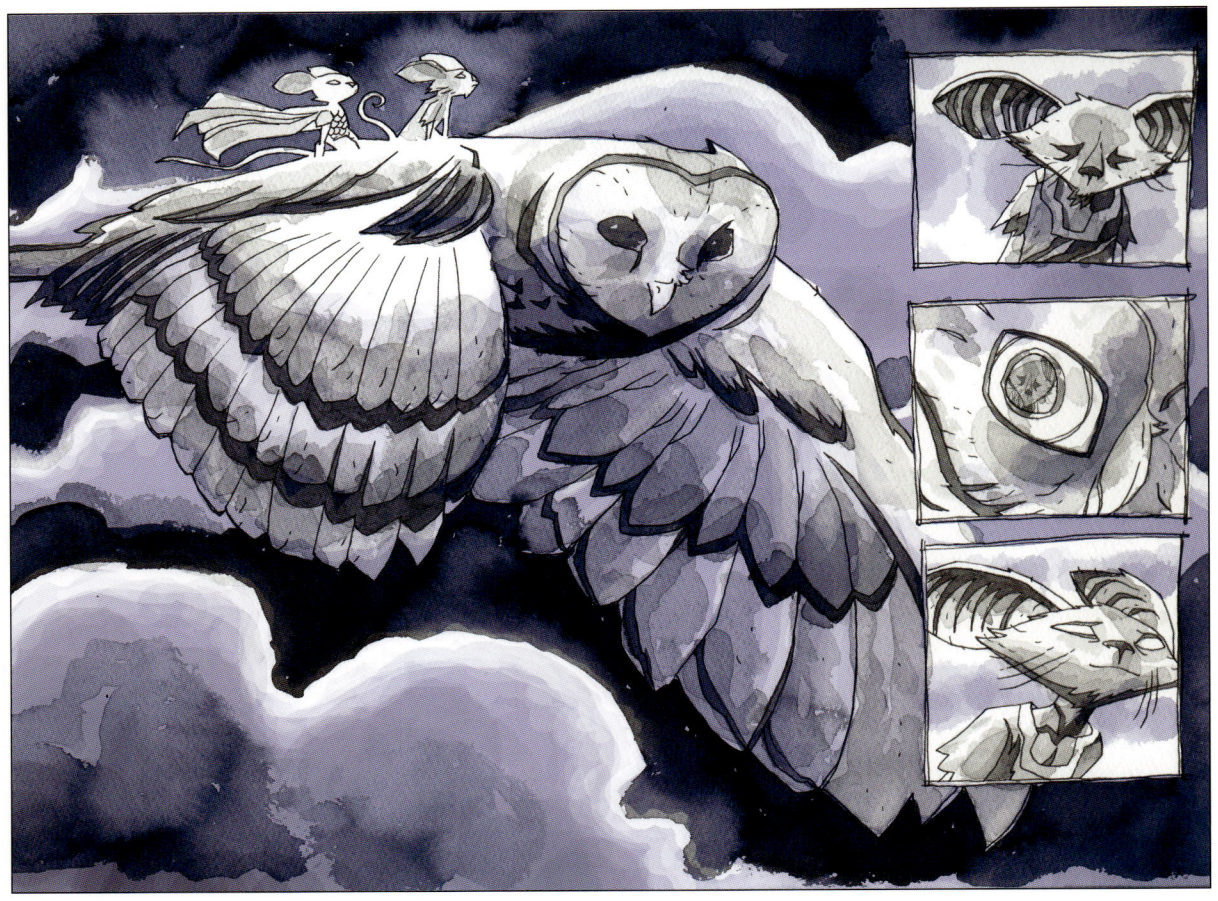

Mice Templar: top, interior spread; bottom, statue designs; following, covers

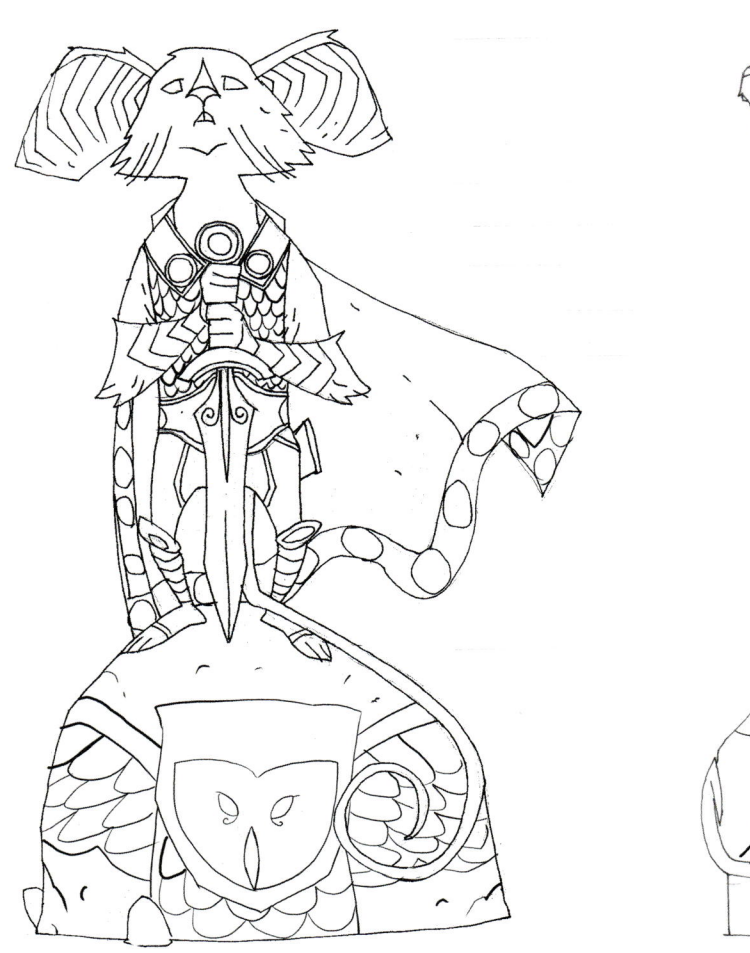
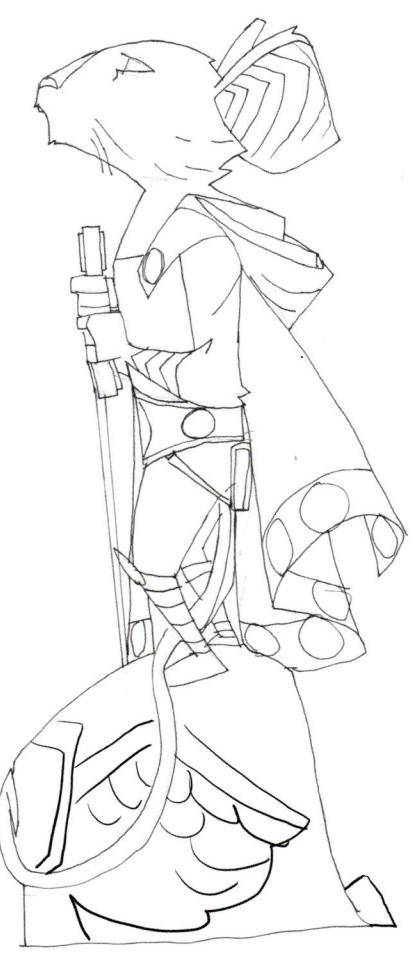

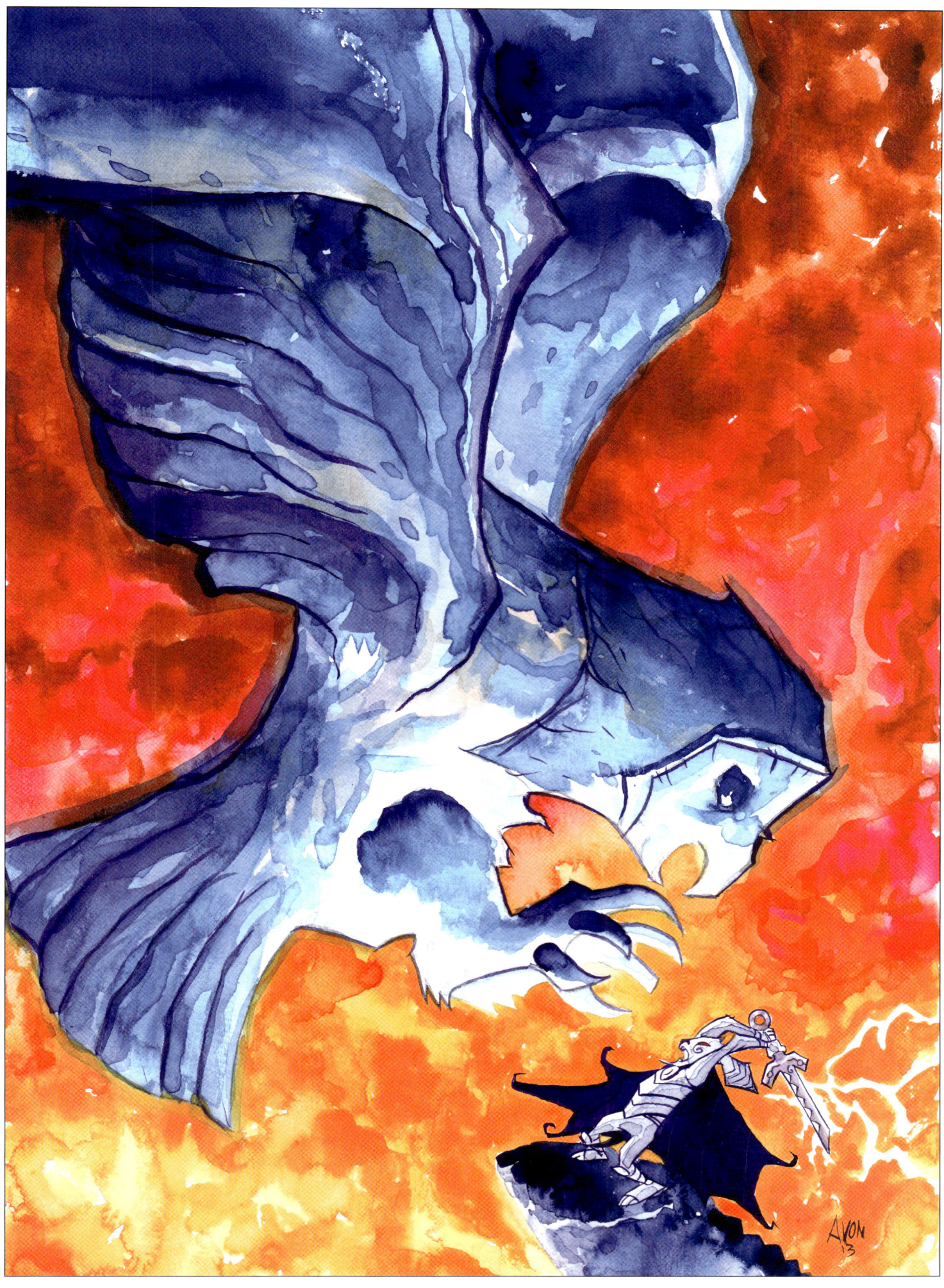

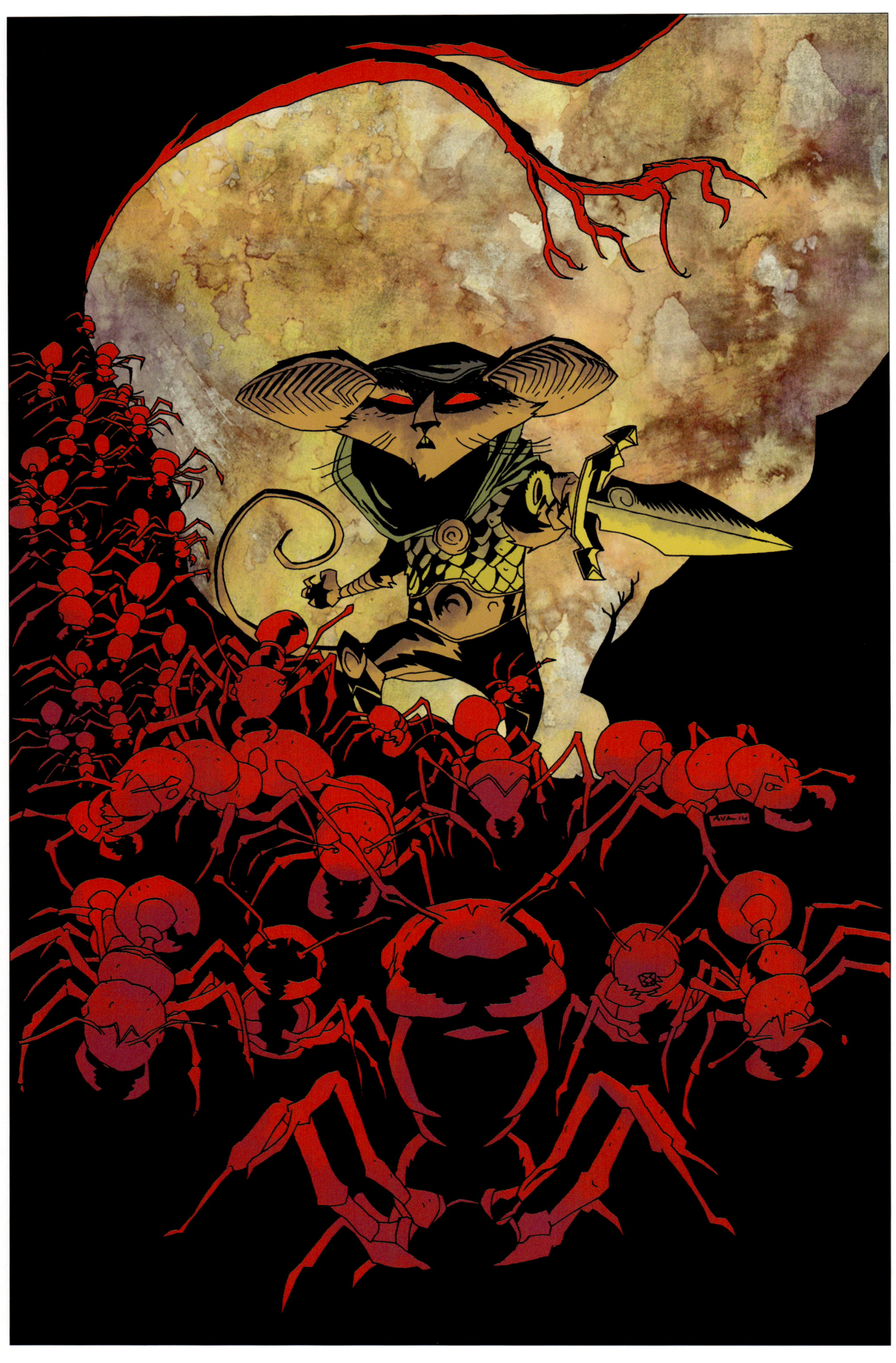

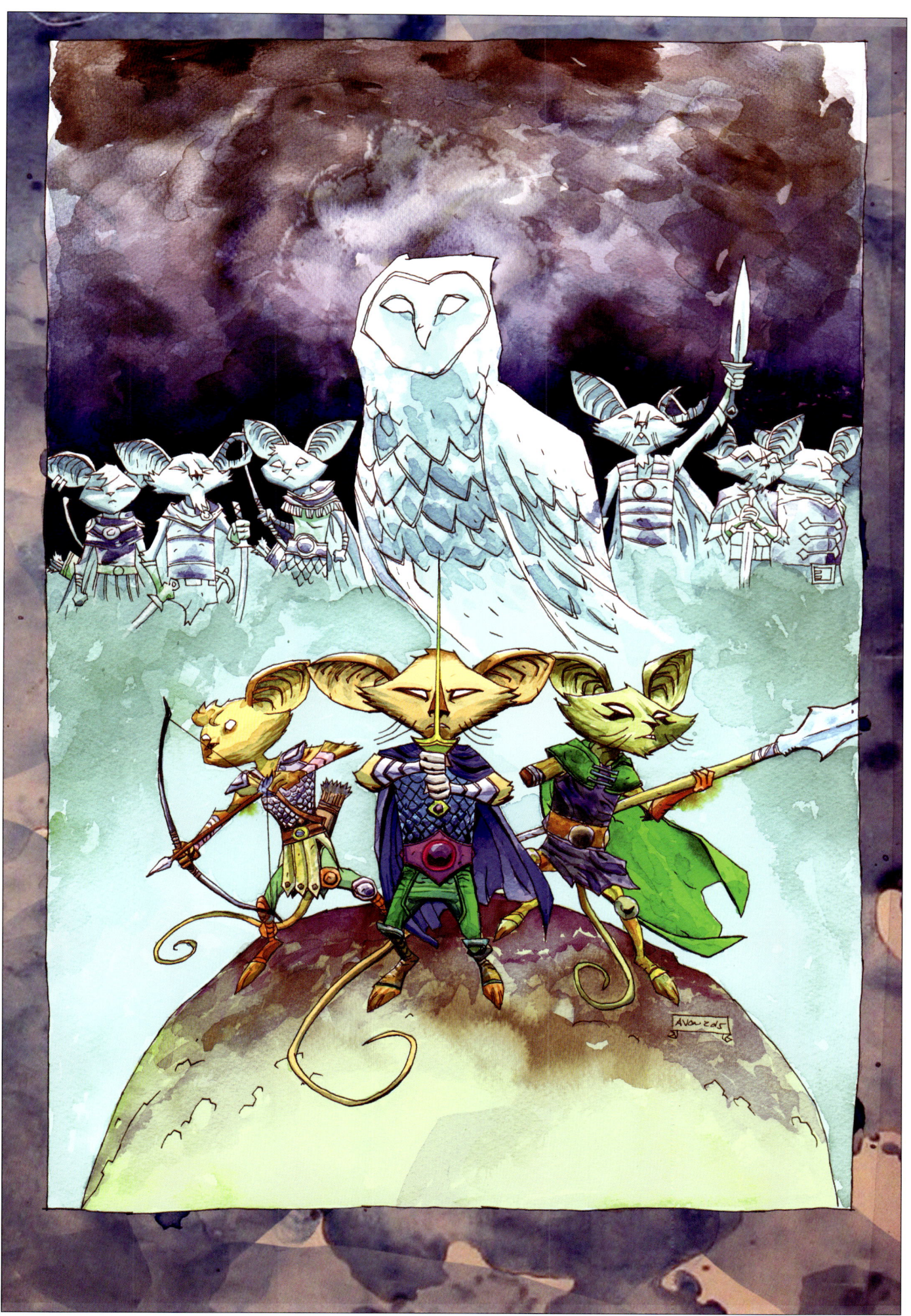

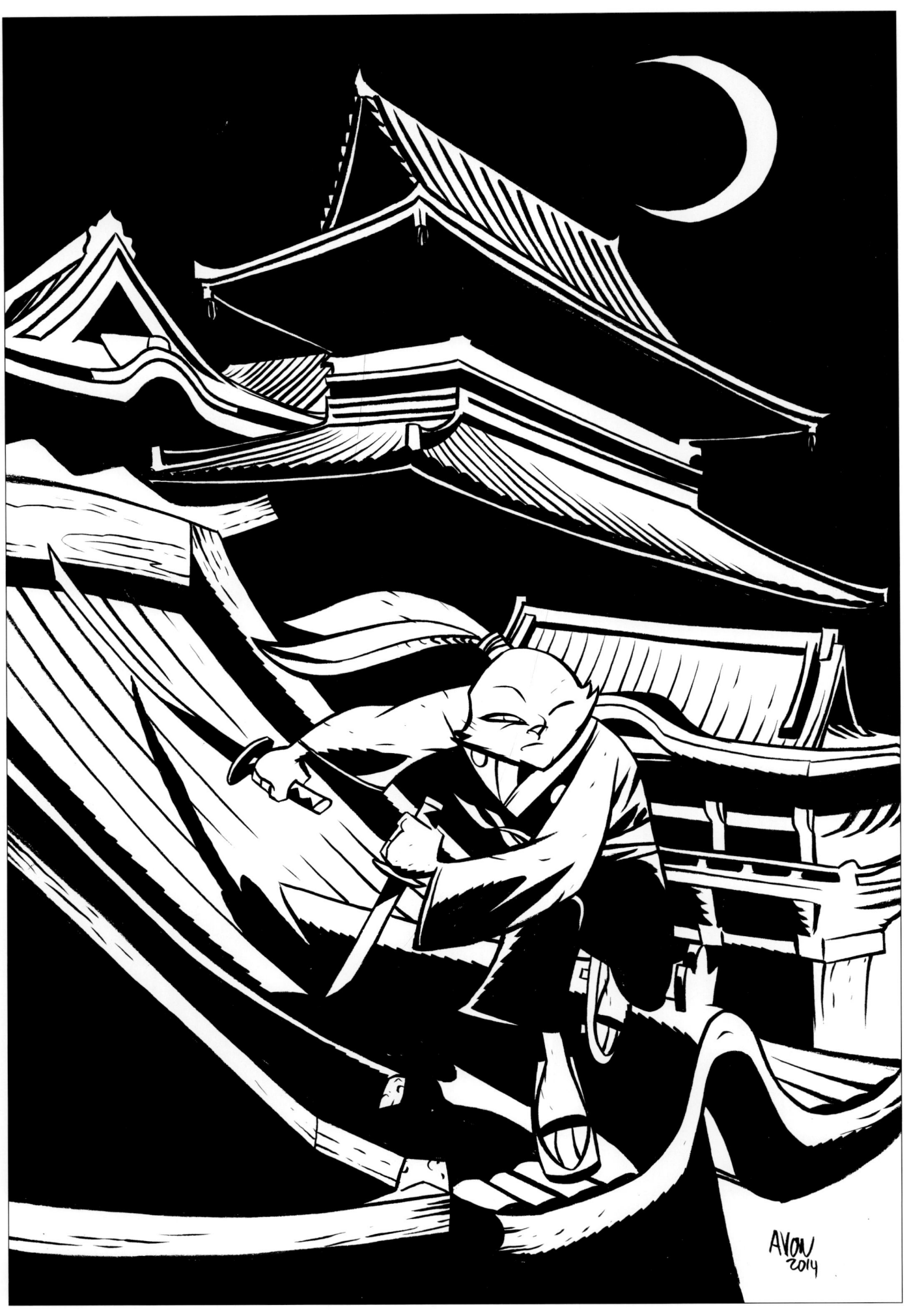

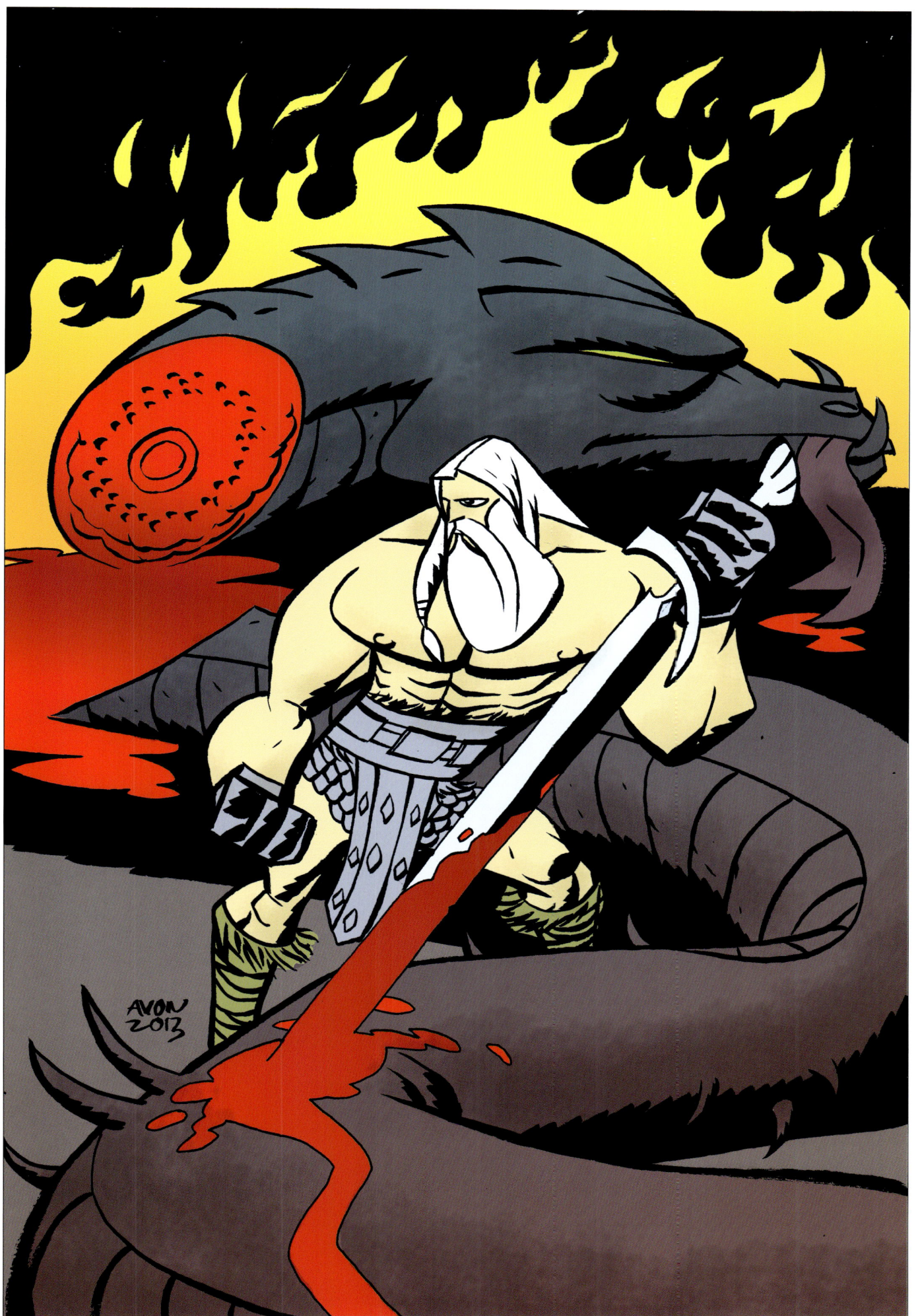

Facing, Stan Sakai's *Usagi Yojimbo*; above, Andrew Maclean's *Head Lopper*

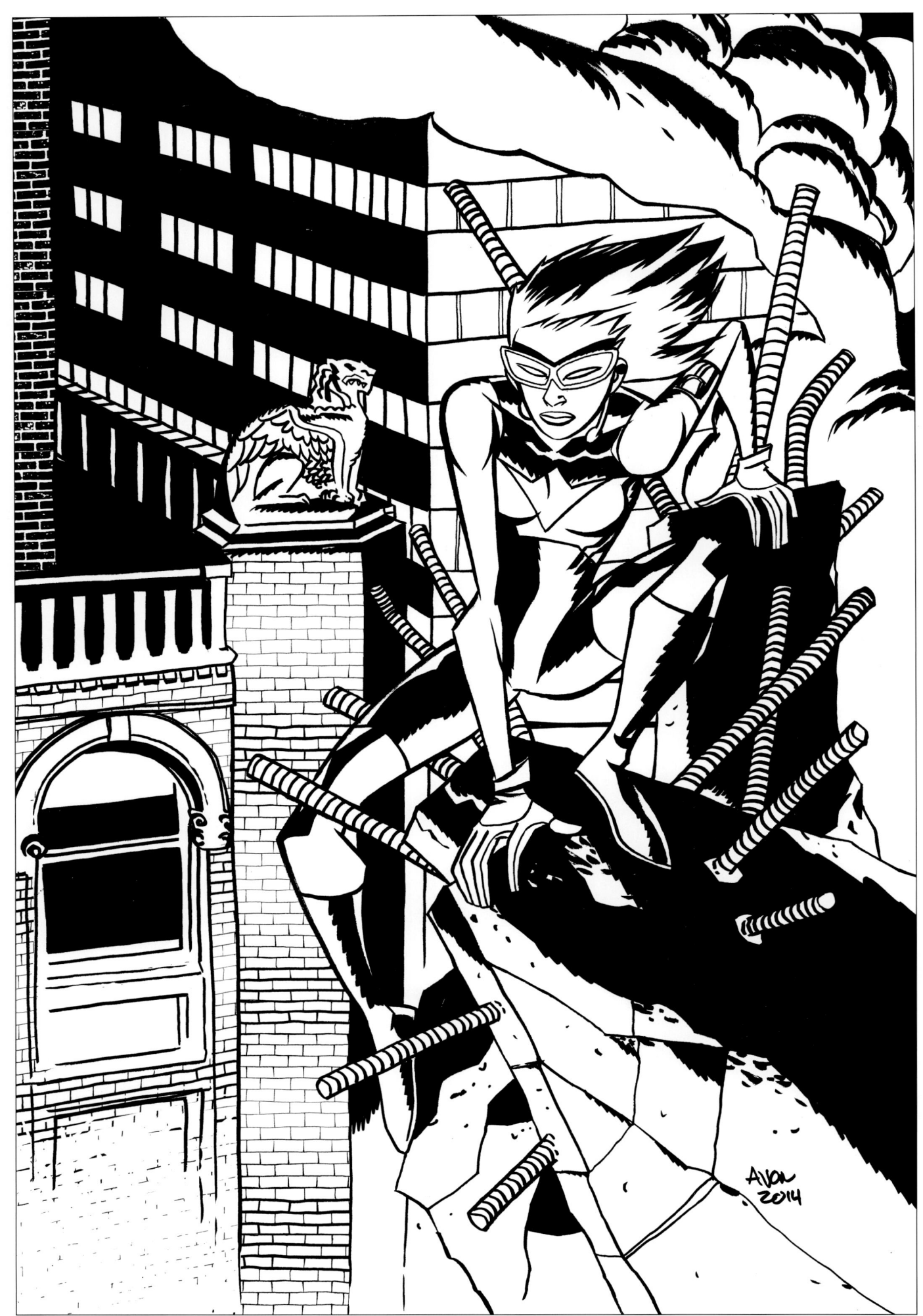

Above, Bryan Glass's *Furious*; facing, in memory of Moebius

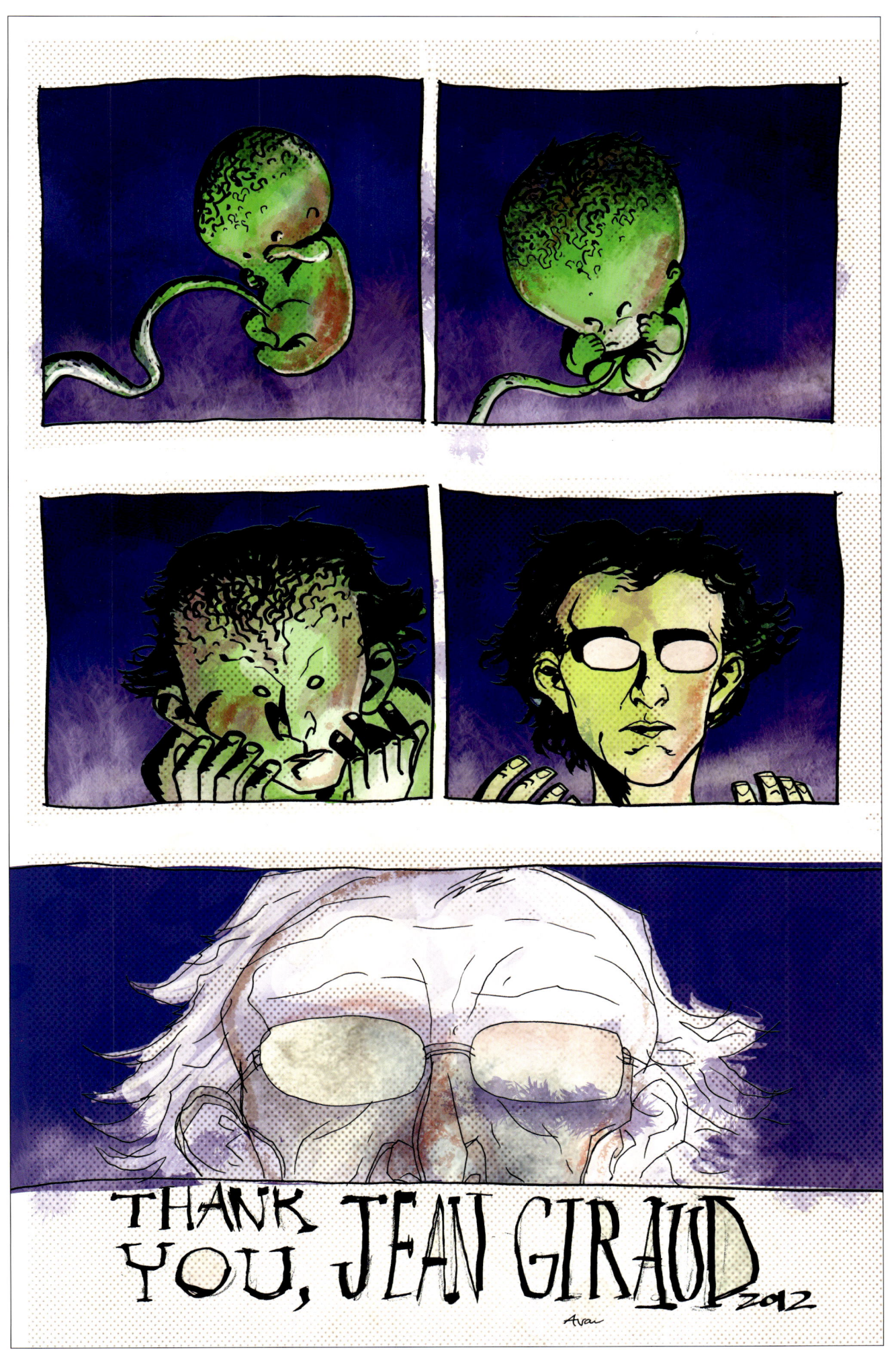

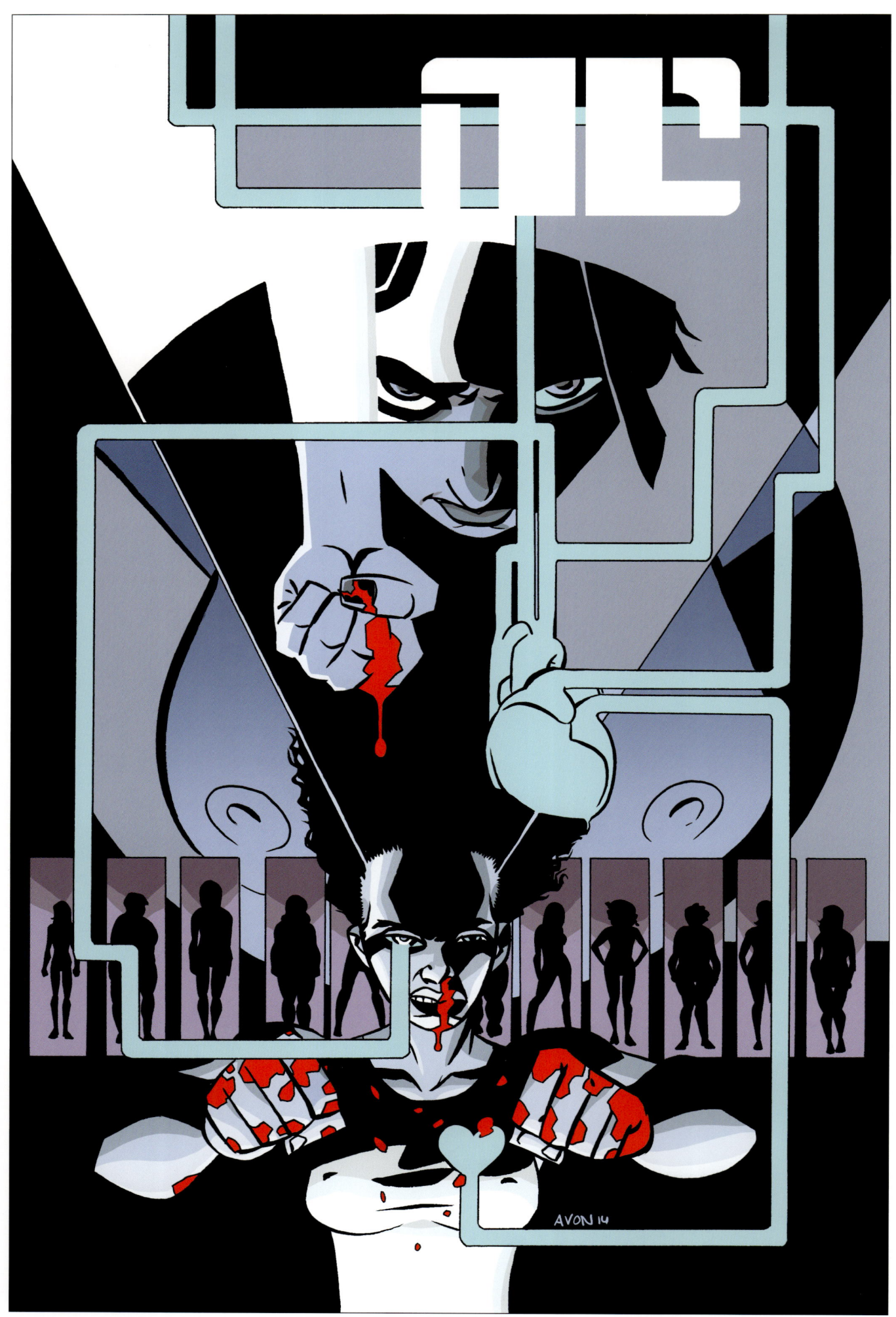

Cover for Kelly Sue DeConnick and Valentine De Landro's *Bitch Planet*

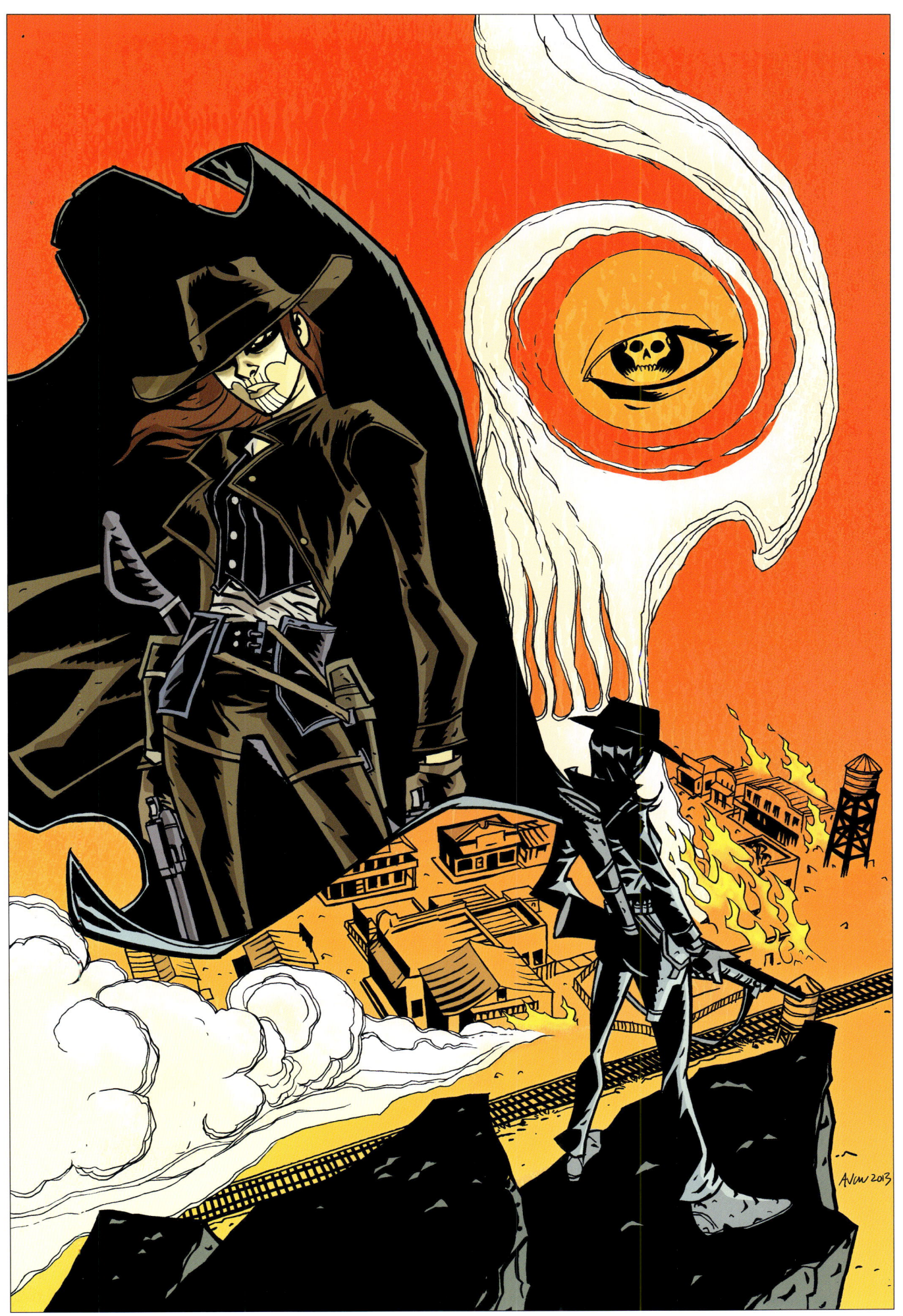

Cover for Kelly Sue DeConnick and Emma Ríos's *Pretty Deadly*

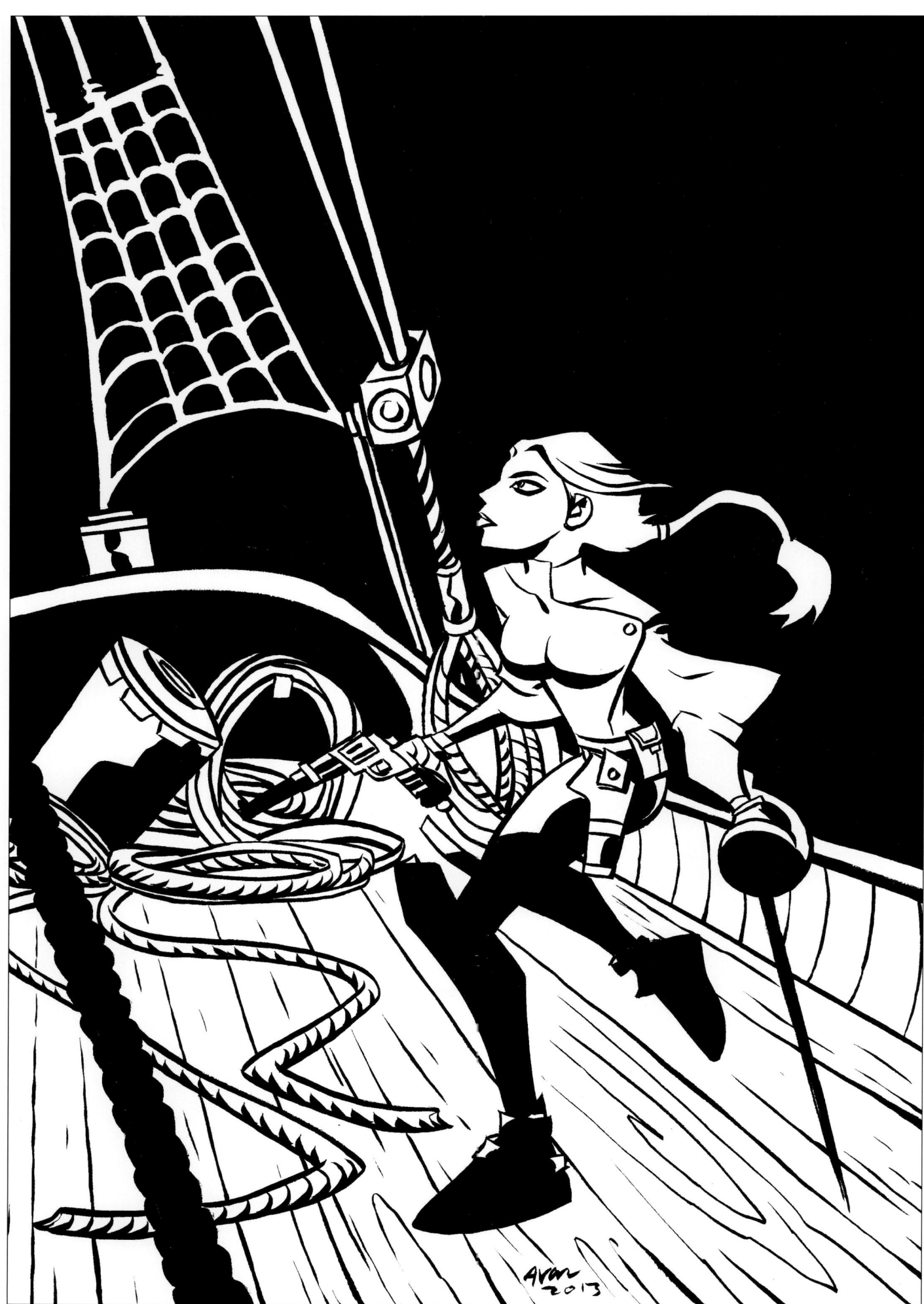

Greg Rucka and Rick Burchett's *Lady Sabre*

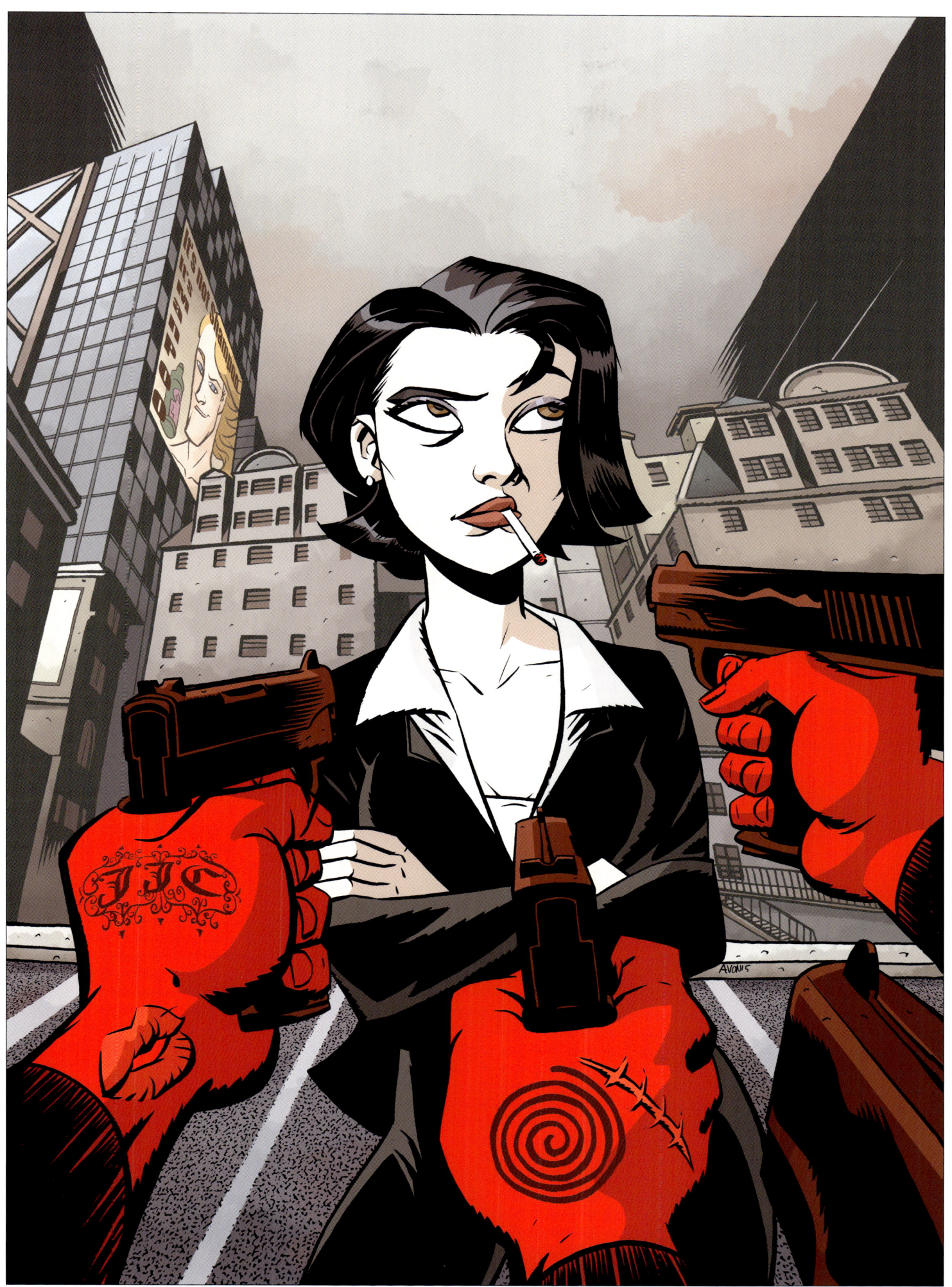
Cover for Chuck Palahniuk's *Fight Club 2*, colored by Dave Stewart

NO PLAN B: THE ART OF MICHAEL AVON OEMING 157

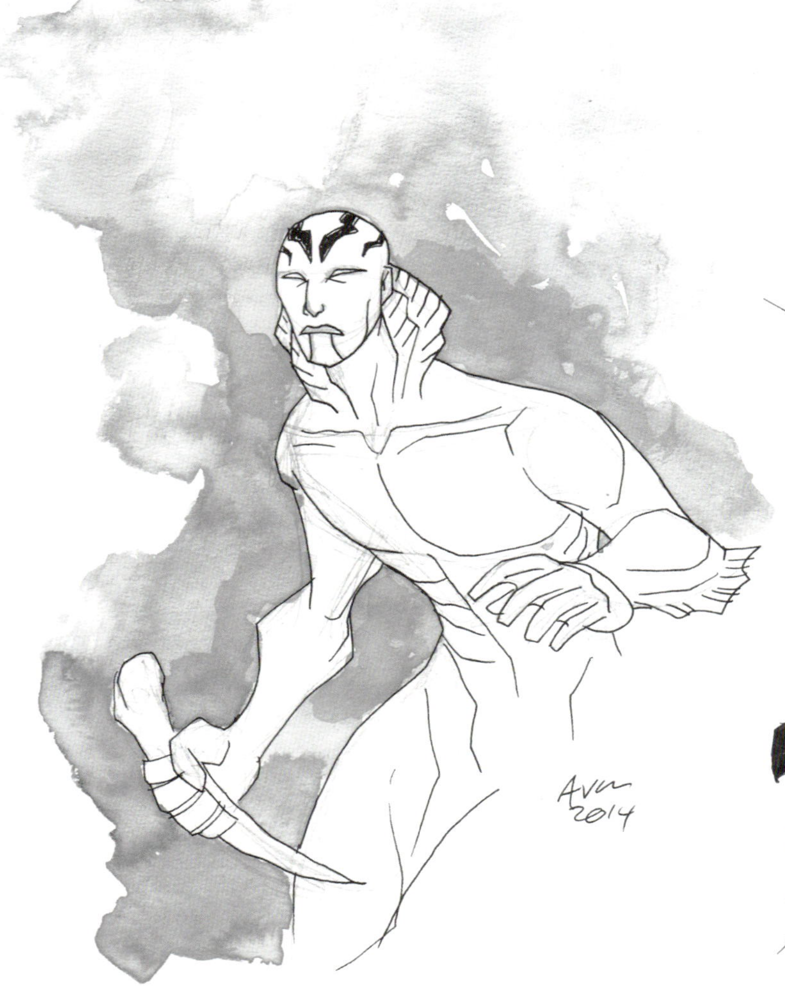

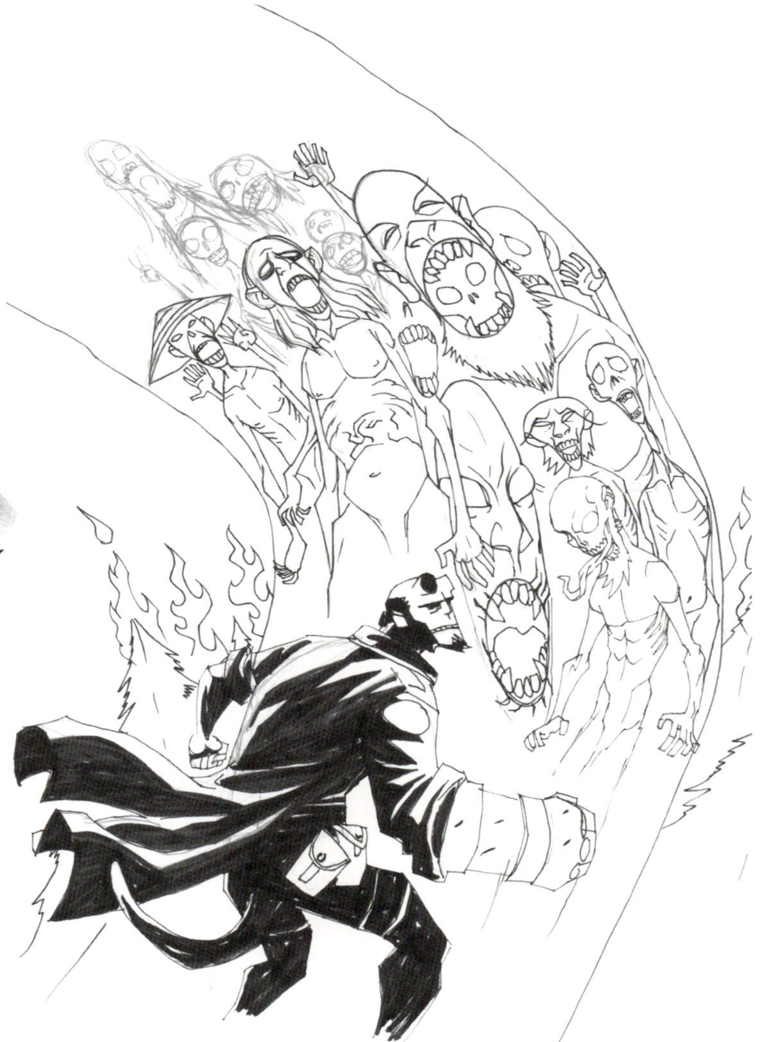

Sketch of Abe Sapien and cover sketch for Mike Mignola's *Hellboy: Winter Special*; facing, finished cover, colored by Dave Stewart
Bottom: Portrait of Scott Allie with Mignola's Hellboy, Abe Sapien, and Johann, Gerard Way and Gabriel Ba's Space Boy, and an unpublished Oeming character, colored by Dave Stewart

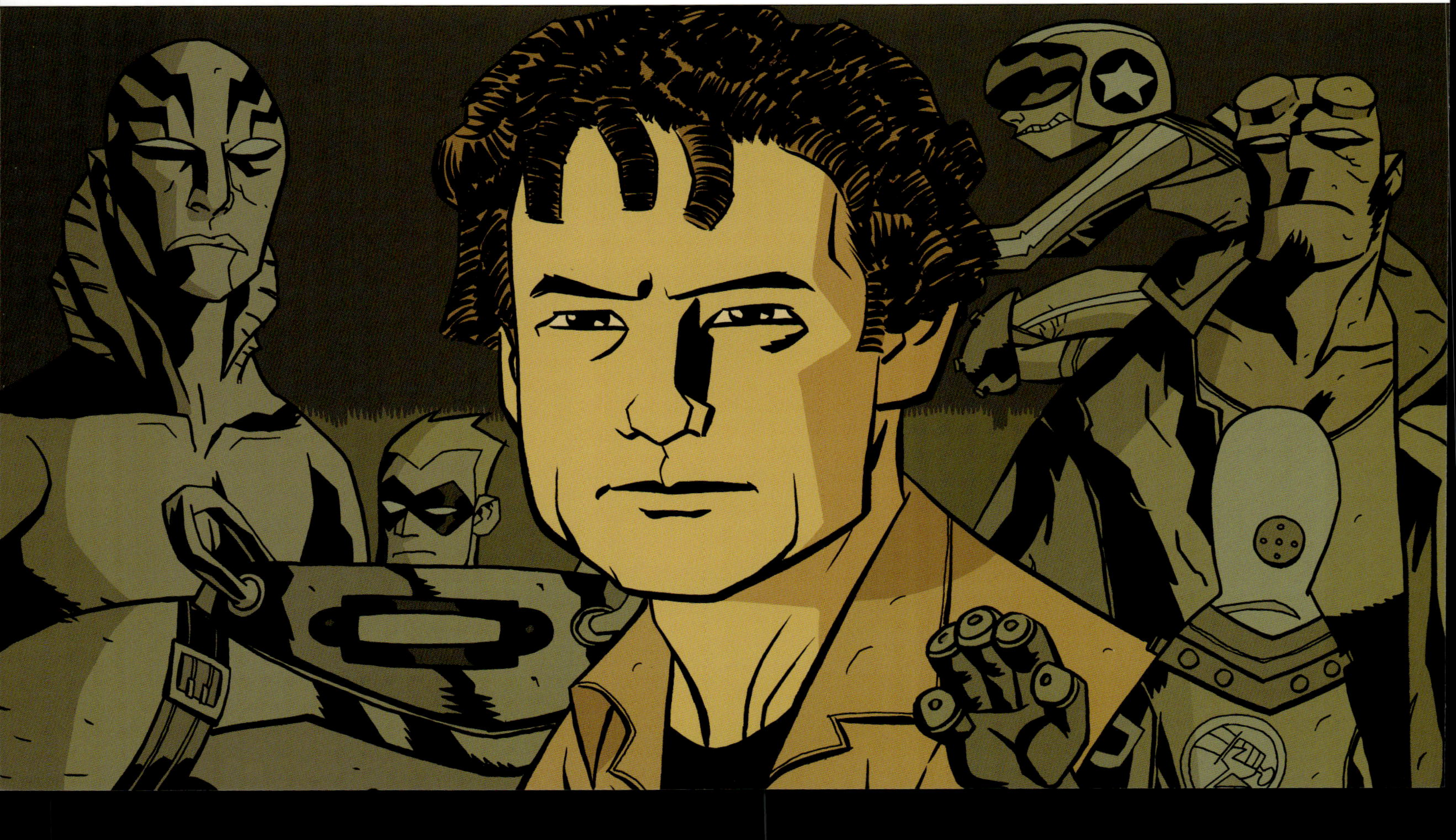

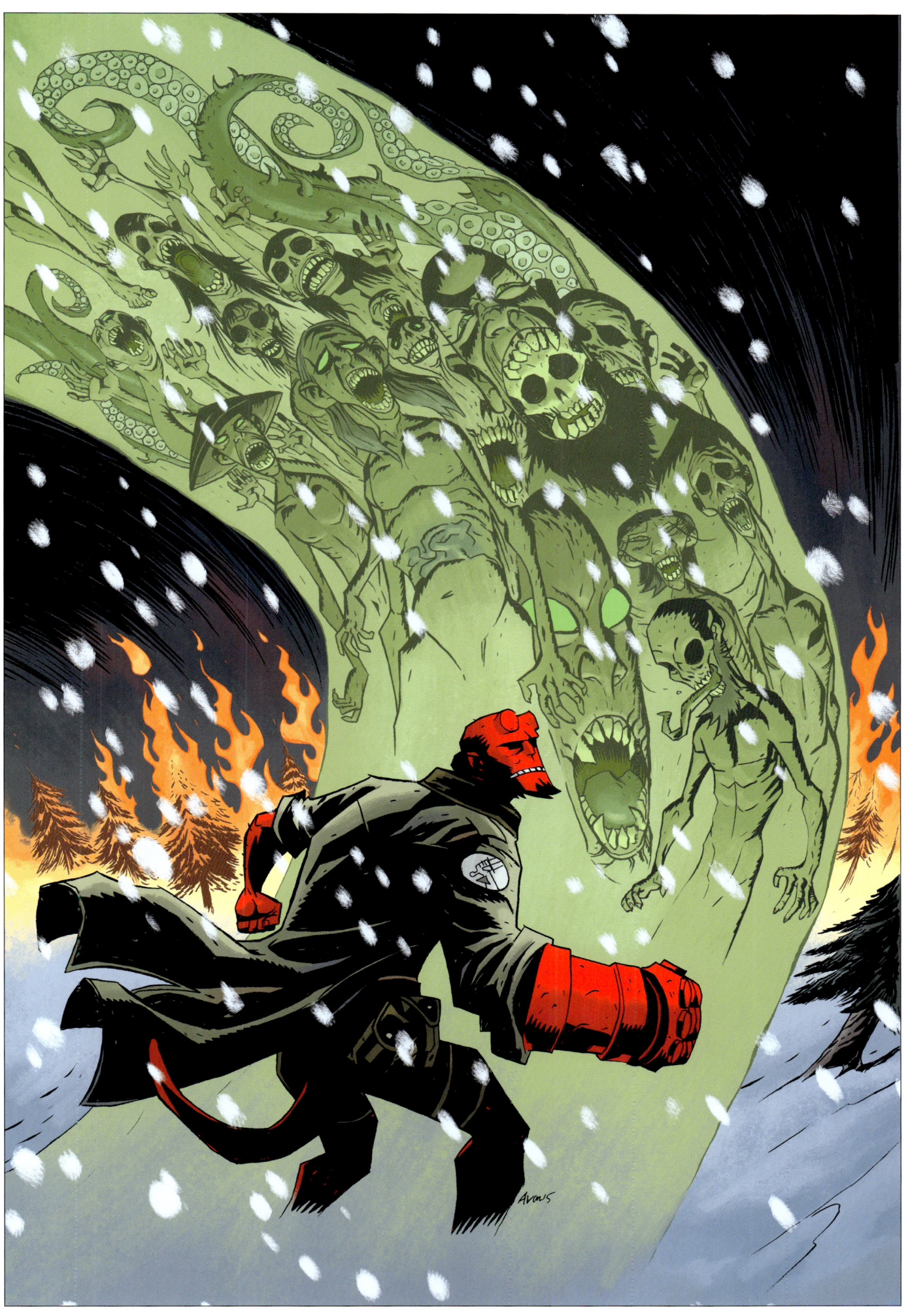

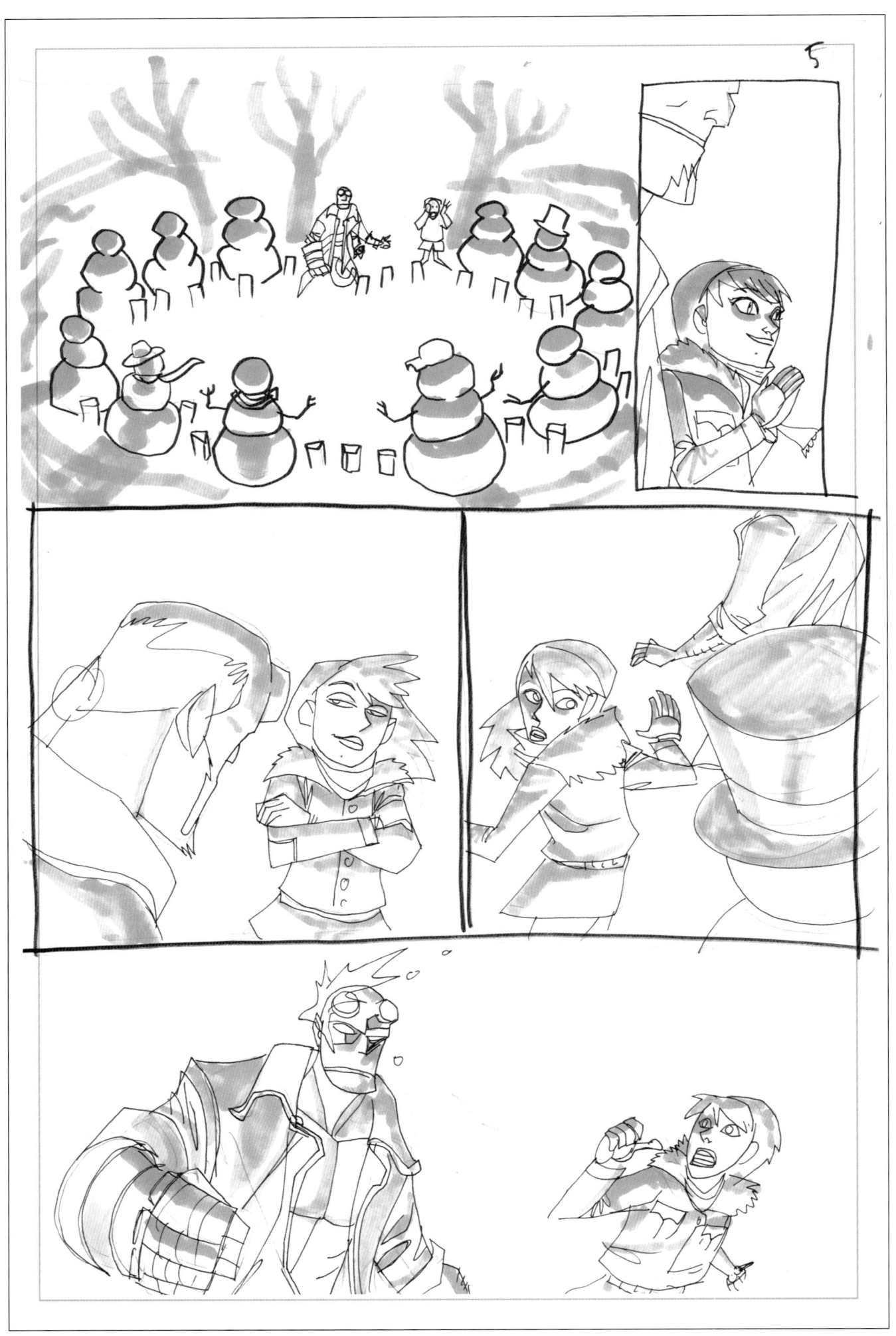

Roughs and (facing) inks for Chelsea Cain's story in *Hellboy: Winter Special*

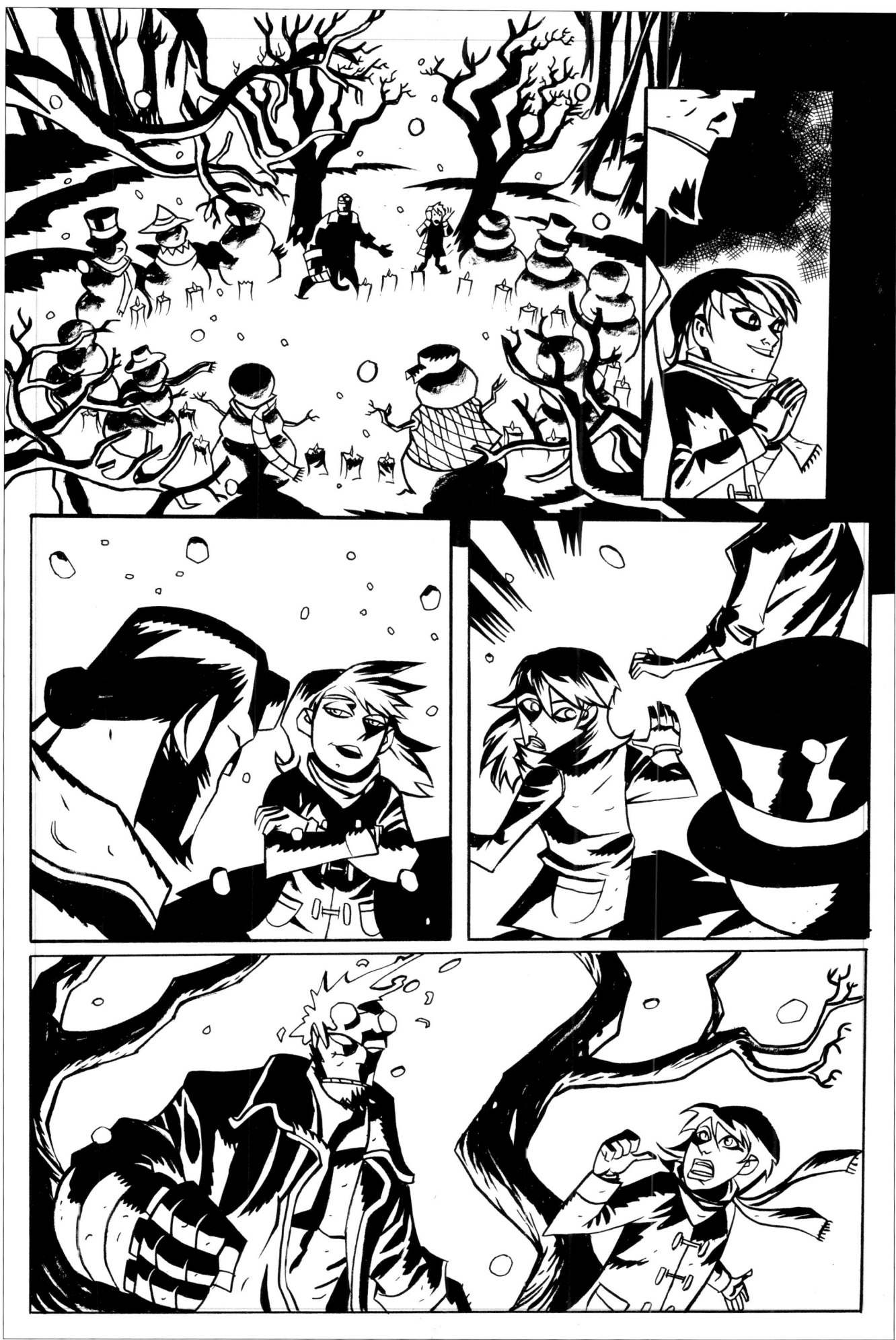

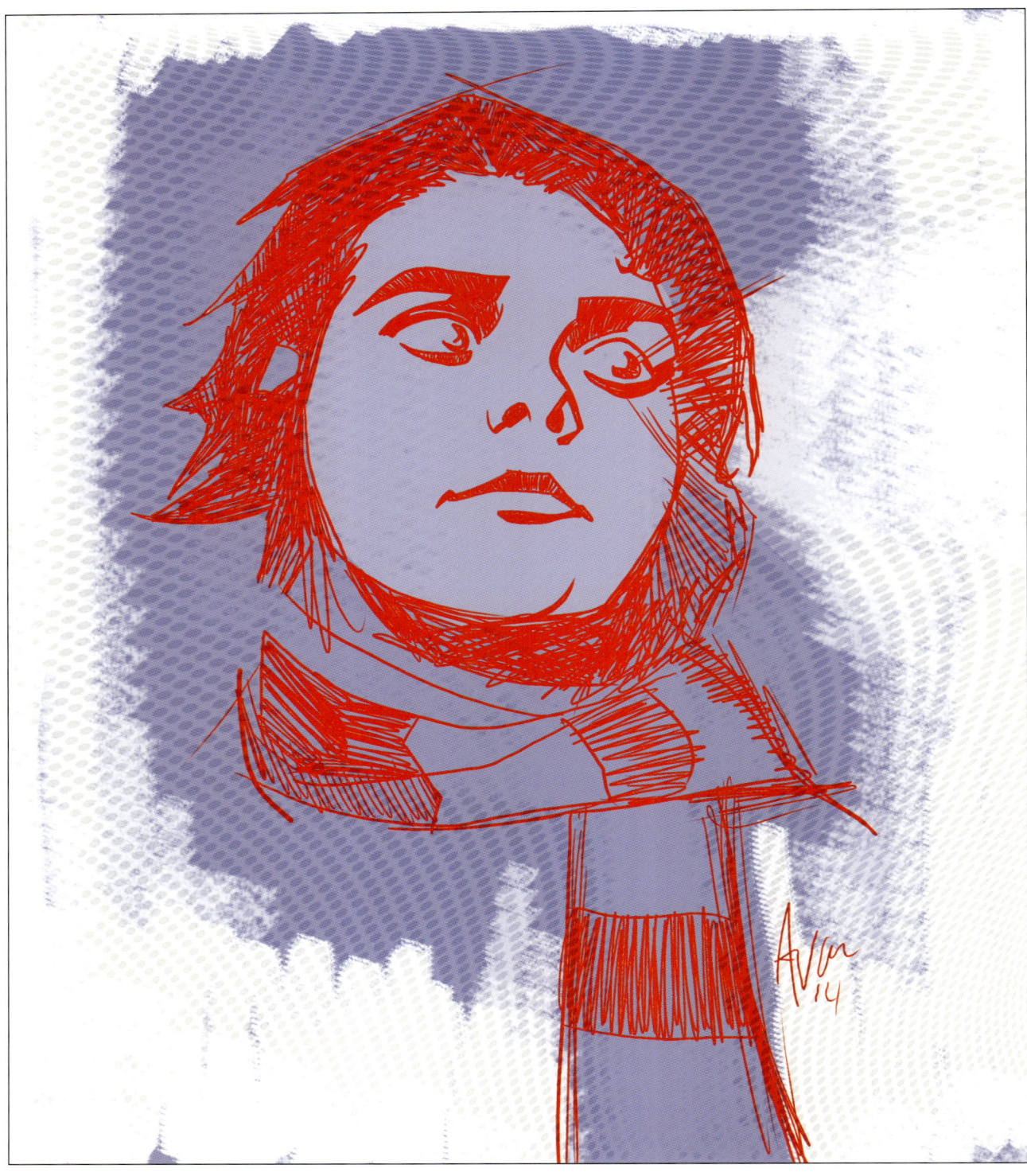

Portrait of Gerard Way

We were waiting to hear about a third season of *Powers* in 2016 when I got the call to work on *Cave Carson Has a Cybernetic Eye* with Gerard Way at DC's Young Animal imprint. I had just finished the Aleister Crowley book with Douglas Rushkoff at Dark Horse and an *Attack on Titan* story and needed a new regular gig when Shelly Bond and Gerard came to me. I knew Gerard back before My Chemical Romance when he was an aspiring comics writer and artist, when we'd worked together on a piece for a Jim Krueger idea.

I assumed *Cave Carson* was a miniseries, but they said it would be an ongoing monthly. I hadn't drawn an ongoing series since *Judge Dredd* in the early nineties, but I threw myself into it. Shelly left DC and our new editor was Molly Mahan, who Taki and I had worked with on *Red Sonja* for Dynamite, and Jamie Rich, who'd edited *Powers* at one point. The best experiences in comics are when you work with people you know.

I showed them all the crazy stuff Nick Filardi had done with our colors on *The Victories*, with Ben Day dots and Zip-a-Tone. His design and coloring ideas made my pages look ten times better. *Cave Carson* doesn't feel like working on a DC book—it feels like a creator-owned project with friends.

I was struck by *Cave Carson*'s Silver Age stories, when Cave was wearing a hard hat. I was interested in how they'd drawn the underworld, the layers below the earth's surface. In those days they didn't have as many reference photos as we do today, so textbooks would show the layers of the earth drawn in a shadowy crosshatch way. One layer would be dots, the next crosshatched. I played around with that idea, but we take it so much further. For Cave's cyber-eye point of view, we start with that and add magic mushrooms, playing with page designs in off-the-wall ways that make sense storywise for this book.

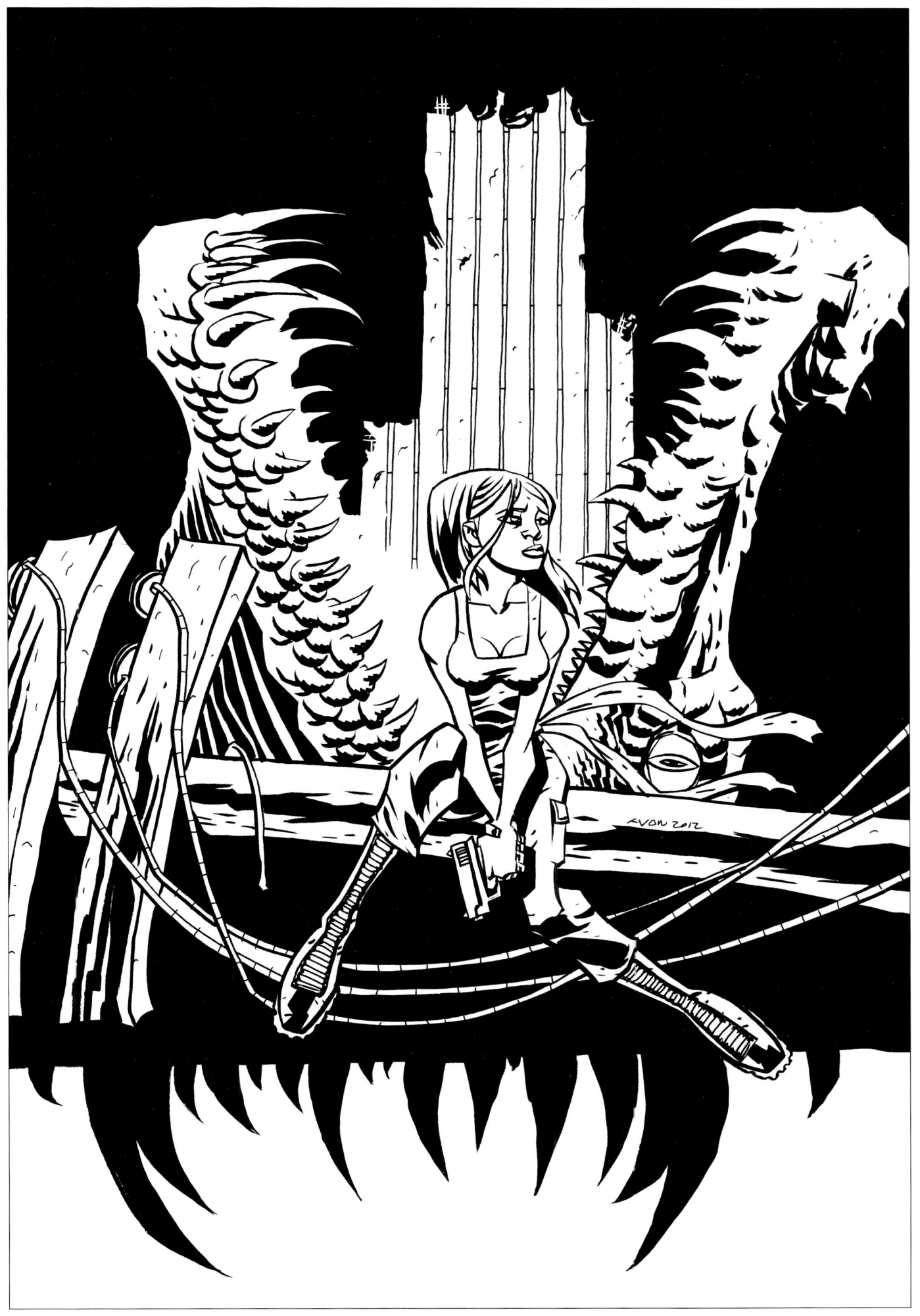

Cover for Tim Daniel's *Enormous*

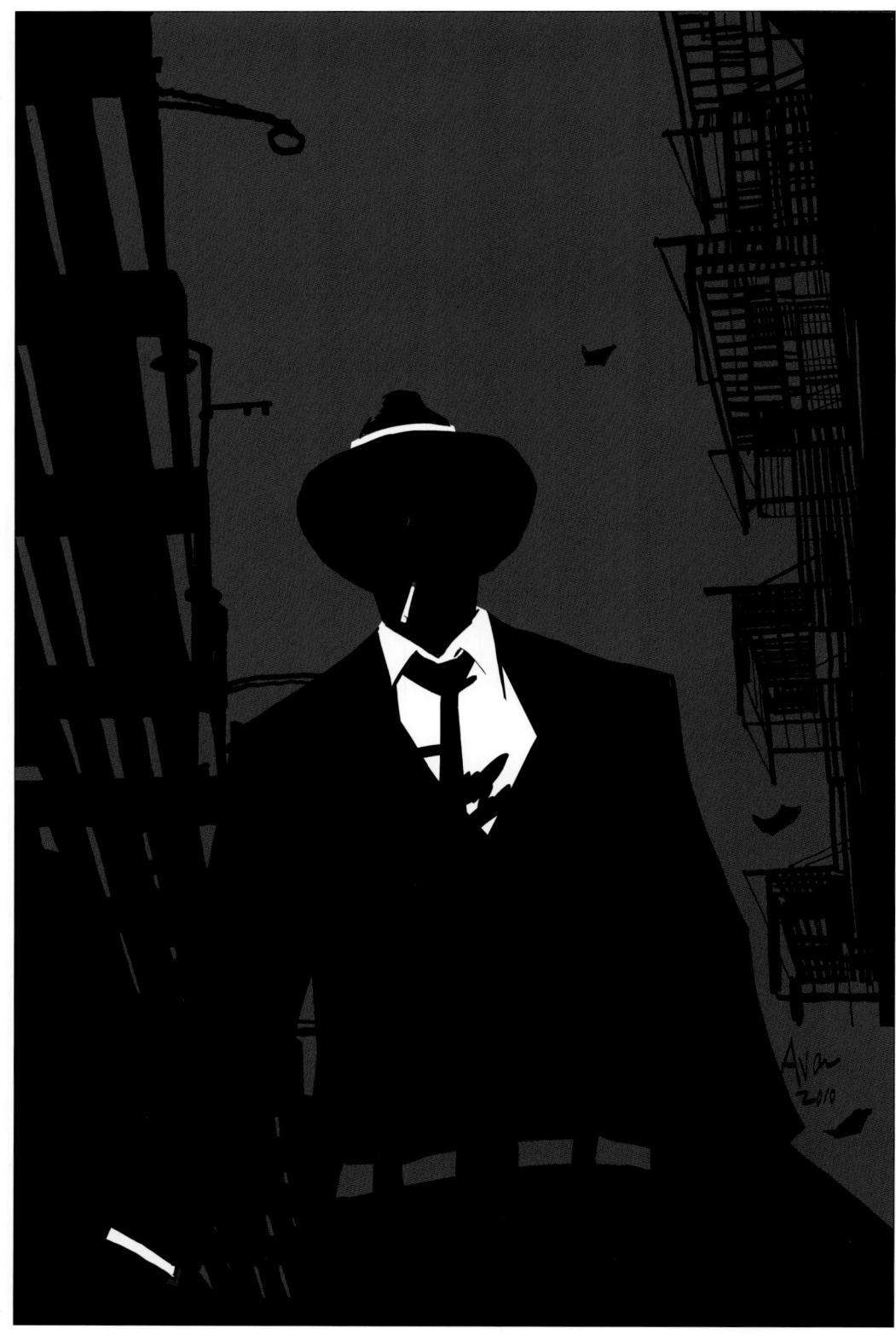

I'm very proud of *United States of Murder Inc.* (Icon, 2014). Not only because it's me and Brian with Taki coloring it—I'm proud of the story concept. Everybody loves mob stories, but it feels like every idea has been done to death. If you can't find something new to say, it falls flat. This idea started at a Halloween party at Randy Bowen's house. Lots of Portland's comics creators were there, like Mike and Laura Allred, David Walker, Matt Fraction, Kelly Sue DeConnick, and Matt Wagner. I casually said to Brian, "What if the mob had never lost its corporate power after the FBI brought them down? If they had no legal opposition, would they be fighting oil companies, or the Vatican?" Brian lit up and said, "That's an amazing idea!"

We called it *Mob World* as a working title, but there was a TV series on TNT called *Mob City*, so we had to change it. "Murder Inc." was the name given to the mob by the press and FBI in the 1930s, and we added the US to show their growth and arrogance in size and power.

Taki hadn't colored a comic before, but we needed to make this creator-owned book on a small budget. We also wanted it to look different from what Nick was doing on *Powers*. Instead of doing the world with desaturated colors and sepias, I wanted saturated flat colors to contrast the blacks I use, almost a throwback to the classic four-color approach used in the early days of comics. Taki came back with examples that told the story in a complexly unconventional way.

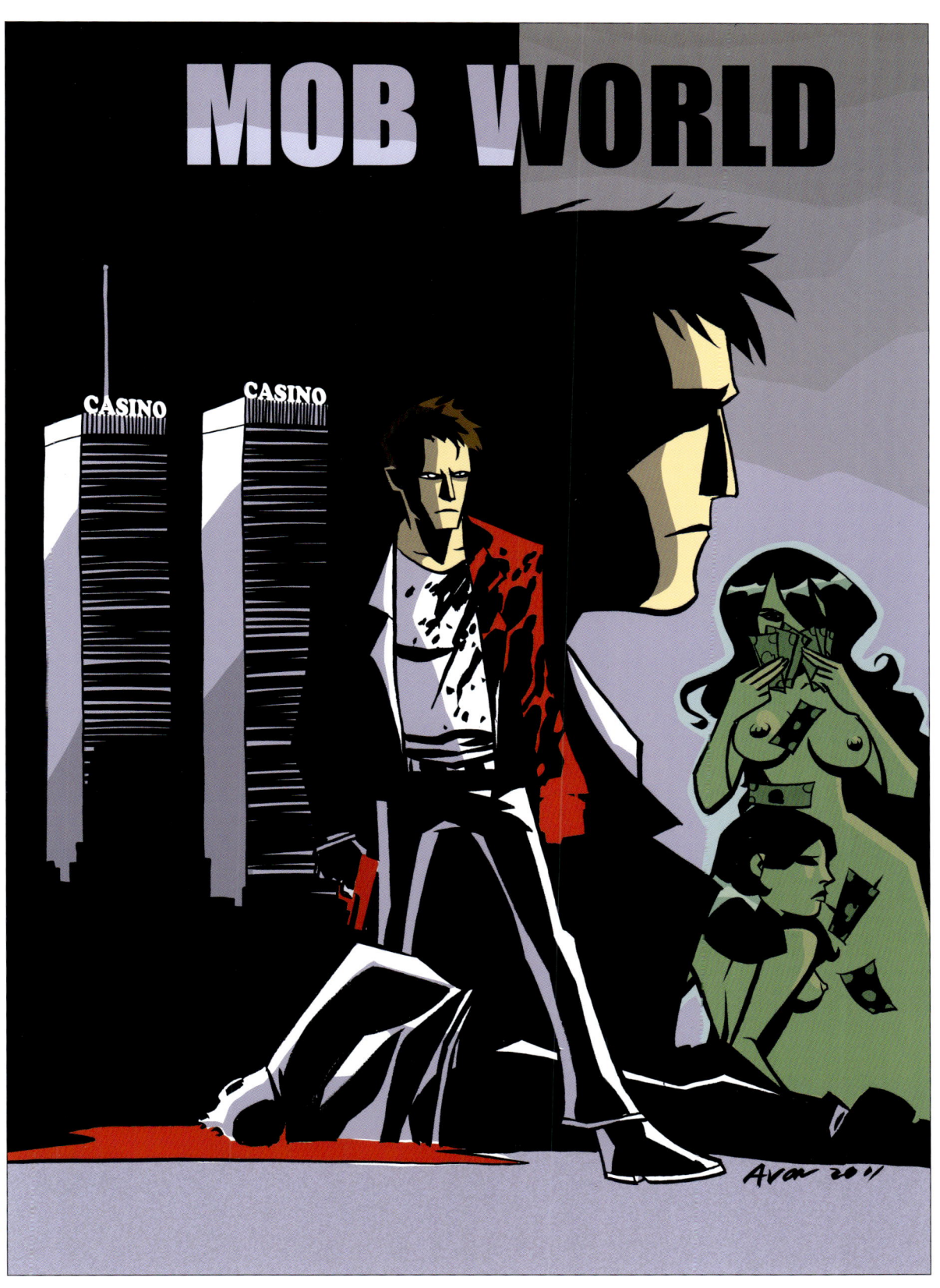

NO PLAN B: THE ART OF MICHAEL AVON OEMING

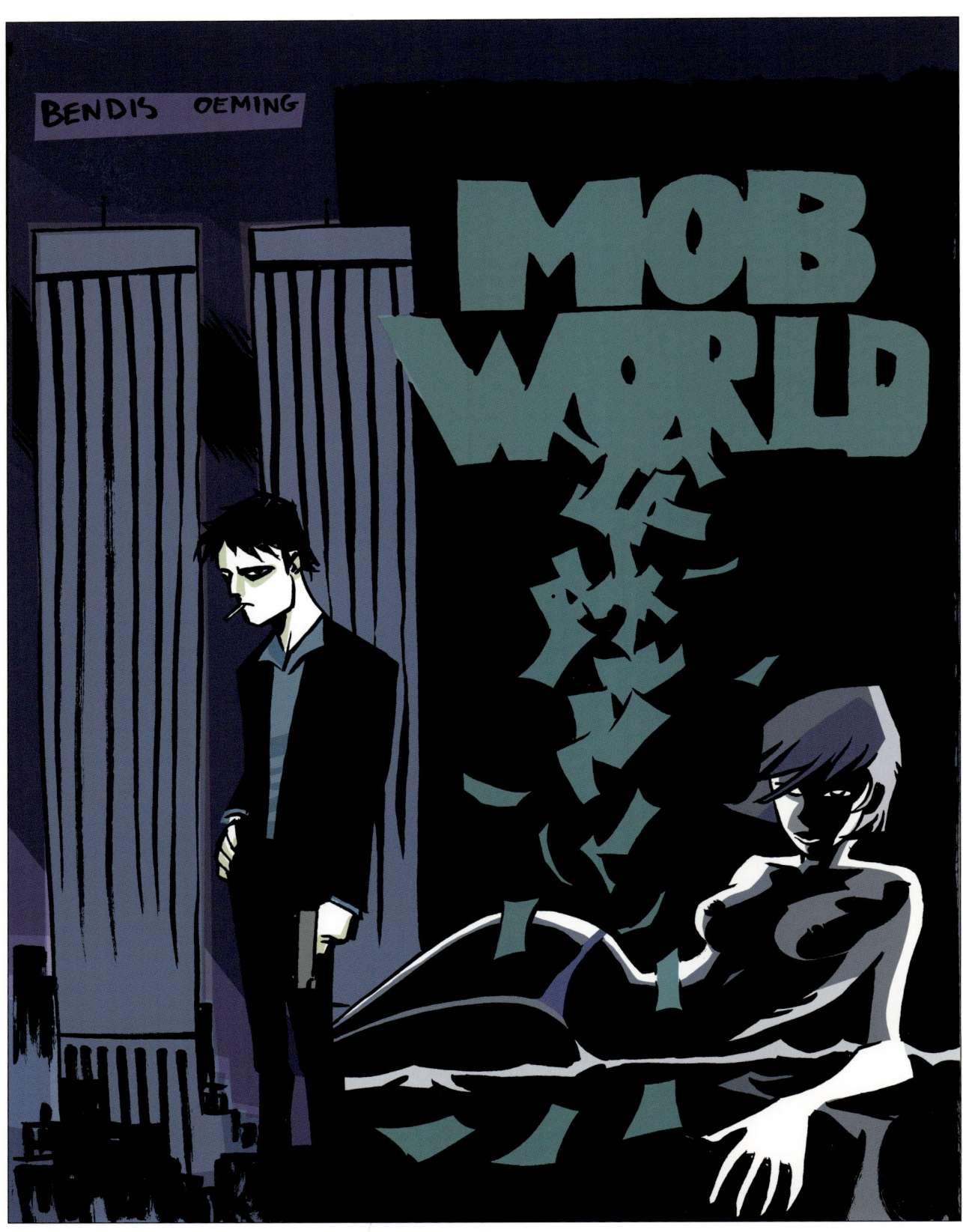

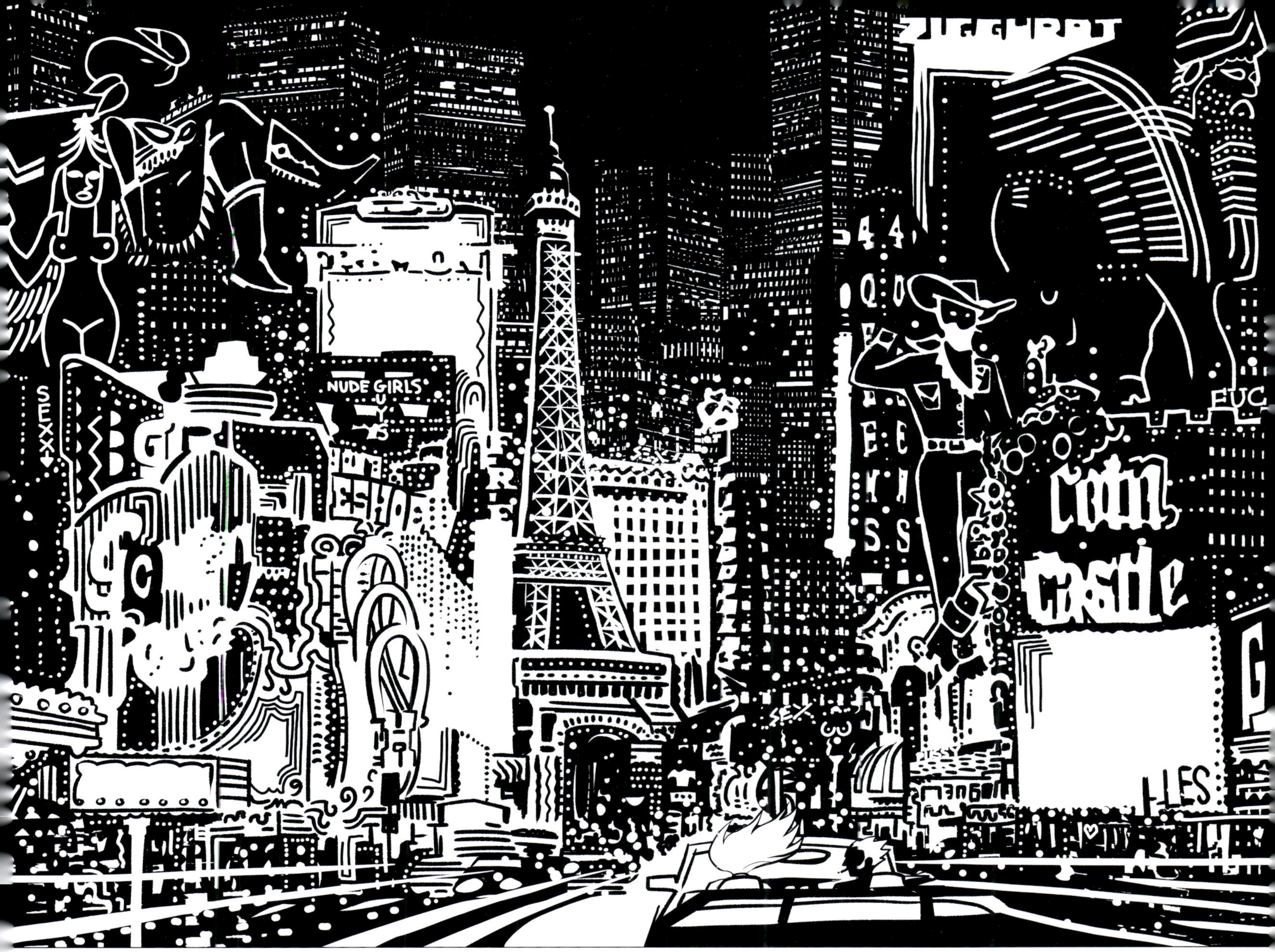

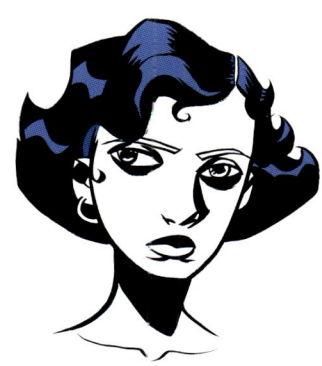
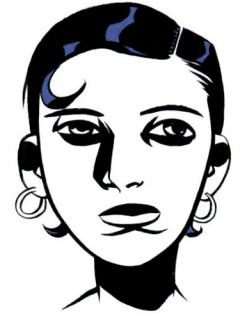
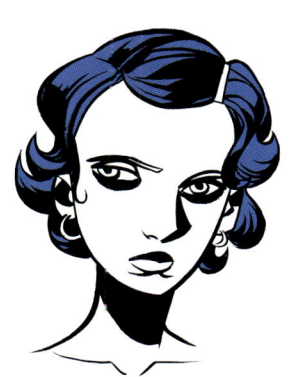
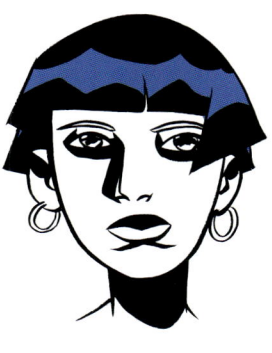
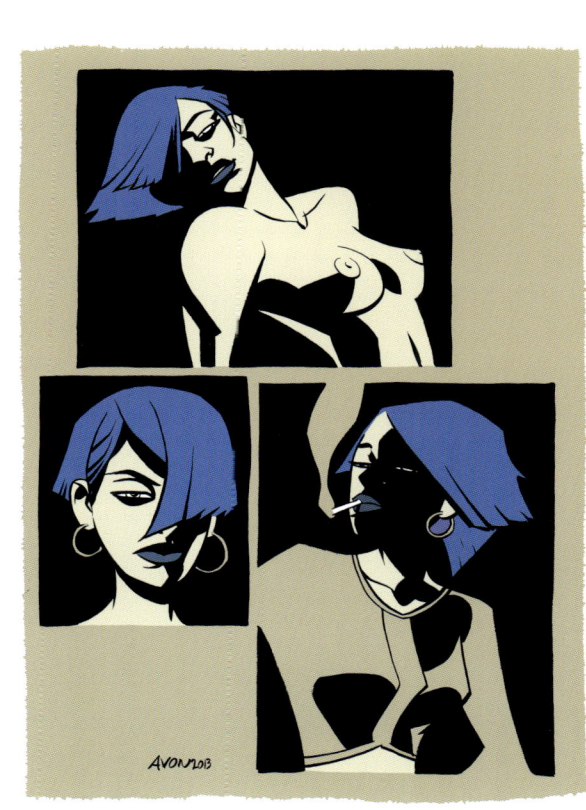

NC PLAN B: THE ART OF MICHAEL AVON OEMING

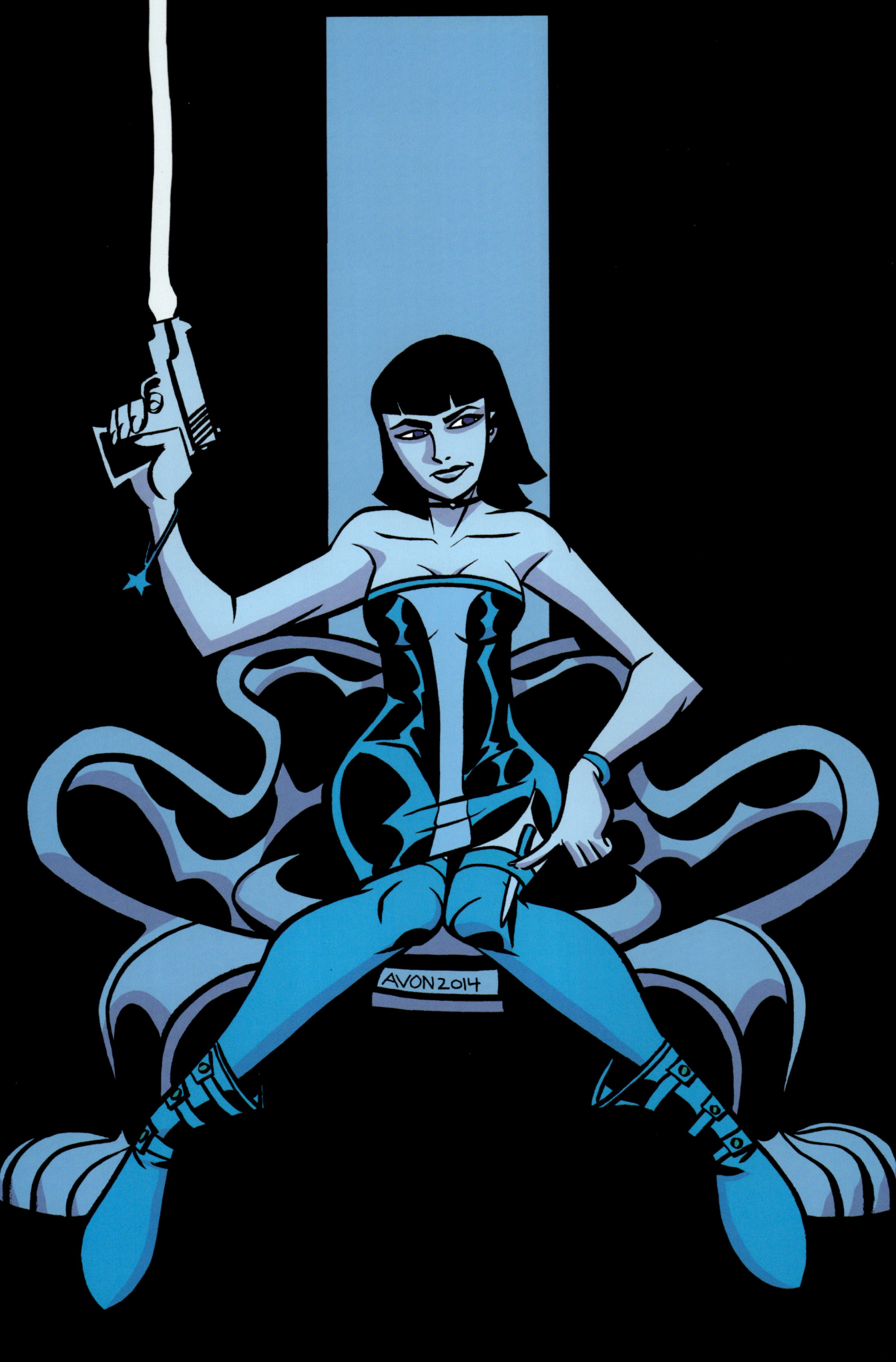

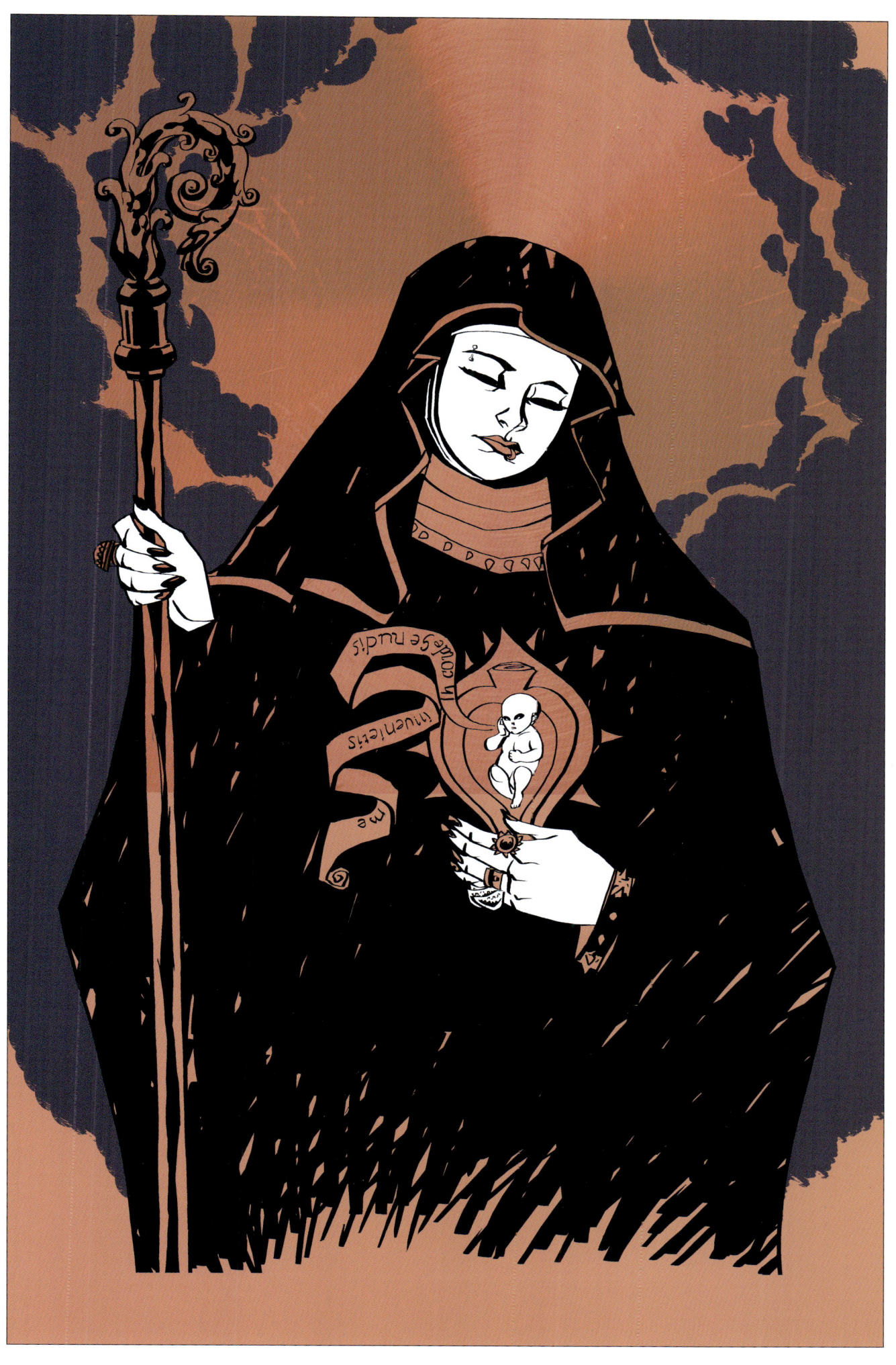

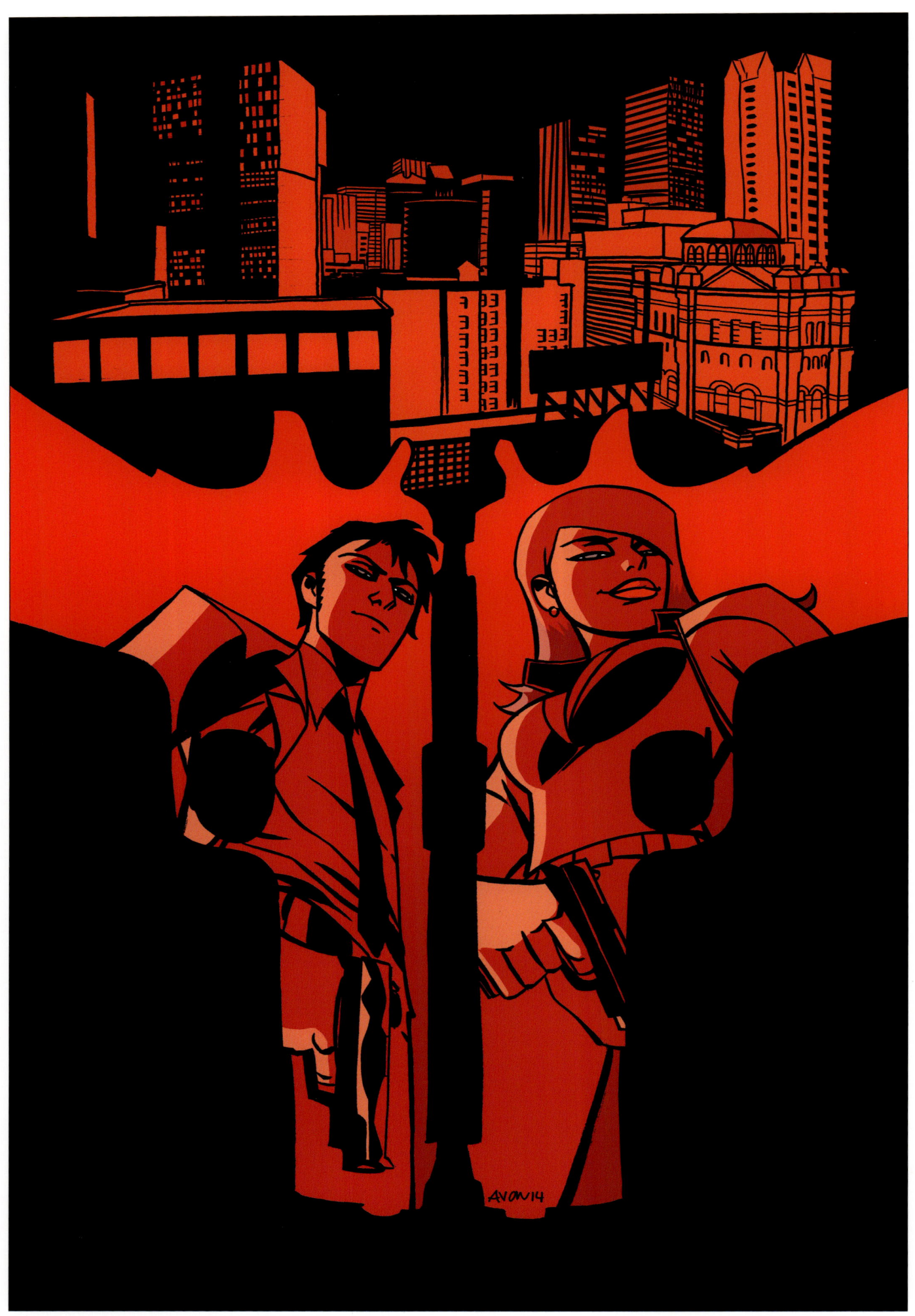

United States of Murder covers

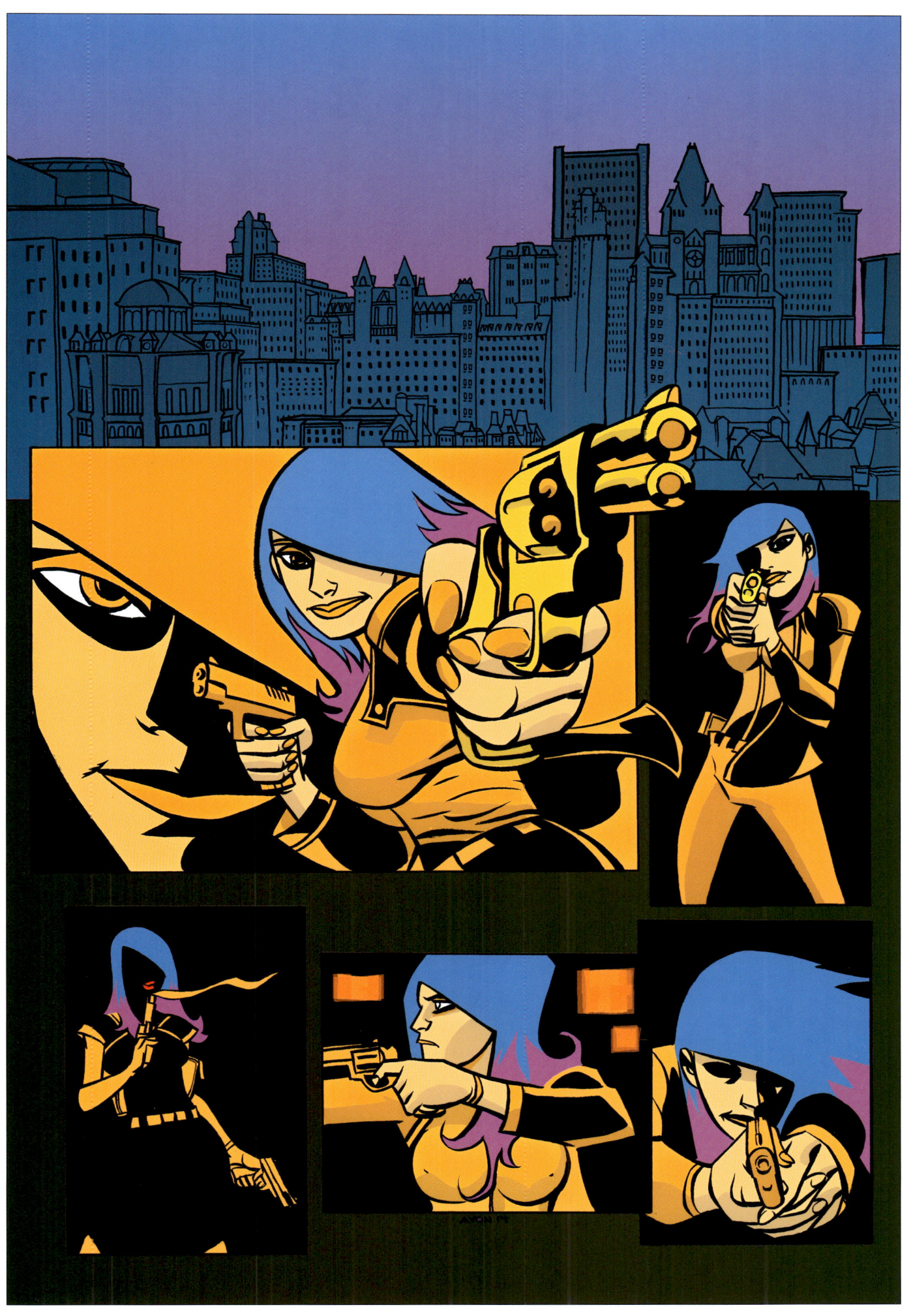

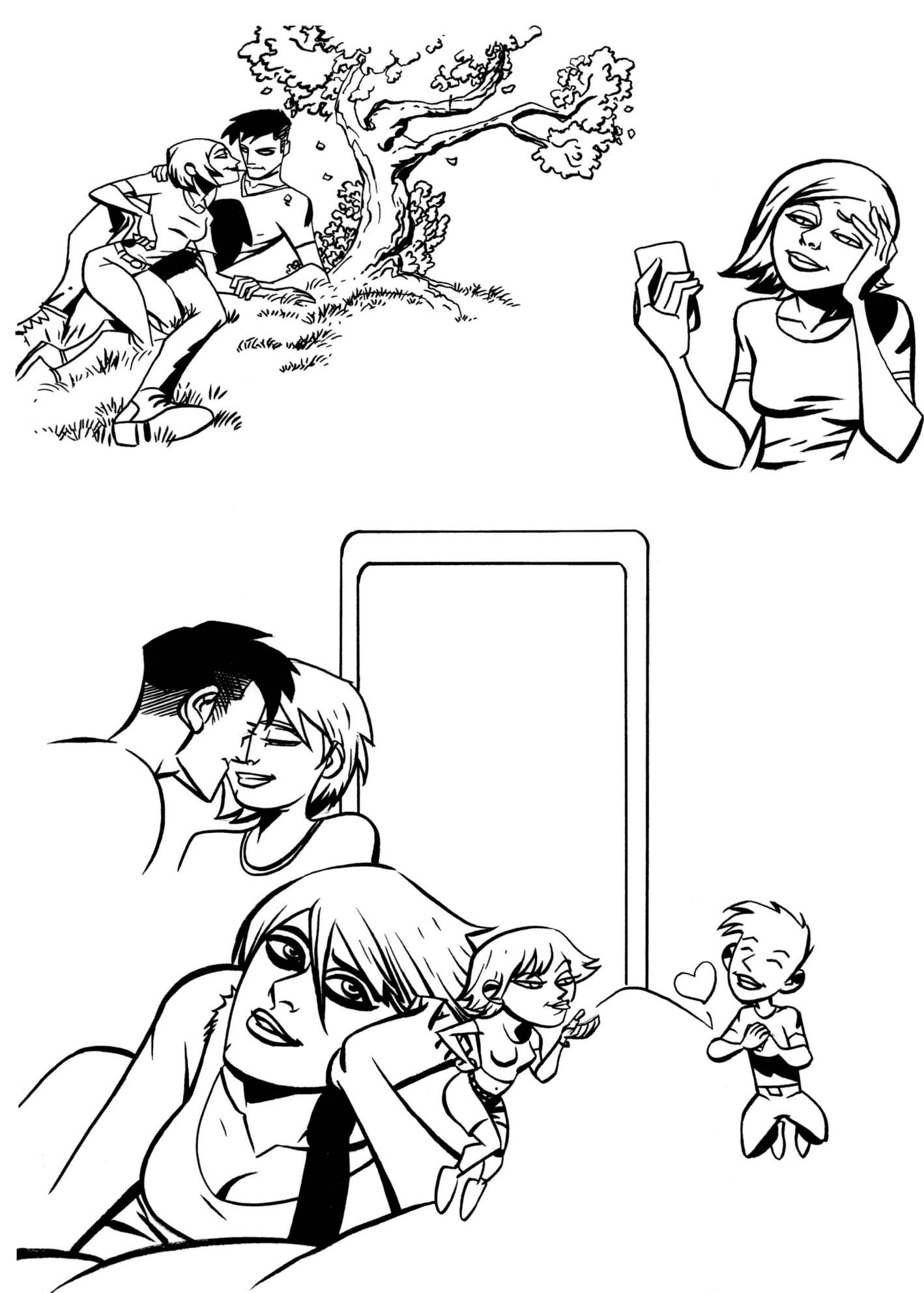

Sinergy character designs

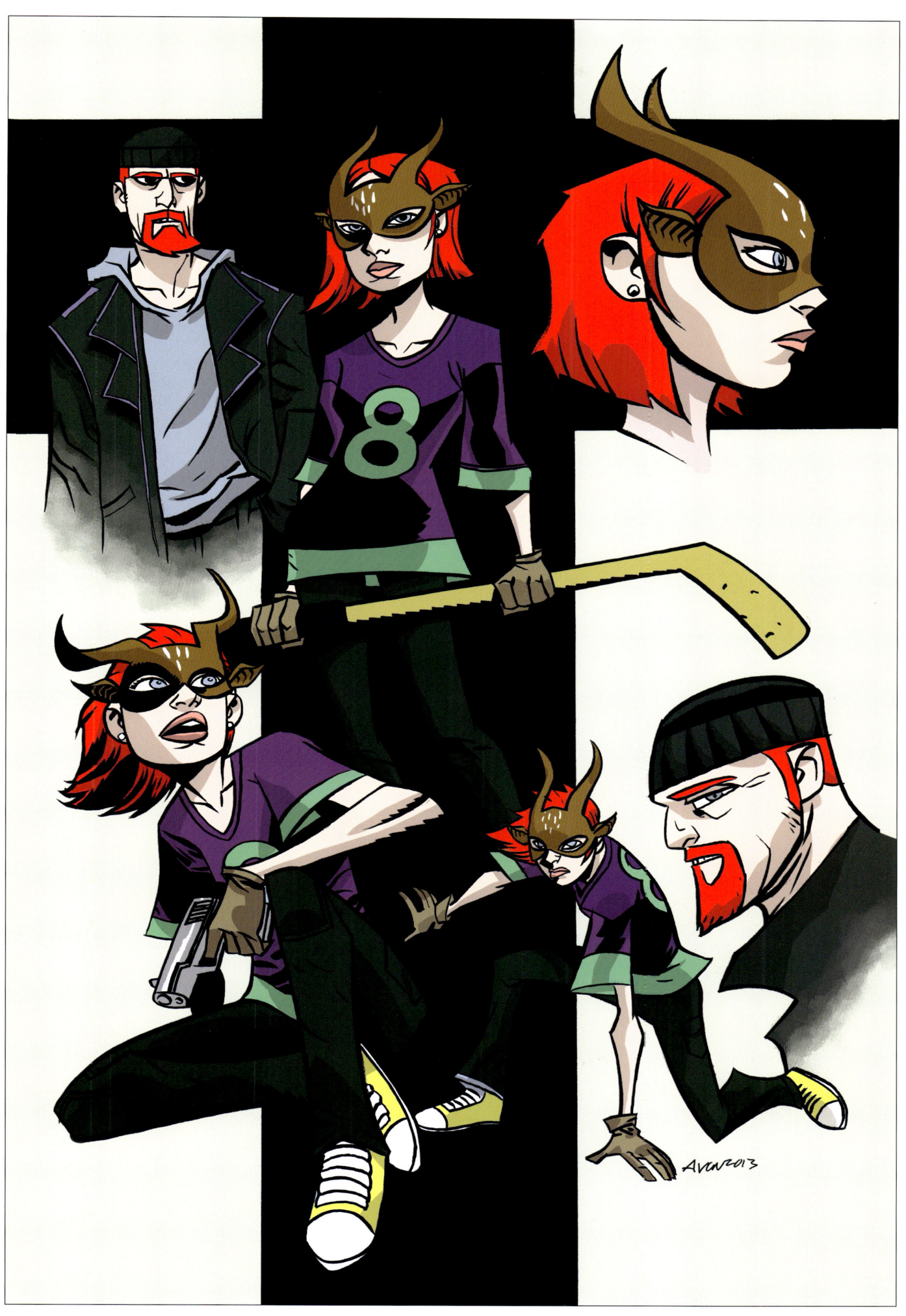

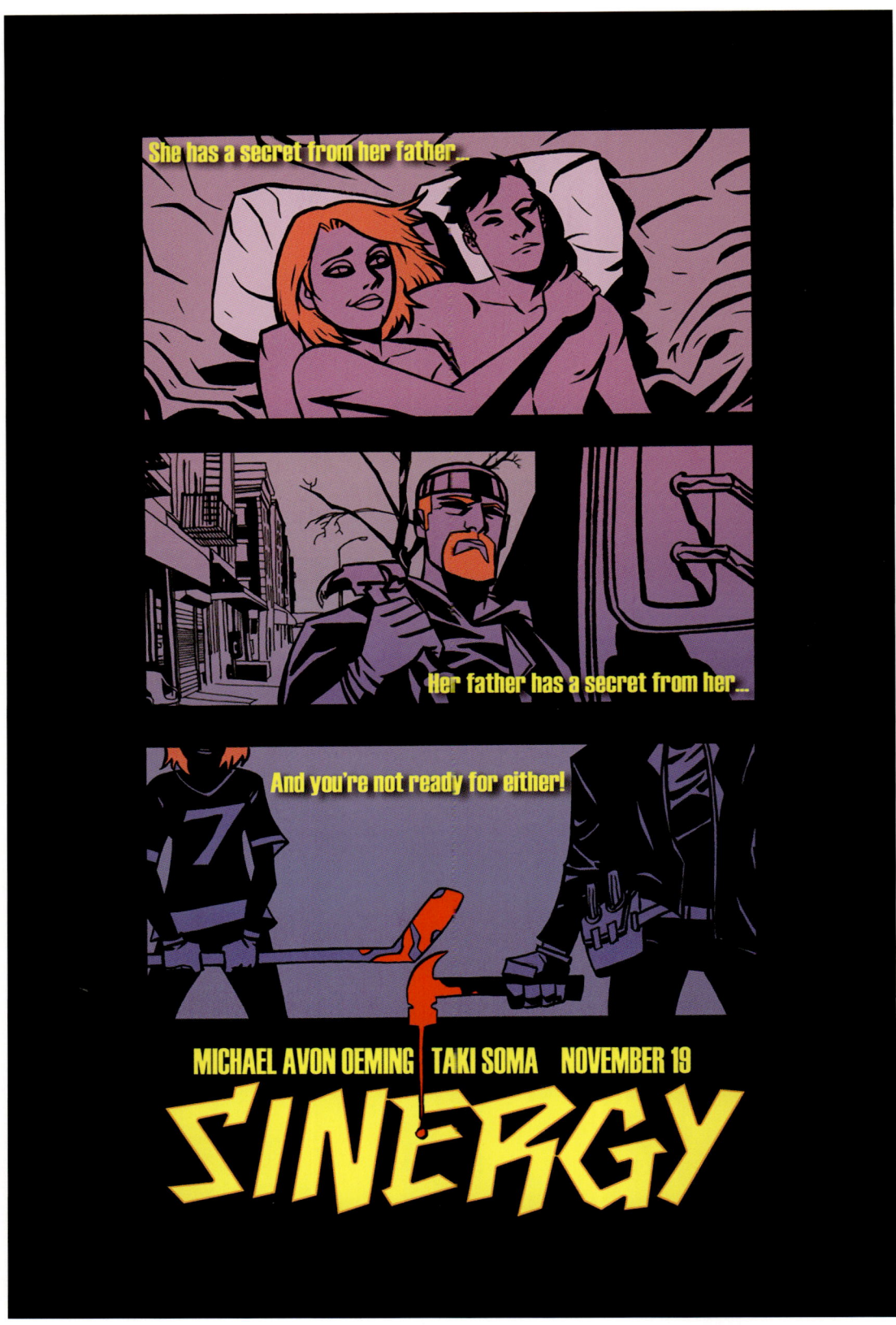

Sinergy is part of the monster-hunting genre I've always loved, with some sort of creature running around, and only a certain type of person can actually see them and protect the rest of the world. That general concept has been revisited so often because it's so cool.

Originally I wanted to do a mother-daughter story, because we don't see much of that. When I got Taki involved, we started talking about her very close relationship with her father, and she felt that that sort of family dynamic is lacking in a lot of dramas. You see a lot of fathers and sons or brothers and sisters, but not a lot of father-daughter genre stories.

We set up this father and daughter's story around monster hunting, but it's really about the two of them. The daughter falls in love with a monster, and the father's desire to kill the daughter's boyfriend in this case is quite literal.

Taki and I got to explore and develop this over a long period of time, finally coming out in 2014 from Image. I had a really good time with the characters. A director from *Powers* is interested in *Sinergy* as a TV series and we're shopping it around now, which will help if we want to do more comics.

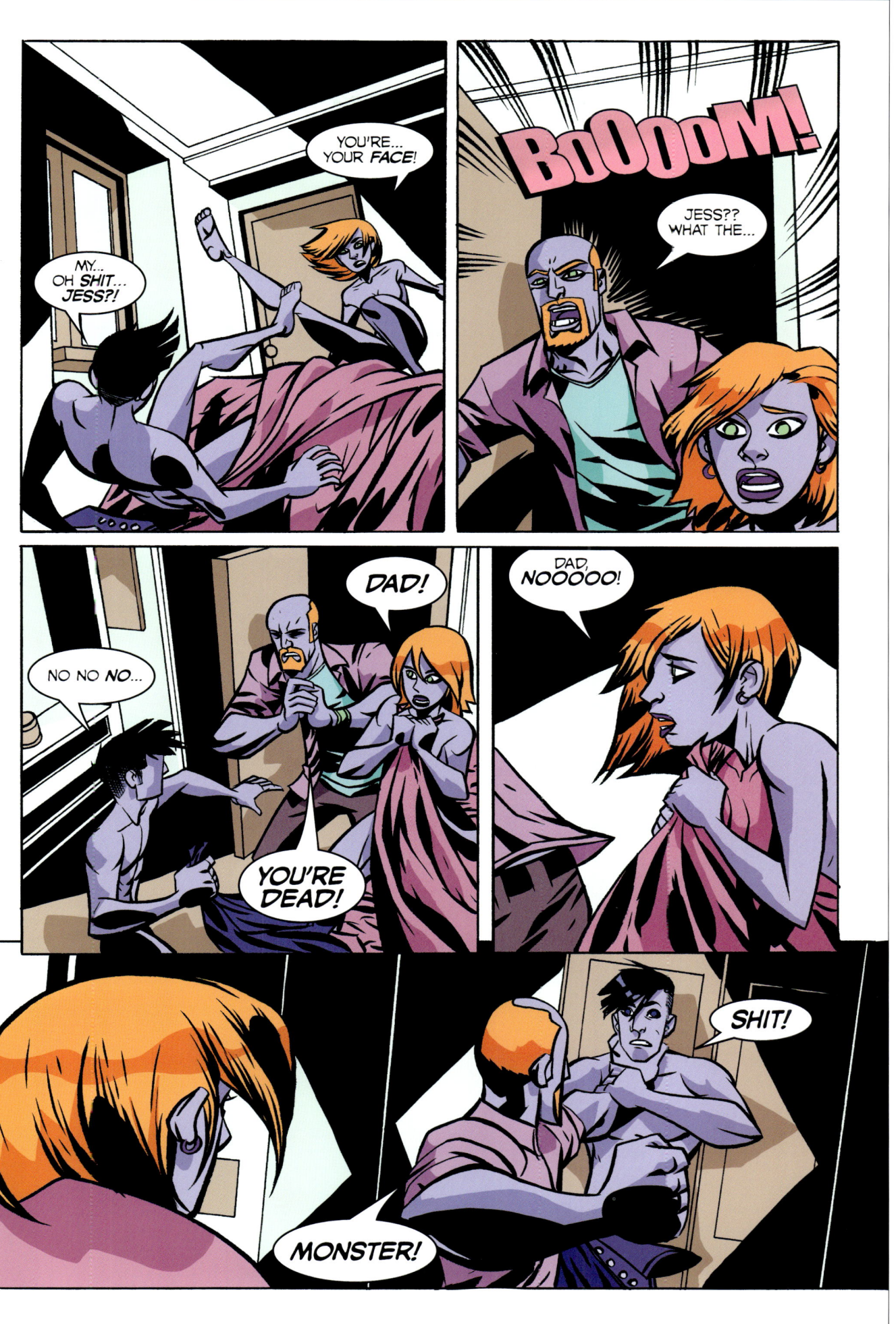

Sinergy interior page, colors by Taki Soma

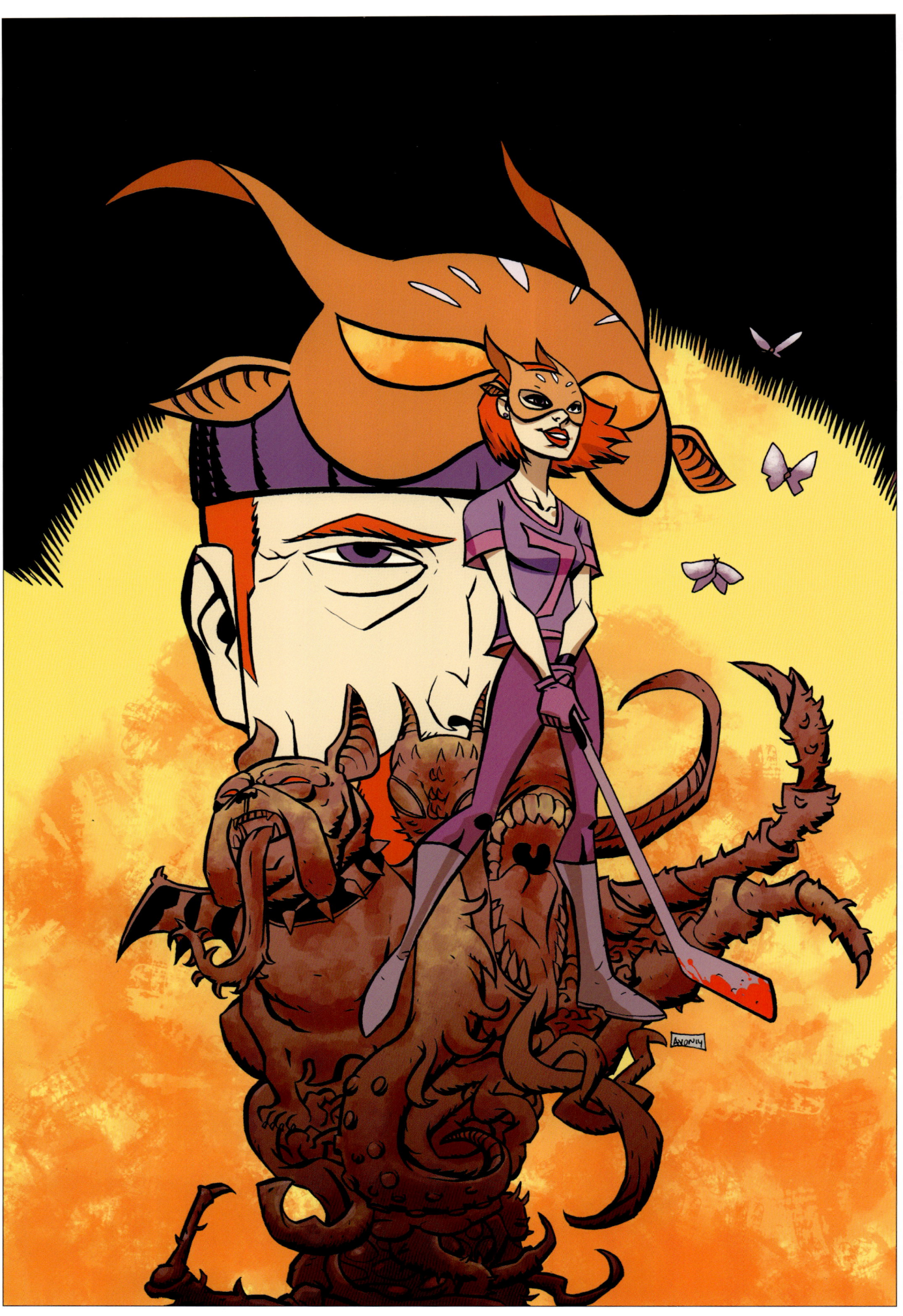

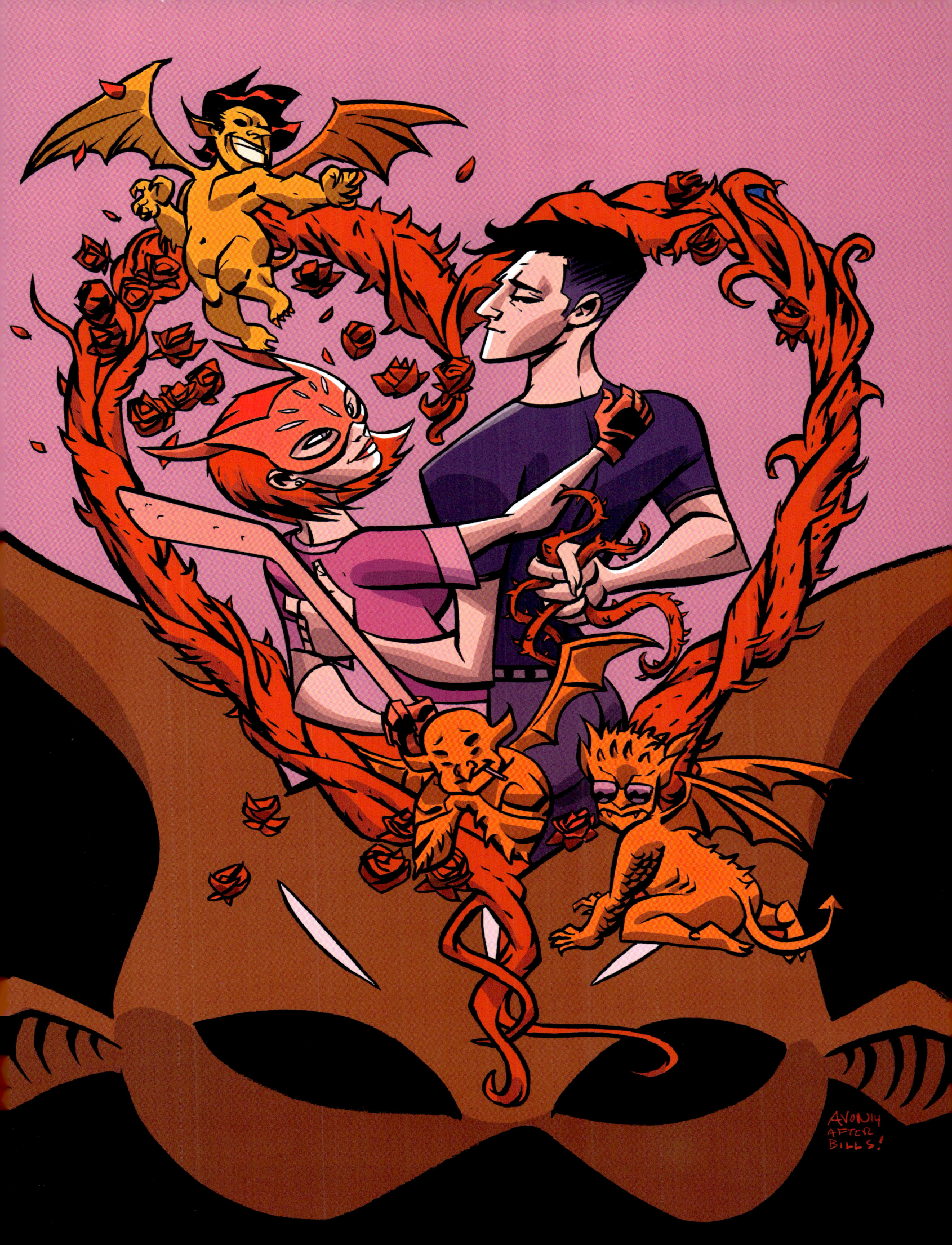

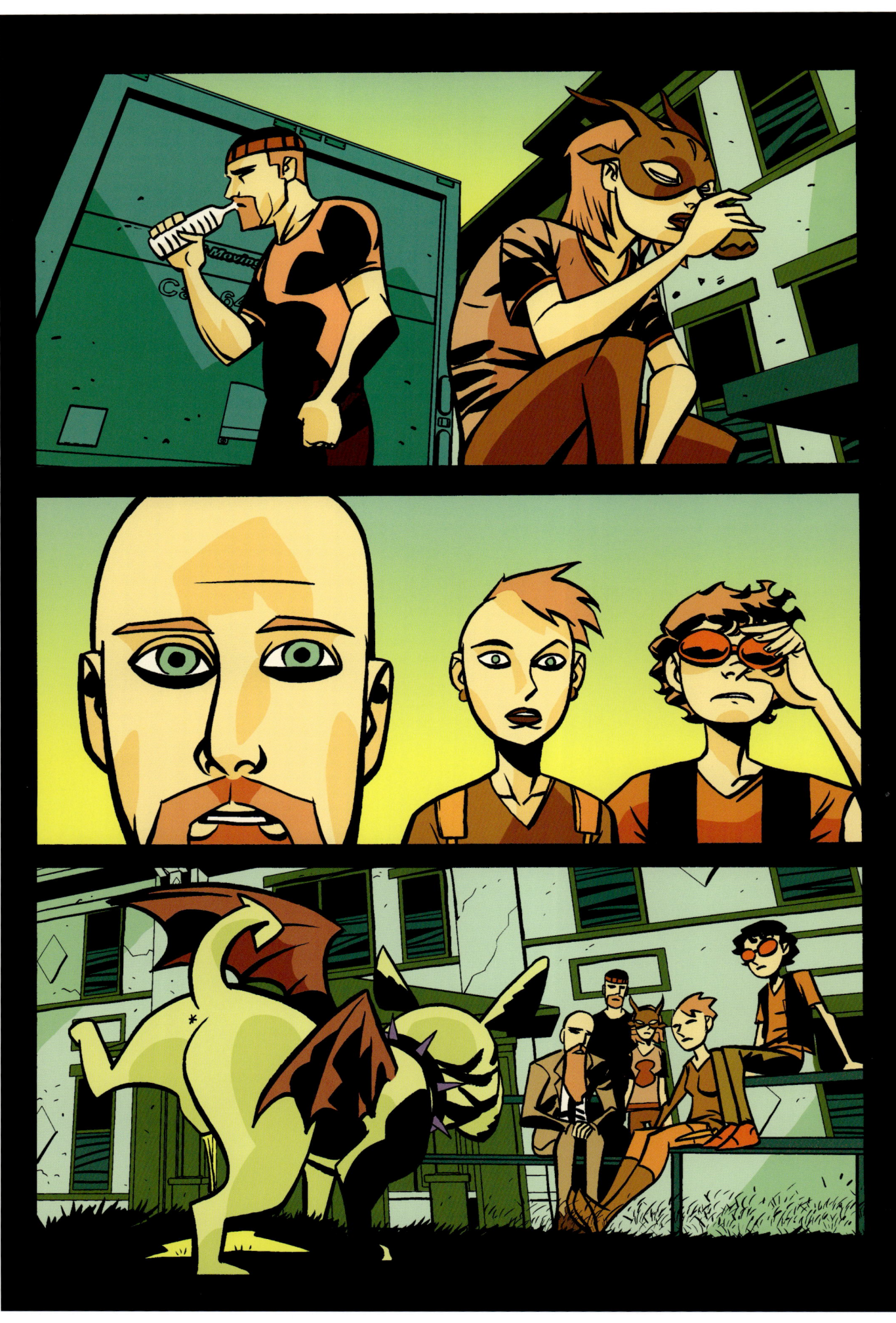

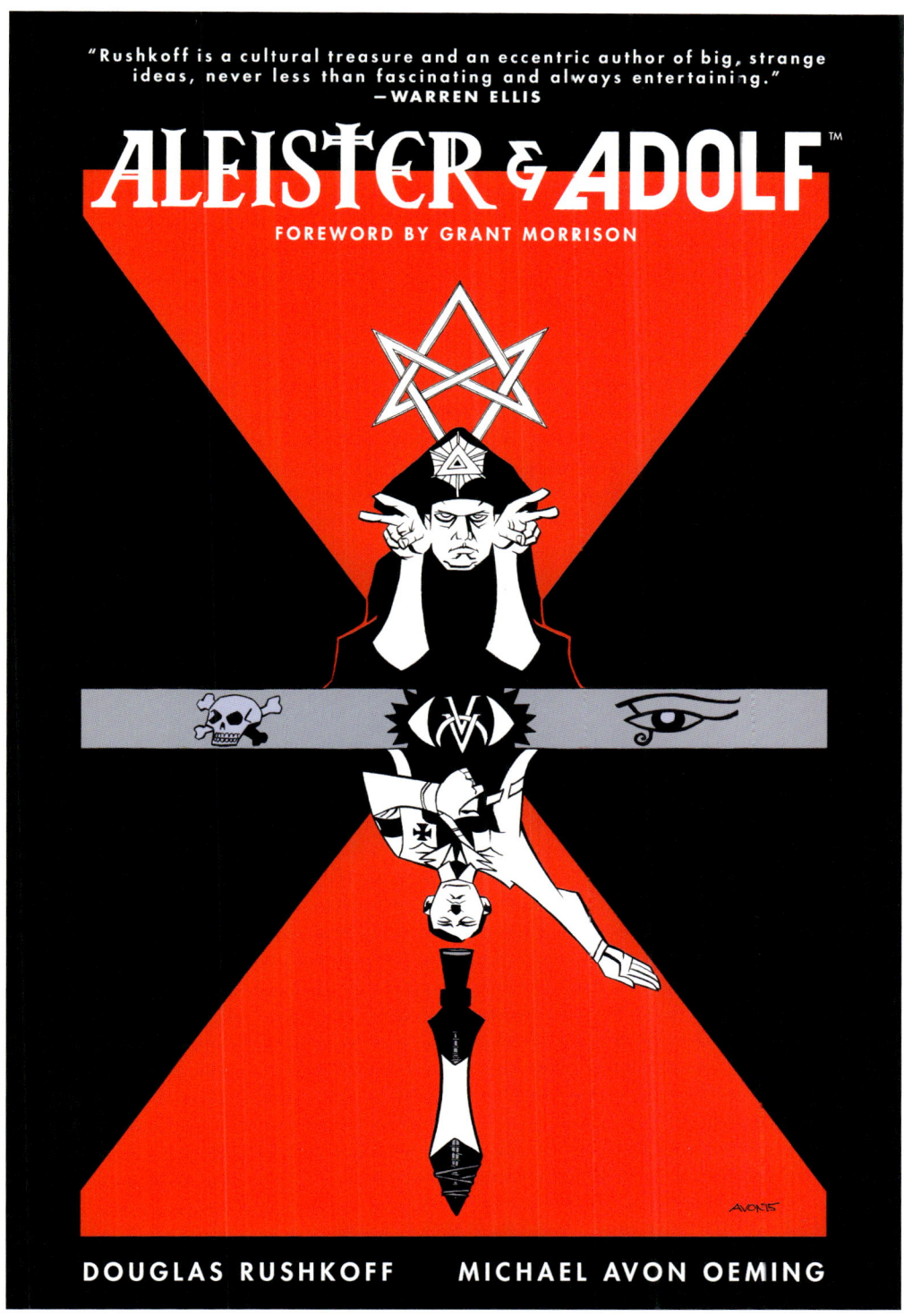

Aleister & Adolf came to me through Dark Horse editor Daniel Chabon. Douglas Rushkoff, a journalist and film producer, has made documentaries for PBS's *Frontline* as one of the foremost thinkers about future technology and how we interact with it. He's written great comics, like Vertigo's *Testament* with Liam Sharp. Liam told me Doug's a standup guy and great storyteller.

This was a book about the evil men do, about how Nazi belief in the occult found its way into everyday society. There are factual accounts of Aleister Crowley working with World War II British intel agents, like future James Bond author Ian Fleming, doing counterespionage against the occult forces within the Nazi party. It sounds like bullshit, but this stuff really happened.

Their ideas were crazy, from looking for the surviving society of Atlantis to searching for the Spear of Destiny, which was used against Christ by a Roman guard and had magic powers. Many Nazis believed so heavily in this mythology and in black magic that they'd consult astrologers to plan out attacks. The Allies hired Crowley to create false astrology charts to manipulate the Nazis' battle plans.

I love subjects like this, but drawing some of the images of occult-based Nazi atrocities was disturbing. They experimented with POWs, amputating limbs to see what they could do for their own soldiers wounded in battle. I was concerned about the tone of the story and my art, not wanting the book to be misconstrued as glorifying or agreeing with any of their actions.

I got to play with different art styles. It came out in November 2016. The book is conventional black and white in the World War II scenes, but when we flash forward to the nineties I used Zip-a-Tone. When magic is used, I'd use watercolors. It was a great book to experiment on, and Douglas and I have become good friends. I hope we work together again soon.

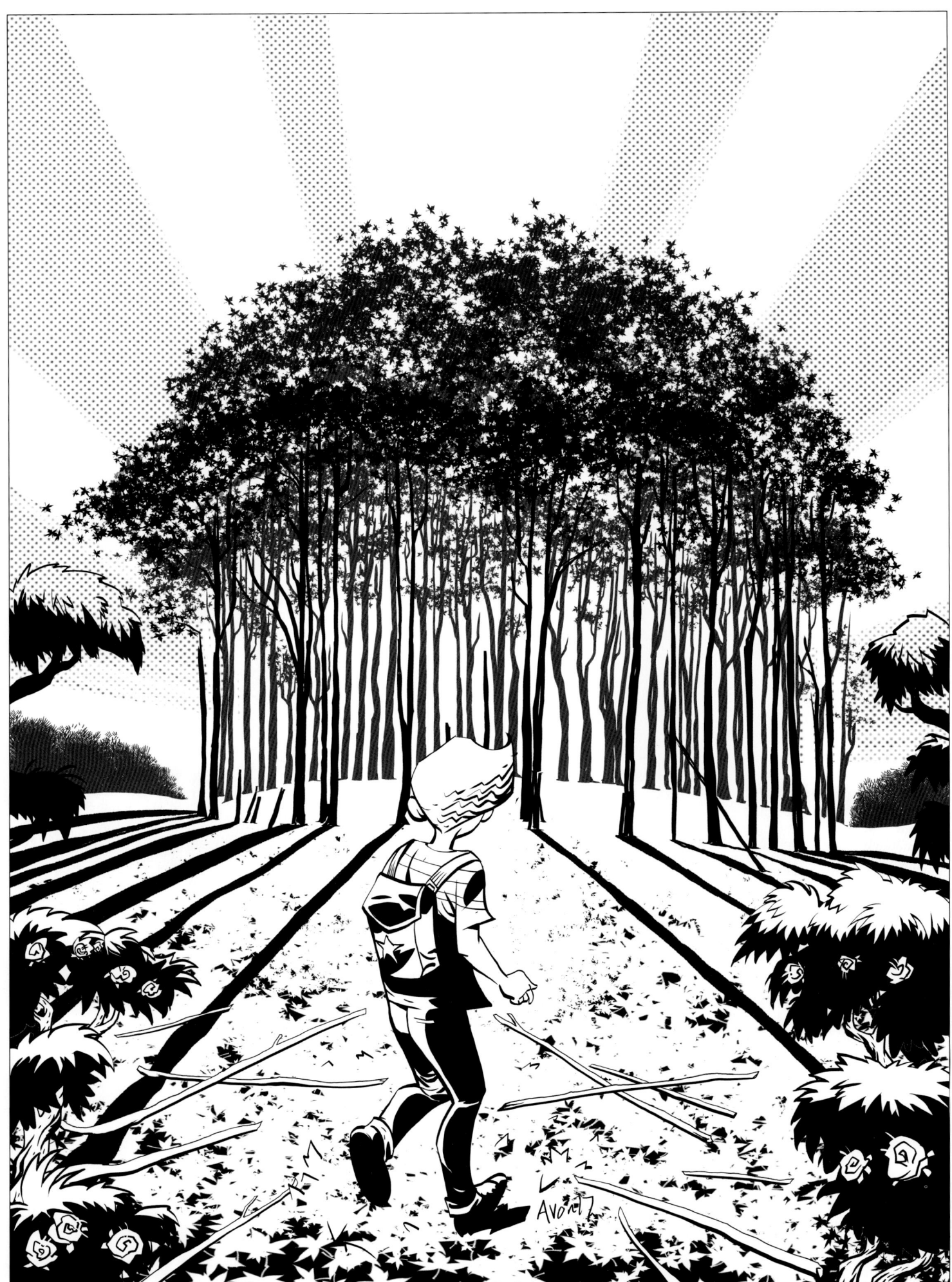
Unpublished Oeming project

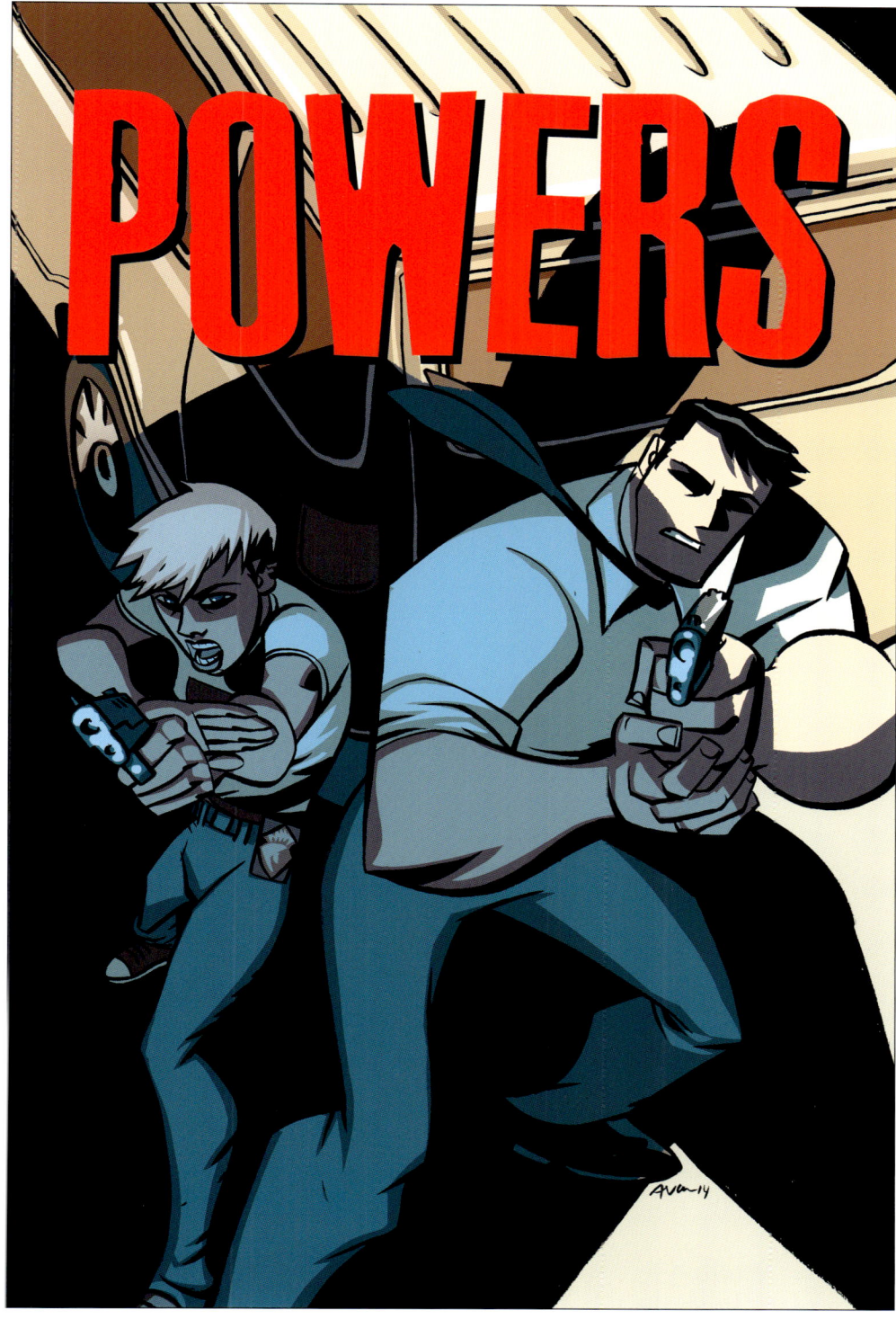

Powers covers, colored by Nick Filardi

It was a long time from when *Powers* was first optioned as a film in 2001 to the beginning of production of the Sony PlayStation series. There was lots of interest in adapting *Powers*, but many attempts missed the point of what we did in the comic, interpreting it as a straightforward superhero story.

At that time comic creators were allowed little or no involvement in the production of an adaptation, way before Robert Kirkman and *The Walking Dead*. It made no sense—Brian got animation, TV, and film writing offers, but was never invited to work on *Powers*. There was an unwritten rule that the concept creators weren't needed in the actual screenwriting process.

Then FX wanted a genre fiction show. They shot a pilot with Jason Patric as Walker, Lucy Punch as Deena, and a cast that included Vinnie Jones, Charles Dutton, and Bailee Madison. Screenwriter Charlie Huston had a background in writing comics as well as TV. He broke the code on *Powers*, writing a great pilot script that finally understood where Bendis was coming from. Charlie was instrumental in explaining to the TV brass that for the series to work, Brian had to be involved in the writers' room.

But eventually FX decided to pass. Sony decided to experiment with its PlayStation box, to compete in the Netflix/Hulu streaming arena. They thought *Powers* would be great as their own streaming TV series, and they looked at us as production partners from the start. Brian was in the writers' room the whole time, and I went in to draw ideas and proof-of-concept sketches.

We had viewing numbers in the millions, combining the online platforms like Crackle and YouTube, but Sony decided not enough viewers were subscribing to the PlayStation platform to get the show, so we ended production after the second season.

NO PLAN B: THE ART OF MICHAEL AVON OEMING 181

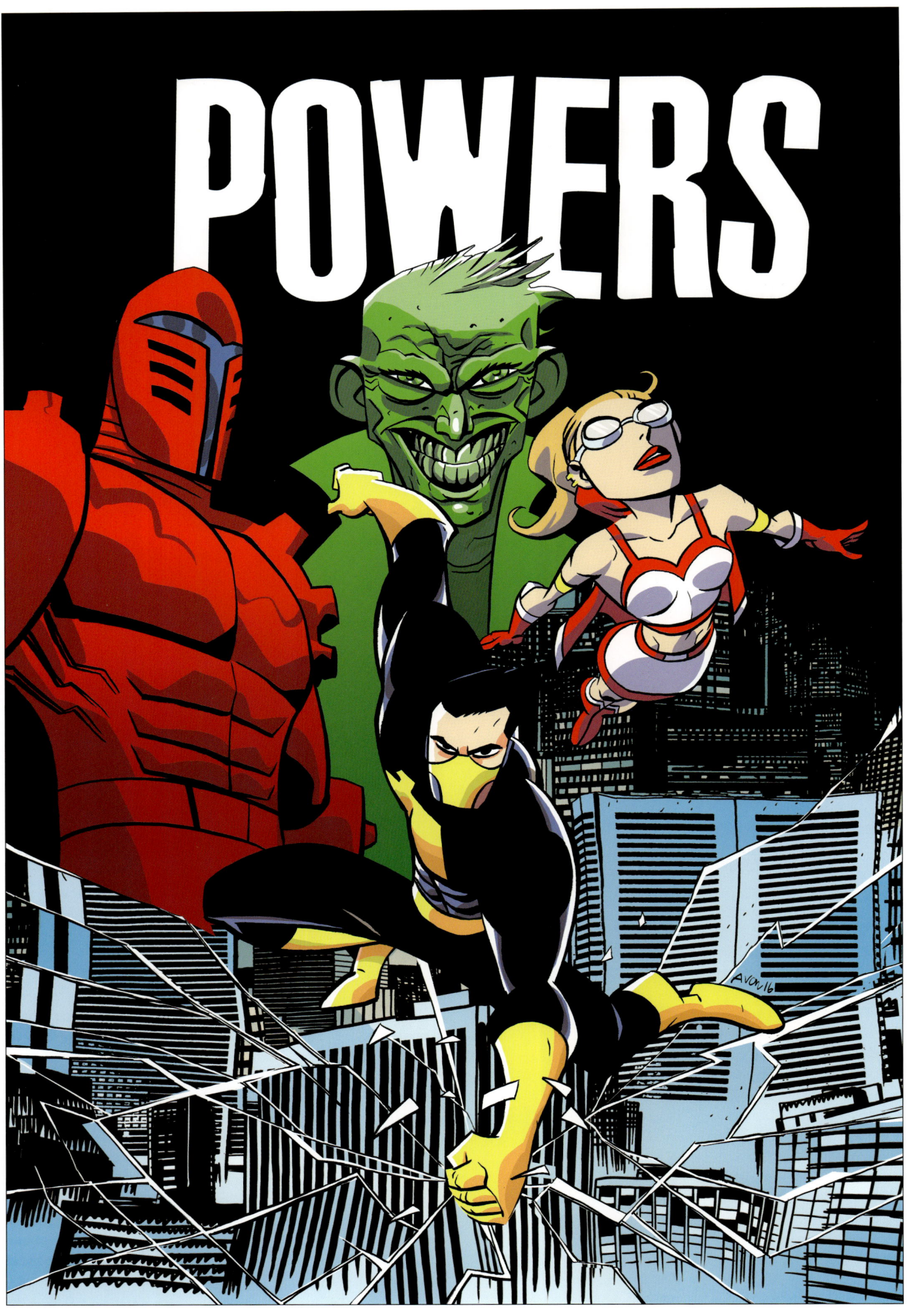

AFTERWORD

By David Mack

The first day that I met Mike Oeming, one of us gave the other a black eye.

We immediately became the closest of friends. In fact, I love Mike Oeming so much that I married him.

1994. We were signing at a comic shop in Philadelphia called Claude's Comics. (Claude was the dog.) Mike walked up to my table and gave me a drawing he'd done of one of my *Kabuki* characters. He drew it so quickly, right there, and it was so good. That was our introduction.

That's Mike. Always drawing, always giving, purity from the idea to the making. Not fussing about it. Just having a thought, making a drawing, and giving it to a stranger.

That evening, Mike and I are talking about our odd childhoods, and it's clear that we are kindred spirits. And then we spontaneously begin wrestling. In the outdoors. In the grass. At night. In Philadelphia.

No one was mad. We just connected like that. With no ego. Like puppy dogs, like bear cubs wrestling, being what we are. Mike is incredibly physical, incredibly strong and quick, and trained as a wrestler. It was clear that we both had a kind of energy that had to daily be worked out of our system. The same way you would walk a dog so that it doesn't eat all your furniture. So although this seems strange to write now, that's how we interacted upon meeting in 1994. Kind of *Fight Club*, pre–*Fight Club*.

Cut to one of us with a black eye, and one a bloody nose, and we decide to stop fighting and talk about art. So there in the grass at night in Philadelphia, one of us bleeding, one of us black and blue, Mike tells me that he sees differently, and that he can right now see an aura radiating from me in heat waves and colors.

I knew I was really going to like this colorful human.

I had met Brian Michael Bendis in 1993, and he and I were already super-close friends, working together. So when Claude's Comics invited me back to sign again, in 1995, I suggested they bring Brian as well. And that was the official meeting of Oeming, Bendis, and me all together.

Brian wasn't inclined to wrestle with Mike and me, but he seemed to get a kick out of us doing it. I remember a time when we were all sharing a hotel room in New York. Oeming and I were wrestling, and I had picked him up and was holding him upside down. Mike kicked me in the face so hard that my gum flew out of my mouth, and the entire room, including Brian and his wife and her friends, gasped in horror, thinking it was my tooth.

That very first art piece that Mike gave me—I painted over it and published it in a *Kabuki* book. Then I wrote some *Kabuki* stories that Mike did the art to in 1996. I love collaborating with Mike. I was always amazed at how naturally the drawings flowed from him.

Mike had a son around this time, and was working hard to make ends meet. He was working as a security guard, drawing his comics in that little security booth. We were all working on our comics and sending faxes to the others to get feedback and share our discoveries and improvements. It was always a joy to get these drawings from Mike in that security booth.

At each convention, Bendis, Oeming, and I would have dinners together and have what we called our MOB meetings. (I think Brian or Mike coined this for Mack, Oeming, Bendis.) We were getting our books published at Caliber Comics, and then we were all making our books at Image Comics. And then, in 2004, we formed the Icon imprint at Marvel and brought our books *Powers* and *Kabuki* there. Through it all we learned from each other and strategized how we each could improve.

And the improvement was not just artistic. Being around Mike makes you want to improve as a human being. It makes you want to be a better person, a better friend, and challenge yourself to grow your kindness and compassion the way Mike exhibits them. Mike has this great sense of fun and presentness with no sense of ego or pretension.

Remember when I said that I love Mike Oeming so much that I married him?

2009. I (as Reverend David Mack) officiated the wedding ceremony between Mike and his talented partner, Taki Soma.

I am so happy to see that Mike and Taki found each other, talented artists who found a way to collaborate with each other so well. Seeing all the struggles that Mike has gone through, and knowing the struggles that Taki also has overcome, I'm so happy that each of them has been life's gift to the other.

A year ago, I was at Mike and Taki's place as they played for me the new episodes of the *Powers* TV show. Mike was drawing and inking. Taki was drawing. I sat on the couch drawing. Each of us drawing as we watched this TV show that had come from the drawings that Mike had made in that little security guard booth.

You know how you see a duck gliding effortlessly on the water? But underneath you know its feet are paddling like crazy? The work in this book gives you a sense of some of that energy of Mike's that is happening underneath the surface.

Like a force of nature.

DAVID MACK

RECOMMENDED READING

RAPTURE
Story by Michael Avon Oeming and Taki Soma
Art by Michael Avon Oeming
978-1-59582-460-8 • $19.99

WILD ROVER FEATURING THE SACRIFICE
Story by Michael Avon Oeming
Art by Michael Avon Oeming and Victor Santos
$2.99

THE VICTORIES VOLUME 1: TOUCHED
Story and art by Michael Avon Oeming
978-1-61655-100-1 • $9.99

THE VICTORIES VOLUME 2: TRANSHUMAN
Story and art by Michael Avon Oeming
978-1-61655-214-5 • $17.99

THE VICTORIES VOLUME 3: POSTHUMAN
Story and art by Michael Avon Oeming
978-1-61655-445-3 • $17.99

THE VICTORIES VOLUME 4: METAHUMAN
Story and art by Michael Avon Oeming
978-1-61655-517-7 • $17.99

ALEISTER & ADOLF
Story by Douglas Rushkoff
Art by Michael Avon Oeming
978-1-50670-104-2 • $19.99

B.P.R.D.: PLAGUE OF FROGS VOLUME 1
Story by Mike Mignola and others
Art by Michael Avon Oeming, Guy Davis, and others
978-1-59582-675-6 • $19.99

ABE SAPIEN VOLUME 9: LOST LIVES AND OTHER STORIES
Story by Mike Mignola, Scott Allie, and others
Art by Michael Avon Oeming and others
978-1-50670-220-9 • $19.99

VALVE PRESENTS: THE SACRIFICE AND OTHER STEAM-POWERED STORIES
Story by various writers
Art by Michael Avon Oeming and others
978-1-59582-869-9 • $24.99

CONAN: THE DAUGHTERS OF MIDORA AND OTHER STORIES
Story and art by Michael Avon Oeming and others
978-1-59582-917-7 • $14.99

KABUKI LIBRARY VOLUME 1
Story and art by David Mack
978-1-61655-677-8 • $39.99

DREAM LOGIC
Story and art by David Mack
978-1-61655-678-5 • $34.99

FURIOUS VOLUME 1: FALLEN STAR
Story by Bryan J. L. Glass
Art by Victor Santos
978-1-61655-468-2 • $17.99

POLAR VOLUME 1: CAME FROM THE COLD
Story and art by Victor Santos
978-1-61655-232-9 • $17.99

THE GOON LIBRARY VOLUME 1
Story and art by Eric Powell
978-1-61655-842-0 • $39.99

FIGHT CLUB 2 LIBRARY EDITION
Story by Chuck Palahniuk
Art by Cameron Stewart
978-1-50670-237-7 • $149.99

VEIL
Story by Greg Rucka
Art by Toni Fejzula
978-1-61655-492-7 • $19.99

THE UMBRELLA ACADEMY VOLUME 1: APOCALYPSE SUITE
Story by Gerard Way
Art by Gabriel Bá
978-1-59307-978-9 • $17.99

ALABASTER: WOLVES
Story by Caitlín R. Kiernan
Art by Steve Lieber
978-1-61655-025-7 • $19.99

EDGAR ALLAN POE'S SPIRITS OF THE DEAD
Story and art by Richard Corben
978-1-61655-356-2 • $24.99

MOEBIUS LIBRARY: THE WORLD OF EDENA
Story and art by Moebius
978-1-50670-216-2 • $49.99

WILL EISNER: THE CENTENNIAL CELEBRATION, 1917–2017
Story and art by Will Eisner and others
978-1-50670-355-8 • $49.99

THE ART OF USAGI YOJIMBO
Story and art by Stan Sakai
978-1-59307-493-7 • $29.95

APOCALYPTIGIRL: AN ARIA FOR THE END TIMES
Story and art by Andrew MacLean
978-1-61655-566-5 • $9.99

CREEPY PRESENTS ALEX TOTH
Story and art by Alex Toth and others
978-1-61655-692-1 • $19.99

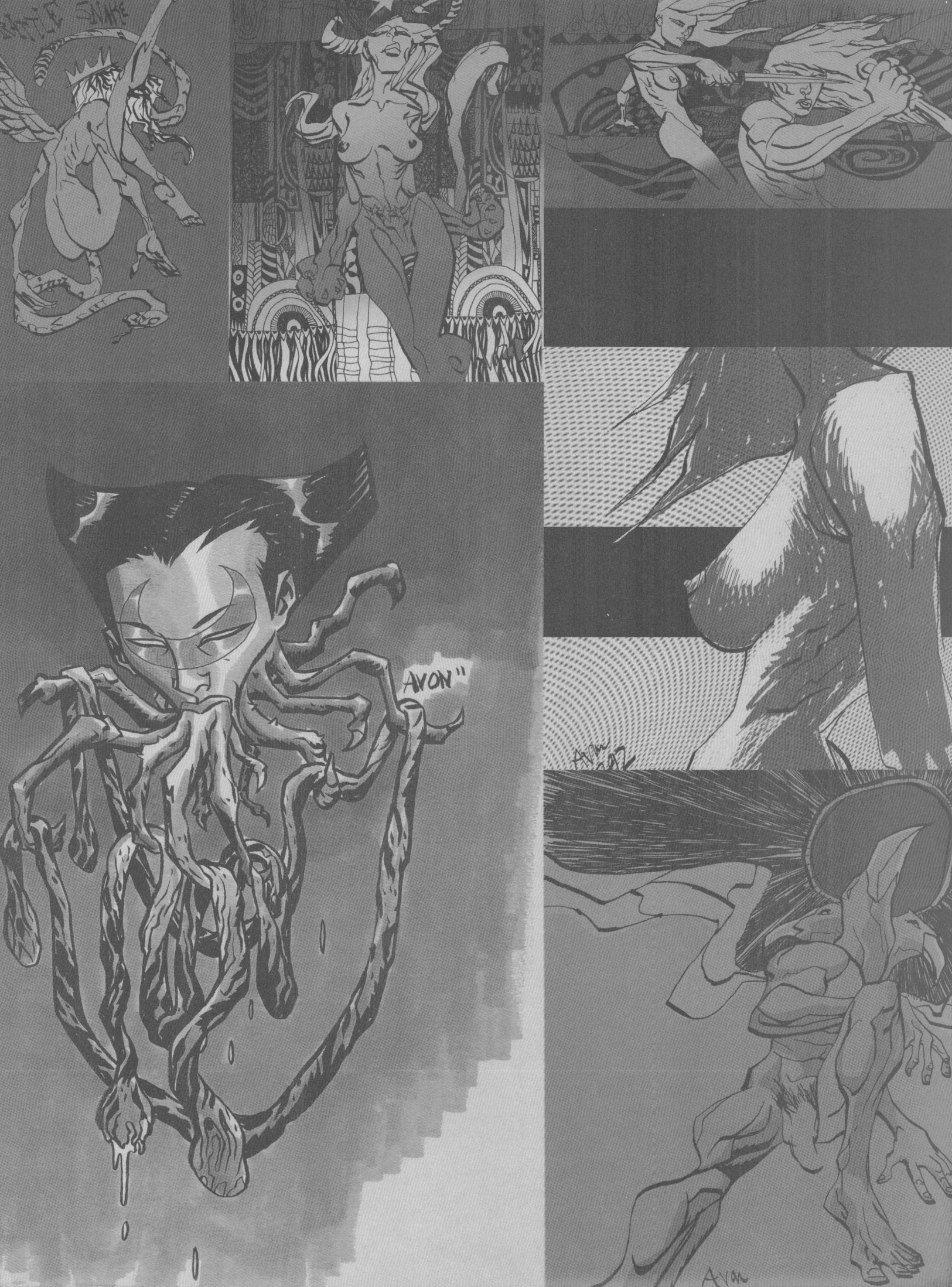

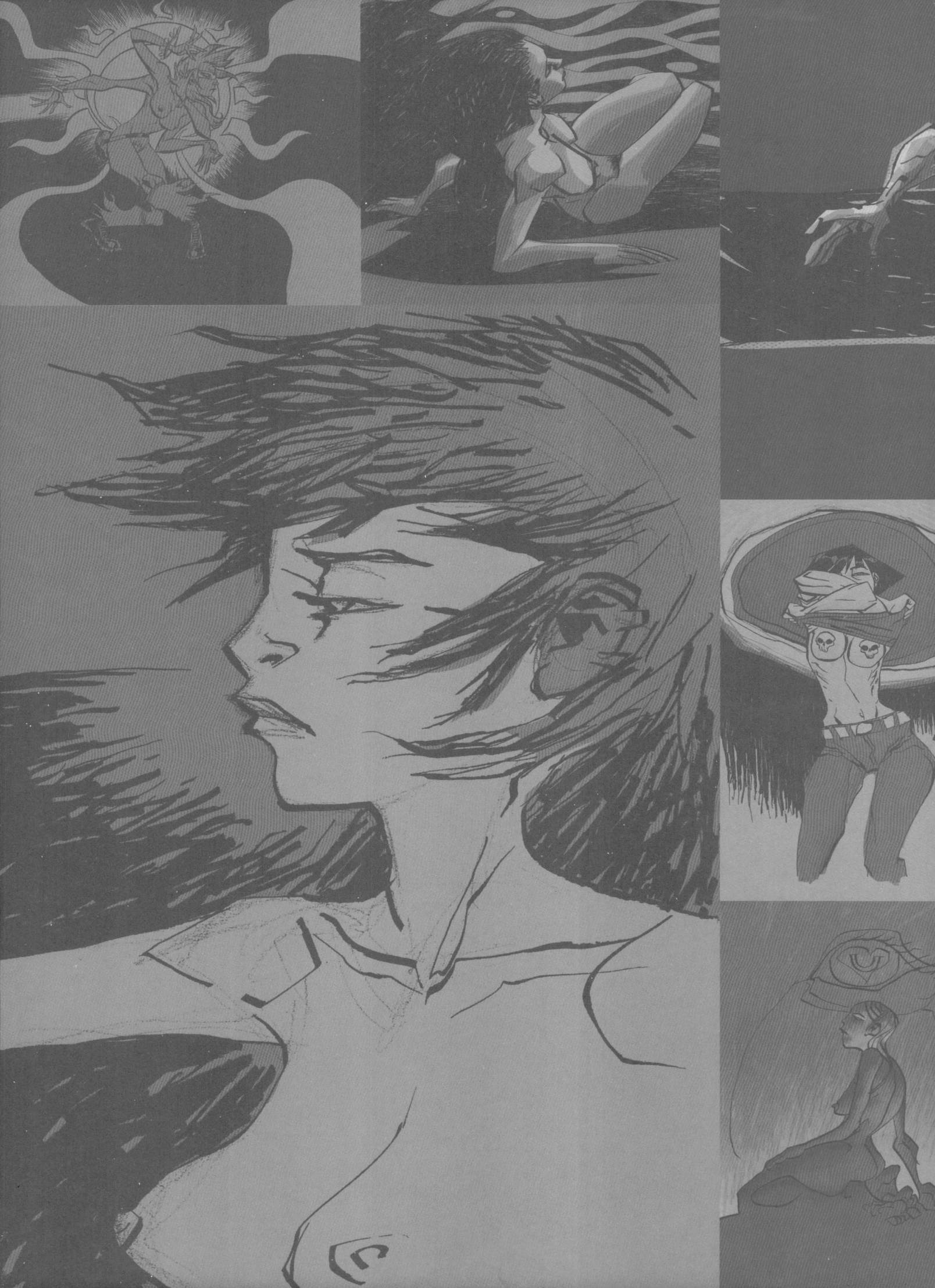